THE OLD RELIGION IN A NEW WORLD

THE OLD RELIGION
in a
NEW WORLD

The History of North American Christianity

Mark A. Noll

William B. Eerdmans Publishing Company

Grand Rapids, Michigan / Cambridge, U.K.

Wm. B. Eerdmans Publishing Co.
255 Jefferson Ave. S.E., Grand Rapids, Michigan 49503 /
P.O. Box 163, Cambridge CB3 9PU U.K.

Printed in the United States of America

06 05 04 03 02   7 6 5 4 3 2

Library of Congress Cataloging-in-Publication Data

Noll, Mark A., 1946-
    The old religion in a new world: the history of North American Christianity /
      Mark A. Noll.
      p.   cm.
    Includes bibliographical references and index.
    ISBN 0-8028-4948-2 (pbk.: alk. paper)
    1. United States — Church history. 2. Canada — Church history. I. Title.

BR515.N744 2002
277 — dc21

                              2001040537

www.eerdmans.com

To Skip Stout

CONTENTS

PREFACE

This book offers an introduction to the history of Christianity in North America. It attempts especially to explain what was *new* about the outworking of organized Christian religion on this continent by comparison with the European origins of that religion. To that end, the book has two main objectives. The first is to provide a broad outline of major events, developments, and occurrences in the history of the Christian churches, either transported from Europe or springing up indigenously, that have filled North America with such remarkable vitality and diversity. The second is to highlight some of the most important interpretive issues in the transfer of the hereditary religion of Europe to the "New World" and its development in that new environment. By contrast with longer accounts, the discussions in this book are intentionally succinct, suggestive, and selective. With its notes for further study, a bibliography, a chronology, and factual material on denominations and the strength of Christian adherence in different American regions, this work is intended to open doors to advanced study. But the primary intention throughout is to meet the needs of curious students and lay readers interested in a broad interpretive overview of the subject.

A word is appropriate at the outset as to how this book differs from my longer textbook, *A History of Christianity in the United States and Canada* (Eerdmans, 1992). A few years ago, a German publisher, the Evangelische Verlagsanstalt of Leipzig, asked me to prepare the volume on North America for its series "Church History in Individual Studies." That book, which I wrote in English, has now been translated and published as *Das Christentum in Nord Amerika*. About half of this new book represented an abridgment and updating of material from my earlier Eerdmans book; about half grew from new research, such as the selective use of opinions and observations by Europeans on Christian life in North America. (The translations in this book of such comments from German and French sources are my own.) In the course of working on the German book, it gradually dawned on me that an effort to introduce Europeans to the history of North American Christianity might also be useful for Americans. *The Old Religion in a New World* is, thus, a further revision and updating of the manuscript originally prepared for publication in Germany. It is a substantially new book with much new material and an entirely new apparatus, along with some pages abridged from the earlier Eerdmans volume.

The burden of *The Old Religion in a New World* is to highlight aspects of North American Christianity that set it apart from patterns of religious experience and organization more common in historic European Christendom. Thus, for example, the separation of church and state that has prevailed in the United States since the late eighteenth century receives considerable attention. Similarly, the book discusses at several points a phenomenon that contrasts sharply with general European patterns: in the United States there has existed a striking *harmony* between the churches and forces of progress, democracy, and pragmatism; the New World did *not* support the characteristic European bond between established churches and conservative social orders. The place of the Roman Catholic Church in the United States is another matter treated as a contrast to the European situation, since it was a parvenu, disadvantaged culturally and sometimes legally because of its late arrival. (In the United States and in Canada outside Quebec, the only churches that ever came close to a position of cultural establishment were Protestant.) To highlight the perspective of the whole, the book begins with a chapter on what it meant for Christianity to spread from Europe to the New World. The eleven chapters making up the rest of the book are divided between some offering a sketch of developments in a specific historical period and others attempting a more general interpretation of a major theme or circumstance in American Christian history. The afterword returns for an assessment of the new forms of American Christianity that sprang from Europe's old religion.

The chronological chapters divide new-world history into the following eras: the period of colonization; the era of nation formation, which was also the era during which distinctly American forms of Christian practice emerged; the middle decades of the nineteenth century, when Protestantism reached the peak of its influence; the period from the end of the Civil War to the beginning of the pentecostal movement in 1906, when the United States experienced a surge in the diversity of its Christian communions; the period from 1906 to 1960, when battles between Protestant fundamentalists and modernists, two world wars, the cold war, and the beginnings of the civil rights movement altered considerably the North American churches; and the years since 1960 to the present, which have witnessed a shifting balance of power among the churches, several new movements of spiritual renewal, and increasing antagonism with some secular elements in the broader culture. The five thematic chapters interspersed in this chronological sequence treat the American separation of church and state; the practice of theology and intellectual life within the North American churches; the instructive contrasts provided by Canada and Mexico to developments in the United States; the fate of ethnic and confessional communities in American Christian experience; and the practices of quotidian Christian life by ordinary believers. The book closes with a list and classification of the Christian denominations in North America with at least 100,000 adherents, a schematic overview of Christian strength in the regions of the United States and Canada, a chronology, and a bibliography.

An ideal treatment of "Christianity in North America" would be constantly alert to the ways in which Canadian and Mexican experience parallels or contrasts with experience in the United States. Unfortunately, academic comparisons for religion in the United States and Mexico are quite rare. While a few efforts to consider the Christian history of the United States and Canada as a single unit do exist, even that kind of work is still in its infancy. As a result, this book concerns primarily the United States, with two exceptions: the first three chapters treat the history of Canada and the United States as a unit, with a few brief remarks on Mexico as well, and the tenth chapter features a comparison of the Christian history of the three nations, with special attention to issues of church and state. In an effort to avoid unthinking, but common, linguistic imperialism, in this book "North America" and "North American" are used to refer to both Canada and the United States; "American," on the other hand, will be used as an adjective referring specifically to the United States.[1]

Books of synthesis like this one depend very heavily on the community of researchers who have worked so diligently and with so much creativity to record and interpret the history of Christianity in North America. I am especially indebted for ongoing instruction, encouragement, and friendship to the scholars who cooperate in the programs of two sub-groups of that community: the Cushwa Center for the Study of American Catholicism at the University of Notre Dame and the Institute for the Study of American Evangelicals at Wheaton College. To Rachel Maxson, a diligent young researcher, I am especially grateful for assistance on the treatment of Mexico. The same degree of thanks is owed to another talented assistant, Jeff Gustafson, who helped prepare the book for publication. Finally, it offers me great pleasure to dedicate the book to a long-time mentor and teacher who is also a long-time friend.

---

1. It is my hope some day to prepare a full revision of *A History of Christianity in the United States and Canada* that expands comparative treatment of Canada and adds significant attention to Mexico as well.

CHAPTER ONE

From Europe to America

The movement of Christianity from Europe to North America was an immensely complex migration, extending over centuries and filled with tragic disillusionment as well as unanticipated successes. It amounted to one of the most important transformations in the entire history of Christianity. In the year 2000 the worldwide affiliated Christian population amounted to approximately two billion people. Of that number, over 15 percent, or more than 300 million, were found in Canada, the United States, and Mexico.[1] Five hundred years earlier, of course, there had been virtually no Christians in North America.

The place of the United States as the world's only remaining super-power magnifies the importance of the Christian history of North America. The spread of American influence around the world has meant that American versions of the nature, purpose, and content of the Christian faith have also spread widely. At the end of the twentieth century the churches of the United States were sponsoring approximately 70,000 overseas missionaries, with another 8,400 from Canada and 2,400 from Mexico.[2] As just one concrete example of America's

---

1. Figures are from David D. Barrett and Todd M. Johnson, "Annual Statistical Table on Global Mission: 2001," *International Bulletin of Missionary Research* 25 (Jan. 2001): 24-25.

2. Patrick Johnstone, *Operation World* (Grand Rapids: Zondervan, 1993).

reach overseas, the American evangelistic organization Campus Crusade for Christ in 1979 produced a motion picture on the life of Christ, based on the Gospel of Luke. As of early 2001, copies of that film had been distributed in 638 separate languages, it was being shown actively in more than a hundred countries, and it had been viewed by over four billion people.[3] Therefore, to inquire about what happened to Christianity in its transplantation from Europe to North America is to raise not only an important historical question but also one with considerable bearing on the worldwide fate of Christianity at the start of the twenty-first century.

For a historical approach to the transplantation of Christianity from Europe to North America, it is instructive to begin with specific cases. Some of these cases present simple stories. Others are more complicated, and complicated in different ways. Together, these narratives underscore the complexities confronting any effort to account for Christianity as it traveled across the Atlantic Ocean to a New World.

The Transportation of Christianity as a Simple Narrative

On June 4, 1893, parishioners who attended the 7:00 a.m. mass at St. Wenceslaus Church in Spillville, Iowa, deep in the American Midwest, heard something remarkable. On the organ a visitor was playing the beloved Czech hymn, "Boze pred tvou velebnosti — O God before Thy Majesty," and the congregation, unaccustomed to music at the daily mass, was being asked to sing along. The organist was Antonín Dvořák, who only the day before had arrived in Spillville for a vacation from his work as musical director of the National Conservatory in New York. He had come to this tiny Midwestern community on the Turkey River in northeast Iowa because of its reputation as a well-maintained enclave of Czech immigrant culture. In New York, as in Europe, Dvořák practiced his Catholicism faithfully, but he was not in the habit of playing the organ for services as he did throughout the summer of 1893 in

---

3. "Jesus Film Passes 4 Billion Mark," *Christian Week*, Feb. 6, 2001, p. 12.

Spillville.[4] For Antonín Dvořák, the transplantation of Christianity from Europe to North America meant no change in the material content of his faith, but deeper emotional satisfaction in its practice.

A similar sense of continuity between European Christianity and North American Christianity, but with much broader effects, is illustrated by events that occurred in the city of Montreal during the early 1840s. Montreal was then (as it is now) a center of French-Catholic civilization in Quebec. Each night from 13 December 1840 through 21 January 1841, Mgr. Charles de Forbin-Janson held a well-attended preaching mission in the new diocese of Montreal. Forbin-Janson, a native of France who had arrived in North America only in 1839, was co-founder of the Missionaires de France (later known as the Fathers of Mercy). Early in his clerical career, at the request of Pope Pius VII, he had devoted himself to public preaching and heightened concentration on the sacraments as means of winning his countrymen back to the church after the disengagements of the French Revolution. Now he was using these same techniques in the New World. Forbin-Janson's preaching had been effective in the United States, but not nearly as successful as it was in Lower Canada, where he enjoyed the dedicated assistance of Mgr Ignace Bourget, soon to be Montreal's second bishop. Shortly after Forbin-Janson's mission ended, Bourget embarked for France, where he recruited a host of Europeans to aid the work of his diocese: Oblates of Mary Immaculate, Jesuits, Sisters of the Sacred Heart, nuns of the Good Shepherd from Angers, clerics of St. Viator, and Fathers, Brothers, and Sisters of the Holy Cross. Historian Louis Rousseau credits a combination of local conditions, the Forbin-Janson mission of 1839-1840, and Bourget's dedicated leadership for a revival of ultramontane Catholicism in Quebec.[5] For Forbin-Janson and Bourget, the transplantation of Christianity from Europe to North America meant an opportunity to create in Quebec one of the most conservative, and one of the most durable, organic Christian societies found anywhere in the world.

4. John Clapham, *Antonín Dvořák: Musician and Craftsman* (New York: St. Martin's, 1966), p. 19.

5. Louis Rousseau, "L'origine d'une société maintenant perdue: le réveil religieux montréalais de 1840," in *Religion et culture au Québec: Figures contemporaines du sacré*, ed. Yvon Desrosiers (Montreal: Fides, 1986), pp. 71-92.

Another Catholic voice can be enlisted, this time with more complexity, to suggest the same sort of continuity. In 1925, Gerald Shaughnessy published his landmark study of Catholicism in the United States, *Has the Immigrant Kept the Faith?* In this generally optimistic account Shaughnessy nonetheless reported that, especially among Italians, there was at least some leakage of immigrants to non-Catholic churches, where, as he reported, Protestants occasionally employed "statues, altars, candles and other similar appurtenances . . . to entrap the unwary and the ignorant" by fooling them into thinking they were attending Catholic churches. Yet despite losses from such underhanded practices, Shaughnessy was able to report that, even among Italian-American immigrants, the rate of Catholic retention was much higher than he and a host of other interpreters had thought possible. For Shaughnessy, the transplantation of Christianity from Europe to North America meant new opportunities for frauds to imitate the one true faith, but also an unprecedented flourishing of the Catholic church, a flourishing that Shaughnessy could only consider "a living, vital, irrefragable, concrete proof of the power and the grace of God."[6]

Many of the Protestants who came to North America felt just as strongly that the movement of Christianity from Europe was a straightforward affair, but one with exactly opposite connotations. Alexander Campbell was born near Ballymena, Country Antrim, Ireland, in 1788, the son of a Seceding Presbyterian minister. After study in Scotland, he came in 1809 to the United States. Immediately upon his arrival in the New World, Campbell abandoned the Presbyterianism in which he had been trained because he found its theology, its polity, and its sacramental restrictions far too confining in the openness of the new American republic. Throughout the long career that followed, Campbell became one of the leaders of the "restorationist" movement that was defined by efforts to promote a Christianity shorn of Old-World excrescences and pared back to the essentials of a simple New Testament faith. For these restorationist purposes, Campbell could not imagine a better place than the United States of America. In one of

6. Gerald Shaughnessy, *Has the Immigrant Kept the Faith?* (New York: Macmillan, 1925), pp. 221n16, 270.

many such statements about his new country, Campbell proclaimed in an 1830 address that the declaration of American independence on July 4, 1776, was "a day to be remembered as was the Jewish Passover. . . . The American Revolution is . . . the precursor of a revolution infinitely more important to mankind[,] . . . the emancipation of the human mind from the shambles of superstition, and the introduction of human beings into the full fruition of the reign of heaven."[7] For Campbell, the transplantation of Christianity from Europe to North America meant an opportunity to strip away the corruptions of Europe, to join Christian faith with liberating aspects of American experience, and so to approach the millennium of Christ's reign on earth.

The Transmission of Christianity as a Complex Narrative

By no means were all migrations of Christian faith to North America such straightforward affairs. Many were far more complex, with a complexity as instructive as the simplicity of the previous examples.

Isaac Buchanan was a Lowland Scot who came to Upper Canada (now Ontario) in the 1830s to pursue his economic betterment. Through a long and active Canadian business career, he nonetheless remained an earnest practitioner of the evangelical Presbyterianism of his youth. Along with many Scots of his day, age, social location, and religion, he looked upon Canada as an extension of Scotland and so easily transferred religious expectations from the Old World to the new. One of the pieces of ecclesiastical baggage that Buchanan brought with him from Scotland to Upper Canada was the conviction that church-state establishments were not only permissible, but essential for the well-being of religion and society. This conviction he maintained in the New World even after the Canadian Presbyterian church imitated a schism in Scotland between Free and established Presbyterians in 1843 and split itself in two. It was not until Buchanan, on trips back to the old country, heard arguments from members of the

---

7. Alexander Campbell, "An Oration in Honor of the Fourth of July, 1830," *Popular Lectures and Addresses* (Cincinnati: Standard, 1863), pp. 374-75.

Scottish Free Kirk attacking church-state establishment, and not until he also applied to ecclesiastical life the arguments he absorbed in Britain about the virtues of free trade, that Buchanan changed his opinion on ecclesiastical establishments. To quote a fine doctoral thesis on Buchanan: "It was in Britain that he first spoke out against church establishment and argued for the complete financial separation of church and state. Only later did he suggest that the granting of financial assistance to religion was as incorrect in the Canadas as it was in the homeland."[8] For Buchanan and the issue of church-state relationships, the transplantation of Christianity from Europe to North America meant that instruction would come from the Old World concerning how to act in the new.

Complex connections between the Old and New Worlds can be observed in other ways as well. The swarming of Scandinavian immigrants to the United States after the mid-nineteenth century resulted in a mass of complicated religious choices. The story of Lars Paul Esbjörn (1808-1870) is one of the most complicated. In Sweden, Esbjörn's ardent advocacy of trans-denominational pietism — complete with active revivalism, temperance societies, Sunday Schools, attacks on slavery, and a willingness to adjust the Augsburg Confession — prevented his rise in the state Lutheran Church. This background of discontent with religion in Sweden led him to migrate to the United States in 1849. In his new land he first came under the influence of a sectarian pietist, Olof Gustav Hedström, and he almost joined Hedström's Swedish Methodist church. Later he sought support for his labors from yet another denomination, the American Home Missionary Society of the Congregationalists. Soon, however, Esbjörn began to be worried about the excesses of religious freedom in his new land, and so he organized a Lutheran church in Andover, Illinois. Later he came out strongly for the defenders of strict confessional Lutheranism who took their stand on an unaltered Augsburg Confession. Fourteen years after Esbjörn came to America, he returned to Sweden, where he accepted a position

---

8. Harry Bridgeman, "Three Scots Presbyterians in Upper Canada: A Study in Emigration, Nationalism and Religion" (Ph.D. dissertation, Queen's University, Ontario, 1978), p. 345.

in the established Lutheran Church, the very church he once had abandoned as hopelessly corrupt.[9] For Esbjörn the transplantation of Christianity from Europe to North America meant at first unprecedented
opportunity to advance an activist pietism, then growing concern
about the excesses of American liberty, and finally a return to traditional European institutions.

Still other voices testified to a different kind of complexity in the
westward movement of Christianity. In 1865, Philip Schaff, the Swiss-
born emigré church historian, returned to Europe from the United
States to lecture before Protestant audiences on the meaning of the
American Civil War. In the course of these speeches, he could barely
contain his enthusiasm for the progress of Christianity in his adopted
land, especially for "its careful observance of the Sabbath," which to
Schaff was one of the most powerful proofs "of the God-fearing and
Christian character of the American nation." Schaff wanted his hearers
to know that the American who honored Sunday, which stilled even the
"otherwise so busy commercial life" of the United States, was "no ju-
daic sabbatarian and slavish legalist." Rather, this was someone who
voluntarily chose to honor the day in the freedom "of the Gospel and of
the Spirit." Sadly, Schaff also felt compelled to tell his European audiences that the peace and sanctity of the American Christian sabbath
was now "being threatened, above all in New York City, by the huge
mass of immigration pouring in from all countries of the Continent."
By mentioning specifically that New York's population of about one
million included 220,000 Irish and 150,000 Germans, and by singling
out the sabbath-despisers' "smoke-filled taverns and pleasure palaces"
as the scenes of greatest sabbath desecration, Schaff left little doubt as
to where he thought the most serious threat was arising to a gloriously
Christian social practice.[10] For Schaff the transplantation of Christianity from Europe to North America meant an opportunity for the faith
to flourish as it was flourishing nowhere else in the world, but also a

9. Esbjörn's story is told in George M. Stephenson, *The Religious Aspects of Swedish Immigration* (1932; reprint, New York: Arno, 1969), pp. 147ff. I am grateful to Louise Bur-
ton for bringing it to my attention.

10. Philip Schaff, *Der Bürgerkreig und das christliche Leben in Nord-Amerika: Vorträge*
(Berlin: Wiegandt und Grieben, 1866), pp. 52-58.

lesson in how a lack of discipline brought from the Old World could undermine piety in the new.

Shortly after Schaff made these comments, an entirely different view was expressed on the fate of Christianity in the United States. Orestes Brownson, after earlier careers as humanist, reformer, Unitarian, and Transcendentalist, had entered the Catholic church in 1844. During the American Civil War (1861-65), he championed the North as promoting both civilization and true religion. Yet afterwards he came to doubt the compatibility between American civilization and the principles of his adopted church. Brownson's disillusionment grew so great that in 1870 he could write: "I defend the republican form of government for our country, because it is the legal and only practicable form, but I no longer hope anything from it. Catholicity is theoretically compatible with democracy . . . , but practically, there is, in my judgment, no compatibility between them. According to Catholicity all power comes from above and descends from high to low; according to democracy all power is infernal, is from below, and ascends from low to high. This is democracy in its practical sense, as politicians & the people do & will understand it. Catholicity & it are as mutually antagonistic as the spirit & the flesh, the Church and the World, Christ & Satan."[11] For Brownson the transplantation of Christianity from Europe to North America created a challenge to preserve the one true faith in an environment alien to that faith.

Finally, the transplanting of Christianity in North America could bring a welter of unexpected burdens as well as opportunities. In the spring of 1913, Johannes Groen was the minister of the largest Christian Reformed Church in Grand Rapids, Michigan. The Christian Reformed Church, a Dutch immigrant denomination, was headquartered in Grand Rapids near the eastern shore of Lake Michigan. Shortly before the state of Michigan held a referendum on the question of giving women the right to vote, Groen made a speech supporting suffrage for women. In so doing, he enlisted the standard intellectual repertoire of his Dutch Calvinist heritage. That repertoire included Scripture diligently perused, reason carefully applied to worldly affairs, and full de-

---

11. *The Brownson-Hecker Correspondence,* ed. Joseph F. Gower and Richard M. Leliaert (Notre Dame, IN: University of Notre Dame Press, 1979), p. 291.

ployment of the organic Calvinism of the Netherlands' Abraham Kuyper, who had paid a triumphant visit to Grand Rapids only fifteen years before. The difficulty for Groen was that the overwhelming majority of his fellow leaders in the Christian Reformed Church were using precisely the same intellectual resources to oppose women's suffrage. For his pains in taking this stand, Groen's lecture was subjected to detailed refutation by his denomination's leading theologian, he was attacked in the local newspaper through a letter signed by all but three of his fellow Christian Reformed ministers in Grand Rapids, and he was forced to defend himself in the local ministerial association. As a last indignity, Groen, while walking along Grand Rapids's Eastern Avenue, encountered an irate parishioner who pulled a gun and shot him. The minister survived, but he had been given a message.[12] For Groen the transplantation of Christianity from Europe to North America meant freedom to follow a traditional expression of Christianity wherever its adherents thought it took them, but also that the same freedom could be used strenuously, even violently, to challenge such a decision.

To query Antonín Dvořák, Charles de Forbin-Janson and Ignace Bourget, Gerald Shaughnessy, Alexander Campbell, Isaac Buchanan, Lars Paul Esbjörn, Philip Schaff, Orestes Brownson, and Johannes Groen about the transplantation of Christianity from Europe to North America is to receive a great variety of responses. Even more, it is to realize that the question is thronged on every side by conceptual conundrums. There is a problem of discriminating between the influences of immigration per se and immigration to North America. There is a problem of comparing how the transportation of Christianity from Europe to America contrasts with the transportation of Christianity from rural to urban areas, for this other movement of peoples was intertwined with the westward, international movement at every stage.[13] There is a prob-

---

12. James D. Bratt, *Dutch Calvinism in Modern America* (Grand Rapids: Eerdmans, 1984), pp. 77-78.

13. See especially Hugh McLeod, "Introduction," in *European Religion in the Age of Great Cities, 1830-1930,* ed. Hugh McLeod (London: Routledge, 1995); and McLeod, "Secular Cities? Berlin, London, and New York in the Later Nineteenth and Early Twentieth Centuries," in *Religion and Modernization,* ed. Steve Bruce (Oxford: Clarendon Press, 1992).

lem in noting the religious factor in the decision of some like Lars Paul Esbjörn to return to Europe. Among many other conceptual difficulties, there is also a problem in discerning how much the new arrivals from Europe were themselves responsible for the shape of the supposedly "North American" Christianity that was developing on this continent.

Explanations

Historians have made considerable headway in providing answers to such questions, particularly as they summarize the many different ways in which the old faith was adjusted to its new environment. Of such summaries, the most notable remains the account by Sydney E. Ahlstrom in his magisterial *Religious History of the American People* (1972). Ahlstrom detailed what he called five "types of accommodation to the American religious situation."[14] In ascending order of ecclesiastical precisionism, Ahlstrom described, first, nominal members of European state churches who, though perhaps joining lodges and other fraternal orders in the New World, used immigration as an occasion to abandon formal religion. Second were sectarians, illustrated by the various migrations of Mennonites, who found in the New World opportunities denied in the old to pursue long-held visions of ecclesiastical purity. Third were what Ahlstrom called "incipient sectarians" who pursued pietistic, perfectionistic, or reformist goals within the European state church, but when they came to America joined denominations of evangelical Baptists, Methodists, Presbyterians, or Congregationalists. Fourth were members of European state churches who, upon arrival in America, founded parallel denominations to those with which they had been pleased at home, like the American Episcopal Church or the German and Dutch Reformed Churches. Fifth were those who created new ecclesiastical bodies in the New World (like the Christian Reformed Church and several Lutheran denominations), but who did so in order simply to replicate churches they had left in the

---

14. Sydney E. Ahlstrom, *A Religious History of the American People* (New Haven: Yale University Press, 1972), pp. 752-54.

old. Because he was concentrating on Protestants, Ahlstrom did not add a necessary sixth category, which could be called North American "branch churches." Of these, the Roman Catholic Church and the various churches of the Eastern Orthodox diaspora were the preeminent examples.

Other historians have, of course, seen the picture in other terms.[15] What is common in their depictions, however, is the conclusion that some things changed while others remained the same when the Christian faith took root in the New World. Continuities and discontinuities differed substantially depending on when migrations took place, where they ended up, and what material conditions shaped them. Varied as the different movements of the old religion to North America were, they shared in common the need to adjust to a substantially new environment for religious practice.

An American Religious Environment

The question of how the North American environment shaped the Christianity that came to the New World may be restated in the following way: With the worldwide history of Christianity as a standard, what is different about North American Christianity because of North America?[16] Because the religious history of Mexico is so distinct from that of

---

15. For other noteworthy efforts to chart the movement of Christianity across the Atlantic, see Martin E. Marty, "Ethnicity: The Skeleton of Religion in America," *Church History* 41 (March 1972): 5-21; Harry S. Stout, "Ethnicity: The Vital Center of Religion in America," *Ethnicity* 2 (June 1975): 204-24; Randall M. Miller and Thomas D. Marzik, eds., *Immigrants and Religion in Urban America* (Philadelphia: Temple University Press, 1977); Timothy L. Smith, "Religion and Ethnicity in America," *American Historical Review* 83 (Dec. 1978): 1155-85; Jay P. Dolan, "The Immigrants and Their Gods: A New Perspective in American Religious History," *Church History* 57 (March 1988): 61-72; George E. Pozzetta, ed., *The Immigrant Religious Experience* (New York: Garland, 1991); Martin E. Marty, ed., *Ethnic and Non-Protestant Themes*, Vol. 8: *Modern American Protestantism and Its World* (New York: K. G. Saur, 1993); and R. Stephen Warner and Judith D. Wittner, eds., *Gathering in Diaspora: Communities and the New Immigration* (Philadelphia: Temple University Press, 1998).

16. Provocative discussions concerning the uniqueness of the American experience

both the United States and Canada, efforts to answer this question will focus on the United States, with Canada as the main complement. At least four aspects of the American religious environment have been especially important: space, race and ethnicity, pluralism, and the absence of confessional conservatism.

Space

Sheer spaciousness should be the first thing that religious historians note about North America, although in an age where the internet and the airplane have conquered space the significance of geography is often neglected. Yet the most obvious reason why the history of Christianity in Canada and the United States differs from the history of Christianity in Europe is that North America is so much bigger than Europe. The huge expanse of North America gave churches the kind of breathing room that simply had not existed before. This breathing room allowed Christian groups that had felt confined in Europe a chance to develop their own religious visions out of their own internal resources. It allowed European religious antagonists to drift apart. It also gave creative souls every possible opportunity to propose new versions of Christianity. Anglicans who hoped to establish their church in North America found, for example, that parishes in Virginia were sometimes larger than dioceses in England.

By the end of the eighteenth century, every Protestant denomination that had been transplanted in any significant way to North America found itself spread over more territory than its parent denomination covered in Europe. The scale of North America is further suggested by the fact that the distance between London and Moscow — with all the thickly packed church history encountered between these

and American character are found in Philip Gleason, "American Identity and Americanization," in *Harvard Encyclopedia of American Ethnic Groups,* ed. Stephan Thernstrom (Cambridge: Harvard University Press, 1980), pp. 31-33; Byron E. Shafer, ed., *Is America Different? A New Look at American Exceptionalism* (Oxford: Clarendon Press, 1991); and Philip Gleason, *Speaking of Diversity: Language and Ethnicity in Twentieth-Century America* (Baltimore: Johns Hopkins University Press, 1992).

two cities — is less than the distance between Montreal and Denver, or Montreal and Houston — distances that traverse a much thinner ecclesiastical history. In yet another way of highlighting differences of geographical scale, the physical space bounded by Rome, Geneva, and Wittenberg — the centers for Catholicism, Reformed Protestantism, and Lutheranism — would fit easily into Arizona or five other American states, and it would be swallowed up in the land area of seven individual Canadian provinces.

The importance of these distances for church history is reinforced by expert recent commentary on European religious strife. The Irish historian David Hempton, for example, has shown how Protestant-Catholic antagonism in Northern Ireland grew directly in proportion to the propinquity of the two religious communities, a propinquity which contributed, in Hempton's phrase, "to an increase in religious competition and sectarian stereotyping."[17] To be sure, the sort of sectarian religious antagonism Hempton charts for Belfast has not been a stranger to North America. Just as the activities of the Orange Order, the strongly loyalist Protestant fraternal organization, have often occasioned rioting in Northern Ireland, so the Orange Orders founded by immigrants from Northern Ireland in North America have also precipitated public disorder. In the New World, however, Orange-connected Protestant-Catholic violence was scattered in places like Conception Bay, Newfoundland; Winnipeg, Manitoba; and New York City. Its ferocity was eventually defused, however, at least in part because of the great spaces separating those who cared about such things.[18] To put this particular problem in concrete terms, it is helpful to remember that the heavily Protestant County Down in Northern

17. David Hempton, "Belfast: The Unique City," in *European Religion in the Age of Great Cities, 1830-1930*, ed. Hugh McLeod (London: Routledge, 1995), 149. See also David Hempton and Myrtle Hill, *Evangelical Protestantism in Ulster Society, 1740-1890* (London: Routledge, 1992).

18. For comparison, see Michael A. Gordon, *The Orange Riots: Irish Political Violence in New York City, 1870 and 1871* (Ithaca, NY: Cornell University Press, 1993); and Paul Laverdure, "The Redemptorist Mission in Canada, 1865-1885" [on Orange rioting in Conception Bay], in *Historical Papers 1993: Canadian Society of Church History*, ed. Bruce L. Gunther (n.p.: Canadian Society of Church History, 1993), pp. 86-87.

Ireland is less than fifty miles from the heavily Catholic County Londonderry. Using the 1990 church census of the Glenmary Research Center in Atlanta to define a contrast, Rhode Island was the state with the highest percentage of Catholics in the United States, and Mississippi was the state with the highest proportion of Southern Baptists (the largest Protestant denomination in America and one historically suspicious of Catholics).[19] Rhode Island and Mississippi are roughly twelve hundred miles apart.

Race and Ethnicity

A children's song popular in many American churches after World War II emphasizes the ideal of God's love reaching out to every race:

> Jesus loves the little children,
> all the children of the world;
> red and yellow, black and white,
> they are precious in his sight;
> Jesus loves the little children of the world.

This song has been popular because it expresses a profound truth of the Bible, but in America it takes on a special meaning for historical reasons.

Of special importance for American Christian history is the fact that from the beginning, settlement by Africans took place alongside settlement by Europeans.[20] Even if the latter were the enslaved victims of kidnapping, the intermingled black-and-white character of society is a permanent part of the American experience. At almost the same time, North America witnessed a mingling of the various British nations — English, Scottish, Irish, and Welsh. In the region that became Canada,

19. Martin B. Bradley, et al., *Churches and Church Membership in the United States, 1990* (Atlanta: Glenmary Research Center, 1992).

20. See David W. Wills, "The Central Themes of American Religious History: Pluralism, Puritanism, and the Encounter of Black and White," *Religion and Intellectual Life* 5 (Fall 1987): 30-41.

French and English settlement coexisted from the early eighteenth century. During the great era of European migration to North America that began in the 1830s, Northern Europeans of all kinds streamed across the Atlantic, soon to be followed by great numbers of Eastern and Southern Europeans as well. Before the start of the twentieth century immigrants from Asia were added to the North American mix, and by the middle decades of the twentieth century a great influx from the Hispanic world (Cuba, Mexico, Puerto Rico, and Central and South America) was added as well. The religious effect of these migrations was to populate North America with a far greater range of ethnicities, and of ethnic churches, than has ever existed in any one nation of Europe, Asia, or Latin America.

Historians of American Roman Catholicism commonly stress the way in which ethnic trajectories intersect the story of their church.[21] By so doing, they show how the histories of English Catholics, French Catholics, Irish Catholics, German Catholics, Italian Catholics, Polish Catholics, Hispanic Catholics, and African American Catholics — to mention only the largest groups — have been distinct from each other, but also influenced by common American circumstances.

Although it is not usually emphasized as much, ethnicity has meant almost as much for Protestant history as for Catholic history. Many of the nation's earliest Protestant churches were as distinctly English as they were Anglican, and the churches founded by non-English Britons could be just as distinctly ethnic. Scottish and Scots-Irish immigrants exercised a kind of ownership over Presbyterian churches for much of their history, and in some areas of the country Welsh communities were as fiercely loyal to their Baptist, Presbyterian, or Methodist churches as to the memory of Wales. Later, Lutheranism in America meant almost exclusively German or Scandinavian Lutheran. Today, Korean Presbyterians, Hispanic Pentecostals, or members of Vietnamese Christian and Missionary Alliance churches often practice a form of

---

21. See, for example, Jay P. Dolan, *The Immigrant Church: New York's Irish and German Catholics, 1815-1865* (Baltimore: Johns Hopkins University Press, 1975); and Dolan, ed., *The Notre Dame History of Hispanic Catholics in the United States,* 3 vols. (Notre Dame, IN: Notre Dame University Press, 1994).

Protestant faith singularly influenced by ethnic background. It has always been so.

The most important ethnic contribution to the history of Christianity in North America, however, has been African American. It is a fact that race as well as ethnicity has figured more centrally in American church history than in Europe. The effect on the churches began with the importation of African slaves in the seventeenth century and continues to this day. Russell R. Menard, a historian of the American colonies, has written that the United States created a different kind of pluralistic society at least in part because "race rather than Old World origins proved the primary determinant of ethnic identity."[22]

Most slaveowners were really not eager to have their slaves hear the Christian message, and many of the slaveowners who did allow Christianity to reach the slaves did so only because they thought it would make slaves better at their tasks. Yet many slaves nonetheless succeeded in learning something about Christianity and went on to form churches for themselves — a crucial contribution to American religious history.[23] African American denominations emerged from humble Northern beginnings around 1800 and received a major boost from emancipated slaves after the Civil War. Notable Christian leaders among African Africans, such as Richard Allen, founder of the African Methodist Episcopal Church, theologian-bishops Daniel Payne and Henry McNeal Turner of the nineteenth-century African Methodist Episcopal Church, and the Baptist Martin Luther King, Jr. have contributed significantly to the general history of American Christianity. But the most notable development for the African Americans was the

---

22. Russell R. Menard, "Migration, Ethnicity, and the Rise of an Atlantic Economy: The Re-peopling of British America, 1600-1790," in *A Century of European Migrations, 1830-1930*, ed. Rudolph J. Vecoli and Suzanne M. Sinke (Urbana: University of Illinois Press, 1991), p. 74.

23. See especially Albert J. Raboteau, *Slave Religion: The "Invisible Institution" in the Antebellum South* (New York: Oxford University Press, 1980); Mechal Sobel, *The World They Made Together: Black-White Values in Eighteenth-Century Virginia* (Princeton: Princeton University Press, 1987); and Sylvia R. Frey and Betty Wood, *Come Shouting to Zion: African American Protestantism in the American South and British Caribbean to 1830* (Chapel Hill: University of North Carolina Press, 1998).

ability of countless slaves, freed slaves, and those threatened by slavery to find dignity, purpose, and resolve in a religion passed on so grudgingly by the slaveowners.

The persistence of legal, cultural, social, and religious divisions between ethnic groups is as much a part of European history as North American history. But the fact that black-white division has been pervasive, deep, and enduring in North America sets American church history apart. Recent surveys show that substantial systematic differences continue to exist between the beliefs and practices of African American Christians and Caucasian Christians. Political differences are most notable, since for several decades African-American Protestants have voted overwhelmingly for the Democratic Party while white Protestants have voted substantially for the Republican Party. In the American presidential election of 2000 the pattern continued, with great support among white churchgoers for Republican George W. Bush and even greater support for Democrat Al Gore from African Americans.[24] The table on page 18 highlights some of the ongoing effects of black-white racial division. It shows great religious similarities between evangelical white Protestants and African Americans, but also considerable social and political differences.[25] The American situation bears some resemblance to the white-black religious situation in South Africa.[26] But American forms of racial division *within the same forms of Christianity* have no direct counterpart in Europe.

24. See Lyman A. Kellstedt and Mark A. Noll, "Religion, Voting for President, and Party Identification, 1948-1984," in *Religion and American Politics,* ed. Mark A. Noll (New York: Oxford University Press, 1990); as well as the many studies of John C. Green, James L. Guth, Corwin E. Smidt, and Lyman A. Kellstedt, for example, *Religion and the Culture Wars: Dispatches from the Front* (Lanham, MD: Rowman & Littlefield, 1996).

25. Information for this table is drawn from the Akron 1996 survey of 4,037 Americans, and is used courtesy of John Green, James Guth, Lyman Kellstedt, and Corwin Smidt. "Evangelical" and "mainline" are explained in Chapter Seven below. Figures from the 2000 presidential election are courtesy of Lyman Kellstedt; voting totals in 2000 are for those who attend church regularly.

26. But see the significant differences spelled out in George Fredrickson, *White Supremacy: A Comparative Study in American and South African History* (New York: Oxford University Press, 1981); and Fredrickson, *Black Liberation: A Comparative History of Black Ideologies in the United States and South Africa* (New York: Oxford University Press, 1996).

**Table 1.   The African-American Difference in Contemporary
American Religion**

	White Evangelical Protestants	White Mainline Protestants	African Americans	Roman Catholics
Pray daily or more	75	61	80	62
Read Bible daily or more	35	14	33	9
Believe Adam and Eve were real people	89	59	80	n.a.
Think more should be spent to fight hunger	46	44	68	52
Believe defense spending should be cut	32	31	37	31
Believe that an Equal Rights Amendment is needed	54	63	81	66
Voted for Bill Clinton (Democrat) for president in 1996	25	39	68	40
Voted for George Bush (Republican) for president in 2000	84	65	4	57

Pluralism

The stupendous array of churches, para-church agencies, forms of Christian worship, and modes of Christian action has often been one of the most striking features of North American religious life to European visitors. In the sardonic account of a lengthy American sojourn that the British Frances Trollope published in 1832, for instance, she marveled at "the innumerable religious sects throughout America," the "almost endless variety of religious factions."[27] The pluriform character of North American Christianity — arising from the plural origins of immigrant churches, the sheer physical size of the continent, and the special spur of populist ideologies — first characterized the United States, but now is also increasingly prevalent in Canada.

Obvious as this North American religious pluralism is, however, it

27. Frances Trollope, *The Domestic Manners of the American* (1832), quoted in *The Voluntary Church: American Religious Life, 1740-1860, Seen Through the Eyes of European Visitors,* ed. Milton B. Powell (New York: Macmillan, 1967), pp. 68-69.

must be qualified both geographically and ideologically. In the first instance, as the British sociologist Steve Bruce has argued, religious pluralism in North America describes a continent-wide situation more precisely than it does the situation in all particular locations.[28] In the nation as a whole and in many major urban centers, the United States exhibits tremendous religious diversity. Similar diversity is found in and around Canadian metropolises like Toronto, Winnipeg, and Vancouver. Nonetheless, considerably less diversity exists in other American and Canadian regions. For example, New Mexico, southern Texas, southern Louisiana, southern Florida, and many areas of the northeastern United States are overwhelmingly Roman Catholic; Utah and southern Idaho are overwhelmingly Mormon; Alabama, Georgia, Arkansas, Mississippi, and many other sub-regions in the South are overwhelmingly Baptist; parts of Minnesota, North and South Dakota are heavily Lutheran; and there are individual counties scattered throughout the nation where Methodists, members of the Churches of Christ, the Dutch Reformed, or even Pentecostals function as an unofficial religious establishment.[29] So strong are some of these informal ecclesiastical establishments that, to take one of the most potent examples, historian Bill Leonard has styled the Southern Baptist Convention "the Catholic church of the South."[30] In Canada, much the same situation prevails, most notably with the historical sovereignty of Roman Catholicism in Quebec, but also with dominating local concentrations of Catholics in some parts of New Brunswick and Ontario, of Baptists and Presbyterians in parts of the Maritimes, of the United Church in some regions of Ontario and on the prairies, and of a wide variety of Mennonites, Lutherans, independent evangelicals, and others in parts

28. Steve Bruce, "Pluralism and Religious Vitality," in *Religion and Modernization: Sociologists and Historians Debate the Secularization Thesis,* ed. Bruce (New York: Oxford University Press, 1992), pp. 170-94.

29. These conclusions are based on color-coded maps indicating the strength of various denominations around the United States produced by the Glenmary Research Center (750 Piedmont Ave., NE, Atlanta, GA 30308). In addition, a few sections of New York and other major cities remain overwhelmingly Jewish.

30. Bill J. Leonard, *God's Last and Only Hope: The Fragmentation of the Southern Baptist Convention* (Grand Rapids: Eerdmans, 1990), pp. 3-4.

of the Canadian West.[31] The effects of travel, television, mobility, the growth of government, and declining rates of church adherence have undercut some of the power of these unofficial local establishments in the United States and even more in Canada. But they remain an important part of North American history, as well as a continuing reality in some areas.

The second qualification about North American pluralism is the observation that, especially in the United States, an ideology of pluralism has sometimes worked against the much-trumpeted virtues of American freedom. As Philip Gleason has shown, the American celebration of diversity has sometimes itself constituted an ideology of pluralism that brooks no rivals.[32] The power-brokers who define pluralism as a public good can also set the boundaries of acceptable pluralism. Gleason points especially to the arena of public education as a historic flashpoint, since this arena has regularly featured a fervent rhetoric of freedom combined with vigorous cultures of coercion. This combination of libertarian rhetoric and hegemonic action explains much about the resentment felt by many Catholics in the nineteenth century: Protestants claimed that their educational institutions promoted a generic freedom, but this "public" education discriminated against Catholics and favored Protestants.[33] Throughout the twentieth century, the schools have become centers of controversy when citizens have protested ideological teaching where others have seen only common-sense facts or ethics.

Canada has historically witnessed the opposite combination: a rhetoric of orderly adherence to authority with a practice of broad religious toleration. It is a striking ideological difference between religion in the United States and Canada that all Canadian provinces have taken for granted some kind of public financial support for Roman Catholic schools, and that all Canadian provinces except Ontario have readily extended that support in some form or other to sectarian

---

31. "Religious Adherence," *Historical Atlas of Canada, Vol. III, 1841-1961* (Toronto: University of Toronto Press, 1990), plate 34.

32. Gleason, *Speaking of Diversity*, pp. 231-300.

33. For a fine overview, see the essay by Virginia Brereton, "Education and Minority Religions," in *Minority Faiths and the Protestant Mainstream*, ed. Jonathan D. Sarna (Urbana: University of Illinois Press, 1998).

Protestant schools. Generally speaking, though, the ideological commitment to pluralism, especially in the United States, has often been
far more prominent than the practice of pluralism.

Necessary qualifications having been made, it is still the case that
North America witnesses a scope of religious diversity hardly matched
anywhere else in the world. This diversity, especially combined with the
great spaces of North America and formal disestablishment, has meant
a real difference for the churches. For all of Europe's traditional confessional denominations, moving to the New World meant at least two
new realities — multiple schisms and ecclesiastical competition. Schism
is far from unknown in Europe, but it has flourished as never before in
North America. It has separated the Polish National Catholic Church
from Roman Catholicism, the Churches of Christ from Presbyterianism, the Lutheran Brethren and the Lutheran Free Church from the
main ethnic Lutheran churches, the Reformed Episcopalians from the
Episcopal Church in the United States, the Protestant Reformed
Church from the largely Dutch-American Christian Reformed Church,
the Ukrainian Orthodox Church of the USA from the Ukrainian Orthodox Church in America, and many, many more — the list is endless.

To be sure, North American forces have also worked in the other direction. Within all major religious traditions, ecclesiastical amalgama-
tions have taken place that were unthinkable in Europe. Again the list
is very long: seceding splinters rejoining larger Presbyterian churches;
Finns, Danes, Swedes, and Norwegians joining Germans and Slovaks in
multi-ethnic Lutheran churches; jaded evangelicals joining recent immigrants from the Middle East in the Antiochean Orthodox Church,
among others. However significant these ecumenical forces have been,
however, the forces of individualization have been greater.

European confessional churches have also had to learn how to
compete democratically if they wanted to survive.[34] After the creation

---

34. See especially Nathan O. Hatch, *The Democratization of American Christianity*
(New Haven: Yale University Press, 1989). Roger Finke, "Religious Deregulation: Origins
and Consequences," *Journal of Church and State* 32 (Summer 1990): 609-26, is more cir-
cumspectly argued than Roger Finke and Rodney Stark, *The Churching of America, 1776-
1990: Winners and Losers in the Religious Economy* (New Brunswick, NJ: Rutgers University
Press, 1992).

of the United States, the religious freedom mandated by the United States Constitution, along with the already-existing pluralism and openness of the nation, left churches to their own ingenuity. In these circumstances, the denominations that were slow to adjust — especially Congregationalists and Episcopalians/Anglicans — found themselves rapidly outstripped by Baptists and Methodists, the denominations that knew best how to frame their message in the ethos of American democracy. As noted in the chronological chapters below, the Congregationalists and Anglicans were the largest denominations at the time of the American founding in 1776. Within less than fifty years they had been far outstripped by the Methodists and Baptists, and they had been matched by the rapid growth of the "Restorationist" movement consisting of Churches of Christ and Disciples of Christ.

If previously established churches in Europe have had to learn how to compete in the New World, the reverse has been true for European sectarian churches. For those Christians who in Europe defined themselves by their rejection of church establishment, there has been space and opportunity in North America to develop freely. Sometimes these sectarian churches have even set up quasi-establishments of their own, as Puritan Congregationalists did in colonial New England and other sectarians have done in regions where they have dominated.

For all Christian bodies transplanted from Europe — whether European establishmentarians or European sectarians — it has been necessary to use American concepts to communicate about themselves in the American environment. Of countless examples, among the most striking in showing this need to "speak American" in the public square has been the diligence of Quakers, Mennonites, and other pacifists in presenting their convictions to governmental authorities during times of war. Another example is the skill with which public representatives of the Roman Catholic Church — from Bishops John Carroll and John England in the early decades of the United States to John Courtney Murray and the editor Richard John Neuhaus in recent decades — have defended Catholic convictions with republican rhetoric. For Canada, a parallel situation has obtained in which, especially since World War II, leaders in the United Church, Roman Catholics, spokespersons for the Evangelical Fellowship of Canada, and still other groups have become expert at using the language of Canadian public discourse to express the distinctive convictions of their religious traditions.

North American pluralism, in short, has never created a simple ecclesiastical free-for-all, but it has nevertheless given a distinctly North American cast to the general history of Christianity. It is for this reason that Ernst Troeltsch's famous distinction between "church" and "sect" possesses only slight utility for the United States.[35] The European distinction between established "churches" that support the status quo and pietistic or mystical "sects" that seek a pure church barely survives in the United States and has only slightly more validity in Canada. Even the archetypal European "church," Roman Catholicism, has in many places and various eras acted in America like a "sect." The most prominent example is the Catholic sponsorship of private schools that remove Catholic children from America's so-called "public education." No American denomination has ever enjoyed the "churchly" prerogatives and responsibilities of a European state church; instead, the American pattern is best described as "denominationalism."[36] Almost all American churches exhibit both "sectarian" traits (they constitute themselves, they exist without state financial assistance, they compete for adherents) and "churchly" traits (some enjoy high social status, many exert direct or indirect influence on public mores or public policy, almost all accept relief from taxation). The "denomination" in America is neither a "church" nor a "sect." Rather, it is a singular product of an environment defined by great space, the absence of formal church-state ties, and competition among many ecclesiastical bodies.

35. See H. Richard Niebuhr, *The Social Sources of Denominationalism* (New York: Henry Holt, 1929); and John Wilson, "The Sociological Study of American Religion," in *Encyclopedia of the American Religious Experience,* ed. Charles H. Lippy and Peter W. Williams, 3 vols. (New York: Scribner's, 1988), vol. 1, pp. 23-24.

36. See Sidney E. Mead, "From Coercion to Persuasion: Another Look at the Rise of Religious Liberty and the Emergence of Denominationalism" and "Denominationalism: The Shape of Protestantism in America," in Mead, *The Lively Experiment: The Shaping of Christianity in America* (New York: Harper & Row, 1963); Russell E. Richey, ed., *Denominationalism* (Nashville: Abingdon, 1977); and Russell E. Richey and Robert Bruce Mullin, eds., *Reimagining Denominations: Interpretive Essays* (New York: Oxford University Press, 1994).

The Absence of Confessional Conservatism

Of many other North American environmental influences that could be explored, a final one is the effect of westward migration on the conservative tradition of the European Christian churches. In Europe, for better and for worse, the churches have long been regarded as conservative bastions — of dogma, of ethics, of traditional social stratification, of inherited ecclesiastical privilege, and so on.[37] In the United States, if not so markedly in Canada, the churches have had to adapt to a prevailing cultural liberalism, with liberalism defined in the nineteenth-century fashion as an affinity for populism, individualism, democratization, and market-making. In 1965, the Canadian savant George Parkin Grant wrote that there has been no room in America "for the organic conservatism that pre-dated the age of progress. Indeed the United States is the only society on earth that has no traditions from before the age of progress."[38] Seymour Martin Lipset glosses Grant's comment by repeating H. G. Wells's assertion from early in the twentieth century that "the Americans' 'right-wing' and 'left-wing' are just different species of liberalism."[39] Churches in North America still attempt to conserve much, but those efforts at conservation are also hemmed in by powerful forces of democratic individualism that simply have not exerted such a strong force in Europe.

The situation that results, especially in the United States, reverses the European pattern. The only way for a denomination to be confessionally conservative is for it to become sectarian — that is, to actively oppose marketplace reasoning; to refuse to abide by the democratic will of majorities; to insist upon higher authorities than the *vox populi;* and to privilege ancestral, traditional, or hierarchical will over individual choice. But to pursue sectarianism — even if sought in such historically "churchly" ways — is to sacrifice those concerns connecting Christian-

37. For an excellent overview, see Hugh McLeod, *Religion and the People of Western Europe, 1789-1989* (rev. ed., Oxford: Oxford University Press, 1997).

38. George Parkin Grant, *Lament for a Nation* (Princeton: D. Van Nostrand, 1965), pp. 64-65.

39. Seymour Martin Lipset, "American Exceptionalism Reaffirmed," in *Is America Different?* p. 38.

ity to society, learning, politics, culture, and home and family that over the course of more than a millennium came to define Christian conservatism in Europe. Chapter Eleven, which discusses particularly the fate of Lutherans and Roman Catholics in the United States, returns to this theme.

These conundrums facing confessional conservatives in a liberal New World have almost completely silenced the voice of conservatism (when defined as Edmund Burke would have defined it for Britons at the end of the eighteenth century). Where Protestants have striven for this kind of conservatism, as, for example, the Presbyterian conservative J. Gresham Machen did in the earlier part of this century, such efforts are almost invariably taken up into varieties of American fundamentalism in which populist individualism overwhelms organic authority.[40] Machen wanted to oppose "modern" pressure toward diluting the Presbyterian confessions; the only allies he could find were fundamentalists. But fundamentalists were using modern forms of populist communication to contest the modernism of theological liberals. In European terms, both fundamentalists and modernists were liberal anti-traditionalists because both cared little for the traditions of inherited confessional Presbyterianism. As a result, a European-style conservative like Machen was ejected from the main body of Presbyterians, but his ideal of Presbyterian confessionalism was also rejected by most of the fundamentalist allies who joined him in battling theological modernism. To be sure, conservatism of a European sort is present in North America among the various branches of Orthodoxy, but whether that conservatism can survive the turn to democracy and the market in Eastern European regions and the emergence of third- and fourth-generation Orthodox adherents in North America is uncertain.

For North American Roman Catholics, the survival of even modified forms of European Christian conservatism is a question as momentous as it is pressing. When the historian John Lukacs returned to

40. See D. G. Hart, *Defending the Faith: J. Gresham Machen and the Crisis of Conservative Protestantism in Modern America* (Baltimore: Johns Hopkins University Press, 1994); and Bradley R. Longfield, *The Presbyterian Controversy: Fundamentalists, Modernists, and Moderates* (New York: Oxford University Press, 1991).

religion in his native Hungary, shortly before the end of World War II and his emigration to the United States, he explained his choice for the Catholic church in these terms: "after everything was said, . . . the Catholic church was, at least in principle, supra-national and not national, . . . it was less bound to the kind of, at worst provincial, at best cultural, nationalism from which Protestants in Hungary could seldom liberate themselves, and from which the Orthodox churches further to the east would not even attempt to liberate themselves."[41] Whether such an analysis will still obtain in the twenty-first century for North American Roman Catholics depends upon the Catholic ability not to be engulfed by the general cultural liberalism that has played such an important role in the North American history of Christianity.

The history of Christianity in North America is a distinct history because of the North American context. It is not unique in a religious or theological sense, but it does reflect distinctives arising from an "American difference." Christian history in the United States, and to a somewhat lesser degree in Canada, differs from its counterparts in Europe because geography matters, because race and ethnicity have shaped religion from the beginning of European settlement, because North America enjoys a singular degree of religious pluralism, and because European patterns of religious conservatism did not survive passage over the Atlantic. If, however, the history of Christianity in North America is distinctive for these reasons, Christian developments in North America still retain organic connections to historic European patterns as well as to the more recent flourishing of Christianity around the globe. Both distinctives and connections play a large role in the chronological and thematic accounts that make up the remaining chapters of this book.

41. John Lukacs, *Confessions of an Original Sinner* (New York: Ticknor and Fields, 1990), p. 33.

CHAPTER TWO

Colonization, 1492-1730

The circumstances of New World exploration and settlement posed extraordinary challenges to European Christians. Although North America was inhabited by a variety of Native American cultures (some quite sophisticated), it lacked completely the traditions of Christian civilization that reached back more than a millennium in much of Europe. European patterns of church-state interaction (whether cooperation or competition) did not export easily to the New World. European ecclesiastical strife (especially the newer tensions created by the Protestant Reformation and corresponding Catholic responses) meant nothing to Native Americans and also possessed a much-altered significance for those who ventured from Europe to North America. European efforts aimed at evangelizing nominal Christians, negotiating the leadership of Christian societies, or addressing theological problems posed by the early scientific revolution possessed little value in the outposts of North America, the Caribbean, and South America. There the need was to secure a foothold for European civilization, to deal with native populations, who were usually indifferent to Christianity, and to provide religious services for European settlers who were often brutalized by life on the frontier. In all European colonies, the rapid sequence of events always outpaced the ability of Europeans to plan coherently for the re-planting of their churches on the other side of the great ocean.

Colonization

A chronological overview of European settlement can suggest both the range of Christian ventures in the New World and the links sustained between New World innovations and the Old World's Christian past. At the dawn of exploration in 1492, Christopher Columbus opened the diary that recorded his journey to America by expressing a hope that his voyage would discover "how their [the Native Americans'] conversion to our Holy Faith might be undertaken."[1] It is important to remember that in the very year Columbus sailed, the Spanish kingdoms of Ferdinand (Aragon) and Isabella (Castile) had been greatly inspired by the completion of the *reconquista* over Islam. When the last Moorish ruler of Alhambra handed over the keys to that city, Columbus was present as a witness. In 1493, when Columbus returned from his first voyage of discovery, Pope Alexander VI granted Ferdinand and Isabella control of the lands he had explored and charged them with the task of converting the native inhabitants to Christianity. The sense of divine purpose that drove Columbus to the New World emerged naturally from Spain's celebrated role as the champion of Catholic Europe.

The first Christian activity in North America advanced in step with momentous religious change in Europe. As Martin Luther prepared to speak before the Holy Roman Emperor at the Diet of Worms in April 1521, a *conquistador* commissioned by Charles in his duties as king of Spain, Hernán Cortés, was laying siege to the Aztec capital at Tenochtitlán in Mexico. The success of that siege meant that, even as Protestantism emerged as a significant force in Europe, Castilian Roman Catholicism was put in place to evangelize the Indians of New Spain. As Protestants began to organize themselves in Germany, Switzerland, France, and England, Spanish missionaries were arriving in Mexico: Franciscans in 1523, Dominicans in 1526, and Augustinians in 1533. They may have baptized as many as ten million Indians in the first two decades of Spanish rule over New

---

1. *The Diario of Christopher Columbus's First Voyage to America, 1492-93,* ed. Oliver Dunn and James E. Kelley, Jr. (Norman: University of Oklahoma Press, 1989), p. 19.

Spain.[2] In 1541, Hernando de Soto came upon the Mississippi River in the center of the North American continent and called it the Río Espíritu Santo (the River of the Holy Spirit). It was the same year that European hopes for Protestant-Catholic reconciliation collapsed with the failure of leading theologians from both sides to find a common ground for unity at the Council of Regensburg. The Huguenots, Protestant refugees from France, reached present-day South Carolina on the Atlantic coast in the 1560s shortly after the first Roman Catholic service book, with hymns and Scripture portions, was printed in Mexico City. When Spanish colonizers from Florida wiped out the fledgling Huguenot colony, it demonstrated how easily the era's sharp Catholic-Protestant antagonism could be exported from Europe to North America.

Settlement of what became the United States and Canada began in the first decade of the seventeenth century: 1604 with the French in Arcadia (the Atlantic provinces of modern Canada); 1607 with an English colony at Jamestown in Virginia (named for Elizabeth, the Protestant virgin queen of England, 1558-1603); and 1608 with the establishment of Quebec by the French explorer Samuel de Champlain. From the start, colonial officials tried to offer Christian nurture for settlers and promote evangelization of the Indians. The former tasks were occasionally successful, the latter almost never.

During the first half of the seventeenth century, as Europe was torn apart by the Thirty Years' War (1618-1648), various forms of Christianity secured a foothold in a number of North American colonies. Jesuits, Franciscan Récollets, and Sulpicians were at work among French settlers and at Indian missions in modern Canada. Jesuits joined Augustinians, Franciscans, and Dominicans in Mexico. New Amsterdam (later New York) was a Dutch colony served by a few ministers of the Dutch Reformed Church. To the English colonies came still other churches. The Protestant Church of England was established as the official religion of Virginia. In New England five separate colonies were formed by the precise Calvinists who had been frustrated in their ef-

---

2. Kenneth Scott Latourette, *A History of the Expansion of Christianity*, 7 vols. (New York: Harper & Bros., 1937-1945), vol. 3, p. 113.

forts to complete the Reformation at home: Plymouth (1620) and Massachusetts Bay (1630), which were united as one colony (the Commonwealth of Massachusetts) in 1691; Connecticut (1636) and New Haven (1638), which were consolidated as the colony of Connecticut in 1662; and New Hampshire, which separated off as a separate government from Massachusetts in 1680. These five were the "Puritan" colonies.

From the other end of the spectrum of Christian churches, Maryland was settled in 1634 as a refuge for English Catholics. The founders of this colony, George Calvert and his son Cecil, had converted to Catholicism after service to England's King James I. Their colony was a reward for that service. Protestants always made up the bulk of Maryland's settlers, and after several decades the colony itself came under Anglican rule. Yet throughout American colonial history, Maryland offered an unusual sanctuary for Roman Catholics in an English world marked by extreme antagonism to the pope. Among Maryland's leading Catholics was the Jesuit missionary Andrew White (1579-1656), whose work in reducing the language of the Piscataway Indians to writing as a vehicle for Christian literature represented a rare success in European dealings with Native Americans.[3]

English Church-State Establishments

As European colonization expanded during the second half of the seventeenth century, the place of the Christian churches grew somewhat more secure. The two forms of Christianity dominant in the English colonies represented variations on European patterns of church-state establishment. Puritan colonies in New England faced a series of challenges: warfare with Native Americans in 1675-1676 that left twelve towns leveled and 2,000 settlers slain (but that also destroyed the Indians as a factor in the region); hysteria over witchcraft in the early 1690s; the imposition upon Massachusetts in 1695 of a new form of govern-

---

3. See "Andrew White and the Beginnings of Maryland," in *American Jesuit Spirituality: The Maryland Tradition, 1634-1900,* ed. Robert Emmett Curran, S.J. (New York: Paulist, 1988), pp. 47-72.

ment that reduced the legal role of the churches; and, by the start of the eighteenth century, the growth of luxury and a new desire to imitate the ways of the English upper classes, especially in Boston. Yet Massachusetts and the equally Puritan Connecticut remained the most cohesive, most religiously self-assured colonies in the New World.

Anglicanism provided the second establishment transplanted to the English colonies, with Virginia eventually being joined by other Anglican establishments: the Carolinas (founded in 1663 with Anglicanism established in 1706); Maryland after 1691; and, after 1693, parts of New York City (where the colony had been taken over from the Dutch in 1664). The Anglican establishments were significantly bolstered by two new societies created under the leadership of Thomas Bray (1656-1730), who served as a minister for a short period in Maryland. The Society for Promoting Christian Knowledge (SPCK, 1698) began as an effort to provide libraries of Christian books for Anglican ministers in the colonies. The Society for the Propagation of the Gospel in Foreign Parts (SPG, 1701) was chartered to promote missionary work among Native Americans but ended by sending most of its missionaries to colonies (like Massachusetts) that were run by non-Anglicans. Despite the commendable work of these two societies, colonial Anglicanism was never able to overcome a debilitating series of obstacles. The immense size of New World parishes posed problems for which parish life in England provided no guidance. The colonial American South was also dominated by a culture of personal honor, including dueling and exalted notions of patriarchal prerogative, that undermined Anglican ideals. The practice of slavery complicated all interpersonal relationships, including those of church and people. And through a combination of imperial unconcern and American complications, it was never possible to secure an Anglican bishop for the colonies. These circumstances prevented colonial Anglicanism from exerting the kind of general influence that eventually radiated from Puritan New England.

Significantly, both Puritan Congregationalists and colonial Anglicans retained the European ideal of a comprehensive, established state church. Both sought the protection of government, assumed a right to influence the state, treated each other's missionaries as civil threats, and opposed efforts by other Christian groups to settle in their colonies. Yet even as the Puritans and Anglicans strengthened their positions, a rising number of alternatives — either to the Protestantism of the English colonies or the assumptions of establishment — were emerging as well.

Alternatives

Important Roman Catholic colonization continued throughout the seventeenth century. Settlement of Quebec advanced more slowly than settlement in New England or along the Chesapeake Bay. Yet under leaders like Quebec's first Catholic bishop, François-Xavier de Montmorency Laval, who assumed that position in 1658, a comprehensive Catholic society was taking shape. In fact, Laval and his associates succeeded in fashioning a tighter bond between church and society, sacred and secular, than virtually anywhere else in the Western world. The continuing desire of Catholic missionaries to evangelize Native Americans was observable in the labors of the French Jesuit Jacques Marquette (1637-75), who accompanied Louis Jolliet's exploration of the Mississippi River Valley in 1673 for the express purpose of preaching the gospel to the vast network of Illinois Indians in the continent's heartland.

The difficulties besetting European efforts at evangelizing Native Americans were revealed starkly by events in the other major Catholic domain, the Spanish Southwest, at about the same time as Marquette's venture. Near Sante Fe, in what would later become the state of New Mexico, Pueblo Indians arose in 1680 under a native religious teacher named Popé and singled out Catholic missionaries and churches for special attack. The slaying of twenty-one of the region's thirty-three missionaries was a sign of profound Indian resentment at the imposition of the Spanish church. In general, often despite heroic efforts by priests and lay religious, French and Spanish efforts at converting the native population succeeded only partially at best.

The English, who arrived in the New World after the Spanish and French, were more successful in the tasks of settlement, primarily because they succeeded in attracting more colonists than their European competitors. One of the reasons for that success was the space minority religious groups found for themselves in the English colonies. Already before the end of the seventeenth century, the Society of Friends (or Quakers) was a powerful presence in Pennsylvania. The Quakers had been one of the radical sects that flourished during the period of the English Civil Wars (1642-1649). They matured under leaders like George Fox (1624-1691) and soon developed a forceful Christian pacifism. They also taught that an Inner Light of Christ could illuminate even the humblest believer. One of the Quakers' most important converts was William Penn (1644-1718), son of a famous British admiral. When in 1681 Penn acquired a huge tract of land in the New World and in 1682 laid out the city of Philadelphia, he set the stage for a significant migration of Quakers to the colonies.

By the time Quakers were moving to Pennsylvania and the nearby colonies that were later consolidated as New Jersey, a number of Dutch Reformed churches were already established in New York. Quite a few churches were also being set up in the middle colonies by Calvinist Protestants from Germany (the German Reformed churches). The first wave of settlers from Scotland, or from Scotland by way of Ireland (the Scots-Irish), were setting up Presbyterian churches in Pennsylvania, New Jersey, and on Long Island. In 1684 Francis Makemie, who was born in Ireland, educated in Scotland, and commissioned in Northern Ireland to serve as a missionary, established the first American Presbytery. At about the same time, several different kinds of Baptist churches were being gathered in New England, New York, and points further south. The foundation in 1707 of the Philadelphia Association of Regular Baptists was a particularly important step for what would later lead to many powerful organizations of Baptists in America.

Beginning in the 1680s, German migration became especially important. Over the next century, perhaps 120,000 German-speaking immigrants entered North America, with the majority arriving in Pennsylvania.[4] These eventually included some Mennonites, Moravians, and Brethren, but most were associated with the state churches in their

---

4. For a discussion of difficulties in determining the number, see A. G. Roeber, *Palatines, Liberty, and Property: German Lutherans in Colonial British America* (Baltimore: Johns Hopkins University Press, 1993), p. 342n23.

places of origin. By the end of the seventeenth century, the effects of pietism were also being felt with increasing force in the American colonies. German Lutherans under pietistic influence emphasized "heart religion" and self-sacrificing service over the formal institutions and creeds of the churches. Yet German pietists also brought different expectations depending on their place of origin. As demonstrated in the work of A. G. Roeber, pietists under the direct influence of Halle and the institutions of August Hermann Francke tended to define "freedom" as a positive opportunity, perhaps to be exercised in concert with a powerful state, for accomplishing broader purposes in society. Correspondingly, property to these pietists was a trust held by individuals to serve larger, public goals. By contrast, pietists from Württemberg and southwestern Germany tended to view freedom as an interior or domestic state defined especially by the absence of state interference in the conventicles of the godly. To Württembergers, property, if it was not used to protect the virtues of a domestic ideal, was considered a temptation drawing believers away from God. In America, these contrasting ideals created tensions among German immigrants. In general, the ideals of Halle tended to prevail throughout the colonial period, especially as promoted by effective Lutheran missionaries like Henry Melchior Mühlenberg (1711-1787), who arrived in Pennsylvania from Halle in 1742; but after the American Revolution, the more private practices of the Württembergers became more important for the German-Americans, especially as they evolved to merge with the rising tide of America's post-Revolutionary democratic liberalism.[5]

The space provided in colonial British America for the immigrants from Germany opened up to many other groups as well. By the middle years of the eighteenth century, even more Protestants — Sandemanians, Shakers, Free Will Baptists, and Universalists, to name only a few — had appeared in the American colonies. Especially in the middle colonies of New York, New Jersey, Pennsylvania, and Delaware, a func-

---

5. Roeber, *Palatines, Liberty, and Property,* especially pp. 65-80. See also Roeber, "Der Pietismus in Nordamerika im 18. Jahrhundert," in *Geschichte des Pietismus,* vol. 2: *Der Pietismus im achtzehnten Jahrhundert,* ed. Martin Brecht and Klaus Depperman (Göttingen: Vandenhoeck & Ruprecht, 1995), pp. 668-99; and F. Ernest Stoeffler, ed., *Continental Pietism in Early American Christianity* (Grand Rapids: Eerdmans, 1976).

tioning plurality of religion was developing with no exact counterpart in Europe.[6] Almost no one embraced religious pluralism as an ideal, but the practice of pluralism was taking root nonetheless. Governor Thomas Dongan of New York in 1687 made an observation about New York City that would soon be apt for other areas in the colonies as well: "Here bee not many of the Church of England; few Roman Catholicks; abundance of Quakers preachers men and Women especially; Singing Quakers, Ranting Quakers; Sabbatarians; Antisabbatarians; Some Anabaptists; some Independents; some Jews; in short, of all sorts of opinions there are some, and the most part [are] of none at all."[7] Many churches were addressing themselves to the problem of settlers without religion. Almost without noticing it, their presence together in one space was breaking up the European ideal of a unified Christendom.

Religious results of European migration to America can be divided into five main categories: (i) The colonies of Spain in Mexico and the American Southwest witnessed an imperial imposition of a relatively monolithic Catholicism upon Native American populations. (ii) The French Catholic colony of Quebec exerted considerable effort in missionary work among Indians, but its long-lasting monument was a "Christendom" more thoroughly integrated than almost any European example. (iii) Anglicans set up church-state establishments in the southern British colonies, but these establishments never succeeded in providing the comprehensive religious framework common to English experience. (iv) The Puritan establishments of New England, as noted below, grew out of much broader popular participation than the other New World establishments, but they too represented more an adaptation of European religious patterns than complete innovation. (v) In

6. See Richard W. Pointer, *Protestant Pluralism and the New York Experience: A Study of Eighteenth-Century Religious Diversity* (Bloomington: Indiana University Press, 1988); and Jon Butler, *Power, Authority, and the Origins of American Denominational Order: The English Colonies in the Delaware Valley, 1680-1730* (Philadelphia: American Philosophical Society, 1978).

7. Quoted by Jon Butler, "Protestant Pluralism," in *Encyclopedia of the North American Colonies,* ed. Jacob Ernest Cooke, 3 vols. (New York: Charles Scribner's Sons, 1993), vol. 3, p. 609.

the British middle colonies, religious pluralism was a definite innovation, even if an innovation into which colonists stumbled.

Indians and Slaves

For two populations, Native Americans and African-American slaves, early efforts at transporting Christianity to North America were far more destructive than constructive. Almost all European colonies sponsored missionary work among Native Americans. But the only missionaries to have even a measure of success were those who stood furthest from the centers of political power. For example, French missionaries in New France did better than Spanish missionaries in New Spain, in large part because the French missionaries were not encumbered with the business of colonial administration. The most effective mission in what would become the United States was carried out by the Unitas Fratrum (the Unity of the Brethren), or Moravians.[8] This body of pietists, who were lightly guided by Count Ludwig von Zinzendorf (1700-1760), succeeded in establishing a relatively successful mission among the Delaware Indians of Pennsylvania. During the French and Indian War (1756-1763), however, hostility from white Pennsylvanians drove the Moravians and their converts into the Western wilderness, where after much further trauma they eventually established a secure settlement in modern Ontario. Native American cultures operated on principles greatly at odds with European culture, for standards of land ownership as well as child rearing, for patterns of dispute settlement as well as methods of warfare. Perhaps the wonder is not that Europeans found it so difficult to evangelize Native Americans, but that *any* of the Indians took the Christian message for themselves.

The first Africans brought to the New World arrived in Virginia as indentured servants in 1619. Soon slavery became the norm for Afri-

---

8. See Hartmut Beck, *Brüder in vielen Völkern: 250 Jahre Mission der Brüdergemeine* (Erlangen: Verlag der Ev.-Luth. Mission, 1981); and Carl John Fliegel, *Index to the Records of the Moravian Mission among the Indians of North America,* 2 vols. (New Haven, CT: Research Publications, 1979).

cans who reached the European colonies, often as objects of plunder. In the seventeenth century, the only North American protest against racial chattel slavery came from a small band of Quakers and German Mennonites in Pennsylvania, who in 1688 asked the pointed question, "Have these poor negers not as much right to fight for their freedom, as you have to keep them slaves?"[9] But such protests were very rare. For their part, slaves and the smaller number of free African Americans originally found Christianity as alien as other aspects of European culture. A combination of masters unwilling to provide religious instruction and slaves alienated from those who did try to preach to them meant that it was not until the early eighteenth century that a few African Americans began to respond positively to the Christian message.[10] One of the ministers supported by the Society for the Propagation of the Gospel in Foreign Parts, Francis Le Jau, preached with some success to slaves in his huge South Carolina parish during the first decade of the eighteenth century. But Le Jau's insistence that conversion did not alter the slave's status, along with the more general clash of African and European cultures, guaranteed scant success for his preaching. Not until the coming of evangelical revivalism in the 1730s would an appreciable number of African Americans be drawn into the churches.

New England Puritanism

The experience of the Puritans in New England was unusual for colonial America because, while other outposts were only getting started, they succeeded in establishing a stable Christian society. In England, Puritans had attempted to reform the lives of individuals, the practice of the national English church, and the structures of English society. Although Puritans (with their Parliamentary allies) succeeded in win-

9. Lester B. Scherer, *Slavery and the Churches in Early America, 1619-1819* (Grand Rapids: Eerdmans, 1975), p. 42.

10. See Sylvia R. Frey and Betty Wood, *Come Shouting to Zion: African American Protestantism in the American South and British Caribbean to 1830* (Chapel Hill: University of North Carolina Press, 1998), pp. 63-79.

ning the English Civil War, and although Oliver Cromwell's tenure as Lord Protector of England (1649-1658) witnessed the triumph of some Puritan principles, these were short-lived victories. The restoration of the monarchy in 1660 ended Puritan efforts at creating the kind of comprehensive Christian society their Protestant understanding of Scripture demanded.

It was different in the New World.[11] Led by ministers like John Cotton (1594-1652) and Thomas Shepard (1605-1649) in Massachusetts, Thomas Hooker (1586-1647) in Connecticut, and John Davenport (1597-1670) in New Haven — as well as by laymen like John Winthrop (1588-1649) of Massachusetts and William Bradford (1590-1657) of Plymouth — the "Puritan experiment" tested whether consistent Reformation Protestantism could flourish in an environment with external enemies removed. Their environment in New England was so free of enemies because disease had greatly reduced the Native American population, and New England contained too few natural resources to be coveted by other European powers.

In New England, these leaders translated their aspirations into reality by constructing a society governed by a comprehensive theology of *covenant*. In Puritan thinking, the basis for individual salvation was God's covenant promise that he would redeem those who placed their trust in Christ. Puritans explained that promise as the outworking of a covenant within the Godhead whereby the Father chose those who would be saved, the Son accomplished their redemption, and the Spirit made it effective. Although not all Puritans agreed on ecclesiology, those who came to New England held that the basis for a thoroughly reformed church was the commitment of its members to God and to each other. In New England this commitment was expressed in the acceptance (or "owning") of a written church covenant. In addition, Puri-

---

11. An outstanding work linking Puritanism in England and America is Stephen Foster, *The Long Argument: English Puritanism and the Shaping of New England Culture, 1570-1700* (Chapel Hill: University of North Carolina Press, 1991). For expert overviews of recent literature, see Charles L. Cohen, "The Post-Puritan Paradigm of Early American Religious History," *William & Mary Quarterly* 54 (Oct. 1997): 695-722; and David D. Hall, "Narrating Puritanism," in *New Directions in American Religious History,* ed. Harry S. Stout and D. G. Hart (New York: Oxford University Press, 1997), pp. 51-83.

tans held that promises made by God to his covenanted people as a whole prepared the way for a healthy society.[12]

The American Puritans displayed their genius in the way they combined these individual, ecclesiastical, and social covenants. In the first years of settlement, ministers and magistrates agreed on a somewhat more visible standard of conversion than had prevailed in England. With religious enemies scarce in the New World, internal spiritual condition came to serve as the criterion for church membership that external opposition had provided in the Old World. New Englanders asked prospective members to testify before the assembled congregation that they had undergone a saving experience of God's grace. Men and women who made this profession became church members; such a profession then entitled men to become freemen (or voters) in the colony as well as members of a church.[13] By this procedure Puritan leaders made the covenants interlocking. The covenant of grace qualified a person for church membership and (for males) a voting role in the colony's public life. Public life could then fulfill the social covenant with God, since freemen selected the rulers and put laws in place that honored God's written word.

Under this general system, the first generation of New England Puritans achieved considerable success. A few complaints did come from protesters like Roger Williams and Anne Hutchinson (1591-1642), articulate leaders who held that the Massachusetts stress on visible profession of faith undercut reliance on divine grace. Toleration, however, was in short supply for those who questioned the Puritan Way. Massachusetts authorities banned Williams and Hutchinson and imposed fines on other dissenters, such as the Baptists.[14] During the period of

12. On the Puritan understanding of the covenant, the classic statement is by Perry Miller, "The Marrow of Puritan Divinity," in Miller, *Errand into the Wilderness* (Cambridge: Harvard University Press, 1956), pp. 48-98; but see also the corrections in George M. Marsden, "Perry Miller's Rehabilitation of the Puritans: A Critique," *Church History* 39 (Mar. 1970): 91-105.

13. See Edmund S. Morgan, *Visible Saint: The History of a Puritan Idea* (New York: New York University Press, 1963).

14. On Anne Hutchinson, see David D. Hall, ed., *The Antinomian Controversy, 1636-1638* (Middletown, CT: Wesleyan University Press, 1968); on persecution of Baptists, see

1659-1661, they also executed (by public hanging) four Quakers who persisted in returning to the colony after they had been sent away.

It was never the case that all New Englanders subscribed fully to the Puritan system, but on balance, the experiment worked well. New England remained at peace, its civilization incorporated Puritan ideals in the ordering of public life, exemplary cooperation existed between magistrates and ministers, the pious reveled in the freedom to hear Puritan sermons, and the political order functioned efficiently. Relative to other seventeenth-century societies, the system also enjoyed an extraordinary degree of popular support.

The looming difficulty for this New England experiment was the younger generation. Increasingly, sons and daughters of the first settlers failed to experience conversion; consequently, fewer and fewer of the second generation presented themselves for church membership. Steadily the fear grew that the Puritans' interlocking network of covenants would unravel. If there were no new converts, there could be no covenanted church; if there was no covenanted church, there could be no godly society. In the face of this crisis, Massachusetts' leaders proposed an ingenious expedient. Meeting as a synod in 1662, the ministers established what later historians called the "Half-Way Covenant." Under this plan, baptized individuals of good behavior could present their children for baptism, but neither they nor their children could take the Lord's Supper unless they made a personal profession of faith. The framers of the Half-Way Covenant hoped to preserve both the integrity of local congregations as the gathering of the elect and the participation of as many people as possible in the Puritan system.[15]

Historians have offered mixed judgments on the Half-Way Covenant. To some, it has seemed a step toward dry religious formalism; to others, it was a creative way of keeping alive historic Puritan aspirations. Almost all have agreed, however, that time was taking its toll on the Puritan experiment in the New World. A theology forged in the cru-

---

Baptist Piety: The Last Will and Testimony of Obadiah Holmes, ed. Edwin S. Gaustad (Grand Rapids: Eerdmans, 1978).

15. See Robert G. Pope, *The Half-Way Covenant: Church Membership in Puritan New England* (Princeton: Princeton University Press, 1969).

cible of English religious strife could survive in America, but only by modifying its original ideals. Fragments of the Puritan experiment might remain, like the later propensity of some citizens of the United States to look upon their nation as a "New Israel" in covenant with God, but not the Puritan system as a whole. In England, an antagonistic state church and their own internal disagreements defeated the Puritan ideal, but in America the passage of time and the mundane problem of replicating faith in the new generations became the Achilles' heel of the Puritans' practical theology. Nonetheless, the American Puritan effort to construct a theologically rooted, comprehensively Christian society remains one of the most intriguing intellectual as well as practical efforts in the early modern history of Christianity.

By the early eighteenth century, New England Puritanism was fading as a comprehensive way of life. As that century developed, widespread economic and intellectual change, quarrels among the churches, and the entrance of political ideas that would later be called "democratic" and "republican" undercut the interlocking power of the covenants. Even so, Puritan traits of earnestness, religious dedication to tasks, and moral seriousness remained alive as powerful influences in New England and much of the United States. These are the traits that later observers have consistently traced back to the Puritans.[16]

Christian Reflection

Christian thinking in early North America featured efforts to accommodate hereditary intellectual habits to radically new environments. To be sure, a few noteworthy exercises in traditional theology were pursued. Catholics in Mexico City as early as the mid-sixteenth century established a center of higher learning on the model of the University of Salamanca. By the middle of the next century, similar foundations were

16. For a fruitful discussion of this heritage by a European observer, see André Siegfried, *America Comes of Age: A French Analysis* (New York: Harcourt, Brace, 1927), pp. 394-95. More generally, see Daniel Walker Howe, "The Impact of Puritanism on American Culture," in *Encyclopedia of American Religious Experience,* ed. Charles A. Lippy and Peter W. Williams (New York: Scribner, 1988), vol. 2, pp. 1057-74.

in place for Catholics in Quebec (Laval, 1663) and Protestants in Massachusetts (Harvard, 1636). As another example of formal theology, Boston minister Samuel Willard (1640-1707) during the 1670s and 1680s produced a massive set of lectures on the Westminster Confession, which had been composed by English Puritans in the 1640s. They were published after Willard's death in 1726 under the title *Compleat Body of Divinity*. But such formal efforts were unusual, since for both Catholics and Protestants practical actions to found churches and preserve the faith among settlers loomed much larger than formal theology. At the same time, however, Christian thought of a practical, problem-solving bent was abundantly present in North America during the sixteenth and seventeenth centuries.

After only a few decades of Spanish and Portuguese exploration in Central and South America, the tragic confrontation between Europeans and Native Americans produced notable reflection. Some came from the highest reaches of Catholicism: in 1537, Pope Paul III issued the bull *Sublimis Deus,* which, in the face of colonial practice to the contrary, defined the Indians as fully human and fully capable of becoming Christians. Firsthand contact with Native Americans was also a spur for rethinking settled European convictions. Bartolomé de las Casas (1474-1566), who lived in several Caribbean and central American regions, was converted in 1514 from his life as a Spanish lord who profited from the virtual enslavement of Indians to a lifetime of advocacy on behalf of the Native Americans. Las Casas, who eventually became a Dominican, published several books defending the Indians and upbraiding Europeans for treating them like animals. Toward the end of his life, he also began a lengthy exposition of missions theology, *The Only Way of Attracting All Unbelievers to the True Religion.* This landmark work, which does not survive in complete form, held out ideals of conversion without coercion, of catechesis before conversion, and of Christian missionaries accommodating (wherever possible) to native culture.[17]

European contact with Native Americans also stimulated Francisco

---

17. See Bartolomé de las Casas, *In Defense of the Indians,* trans. Stafford Poole (DeKalb: Northern Illinois University Press, 1992); and Bartolomé de las Casas, *The Only Way,* ed. Helen Rand Parish (New York: Paulist, 1992).

de Vitoria (1483-1546), professor at the University of Salamanca in Spain. In 1538 and 1539, Vitoria published two lectures on "the Indies" that outlined principles of international law he hoped could guide the actions of all nations. Influenced by the Scottish theologian John Major, Vitoria undermined much of the rationale justifying Spanish conquests in the New World, defended the sovereignty of Indian rulers in their own domains, and spelled out conditions in which it might be appropriate for a European power to wage a just war on non-Europeans.[18]

In the New World itself, Jesuits, perhaps because of their earlier efforts to negotiate the cultural divide between European and non-European cultures in the Far East, set the pace in practical efforts to contextualize the Christian message. The most notable example of such contextualization was the French Jesuit mission to the Huron Indians in what is now Ontario, Canada. Led by Father Jean de Brébeuf (1593-1649), the Jesuits enjoyed nearly two decades of labor among the Hurons before intra-Indian warfare led to the martyrdom of Brébeuf along with several of his colleagues and to the end of the mission. Brébeuf took special pains to prepare appropriate Christian literature in the Huron language, including the Christmas carol, "Twas the moon of wintertime when all the birds had fled, That mighty Gitchi Manitou sent angel choirs instead."[19] He also provided specific instructions to Jesuit recruits concerning the life to which they were called: "Instead of being a great master and great Theologian as in France, you must reckon on being here a humble Scholar, and then, good God! with what masters! — women, little children, and all the Savages, — and exposed to their laughter. The Huron language will be your saint Thomas and your Aristotle; . . . You must have sincere affection for the Savages, — looking upon them as ransomed by the blood of the son of God, and as our brethren, with whom we are to pass the rest of our lives."[20]

18. Francisco de Vitoria, *Political Writings,* ed. Anthony Pagdan and Jeremy Lawrance (New York: Cambridge University Press, 1991).

19. Quoted from the 1918 Canadian Anglican *Book of Common Prayer and Common Praise.*

20. *The Jesuit Relations and Allied Documents: Travels and Explorations of the Jesuit Missionaries in New France, 1618-1791,* ed. Reuben Gold Thwaites (1896; reprint, New York: Pageant, 1959), vol. 10, p. 93; vol. 12, p. 117.

Movement beyond European Christendom also forced settlers to rethink questions of toleration. Much in advance of Europe, American settlement opened an opportunity to consider whether different kinds of Christians could live together in one society. Roger Williams (ca. 1603-1683), the Calvinist Separatist who tormented the Puritan establishment in Massachusetts, founded the colony of Rhode Island on the principle that government should not coerce religious practice or belief. On a visit to England during the early days of the Puritan rebellion against Charles I, Williams published his famous tract *The Bloody Tenent of Persecution for Cause of Conscience in a Conference between Truth and Peace* (1644). Despite its convoluted prose, the work set out a sharp-edged biblical argument for the free exercise of religion.[21]

New World conditions stimulated similar concerns in two other English colonies. In Roman Catholic Maryland, the force of circumstances led to a short-lived but important experiment. After Parliament and the Puritans had gained the upper hand in England's Civil War, Maryland's Catholic assembly passed an Act of Toleration (1649) in hopes of preserving the right to practice Catholicism. Although this act would soon be repealed, Maryland's innovation marked a breakthrough in imagining a single polity where Catholics and Protestants could live together in peace. For his part, William Penn came to convictions about toleration from his beliefs as a Quaker. In such works as *The Great Cause of Liberty of Conscience* (1670), Penn extended the Quaker sense of individual religious competence into an argument against state mandates for religion. As Penn put these principles to work in the New World colonies of New Jersey and especially Pennsylvania, he created what was, after Rhode Island, the most tolerant civil government in the Christian world. Penn's commitment to religious freedom was also the reason Pennsylvania proved so attractive to immigrants from Germany and elsewhere on the Continent who sought freedom to practice religion as directed by their consciences.

In the English colonies of the seventeenth century, toleration first appeared as a practical expedient. For Roger Williams, it was a way of

---

21. See Edmund S. Morgan, *Roger Williams: The Church and the State* (New York: Harcourt, Brace & World, 1967).

protecting his thoroughly Calvinist understanding of salvation (in which only God, and no human ecclesiastical structure, could mediate redemption). For Catholics in Maryland, toleration was a way of protecting their own existence in a Protestant English system. As with other spheres of practical Christian activity in the New World, however, the practice of toleration led almost inevitably to self-conscious thoughts about the idea of toleration. By the time of William Penn, earlier experiments were broadening out into positive principles. In 1700 very few residents of North America agreed with Penn that religious liberty and the loosening of church-state ties was a positive good. Yet American practice was moving in that direction. When pietistic and evangelical forms of Protestantism began to spring up in the New World during the 1730s and 1740s, latent differences with European practice became even more obvious.

Early American Protestantism and the Religious Future of the United States

For the religious development of the United States, it was significant that Protestantism predominated in the early English colonies. Comparisons with settlement patterns in New France and New Spain, where versions of early modern Roman Catholicism shaped colonial experience, are very useful: in particular, they demonstrate that the distinctive American combination of strong Protestant allegiance and a liberal social polity was not the only possibility for Christianity in the New World. (Regrettably, for the sake of space, notice of Mexico and Canada will now largely drop out of this narrative until Chapter Ten.)

For the United States, however, it is not enough to note that early settlement was Protestant; it is also important to note the kind of Protestantism that prevailed. The earliest American Protestants were predominantly from the British Isles rather than from the Continent. They were also more likely to be Reformed (that is, Calvinist) than either Lutheran or Anabaptist. In the famous phrase of the German sociologist Max Weber, these Protestants practiced a "this-worldly asceticism." Like the medieval religious, they practiced asceticism, or the disciplined organization of all life and attitudes for the glory of God. But unlike the monks and nuns of the Middle Ages, these Protestants thought that discipline for God should be exerted *in* the world. Family life, business practices, political decisions, management of leisure time — all such concerns should be pursued with religious seriousness. Thus it was that, as these Reformed Protestants came to America, they were seeking not a private space to be religious but a free space for their religion to transform. Later contributions by Protestants to American democracy, capitalism, individualism, and voluntary associations all sprang — sometimes for good, sometimes for ill — from the character of the sixteenth-century Reformation.

For later American history, it is also important that most of the Protestants who came to America in the colonial period were Reformed.[22] Lutherans on the Continent and as immigrants to America retained considerable ambiguity about life in the world, for Luther's theology of "two kingdoms" had taught that the affairs of the church could be separated from affairs of society. Yes, God ruled over all, and yes, Christians should be active in society. But according to Luther, the rules for Christian engagement with society were different from rules for the church. Anabaptists, such as the Mennonites, drew an even sharper distinction between church and world. As pacifists and as opponents of infant baptism, they sought nearly complete separation from the world around them. In the Anabaptist ideal — which Mennonites in Canada and the United States would embody with distinction — the church influenced society primarily through its example of separation from the world.

Reformed or Calvinistic Protestants were different. Already in Europe, Calvinists had become the most "successful" Protestants, primarily because they so effectively integrated religion and society. Their view of God as ruler over all meant that doing God's will in every possible respect was the appropriate approach to the world. Church and society

22. For an extended discussion, see Baird Tipson, "Calvinist Heritage," *Scribner's Encyclopedia*, vol. 1, pp. 451-66; Daniel Walker Howe, "The Impact of Puritanism on American Culture," *Scribner's Encyclopedia*, vol. 2, pp. 1057-74; and Mark A. Noll, *One Nation Under God? Christian Faith and Political Action in America* (San Francisco: Harper & Row, 1988), pp. 14-31.

might be distinct spheres, but both were under God's direct control, and the people of God were supposed to exert that control. These were the convictions that the New World's most influential Protestants brought with them. They were grounded in the Reformation generally, but refined by the specific influence of Calvinist theologians and shaped by the specific experiences of the Reformed Puritans in Britain. Many, many religious influences would come to bear on North America, but Reformed influences, taken in this general sense, would never lose their prime importance.

CHAPTER THREE

The Churches Become American, 1730-1830

In 1769 the first preachers commissioned by John Wesley for service in America arrived in the New World. Wesley's movement for reform and renewal within the Church of England had already been given the name "Methodist," since it emphasized a systematic approach to Christian piety and self-sacrificing social service. Although Methodism spread quite slowly in America until after the American War for Independence (1775-1783), the arrival of those first itinerant (or traveling) preachers was extremely significant. After the American Revolution, Methodism became by far the fastest-growing form of Protestantism in America, and Methodist standards of piety, worship, and service exerted a huge impact on American religious life. The reasons for the rise of the Methodists and the nature of their expansion explain much of the nature of Christianity during the founding era of the United States.

A Colonial Revival

The Methodists, however, were not the first to promote the new evangelical style. Rather, they were following where leaders of the colonial Great Awakening had led. The Awakening, which is usually dated 1735-1755, arrived at a time of transition in the Christian history of colonial

America. In the early decades of the century the number and variety of churches continued to expand, but a series of developments pointed to difficulties for the transplanting of European-style Christianity to America. For one thing, both population and the spread of population were growing more rapidly than the churches. Thus, even though the number of congregations was increasing, the number of people per colonial church was increasing even more rapidly. The rapid spread of the population also meant that each church was responsible, on average, for ever-greater amounts of territory.[1]

There were also intellectual difficulties. To be sure, formal education in the colonies was still Protestant, with all the colonial colleges operating under the influence of regional Protestant denominations: Congregational influence was dominant at Harvard and Yale in New England, Presbyterian influence guided the College of New Jersey (later Princeton University), Anglican influence prevailed at the College of William and Mary in Virginia, and a variety of informal Protestant influences came together to form the institutions that later merged as the University of Pennsylvania in Philadelphia.[2] Yet the larger intellectual picture was not so comforting for traditional Protestants. From the end of the seventeenth century, new voices in Britain were modifying traditional beliefs about God's activity in the world, about the Christian Trinity, and about human nature. The English thinker John Toland, for example, published a book in 1696 entitled *Christianity Not Mysterious*. It argued that human reason was adequate for many of the supernatural tasks that had been traditionally assigned to God. Such "deist" views never overwhelmed the Protestants in America, but they were read by some elite groups and would be taken up by some of the

1. On the difficult task of ascertaining the number of church members (and adherents, which was always larger), see Patricia U. Bonomi and Peter Eisenstadt, "Church Adherence in the Eighteenth-Century American Colonies," *William and Mary Quarterly* 39 (1982): 245-86; Jon Butler, *Awash in a Sea of Faith: Christianizing the American People* (Cambridge: Harvard University Press, 1990), pp. 191-93; and Rodney Stark and Roger Finke, "American Religion in 1776: A Statistical Portrait," *Sociological Analysis* 49 (Spring 1988): 39-51.

2. See J. David Hoeveler, *The American Colonial Colleges: Intellect and Politics* (Lanham, MD: Rowman & Littlefield, 2001).

important founding fathers of the United States, such as Thomas Paine, Benjamin Franklin, and Thomas Jefferson.[3]

The major difficulty for eighteenth-century American Protestants, however, was the reality of religious pluralism. Overwhelmingly the organizing principle of religious life in Europe remained the ideal of one church for one place. It was this pattern that the Puritan colonies of New England and the Anglican colonies in the South tried to replicate. By the mid-eighteenth century, however, the European pattern was breaking down fast. Not only were Baptists, Presbyterians, Methodists, and others seeking their own space in Congregationalist Massachusetts and Anglican Virginia, in the middle colonies of New York, New Jersey, and Pennsylvania, so many different Protestant groups had taken root that it had become a practical impossibility to favor any one of them over the others. Dissenting churches soon gained the support of political leaders like Thomas Jefferson and James Madison. These leaders, however, favored disestablishing the churches more from a general concern for liberty than for religious reasons.

A count of churches suggests the tide of Protestant diversity that was rolling into America. In 1700, Congregationalists and Anglicans constituted almost two-thirds of all churches in the thirteen colonies; by 1780 the proportion of Congregational and Anglican was reduced to approximately one-third. It was not that these two seventeenth-century denominations had stopped growing. The number of Congregationalist churches, for example, increased from 146 in 1700 to 749 in 1780. It was, rather, that the number of other churches was growing much faster. As an example, in 1700 the total of colonial Presbyterian, German Reformed, and Dutch Reformed churches was 54; by 1780 that number was 823.[4]

At this point it is worth pausing to note that the churches in colo-

---

3. For early American promoters of similar ideas, see John Corrigan, *The Hidden Balance: Religion and the Social Theories of Charles Chauncy and Jonathan Mayhew* (New York: Cambridge University Press, 1987); for the survival of these ideas in the early history of the United States, see Kerry S. Walters, *The American Deists: Voices of Reason and Dissent in the Early Republic* (Manhattan: University Press of Kansas, 1992).

4. Edwin S. Gaustad, *Historical Atlas of Religion in America* (rev. ed., New York: Harper & Row, 1976).

nial America were almost all Protestant. At the time of the American Revolution, there were only about fifty Roman Catholic churches in the thirteen colonies, and only a few scattered Jewish settlements, mainly in New York, Rhode Island, and Philadelphia. Representatives of other non-Christian religions were still virtually unknown in America.

In this shifting ecclesiastical situation, a major change occurred in the character of Protestantism. That change was partly a response to the religious diversity that had already emerged in the colonies, but it was also a result of the major shift in the character of Christianity itself during the eighteenth century. The new element is usually identified as "pietism" on the Continent or as "evangelicalism" for Britain and North America. The essence of pietism or evangelicalism was a movement away from formal, outward, and established religion to personal, inward, and heartfelt religion. In the American colonies, the coming of evangelicalism sparked a religious revival.

The most visible symbol of the new evangelicalism was the traveling Anglican preacher George Whitefield (1715-1770).[5] Whitefield had been an Oxford undergraduate of very modest means when he was recruited into the "Holy Club" where John Wesley and his brother, the hymn writer Charles, were prominent. In his student years, Whitefield underwent a conversion of the conventional Puritan kind. But from the mid-1730s on, Whitefield's efforts to promote Christianity were anything but conventional.

For one thing, he preached wherever the people could be gathered, which was usually outside of the churches, often not on Sunday, at any hour of the day or night, and sometimes to immense crowds. For another, he wore his Anglican ordination lightly and eagerly cooperated with Protestants of every sort who would support his work: Baptists, Presbyterians, Congregationalists, Moravians, the early Methodists, and more. Whitefield prepared his sermons carefully, but in a sharp break with standard practice he delivered them extemporaneously,

---

5. See Arnold Dallimore, *George Whitefield*, 2 vols. (London: Banner of Truth, 1970-1980); Harry S. Stout, *The Divine Dramatist: George Whitefield and the Rise of Modern Evangelicalism* (Grand Rapids: Eerdmans, 1991); and Frank Lambert, *Pedlar in Divinity: George Whitefield and the Transatlantic Revivals, 1737-1770* (Princeton: Princeton University Press, 1994).

talking directly to the people. In yet another innovation, Whitefield and his associates became expert exploiters of newspapers, pamphlets, and other print media.

Whitefield's message featured the "New Birth," a phrase taken from Jesus' dialogue with the Jewish leader Nicodemus as recorded in the third chapter of the Gospel of John. In Whitefield's sermons, the new birth grounded a compelling appeal to be converted. Whitefield was a riveting preacher with great rhetorical skills; when he thundered forth the stern demands of God's law, when he wept at the pitiful state of lost sinners, when his face turned radiant in describing the glories of union with Christ, people listened. They listened in England, Wales, Scotland, and Ireland, and they listened throughout his seven trips to the colonies.

During his second visit in 1740, Whitefield preached extensively at his home base in Savannah (where he ran an orphanage), in Charleston, Philadelphia, New York, Boston, and many smaller sites in between. His tour of New England that fall was one of the most dramatic events in American religious history. For more than a month, Whitefield preached almost every day to crowds of up to eight thousand spellbound listeners at a time when the whole population of Boston, the region's largest city, was not much larger than that.

In traditional historical accounts, Whitefield is the central figure of the Great Awakening. As a few recent historians have pointed out, however, the Awakening with which Whitefield is associated was not a tightly organized movement with discrete boundaries.[6] It was rather a general movement toward a more personal, emotional, inward, and experiential religion that fed upon dramatic preaching occasions featuring Whitefield and his many imitators.

In simplest terms, the shift represented by Whitefield marked the passing of Puritanism and the rise of evangelicalism as the dominant Protestant expression in America. In this new form, loyalty to a particu-

---

6. See Jon Butler, "Enthusiasm Described and Decried: The Great Awakening as Interpretive Fiction," *Journal of American History* 69 (Sept. 1982): 305-25; but see also the response by Frank Lambert, *Inventing the "Great Awakening"* (Princeton: Princeton University Press, 1999).

lar church was less important than a vibrant religion of the heart. In fact, groups inspired by Whitefield's kind of preaching created fragmentation in New England's traditionally unified churches. The careful theological writing of Jonathan Edwards, which is examined at greater length in Chapter Nine, both explained the dynamics of the revival and encouraged the fragmentation of the church. Some of those who had been born again in the revival left their town's Congregational churches to form Baptist or "Separate" societies where fellowship was restricted to people who could testify to a work of divine grace in their lives.[7]

Outside of New England, by contrast, the revival fires associated with the Great Awakening did more to constitute churches than to fragment them. These new churches were founded with scant concern for church-state establishment; in fact, sometimes they were formed in opposition to the principle of establishment. They were created by Baptists in the middle colonies and the South, Presbyterians in Virginia, German immigrant congregations in Pennsylvania, and soon Methodists everywhere.

This new form of Protestantism was much more attuned to the expanding, market-oriented societies of the eighteenth century than to the ideals of stable church establishments from Europe. Whitefield took his dynamic message to the people. He masterfully exploited the press — especially controversy in the press. Twentieth-century historians use a vocabulary he would not have recognized to call him a master "salesman" for his "product." These words are nonetheless apt in the sense that Whitefield seemed intuitively to grasp that in a new era of commerce, trade, growing cities, and breakdown of European traditions, dynamic new techniques were needed to promote the Christian message.[8]

In the wake of George Whitefield and the broader colonial Awakening, many changes were immediately evident in the churches. Religious bodies that stressed freedom from state control, such as the Baptists, or

7. See C. C. Goen, *Revivalism and Separatism in New England, 1740-1800* (New Haven: Yale University Press, 1962).

8. See Timothy D. Hall, *Contested Boundaries: Itinerancy and the Reshaping of the Colonial American Religious World* (Durham, NC: Duke University Press, 1994).

that relied on their own initiative rather than state connections, such as the Methodists, flourished. A new form of hymnody, with fresh melodies and direct, affecting lyrics, rejuvenated corporate worship. Samuel Davies of Virginia (1723-1761) was an author of such hymns; Davies, who planted numerous Presbyterian churches as the first major representatives in Virginia of a religion other than Anglicanism, hoped that all ages, both sexes, and all races (Indian and African American as well as white) could be joined in the hymns they sang together.[9]

The revivalism promoted by Whitefield was also a religion that could be transported easily to the frontier. It required only an earnest preacher and an audience of individuals who were concerned about their souls before God. The older established churches struggled when they tried to expand to the frontier. But revivalists succeeded, at least in part, because they abandoned establishments, formal educational requirements for ministers, and other habits of European religion.

The older pattern of church establishments and religion conceived in terms of a whole community did not pass away immediately. Connecticut and Massachusetts retained vestiges of their church-state connections far into the next century. In addition, the most active Protestants among America's founding fathers all tried at first to devise some scheme for having governments support the churches. John Witherspoon, the Presbyterian president of Princeton, was the only clergyman to sign the United States' Declaration of Independence in 1776. Soon thereafter he proposed a plan for government to establish more than one religion in a single region, a plan similar to one advocated in Virginia by the patriotic orator Patrick Henry, an active Anglican. But these proposals did not succeed. Religious leaders shaped by the colonial revivals joined founding fathers like Jefferson and Madison in working toward the First Amendment to the United States Constitution (1789), which prohibited the national government from establishing any one particular religion even as it guaranteed to all citizens protection for the free exercise of religion.

Immediately after the founding of the United States, Protestants

---

9. See George William Pilcher, *Samuel Davies: Apostle of Dissent in Colonial Virginia* (Knoxville: University of Tennessee Press, 1971).

undertook a major mobilization effort. That mobilization was based largely on the new pattern described above, with an appeal to individuals and creation of voluntary agencies to achieve religious and civic goals. In the events that led to these new religious patterns, the shift of sensibilities that Whitefield pioneered was the key.

Christianity Engages the African-American Community

Social, political, and economic changes also opened new possibilities for colonists not of British origin. Some attention to the religious needs of African Americans, for example, had been apparent in the early colonies, but not much. Slavery, which became well established in the southern colonies, and which also existed or was promoted in the middle and northern colonies, came into existence without a great deal of conscious reflection. Cultural paternalism was the order of the day, with only occasional pangs of conscience about religious institutions for the slaves.[10] This situation began to change during the Great Awakening. Whitefield, though himself a slave owner, went out of his way to preach to African Americans and also encouraged black converts to take an active part in colonial churches. Samuel Davies of Virginia was only one of several other proponents of the new evangelicalism who tried to incorporate African Americans into churches. In the years after the Awakening, several of Jonathan Edwards' students, including Samuel Hopkins, a minister in Newport, Rhode Island, advanced religious arguments against slavery. They held that it was a violation of the "being" of humans of any sort to be held in bondage by others. Hopkins and his fellows were joined by a few ministers who opposed the enthusiasm of the revivalists but who agreed that Christians should not tolerate slavery. Ezra Stiles, a Congregationalist minister with Hopkins in Newport, was the most articulate of these advocates.[11]

10. A classic account is Edmund S. Morgan, *American Slavery, American Freedom: The Ordeal of Colonial Virginia* (New York: Norton, 1975).

11. See James D. Essig, *The Bonds of Wickedness: American Evangelicals Against Slavery, 1770-1808* (Philadelphia: Temple University Press, 1982).

Major breakthroughs for the spread of Protestant Christianity among African Americans did not occur, however, until the era of the American Revolution.[12] The formation of black churches was beset with every kind of social prejudice and legal disadvantage, but emerge they did. The first continuing black church was the Silver Bluff Church in Aiken County, South Carolina, where an African-American preacher, David George (1742-1810), established a congregation around 1773 or 1774. George's pilgrimage marked him as one of the most remarkable religious figures of his century. After serving as a slave, he was converted through the influence of another slave named Cyrus. Soon George began to exhort his fellow bondsmen, an activity that led to his becoming, in effect, the pastor of the Silver Bluff Church.

As for many other slaves, the American Revolution was a blessing in disguise for George. American patriots were trying to throw off the "slavery" of Parliament, but for those in chattel bondage like David George, the British were the agents who combated racial, chattel slavery. When the British abandoned Savannah, George went with them to Nova Scotia, where he helped establish the first black Baptist churches in what would later become Canada. Then in 1793 George immigrated with a small company of other Nova Scotian blacks to the west coast of Africa, where he helped found Baptist churches in the nation of Sierra Leone. George was thus instrumental in beginning the first black Baptist churches to three very different parts of the world.[13]

Several other African American churches were founded in and around Savannah during the Revolutionary period. One of these was by Andrew Bryan (1737-1812) who, with his wife Hannah, opened the "Ethiopian Church of Jesus Christ" in Savannah (which exists to this day as the First African Baptist Church). Bryan nurtured this church under the British and then under the American patriots, who some-

12. Mechal Sobel, *Trabelin' On: The Slave Journey to an Afro-Baptist Faith* (rev. ed., Princeton: Princeton University Press, 1988); and Sylvia R. Frey and Betty Wood, *Come Shouting to Zion: African American Protestantism in the American South and British Caribbean to 1830* (Chapel Hill: University of North Carolina Press, 1998), pp. 80-148.

13. See Grant Gordon, *From Slavery to Freedom: The Life of David George, Pioneer Black Baptist Minister* (Hantsport, Nova Scotia: Baptist Historical Committee for the Atlantic Provinces, 1992).

times took extreme measures to frustrate his work as a pastor. In 1790 he was briefly imprisoned with about fifty members of his congregation for refusing to heed the guidelines of the slave system. Bryan's own master was more sympathetic and helped him re-establish the church just outside Savannah. Eventually Bryan purchased his own and his wife's freedom. By 1800 their congregation numbered seven hundred strong, and soon the Second and Third Baptist churches of Savannah arose from his work.

The significance of such preliminary efforts at founding African American churches was profound. From the religion of the slaveholders, slaves caught a message of liberation. To those whom colonial elites considered the dregs of society, the Christian faith conveyed a message of hope, dignity, and purpose.

The American Revolution

A rich historiography now exists for the question of how the churches and religious rhetoric contributed to the American break from Britain.[14] Less work has been devoted to the impact of the Revolution on the churches, even though that is the critical issue for a history of Christianity.[15] The kind of revivalism advanced by George Whitefield certainly promoted themes of spiritual liberty that later appeals for political liberty paralleled. Tom Paine's famous tract from early 1776, *Common Sense,* has long been recognized as one of the most important

14. See especially Nathan O. Hatch, *The Sacred Cause of Liberty: Republican Thought and the Millennium in Revolutionary New England* (New Haven: Yale University Press, 1977); Ruth H. Bloch, *Visionary Republic: Millennial Themes in American Thought, 1756-1800* (New York: Cambridge University Press, 1985); Patricia U. Bonomi, *Under the Cope of Heaven: Religion, Society, and Politics in Colonial America* (New York: Oxford University Press, 1986), pp. 187-222; and Melvin B. Endy, Jr. "Just War, Holy War, and Millennialism in Revolutionary America," *William and Mary Quarterly* 42 (1985): 3-25.

15. But see Nathan O. Hatch, *The Democratization of American Christianity* (New Haven: Yale University Press, 1989); and Mark A. Noll, "The Revolution in the Churches," in *A History of Christianity in the United States and Canada* (Grand Rapids: Eerdmans, 1992), pp. 143-62.

factors moving the colonists to support independence from Britain. To a student of colonial religion, it is remarkable for its lengthy citation of Scripture and the fervor of its address, for these were characteristics popularized by evangelical revival preachers that the deist Paine nevertheless knew how to exploit for his own purposes. More religious debate occurred about whether to support the Revolution than most of the American churches remembered, since after independence was achieved the churches were eager to demonstrate their solidarity with the new nation. Yet loyalty to Britain, which was often rooted in religious convictions, led to the migration of many to Canada or Britain. Most of the Anabaptists and many of the Quakers in the colonies remained true to their pacifist principles and so were sometimes harassed by both patriots and loyalists. At the same time, leading clergy of the most visible denominations — especially Congregationalists and Presbyterians — favored the patriot cause, and some of these preachers were among the most vociferous supporters of American independence.[16]

As an ideological force, the Revolution promoted republican principles of checks and balances on the exercise of power, suspicion of accumulated power, and ideals of disinterested public service. Increasingly, it also encouraged democratic ideals for public life. Such emphases eventually exerted considerable influence in the churches. European assumptions about inherited authority, patterns of deference to tradition, and the power of historical precedent became as suspect in religion as they were in political life.

At the same time, the fixation on liberty could also produce ironic results. At least in some of the churches, public mobilization to secure American liberties from Britain had an unexpected effect on relations between men and women. Churches that had been influenced by the colonial revivals often paid less attention to traditional male authority while offering converted women considerable room for speaking and even guiding the churches. When, however, male leaders of these churches were drawn into the dispute with Britain, the political stan-

---

16. Mark A. Noll, *Christians in the American Revolution* (Grand Rapids: Eerdmans, 1976).

dards of liberty they defended encouraged them to show more concern for their own prerogatives as public spokesmen. The result in the churches could be a restriction of women's opportunities, a silencing of women in church discussions, and a new monopoly for men of the churches' disciplinary powers.[17] For the arena of public ideology as well as the arena of relationships among American citizens, the far-ranging changes of the Revolution extended into the churches along with all other colonial institutions.

After the American War for Independence and the framing of the new United States Constitution, Christianity in America entered a new era, like the new nation itself. European assumptions about how religion should function were largely set aside; revivalism as promoted by George Whitefield provided new norms for ecclesiastical practice. For churches, the Revolution ushered in an era of exploring the possibilities of "American" religious practice.

Methodism and the Mobilization of American Protestantism

Whitefield and his colleagues in the colonial Great Awakening planted the seed that the Methodists harvested. The mobilization of Protestant energies in the early United States is best exemplified by the great early leader of the Methodists, Francis Asbury (1745-1816).[18] Asbury was an English follower of John Wesley who at age thirteen began his career as an itinerant preacher. In 1771 Wesley asked for volunteers to go to America, and Asbury responded eagerly. Soon after his arrival, Asbury became the central figure in the American Methodist movement. An early impediment was the Methodist reputation as loyalists to Britain, since Wesley made no secret of opposing the American Revolution. After the War for Independence was over, however, Asbury immediately

17. See especially Susan Juster, *Disorderly Women: Sexual Politics and Evangelicalism in Revolutionary New England* (Ithaca, NY: Cornell University Press, 1994).

18. No satisfactory biography of Asbury exists, but see Frank Baker, *From Wesley to Asbury: Studies in Early American Methodism* (Durham, NC: Duke University Press, 1976); and Francis Asbury, *Journals and Letters*, 3 vols. (Nashville: Abingdon, 1958).

resumed the arduous rounds of preaching, encouraging, writing, and organizing that he pursued for the rest of his life. Before he died, Asbury traveled nearly 300,000 miles, mostly on horseback. His trips took him into all of the thirteen colonies that became the original United States and then into the new states of Tennessee and Kentucky that entered the Union in the 1790s. His own plan of action followed the advice he later gave to younger Methodist itinerants: "Go into every kitchen and shop; address all, aged and young, on the salvation of their souls."

In December 1784, Asbury and his associates met in Baltimore to establish a formal organization, and for the next century the Methodists were the driving religious force in America.[19] To an unusual degree Methodism combined the democratic style of the New World with a measure of control reminiscent of the Old. Methodist preachers aimed their message directly at the common people and were eager to set up small class meetings and local church services where lay people were expected to do much of the work. At the same time, Asbury himself kept close control of the itinerating preachers, and through that control he ensured uniform discipline in this widely dispersed movement. In many ways, the concerns, emotions, and lay involvement of Methodism followed the path blazed by Pietists on the Continent like Philipp Jacob Spener and August Hermann Francke.

Asbury was joined in his work by hundreds, and then thousands, of eager co-workers. The life of a Methodist itinerant was anything but easy. Itinerants were usually young, and as a result could be despised for violating the prerogatives of age. They were often intense preachers who were as likely to alienate audiences as to win them over. Their free use of emotion made them objects of distrust by those who remembered a more orderly faith. Some husbands and fathers thought that the itinerants' appeal to their wives and daughters undermined the good order of patriarchal authority. And everywhere they traveled, the

---

19. See Nathan O. Hatch, "The Puzzle of American Methodism," *Church History* 63 (June 1994): 175-89; and Donald G. Mathews, "Evangelical America — The Methodist Ideology," in *Perspectives on American Methodism*, ed. Russell E. Richey, Kenneth E. Rowe, and Jean Miller Schmidt (Nashville: Abingdon, 1993), pp. 17-30.

itinerants were troubled by bad weather, recurrent illness, the absence of roads, and the other harsh realities of the frontier.[20]

Yet as a body they persevered. Their ability to present Christianity as a reconciliation with God that could stabilize the often daunting realities of day-to-day existence was rewarded with the creation of thousands of local classes and then thousands of churches.[21] When Asbury arrived in America, there were four Methodist ministers looking after about 300 laypeople. By the time of his death in 1816, there were 2,000 ministers and over 200,000 members of Methodist congregations, and this rate of expansion continued after Asbury left the scene. The Methodists maintained about 30 churches (or preaching stations) in 1780; that number rose to 2,700 by 1820, and to an incredible 19,883 by the start of the Civil War in 1861. By 1860 there were almost as many Methodist churches as United States post offices.

Rapid Methodist growth did not proceed without important changes taking place in the movement.[22] So long as Asbury lived, the norm for a Methodist minister was incessant travel, poverty, and a spartan life. As Methodism grew, especially in the cities, there was an increasing desire for a "settled" clergy, with ministers who served a single congregation and oversaw the construction of regular church buildings. Some historians have seen spiritual decay in this process, since the settled Methodist pastors gradually came to resemble the upwardly mobile ministers of other denominations. The intense focus of the laity in meeting together to read the Scriptures, confess their faults to each other, and encourage one another in godly living gradually gave way to a religion organized around public services in a church building under

20. See especially Christine L. Heyrman, *Southern Cross: The Beginnings of the Bible Belt* (New York: Knopf, 1997).

21. Good general books are now appearing rapidly. See John H. Wigger, *Taking Heaven by Storm: Methodism and the Rise of Popular Christianity in America* (New York: Oxford University Press, 1998); Cynthia Lynn Lyerly, *Methodism and the Southern Mind, 1770-1810* (New York: Oxford University Press, 1998); and Dee E. Andrews, *The Methodists and Revolutionary America, 1760-1800* (Princeton: Princeton University Press, 2000).

22. See Russell E. Richey, *Early American Methodism* (Bloomington: Indiana University Press, 1991); and A. Gregory Schneider, *The Way of the Cross Leads Home: The Domestication of American Methodism* (Bloomington: Indiana University Press, 1991).

the oversight of a formally trained minister. Methodists may have paid a price, but it was the price of success. More than any other single event, this expansion of the Methodists was responsible for the wide cultural influence that evangelical Protestantism exerted in nineteenth-century America.

Revivalism and the Baptists

However dynamic they were, the Methodists were only one part of a great Protestant mobilization that historians sometimes call "the Second Great Awakening."[23] In every dimension, this mobilization relied heavily on the techniques of revivalism. Revivalism could take many forms. In the 1790s, for instance, the scholarly president of Yale College in Connecticut, Timothy Dwight, encouraged his students to experience evangelical conversions and then helped some of them find positions as pastors of already existing churches. Dwight's emphasis was on an orderly, disciplined response to the gospel that several of his famous students, like Lyman Beecher and Nathaniel W. Taylor, maintained in their own productive careers.[24]

At about the same time, on the Western frontier, revival was much more exuberant. At one of the most memorable meetings, which occurred at Cane Ridge, Kentucky, in August 1801, thousands of individuals congregated for a "camp meeting."[25] This gathering featured preaching day and night from Presbyterian, Baptist, and Methodist ministers,

23. For good overviews, see Donald G. Mathews, "The Second Great Awakening as an Organizing Process, 1780-1830," *American Quarterly* 21 (1969): 23-43; and John B. Boles, *The Great Revival, 1787-1805: The Origin of the Southern Evangelical Mind* (Lexington: University Press of Kentucky, 1972).

24. The best local study is David W. Kling, *A Field of Divine Wonders: The New Divinity and Village Revivals in Northwestern Connecticut, 1792-1822* (University Park: Pennsylvania State University Press, 1993).

25. See Paul K. Conkin, *Cane Ridge: American Pentecost* (Madison: University of Wisconsin Press, 1990), which puts to good use Leigh Eric Schmidt, *Holy Fairs: Scottish Communions and American Revivals in the Early Modern Period* (Princeton: Princeton University Press, 1989).

and from exhorters both black and white. The results were electrifying, with many participants falling down as if struck dead, while others laughed out loud, barked like dogs, or experienced "the jerks." After the excitement wore off, longer-term results were seen in the creation of many new churches, especially Methodist and Baptist churches.

The essence of revivalism was direct appeal by a dedicated (often passionate) preacher to individuals who gathered expressly for the purpose of hearing the revivalist's message. Most revivalists were men, although there were also some lively women preachers, such as Elleanor Knight, Julia Foote, Rebecca Miller, and Harriet Livermore. In January 1827, Livermore became the first woman to preach in the United States Congress.[26] The purpose of the revival meeting, though approached in many ways, was always the same: to convert lost sinners to faith in Christ and, through the reformed behavior of the converted, to improve society.

Revivalism was thus a perfect complement for dominant social and political norms in the new United States. Revivals were democratic in their appeal to all types and levels of society. They were egalitarian in preaching the same message to all. They were "liberal" in the nineteenth-century sense of the term because they based organization and social activity on the determined action of individuals. But they were also traditional in providing a picture of God similar to what many heard in the older churches.

As with the success of the Methodists, those who exploited revival most thoroughly incorporated its ecstatic elements into structures and institutions that kept the religious spark from burning out of control. For most of the middle and Southern United States, the Protestants who knew how to put revivalism to fullest use were the Baptists.

The writing of Baptist history has never been as impressive as the Baptist movement itself.[27] There are a number of reasons for this im-

---

26. See Catherine A. Brekus, *Strangers and Pilgrims: Female Preachers in America, 1740-1845* (Chapel Hill: University of North Carolina Press, 1998).

27. But see Leon McBeth, *The Baptist Heritage* (Nashville, TN: Broadman, 1967); Timothy George and David Dockery, eds., *Baptist Theologians* (Nashville, TN: Broadman, 1990); and Bill J. Leonard, ed., *Dictionary of Baptists in America* (Downers Grove, IL: InterVarsity Press, 1994).

balance between weak histories and strong churches. Baptists have always featured religion in local settings. Baptist leaders have usually worked to construct local or regional networks and so have escaped the gaze of historians looking for individuals of national prominence. This stress on local congregations grew out of early Baptist suspicion of the established churches and their rejection of all governmental coercion in religion. Baptist churches grew slowly in the colonial period but spread like wildfire in the new republic.

The Baptist message was a time-honored one of sinners needing to find grace in Christ. A Baptist distinctive, as the name implies, was that individuals had to profess Christian faith for themselves and then, on the basis of that profession, be baptized by immersion. Baptist notions of responsibility stressed the freedom of local groups from outside influence. Baptists also developed many strong local leaders — often laypeople — who, with or without formal education, took the initiative in forming new churches. Thus Baptists were uniquely situated to stress the liberating, individualistic aspects of both the Christian message and the politics of the new United States. They were also favorably disposed to show how revived individuals might band together to form strong local churches. "Farmer-preachers" became the characteristic symbol of Baptist strength in the early United States; such ministers were part of the citizenry during the week, but then assumed the role of preacher and pastor in the formal church services, while still remaining very much "of the people."

The growth of the Baptists was only slightly less sensational than the growth of the Methodists. Where there were only about 460 Baptist churches in the country at the end of the American Revolution in 1780, that number had risen to well over 12,000 by 1860.

Baptist leadership, although usually intensely local, did include several preachers and educators who gained national recognition. Richard Furman (1755-1825) was the long-time minister of the First Baptist Church in Charleston, South Carolina, who pioneered a number of Baptist organizational ventures.[28] In 1814, for example, he became the

28. See James A. Rogers, *Richard Furman* (Macon, GA: Mercer University Press, 1985).

first president of the Baptist Triennial Convention, a national body organized to send Baptist missionaries to foreign countries and to frontier regions of the United States. Furman also convinced South Carolina Baptists to relax some of their vigorous localism and support the principle of a statewide organization for the promotion of education, social benevolence, and missions. To indicate the range of Furman's concerns, he was a lifelong promoter of education at every level, and he was also the author of a major defense of slavery based on his interpretation of the Bible. When the Southern Baptist Convention was formed in 1845 over a dispute concerning slaveholding, its organization was derived from principles he had earlier proposed. Within a century of its founding, the Southern Baptist Convention had become the largest Protestant denomination in America.

Something of a northern counterpart to Furman was Francis Wayland (1796-1865), the long-time president of Brown University in Providence, Rhode Island.[29] Like Furman, Wayland was an ardent advocate of missions and education; he urged Baptists to be more active in carrying out their duties as citizens; and he encouraged Baptist organization at the state and national levels. Wayland was the author of several books on ethics, politics, and philosophy that were used very widely as college texts throughout the United States. To suggest the way in which region shaped religious perceptions, Wayland, like Furman, authored a major study on the Bible and slavery, but in it he concluded that the Bible *opposed* the institution.

Energetic labors of leaders like Asbury, Furman, and Wayland, as well as countless others who were not so well known, explain why the Methodists and Baptists expanded so rapidly in the early nineteenth century. The religious message they promoted grew out of traditional Protestant faith but was also powerfully adapted to the American environment.

---

29. See Francis Wayland and H. L. Wayland, *A Memoir of the Life and Labors of Francis Wayland* (New York: Sheldon, 1867).

New "American" Denominations

The same kind of energy also appeared in several denominations freshly minted in the new American nation, with similar results. The most important of these were the churches of the Restorationist movement.[30] This movement sought, in effect, to begin Christianity over again by stripping away the accumulated baggage of the centuries. Its name comes from the effort to "restore" Christianity to the purity of the New Testament. Its leaders included a father and son who emigrated from Scotland by way of Ireland: Thomas (1763-1845) and Alexander (1788-1866) Campbell. They were joined by Barton W. Stone (1772-1844), a plain-speaking Marylander who participated in the great western migration into Kentucky of the 1790s. The Campbells and Stone shared a disillusionment with traditional churches, which they felt were too much constrained by stale European traditions. After affiliating for brief periods with existing denominations, they eventually broke away and set about recovering the primitive Christianity they thought they could see in the New Testament's Book of Acts. Alexander Campbell and Barton Stone created separate movements called "Christians Only" (Stone) and "Disciples of Christ" (Campbell); the names were deliberately chosen to emphasize liberation from the historic denominations. The parallel movements were also alike in seeking to follow the New Testament literally, in practicing baptism by immersion for adult converts, and in stressing the autonomy of local congregations. In the early 1830s, the churches inspired by Stone's and Campbell's ideals joined together as the Christian Church (Disciples of Christ). Church statistics again reveal the strength of an appeal to anti-traditional, lay-oriented, self-starting religion in the early days of the new American nation. By the time of the Civil War, there were just about as many Disciples churches (2,100, concentrated mostly in the upper South and the lower North) as there

---

30. See Richard T. Hughes, *Reviving the Ancient Faith: The Story of the Churches of Christ in America* (Grand Rapids: Eerdmans, 1996); and David Edwin Harrell, *Quest for a Christian America: The Disciples of Christ and American Society to 1866* (Nashville, TN: Disciples of Christ Historical Society, 1966).

were of the older colonial churches, Episcopalian (2,150) or Congregationalist (2,240).

In their later development, the Restorationist churches divided into denomination-like networks known as the Churches of Christ, the Christian Church, and the Disciples of Christ, each of which retains considerable vigor in selected areas of the United States. Together these churches are the living legacy of indigenous religious energies unleashed by the open geography and liberal ideologies of the new United States.

Voluntary Societies

The religious efforts of those who led the Methodists, Baptists, and Restorationists would not have influenced American society so directly if religion had remained neatly separated from the wider world. As it happened, however, American Protestants developed an innovative and powerful vehicle to link private faith and public life. That vehicle was the voluntary society, which became an ideal means for taking advantage of the constitutional separation of church and state. Protestant voluntary societies had existed in Britain for some time, but they came into their own in America during the early decades of the nineteenth century.[31]

Voluntary societies were organizations set up independently of the churches and governed by self-sustaining boards for the purpose of addressing a specific problem. Their genius lay in providing individuals from different denominations a way to pool their concerns, energies, and money in order to provide a flexible response to the changing needs of a rapidly developing American society. Not all such agencies were religious, but the Protestant churches were the leaders in creating these organizations and, through them, exerting real influence in many parts of the rapidly expanding country.[32]

31. See especially Andrew Walls, "Missionary Societies and the Fortunate Subversion of the Church," in *The Missionary Movement in Christian History* (Maryknoll, NY: Orbis, 1996), pp. 241-54; and William H. Brackney, *Christian Voluntarism in Britain and America: A Bibliography and Critical Assessment* (Westport, CT: Greenwood, 1995).

32. See John R. Bodo, *The Protestant Clergy and Public Issues, 1812-1848* (Princeton: Princeton University Press, 1954); Charles I. Foster, *An Errand of Mercy: The Evangelical*

The rapid expansion of the United States created the need for such flexible agencies as voluntary societies. Between 1790 and 1830, the population of the United States mushroomed from slightly under four million to almost thirteen million. By 1840 there were more people in the United States than in England, and within twenty more years the American population was almost equal to the national populations of France and of Germany (defined as the constituent parts of the 1870 German empire). Yet rapid as that population growth was, the physical dimensions of the country posed even greater difficulties for coherence, communication, and community. After the Louisiana Purchase from France in 1803 doubled the size of the country, the United States possessed a landmass four times the size of modern-day France, Germany, and the United Kingdom combined. The incredible dimensions of national expansion were a daunting challenge, and the ecclesiastical response was the voluntary society.

Methodists and Baptists were doing much of the work in ministering to local populations throughout this vast new land, but representatives of the older churches were the driving forces behind the voluntary societies. Congregationalists from New England took the lead (often as they moved out to upstate New York or to the region then known as the West, which was the Ohio River Valley). Soon they were joined by many Presbyterians, representatives of the German and Dutch Reformed Churches, and some Episcopalians, Methodists, Quakers, and Baptists. The first large voluntary agencies had distinctly religious purposes, like the American Board for Foreign Missions (1810) and the American Bible Society (1816). But soon somewhat broader purposes were also served by such organizations as the Colonization Society for liberated slaves (1817), the American Society for the Promotion of Temperance (1826), and the American Antislavery Society (1833). The annual budgets for some of these associations equaled those of the country's largest businesses. Whether providing books and Bibles through traveling

United Front, 1790-1837 (Chapel Hill: University of North Carolina Press, 1960); and Clifford S. Griffin, *Their Brothers' Keepers: Moral Stewardship in the United States, 1800-1865* (New Brunswick, NJ: Rutgers University Press, 1960); with a correction to their interpretation by Lois W. Banner, "Religious Benevolence as Social Control: A Critique of an Interpretation," *Journal of American History* 60 (June 1973): 23-41.

vendors, organizing to improve the treatment of the insane, or reaching out to prostitutes and other social outcasts, the Protestant voluntary agencies aimed at the social conversion of the United States.

As they did so, they opened up unusual opportunities for religious women. The sisters Sarah (1792-1873) and Angelina Grimké (1805-1879), for example, were born in South Carolina near the start of the century and raised as slave-holding Episcopalians,[33] but when the family moved to Philadelphia and the sisters joined the Quakers, they began to speak out against slavery and other social ills. Angelina Grimké's tract arguing for the end of slavery, *An Appeal to the Christian Women of the South* (1836), won her immediate recognition in the new abolitionist movement, but also led many in both North and South to consider her a dangerous radical. Later both sisters became public speakers for the American Antislavery Society. When such speaking in public by women was attacked, Sarah responded with a biblically based defense in her *Letters on the Equality of the Sexes, and the Condition of Women* (1838). The avenue provided the Grimké sisters by voluntary associations was an avenue opened up for many who had earlier performed religious duties only in private.

It is important to realize, however, that not all Protestants participated in the coordinated activities of what has been called "the Protestant United Front."[34] A long-standing resentment of "Yankee meddling" inspired many church people, especially in the South and West, to resist the voluntary societies. The leaders of the societies were usually Northern Congregationalists or Presbyterians; Baptists and Disciples often received them with suspicion because they worried about the effect of the agencies on the independence of local churches. Many others, especially in the South, felt that Northern arguments about slavery represented an unwarranted, uninformed intrusion. So it was, for example, that among Baptists in the middle and Southern states, loosely organized associations came into existence called "Anti-

---

33. See Katharine Du Pre Lumpkin, *The Emancipation of Angelina Grimké* (Chapel Hill: University of North Carolina Press, 1974); and Gerda Lerner, *The Grimké Sisters from South Carolina* (Boston: Houghton Mifflin, 1967).

34. Those who did not participate are well surveyed in Curtis D. Johnson, *Redeeming America: Evangelicals and the Road to Civil War* (Chicago: I. R. Dee, 1993).

Mission," "Old School," "Landmark," or "Primitive." All of them frowned on coordinated missionary, educational, and reform activities that took funds or personnel out of the control of individual churches. The sentiments of these populist groups were reinforced by the carefully reasoned opinions of a few Presbyterian and Episcopalian ministers who also worried about national religious coercion. Theologians like the Presbyterian James Henley Thornwell of South Carolina, for example, defended a doctrine known as the "spirituality of the church."[35] It emphasized that Christian activity must not stray into enterprises not specifically mandated by the words of Scripture. Resistance to the voluntary societies was never as successful at shaping public opinion as were the societies themselves, but this resistance represented an important counter-theme in Protestant life after the start of the nineteenth century. Such differences, when combined with political antagonism between the Northern and Southern states, also became a factor in the American Civil War that began in 1861.

During the decades surrounding the American War for Independence, the American religious landscape was transformed every bit as much as the political landscape. Most obviously, Americans set aside over a millennium of establishmentarian history to organize their churches on the basis of liberty. To be sure, if you were not an English-speaking white Protestant, the fixation on liberty appeared hypocritical;[36] the burning of an Ursuline convent by a Boston mob in 1834, for example, indicated how close to the surface ancient anti-Catholic sentiments remained. Yet compared to the rest of the world, the American religious scene was marked by an unusual measure of liberty.

When Alexis de Tocqueville paid his lengthy visit to North America in the early 1830s, the harmony between religion and liberty was one of the things that most impressed him. At a time when de Tocqueville's

35. See James O. Farmer, Jr., *The Metaphysical Confederacy: James Henley Thornwell and the Synthesis of Southern Values* (Macon, GA: Mercer University Press, 1986).

36. A recent book that examines those protests of liberty with considerable skepticism is Steven J. Keillor, *This Rebellious House: American History and the Truth of Christianity* (Downers Grove, IL: InterVarsity Press, 1996).

France was experiencing growing tension between promoters of liberty and promoters of Christianity, he found in America something quite different. The enduring religious legacy of the American Revolution was, in fact, what so impressed de Tocqueville:

> Anglo-American civilization . . . is the result . . . of two distinct elements which in other places have been in frequent disagreement, but which the Americans have succeeded in incorporating to some extent one with the other and combining admirably. I allude to the *spirit of religion* and the *spirit of liberty.* . . . On my arrival in the United States the religious aspect of the country was the first thing that struck my attention; and the longer I stayed, the more I perceived the great political consequences resulting from this new state of things. In France, I had always seen the spirit of religion and the spirit of freedom marching in opposite directions. But in America I found they were intimately united and they reigned in common over the same country.[37]

37. Alexis de Tocqueville, *Democracy in America,* ed. Thomas Bender (New York: Modern Library, 1981), p. 185.

CHAPTER FOUR

The Separation of Church and State

The United States Constitution, which was written in 1787 and fully implemented in 1789, contains almost no mention of religion. Political leaders at the time took for granted that this document was intended to define the powers of the national, or federal, government. Under the Constitution, the individual states retained wide latitude to determine many matters for themselves, including religion. Thus it was that, when the First Amendment to the United States Constitution went into effect in 1791, contemporary observers realized that its provisions for the separation of church and state applied only to the national government. The amendment's famous stipulation was that "Congress shall make no law respecting an establishment of religion, or prohibiting the free exercise thereof." This provision guaranteed that the *federal* government would not be entangled with the institutions of religion. At the level of the states, however, it was a different story. Five of the nation's fourteen states (Vermont had joined the Union earlier that year) made provision for tax support of ministers, and those five plus seven others continued religious tests for public office. Only Virginia and Rhode Island practiced the kind of separation of church and state that has since become common in America — where government provides no money for churches and poses no religious conditions for participation in public life. With less than a handful of exceptions, even the defenders of religious liberty in Rhode Island and Virginia did not object when Congress or the president proclaimed national days of prayer, when branches of the federal government began their meetings with prayer, when Roman Catholics were discriminated against in state and federal public life, or when military chaplains were appointed and funded by law.[1]

From an American standpoint early in the twenty-first century, the amendment's sweeping endorsement of religious liberty on the national level coexisting with governmental support for churches and religiously inspired legislation in the states may appear to be an anomaly. But from the standpoint of colonial history, it was not a surprising combination at all. Rather, the situation reflected the colonists' allegiance to varied meanings of liberty, which they defined, in terms differentiated by the social philosopher Isaiah Berlin, both "negatively" (as the absence of external political coercion) and "positively" (as the opportunity to govern their lives as they desired).[2] Even more, it reflected the complicated tangle of negotiated local compromises that had been worked out with nearly infinite variation since the first days of European colonization. These were compromises dictated much more by problems of getting along in the New World than by philosophical or theological consistency. Only later in American history would the words of the First Amendment be applied systematically as legal principles that affected directly the religious lives of American citizens.

Nonetheless, from the passage of the United States Constitution, the separation of spheres that were usually bound together in Europe remained a distinctive feature of American religious life. Many European countries would retain, even to the present day, governmental tax collections for churches, monarchs who functioned as symbolic heads of church as well as state, or occasional support for teaching religion in public schools. These were church-state ties that Americans gave up. As

1. This chapter owes a great deal to the finest study of the early periods, Thomas J. Curry, *The First Freedoms: Church and State in America to the Passage of the First Amendment* (New York: Oxford University Press, 1986); and to the outstanding bibliographical essays in John F. Wilson, ed., *Church and State in America: A Bibliographical Guide,* 2 vols. (New York: Greenwood, 1986-87).

2. Isaiah Berlin, "Two Concepts of Liberty," in *Four Essays on Liberty* (New York: Oxford University Press, 1969).

we note below, even Canada, which shares many values with the United States, has never been so fastidious about the separation of church and state.

In order to explore this feature, the following chapter surveys developments in the colonial era, the influence of the Great Awakening and the principles of the Enlightenment, the broader results of Constitutional separation, the fate of the informal Protestant establishment of the nineteenth century, and the major changes of the twentieth century. The separation of church and state has remained a singular feature of American history, even if the principle has always been more ambiguous in practice than in theory.

The Colonial Period

Despite a persistent American mythology that features "religious liberty" as a main stimulant for British migration to North America, the first colonies actually instituted a tighter governmental control of religion than existed in the Old World.[3] As we have seen, New England's "Puritan way" was premised on an ingenious plan that, while it liberated the settlers from Britain's style of church-state entanglement, constructed a new basis for connecting religion and politics. In Virginia the Anglican establishment followed more closely the common European pattern of a top-down merger of political and religious authority. In both New England and the Chesapeake, the kind of freedom that mattered most turned out to be "positive liberty" that enabled colonists to structure their lives as they had been prevented from doing in Great Britain, not "negative liberty" where all were free to do as they pleased.

Before the mid-eighteenth century, church and state were bound together more closely in New England (with the exception of Rhode Island) and the Chesapeake colonies of Virginia and Maryland (along with South Carolina) than they were in England at the same time. As

---

3. See John M. Murrin, "Religion and Politics in America from the First Settlements to the Civil War," in *Religion and American Politics*, ed. Mark A. Noll (New York: Oxford University Press, 1990), pp. 19-43.

part of the settlement of William and Mary as British monarchs in 1689, Parliament passed "An Act for exempting their Majesties Protestant subjects, dissenting from the Church of England, from the penalties of certain laws." This Act guaranteed freedom of worship to Trinitarian Protestant Nonconformists, even as it reaffirmed existing laws prohibiting the dissenters' entrance to the universities, membership in Parliament, or service as officers in the army and navy. (Roman Catholics and Unitarian Protestants continued to suffer harsher disabilities.) The New England and Chesapeake colonies acknowledged this Act of Toleration, but in practice they restrained New England's non-Puritans and the Chesapeake's non-Anglicans more closely than non-Anglicans were restrained in England.

If the history of New England and Chesapeake colonies explains much of the intermingling of church and state that remained in the American states of 1791, where, then, did advanced notions about the separation of church and state, as embodied in the First Amendment, come from? Part of the answer is contained in the history of these vigorous establishments themselves. Such lonely voices as Roger Williams's and momentary outbursts of toleration like the Maryland Act of 1649 did point, however feebly at the time, to what would follow.[4] More direct support for non-traditional relations between church and state appeared in the colonies founded after the Restoration of Charles II in 1660.

The path to religious toleration, looser connections between church and state, and, finally, religious freedom (in the negative sense of the term) began most clearly in New York, New Jersey, Pennsylvania, and Delaware. In these middle colonies, populations were diverse from the beginning. In particular the wide range of peoples attracted to New York City and Philadelphia, the colonies' main crossroads of commerce and settlement, overwhelmed inherited ideals of church-state religious uniformity.

Under its original Dutch settlement, New York church regulations were as tight as, or tighter than, in Massachusetts and Virginia. But

---

4. See Edwin S. Gaustad, *Liberty of Conscience: Roger Williams in America* (Grand Rapids: Eerdmans, 1991).

when in 1664 the brother of Charles II, James (the Duke of York), mounted a successful expedition against New Netherlands and gained the colony for England, one of the first changes was to allow religious toleration. In 1642 a Jesuit missionary had recorded eighteen different languages among the still tiny population of the province. Under the new English regime, a freedom of worship to match this diversity of tongues soon became the norm. In New York, religious toleration was regularly challenged by those who upheld the principles of Dutch or English establishment, but by the 1730s a functioning freedom of religion was in place.[5]

Here New York demonstrated the pattern that led directly to the First Amendment. Diversity of churches was simply too great to allow one denomination to be favored by law. Principles of liberty were expanding too rapidly to allow defenders of institutionalized church-state bonds a chance to recover. As some historians have suggested, English cultural forms and social mores continued to grow more attractive in New York and other urban areas throughout the eighteenth century.[6] But attachment to the principle of establishment was growing weaker.

A similar story, with different local issues predominating, led to the same resolution in New Jersey, Pennsylvania, and Delaware. In New Jersey, Quakers, Anglicans, and Presbyterians enjoyed strong constituencies, but none was strong enough to control the others. In Pennsylvania and Delaware, the effects of William Penn's more liberal attitudes made a difference from the first. Penn did envisage Quaker control of the colony, but also a wide measure of toleration for other Christians. Quakers dominated the Pennsylvania assembly from the colony's founding in 1681 until 1756.[7] In later years, a crisis brought on by warfare with France and its Indian allies made it impossible for Quaker pacifists to continue to govern. But from the start, Penn's policy of religious toleration encouraged the settlement of diverse groups from Britain and the Continent. The "Pennsylvania Charter of Liberty"

---

5. See the references in Chapter Two, note 6.

6. See John M. Murrin, "Anglicizing an American Colony: The Transformation of Provincial Massachusetts" (Ph.D. dissertation, Yale University, 1966).

7. See Frederick Tolles, *Quakers and the Atlantic Culture* (New York: Macmillan, 1960).

(1682) provided that all officials of the colony "shall be such as possess faith in Jesus Christ." But it also stated without equivocation, "That all persons living in this province, who confess and acknowledge the one Almighty and eternal God, to be the Creator, Upholder and Ruler of the World; and that hold themselves obliged in conscience to live peaceably and justly in civil society, shall, in no ways, be molested or prejudiced for their religious persuasion, or practice, in matters of faith and worship, nor shall they be compelled, at any time, to frequent or maintain any religious worship, place or ministry whatever."[8] Unlike Maryland's similar declaration in 1649, the Pennsylvania proclamation of toleration stuck.

In his provisions for religion, William Penn was literally more than a century ahead of his time. By requiring citizens to be theists and by promoting religious observances common to Christian denominations, while at the same time guaranteeing a wide religious toleration within those bounds, he pointed the way to the church-state arrangements that prevailed in most of the states during the first decades after national independence. In the context of the eighteenth century, it was a testimony to the liberality of Penn's vision that Pennsylvania was the only one of the thirteen colonies where Roman Catholics were allowed the freedom for public worship. That kind of toleration was denied under even some of the first state constitutions.

Awakening and Enlightenment

If the religious pluralism of the middle colonies and the encouragement of liberal principles paved the way for the First Amendment to the Constitution, so also did other circumstances of the eighteenth century. From opposite ends of the ideological spectrum — the upsurge of Calvinist piety known as the Great Awakening and increasing American attachment to ideals of the European Enlightenment — came grow-

8. "Pennsylvania Charter of Liberty" (1682), in *The Founders' Constitution*, 5 vols., ed. Philip B. Kurland and Ralph Lerner (Chicago: University of Chicago Press, 1987), vol. 5, p. 52.

ing support for principles of toleration and religious freedom. The Great Awakening had two major consequences for questions of church and state. First, by fragmenting the traditional Congregationalist churches in New England, it created some of the same religious diversity that was propelling the separation of church and state in the middle colonies. Second, by effectively spreading the message of "heart religion" in the Chesapeake, it created forceful opposition for the Anglican establishments.

The New England establishments did not give way easily. It was not until well after the Revolution, with its addition of potent political arguments to the religious impulses of the Awakening, that Congregationalism was completely disestablished in Connecticut (1818) and Massachusetts (1833).[9] Yet the push for disestablishment gained force as the leaders of New England's Congregationalism themselves began to complain about the unjust oppression of the British parliament. In 1774 the New England Baptist leader, Isaac Backus, led a group of his fellow-religionists to the First Continental Congress in Philadelphia, where he sought an interview with the Massachusetts delegation that included John Adams and Sam Adams, both of whom were almost as staunch in their support of established Congregationalism as they were in opposition to the rule of Britain. In a spirited exchange, Backus tried to convince the Adams cousins that the Baptists' complaints against Congregationalist oppression were just as righteous as complaints by the colonial patriots against the British parliament. If it was wrong for Parliament to tax the colonies without their representation, Backus argued, it was also wrong for Massachusetts Congregationalists to tax Baptists without their consent for the sake of building Congregational churches. John Adams conceded that there was an establishment in Massachusetts, but contended that, because it was possible for Baptists and other dissenters to petition for exemption from its provisions, it was "a very slender one, hardly to be called an establishment." When Backus pushed further to complain about the need for such exemp-

9. See John Witte, "How to Govern a City on a Hill: Religion and Liberty in the 1780 Massachusetts Constitution," in *Religion and the Founding of the American Republic,* ed. James Hutson (Lanham, MD: Rowman and Littlefield, 2000).

tions, Adams retorted that "we might as well expect a change in the so-
lar system as to expect they would give up their establishment."[10] In the
short run, Adams was right; in the long run, Backus's views prevailed.

The effects of the Great Awakening in the South were almost as direct. The arrival of Baptists and Presbyterians in the backcountry of
Virginia and the Carolinas set up an immediate challenge to Anglican
hegemony. Anglican officials took steps at once to stop the itinerations
of revivalist ministers. But just as soon came a reply: in 1752 Samuel
Davies, the powerful Presbyterian preacher, petitioned the Bishop of
London, nominal supervisor of Virginia's Anglicans, for relief from the
colony's establishmentarian laws. To Davies it was clear that "the liberties granted by the Act of Toleration" should extend to the colonies.[11]
Anglicans took these sectarian admonitions with even less good grace
than did Massachusetts' defenders of its establishment. Through and
beyond the time of the Revolution, Baptist and other dissenting conventicles were occasionally, and sometimes brutally, disrupted by Anglican ministers and their gentry allies.[12]

Not all of Virginia's elite approved of such violence, however. Led
by Thomas Jefferson and James Madison, a growing number of Virgin-
ians joined others throughout the colonies in applying principles of
the Enlightenment against traditional coercive establishments. Madison, for example, wrote a college classmate in January 1774 that of all
the problems under which Virginia labored, the worst was "that diabol-
ical Hell conceived principle of persecution rages among some and to
their eternal Infamy the Clergy can furnish their Quota of Imps for
such business."[13] Similar feelings about the evil of religious establish-

---

10. Curry, *First Freedoms,* pp. 131-32. See also William G. McLoughlin, ed., *Isaac
Backus on Church, State, and Calvinism: Pamphlets, 1754-1789* (Cambridge: Harvard University Press, 1968).

11. "Samuel Davies on Behalf of Dissenters in Virginia," in *Church and State in American History,* ed. John F. Wilson and Donald L. Drakeman, 2nd ed. (Boston: Beacon,
1987), pp. 39-40.

12. See Rhys Isaac, *The Transformation of Virginia, 1740-1790* (Chapel Hill: University
of North Carolina Press, 1982).

13. "James Madison to William Bradford, 24 Jan. 1774," in *Founders' Constitution,*
vol. 5, p. 60.

ments lay behind Jefferson's efforts to promote complete freedom of religion in Virginia, a goal that was reached with the Virginia Act for Establishing Religious Freedom of 1785.[14]

One of the conflicts that pushed all of the colonies in the direction that Virginia eventually took was strife over Anglican efforts to secure a bishop in the colonies. Such efforts increased from the mid-eighteenth century, but they were met with ferocious opposition. That opposition increased colonial resentment against the mother country and was a factor in the War for Independence. It also paved the way for later protests against other forms of Protestant state-church union.[15] The nation's founders retained the conviction that religion in general was a necessity for public well-being, but they had reached the point of rejecting the kind of establishments favoring one particular church that were still the norm in Europe.

Minority religious groups that had not been allowed to exercise a significant public role in the development of the British colonies continued for some time in an ambiguous situation under the new United States government, even after the passage of the First Amendment. In the colonial period, Roman Catholics enjoyed full civil rights only in Pennsylvania, Rhode Island, and (for a relatively few decades) in Maryland. The link between France and Catholicism had exacerbated the problem of Catholic civil rights during and after the French and Indian War. Sam Adams, otherwise a stalwart for liberty, in 1772 proclaimed that Catholics could not be granted official toleration because they teach "Doctrines subversive of the Civil Government under which they live."[16] Popular attitudes that underlay the resistance to Catholic civil rights spurted to the surface with a vengeance when in 1774 the British parliament granted the Roman Catholic hierarchy in Quebec many of

---

14. See Edwin S. Gaustad, *Sworn on the Altar of God: A Religious Biography of Thomas Jefferson* (Grand Rapids: Eerdmans, 1996); and Merrill D. Peterson and Robert C. Vaughan, eds., *The Virginia Statute for Religious Freedom: Its Evolution and Consequences in American History* (New York: Cambridge University Press, 1988).

15. See Carl Bridenbaugh, *Mitre and Sceptre: Transatlantic Faiths, Ideas, Personalities, and Politics* (New York: Oxford University Press, 1962).

16. "Samuel Adams, The Rights of the Colonists, 20 Nov. 1772," in *Founders' Constitution,* vol. 5, p. 60.

the prerogatives of an established church. Yet in a development that anticipated much later pragmatic cooperation, when New England Protestants actually confronted Quebec Catholics during the Revolutionary War, they found that they got along more peacefully than earlier protesters could have imagined.[17]

For their part, colonial Catholics went out of their way to show that they could be solid supporters of religious freedom. The first American Catholic bishop, John Carroll, devoted several pages of a 1784 apology to rebutting the charge that Catholics stifled free inquiry.[18] In the next generation, Bishop John England of South Carolina was a leading Catholic voice proclaiming the compatibility of Roman Catholicism and republican values.[19] This line of argument has continued into the late twentieth century, with the Jesuit theologian John Courtney Murray (1904-1967) and the convert from Lutheranism to Catholicism Richard John Neuhaus (b. 1936) becoming the leading Catholic defenders of the compatibility of American forms of democracy and historic Roman Catholicism.[20]

For reasons having more to do with prejudicial ignorance than active opposition, Jews were in roughly the same civil situation as Roman Catholics. Protestant attention to Jews was minimal in the British colonies, mostly because there were so few. In New York, Jews found a relative toleration in practice, and in 1710 a rabbi was even emboldened to petition the governor for the same kind of civil exemptions enjoyed by Protestant clergymen (the response does not survive). Yet in Rhode Island, where Jews had been present since the mid-seventeenth century, worshipped without restraint, and built a synagogue, they could still not vote or hold colonial office.

---

17. See Charles P. Hanson, *Necessary Virtue: The Pragmatic Origins of Religious Liberty in New England* (Charlottesville: University Press of Virginia, 1998).

18. John Carroll, *An Address to the Roman Catholics of the United States of America* (Annapolis: Frederick Green, 1784).

19. See Patrick Carey, *An Immigrant Bishop: John England's Adaptation of Irish Catholicism to American Republicanism* (Yonkers, NY: U.S. Catholic Historical Society, 1979).

20. Robert P. Hunt and Kenneth L. Grasso, *John Courtney Murray and the American Civil Conversation* (Grand Rapids: Eerdmans, 1992); and Richard John Neuhaus, *The Catholic Moment* (San Francisco: Harper & Row, 1987).

During the Revolutionary period, however, the small group of Jews in America readily adopted the language of liberty for themselves. In December 1783 five members of the Philadelphia Synagogue petitioned Pennsylvania's Council of Censors, which performed ombudsman functions, for full civil rights under the new regime. Pennsylvania had decreed that belief in the Old *and the New* Testaments should be qualifications for holding office. The memorialists responded with republican language to suggest that, "[a]lthough the Jews in Pennsylvania are but few in number," they were "as fond of liberty as their religious societies can be." Moreover, Jews throughout the states had "always tallied with the great design of the Revolution," and the Jews of Pennsylvania especially could count as many "Whigs" as any other group "in proportion to the number of their members."[21] Although the council was not empowered to act on this petition, it did receive favorable comment in the Philadelphia press.

The experiences of the colonial and Revolutionary periods created the following situation in the early United States: The national government would have no formal connections with religious institutions, yet in the individual states, various arrangements existed that privileged a single Protestant denomination or the beliefs of a generic Protestantism. In addition, governments at all levels offered various forms of assistance to churches and religious activities that fell short of a full establishment. In all of the states, public opinion was moving in the direction of granting more and more rights to more and more religious groups.

At the start of the national period, "no establishment" meant not having the church-state situation that Southern Anglicans and New England Congregationalists had once enjoyed. "Religious liberty" meant several things: for almost all Protestants it meant the negative freedom of worshipping as one pleased, but for many of the states it also meant a positive freedom to restrict the rights of non-Protestants

---

21. Jonathan D. Sarna and David G. Dalin, eds., *Religion and State in the American Jewish Experience* (Notre Dame: University of Notre Dame Press, 1997), pp. 72-73; this insightful volume reprints other similar documents along with a full discussion (pp. 61-80).

or non-Christians. In fact, between the proclamation of the Declaration of Independence in 1776 and the start of government under the Constitution in 1789, the U.S. Congress itself entertained proposals for a wide range of practical procedures to encourage religion without setting up a European-style church establishment.[22]

Effects of Church-State Separation

Gradually the principle that the institutions of the church and the institutions of the government should be separate spread further. In the nineteenth century, the main area of conflict remained treatment of Roman Catholics. In the twentieth century, consideration of the rights of non-Christians took center stage, as did the corresponding question of rights for the Christian communities that, taken together, still constituted the vast majority of the population. From the 1790s on, the principle of "religious freedom" began to be celebrated as critical for American democracy. This celebration sometimes hid the fact that complicated questions of jurisprudence remained in fleshing out what the ideal of "religious freedom" actually meant in practice.

Almost no one in the early United States took this separation of church and state to mean the absence of religious influence on public life. Nevertheless, wide agreement existed that the churches as such should be separated from the government. Sectarian Protestant bodies had been strong supporters of this step — especially the Baptists, who in all regions of the country campaigned hard for the division of church and state. The rapid growth of Baptist memberships in the early decades of the new United States showed how ready Baptists were to take advantage of the principle of religious freedom. But even Congregationalists and Anglicans who had been nervous about the separation of church and state very soon joined the Baptists in supporting the concept.

So it was that a religious environment came into existence that was very different from the situation in Europe. This new environment be-

---

22. See Derek Davis, *Religion and the Continental Congress, 1774-1789: Contributions to Original Intent* (New York: Oxford University Press, 2000).

came the stage for several important religious developments. In the first instance, since the denominations could no longer rely on the state for support, they were forced to compete for adherents. In a competitive environment, churches and denominations that mastered the techniques of persuasion flourished.[23] Methodist, Baptist, and Restorationist churches advanced rapidly in the early nineteenth century because these groups were expert at direct appeals to the people. Churches and denominations that trusted in such European techniques as government funding for new churches or state-supported educational institutions fell behind. For example, a minister's formal education (which was very important in the European pattern) meant far less in the new America than a minister's ability to command a crowd and compel assent. One reason that revivals became the standard American way of drawing a crowd and then building up the churches was that they were self-generated. They did not rely on the agency of the state or a certificate of approval from some higher cultural authority, as the church in Europe often did. They relied instead on the vigor, dedication, and persuasive skill of each revivalist.[24]

The negative results of this polity were a neglect of tradition and a devaluation of formal learning; the positive result was success in reaching ordinary people with the Christian message. At the very same time that European churches began to lose touch with common women and men, American churches were gaining increased loyalty from ordinary people. In particular, where European state churches were usually slow to build churches in new manufacturing areas, at least some American denominations moved in alongside the new urban population. Where only a few groups of European churches took advantage of newspapers, pamphlets, and cheap books, many American religious movements exploited these means, reaching a broader, more democratic audience.[25]

23. See especially Nathan O. Hatch, *The Democratization of American Christianity* (New Haven: Yale University Press, 1989).

24. See Roger Finke & Rodney Stark, *The Churching of America, 1776-1990: Winners and Losers in Our Religious Economy* (New Brunswick, NJ: Rutgers University Press, 1992); and Roger Finke, "Religious Deregulation: Origins and Consequences," *Journal of Church and State* 32 (1980): 609-26.

25. Compare Hatch, *Democratization of American Christianity;* and Hugh McLeod, *Re-*

It is especially important to note that accepting the separation of church and state made many American church leaders into innovators in communication. If it was necessary to promote a religious message oneself in order to have a church of any kind, then it was imperative to be always inventing and improving new ways of promoting the message. Throughout American history, evangelical Protestants have been at the forefront of new communication strategies, but representatives of other Christian traditions have never been far behind.[26] In the eighteenth century, George Whitefield was a pioneer in the use of newspapers for publicizing his cause. The American Bible Society in the early nineteenth century innovated with high-speed presses and networks of sales agents.[27] Religious publishers in that same century were among the earliest to exploit advertising in magazines.[28] In the early twentieth century, religious entrepreneurs like Paul Rader in Chicago were some of the first successful exploiters of the radio.[29] Only with television have Protestants not been on the cutting edge. With that medium, it was a Catholic Bishop, Fulton Sheen (1895-1979), who showed the way with a very popular program, "The Catholic Hour," in the 1950s and 1960s.

The Informal Protestant Establishment

Early American practice and the United States Constitution constructed a broad concept of religious liberty, but for the first century of United States history, that liberty was enjoyed primarily by Protestants.

---

ligion and the People of Western Europe, 1789-1989, 2nd ed. (New York: Oxford University Press, 1997).

26. See Leonard I. Sweet, ed., *Communication and Change in American Religious History* (Grand Rapids: Eerdmans, 1993).

27. See Peter J. Wosh's study of the American Bible Society, *Spreading the Word: The Bible Business in Nineteenth-Century America* (Ithaca, NY: Cornell University Press, 1994).

28. See R. Laurence Moore, *Selling God: American Religion in the Marketplace of Culture* (New York: Oxford University Press, 1994).

29. See Larry K. Eskridge, "Only Believe: Paul Rader and the Chicago Gospel Tabernacle, 1922-1933" (M.A. thesis, University of Maryland, 1985).

Sunday religious services were held in Washington, D.C.'s federal buildings, with only Protestant worship leaders until the late 1820s and then mostly Protestant leaders thereafter. State and federal governments provided subsidies for missionary work among Indians, sometimes provided Bibles and even land for rural churches, passed a great deal of legislation to protect Sunday as a day of rest, observed major Christian holidays, sponsored chaplains in the military and official prayers for many government meetings, and in other ways offered much state support for religion, without establishing one denomination as the church of the land.[30]

Behind this way of interpreting "the separation of church and state" was a religious-political consensus inherited from the founding era.[31] The national government would not sponsor any particular denomination and it would also try to ensure the broadest possible space for the exercise of religion. In turn, the churches as such were expected to give up overt political action. But both the founding fathers and major Protestant spokesmen appealed for the churches to strengthen the moral character required for a republican government. Writers and speakers regularly appealed to the slippery term "virtue" to make this argument. Sometimes "virtue" was defined as a self-sacrificing attitude toward public service, sometimes as private holiness before God. In either case, Americans, as good republicans, held that "virtue" in the citizenry was required to preserve liberty, to restrain the natural tendency of governmental power to expand, and to make the checks and balances of the Constitution actually work for the well-being of society. The great difference of opinion between those who eagerly embraced the national plans of the (mostly Northern) voluntary societies and those who resented their activities (often Southerners) concerned the fate of virtue under the influence of these societies. Their defenders re-

30. For a summary of those government-sponsored activities, see the well-documented article by John Witte, Jr., "The Essential Rights and Liberties of Religion in the American Constitutional Experiment," *Notre Dame Law Review* 71 (1996): 405-7; and more generally, Witte, *Religion and the American Constitutional Experiment: Essential Rights and Liberties* (Boulder, CO: Westview, 2000).

31. This account follows John G. West, *The Politics of Revelation and Reason: Religion and Civic Life in the New Nation* (Manhattan: University Press of Kansas, 1996).

garded national organization as an efficient, non-establishmentarian way to encourage citizens in the pursuit of personal and public virtue. Their opponents saw the same agencies as bloated monsters threatening the liberty and virtue of people in their local settings.

In the United States' earliest decades, this republican-religious reasoning was usually applied by Protestants for Protestants. But gradually the reasoning broadened to include non-Protestants, and then non-Christians. Debates over the reading of Scripture in public schools showed how the pressures of an increasingly diverse society began to break down the informal Protestant establishment long before the modern judicial era witnessed the introduction of new principles for interpreting the Constitution.[32]

Throughout the nineteenth century, almost all of America's publicly funded primary schools provided for readings from the Bible. Invariably these Bible readings were from the King James Version (KJV), which was the nearly universal Bible of choice for America's Protestants. Catholic opposition to Bible readings from the KJV in the public schools represented the first significant challenge to Protestant hegemony in the American public square.[33] That opposition, however, resembled the steps that Jewish citizens would also take against a practice they held to violate the separation of church and state. Unlike Jews, Catholics generally supported Christian Bible readings, but not from the KJV. But like Jews, Catholics wanted public practice to be as free for them as it was for the nation's Protestant majority. The efforts of Catholics and Jews illustrate the logic by which "religious freedom" expanded in nineteenth-century America.

In 1886 Catholic parents in Edgerton, Wisconsin, petitioned their

32. An overview keyed to legal decisions of the 1950s and 1960s is Donald E. Boles, *The Bible, Religion, and the Public Schools,* 3rd ed. (Ames: Iowa State University Press, 1965). Several contemporary arguments concerning Bible reading in the public schools are found in Lamar T. Beman, ed., *Religious Teaching in the Public Schools* (New York: H. W. Wilson, 1927). See also David L. Barr and Nicholas Piediscalzi, eds., *The Bible in American Education* (Philadelphia: Fortress, 1982).

33. See Jay P. Dolan, *The American Catholic Experience* (Garden City, NY: Doubleday, 1985), p. 267; and James Hennesey, S.J., *American Catholics* (New York: Oxford University Press, 1981), pp. 122, 125, 166.

local school board to stop daily readings from the KJV. The board replied that, by reading the KJV without comment, it was giving all children the right to interpret the Bible for themselves. To read the Bible without comment, the board believed, was non-sectarian; to stop reading it because it offended Roman Catholics was sectarian. This reasoning incensed Humphrey Desmond, for fifty years the editor of the *Catholic Citizen* of Wisconsin, who galvanized support to save parents and their children "from the sectarian inquisition presently established in the tax-payers' public school." To suggest the absurdity of the mainstream position, he wrote in February 1887: "Where in the whole land is the Catholic Bible read in the public school each morning; where is the Ave Maria compulsorily recited by Protestant pupils . . . ? On the other hand, we have public Normal Schools in this state run as part of the Methodist Book Concern; public school establishments turned into Protestant ecclesiastical machines; . . . and proselytism at the expense of Catholics whose children are being proselytized." A local judge ruled against the parents, stating that the KJV's "very presence, as a believed book, has rendered the nations having it, a chosen race; and then too, in exact proportion as it is more or less generally known and studied." But the Wisconsin Supreme Court reversed that ruling, favoring instead the parents and forbidding local boards to mandate readings from the KJV.[34]

For Jews, mandated readings from the KJV in the public school were almost always felt as a civil and religious imposition.[35] Before the Civil War, one of the nation's leading rabbis, Isaac Leeser, had complained that making Jews obey Sunday legislation was the same thing as forcing them to attend church or receive baptism.[36] Much the same

34. John O. Geiger, "The Edgerton Bible Case: Humphrey Desmond's Political Education of Wisconsin Catholics," *Journal of Church and State* 20 (Winter 1978): 13-28 (quotations on pp. 16, 19).

35. For succinct orientation to the general subject, see Jonathan D. Sarna, "Christian America or Secular America? The Church-State Dilemma of American Jews," in *Jews in Unsecular America*, ed. Richard John Neuhaus (Grand Rapids: Eerdmans, 1987), pp. 8-19.

36. Naomi W. Cohen, *Jews in Christian America: The Pursuit of Religious Equality* (New York: Oxford University Press, 1992), p. 5.

reasoning was applied to Bible reading in public schools, especially after the great increase in Jewish immigration during the last third of the twentieth century.

In a famous Cincinnati case of 1869-1870, the two Jews on the Cincinnati school board divided over a decision by the board to exclude Bible readings. But the prominent leader of Reform Judaism, Isaac Wise, was joined by another prominent Reform rabbi, Max Lilienthal, to support the board's effort to eliminate Bible readings altogether from the public schools. As Wise put his position around that time: "We are opposed to Bible reading in the schools. We want secular schools and nothing else. . . . Having no religion [the state] cannot impose any religious instruction on the citizen."[37]

Jewish sensitivity to the way Bible reading in public schools imposed civil and religious burdens remained keen into the twentieth century. In 1906 the Central Conference of American Rabbis published a pamphlet setting out its reasons why, as the title put it, *The Bible Should Not Be Read in Public Schools.* The next year the Union of Orthodox Jewish Congregations succeeded in having the New York City Board of Education end teaching of religion in the city's public schools.[38] For several years near the start of the First World War, *The American Jewish Yearbook* catalogued instances where courts or legislators mandated, eliminated, or discussed Bible reading in the schools. In its listings — alongside notices concerning legal action on general religious education in public schools, the observance of Sunday as a holy day, and provision for Jewish religious observances — the *Yearbook* noted twenty-six Bible rulings in thirteen states in just three years.[39]

Readings from the King James Version in public schools, along with other Bible-related offenses (like rampant anti-Semitism in popular biblical fiction) and more general efforts of mainstream Protestants to define the United States as a Christian nation (like an effort by the National Reform Association to amend the Constitution and recognize

37. Quoted in Cohen, *Jews in Christian America,* p. 83.
38. Jacob Rader Marcus, *United States Jewry, 1776-1985,* 4 vols. (Detroit: Wayne State University Press, 1993), vol. 3, p. 186.
39. *The American Jewish Yearbook* 16 (5675 [1914]): 138; 17 (5676 [1915]): 203-4; 18 (5677 [1916]): 84-85.

the rule of Christ over the nation), sharpened Jewish understanding of what they themselves desired from the Scriptures.[40] One Jewish response to the informal Protestant establishment was similar to that of many Catholics: separate, privately financed schools, in which study of the Hebrew Scriptures could be undertaken in their own versions and according to their own convictions.[41]

To Catholics, Jews, and other non-Protestants, the expansion of religious liberty represented only good logic. They could not see how the United States could both promote civil liberty and bestow special privileges on the King James Version of the Bible. For those areas of the country where Catholic and Jewish population was substantial by the early twentieth century, this argument was generally accepted. Later judicial rulings would expand the logic into areas where Protestant majorities continued to hold sway.

The special case of Jews in an America populated overwhelmingly by Christians requires further comment.[42] While Jews in America have almost all sought "equal footing" before the law, the meaning of "equal footing" has differed widely for Jews, depending upon time, place, and circumstance. For example, until the last third of the nineteenth century, almost all public Jewish voices expressed themselves *in favor* of government support for religion — whether in education, the military (through chaplains), or other venues. The difficulty for Jews in roughly the first century of United States history was to overcome laws and deeply engrained cultural habits that, in effect, forced American citizens to act like Christians. Thus, Jews opposed test acts requiring office holders to believe in the New Testament, they protested when "public schools" mandated praying the Lord's Prayer or promoting faith in Christ, and they urged the right to name rabbis as chaplains during the

40. On anti-Semitism in fiction, see Naomi A. Cohen, ed., *Essential Papers on Jewish-Christian Relations in the United States* (New York: New York University Press, 1990), pp. 112-13; on the Reform Association, see Howard M. Sachar, *A History of the Jews in America* (New York: Knopf, 1992), pp. 81-82.

41. Virginia L. Brereton, "The Public Schools Are Not Enough: The Bible and Private Schools," in Barr and Piediscalzi, *The Bible in American Education*, pp. 43-45.

42. The next paragraphs depend heavily on Sarna and Dalin, *Religion and State in the American Jewish Experience*.

Civil War alongside Christian clergymen. In these protests, Jews worked against the American grain of the period, but as promoters of a more equitable approach to religion in public rather than as opponents of religion in all public life.

Beginning with the large-scale Jewish immigrations from central and eastern Europe after the Civil War, more and more Jews became advocates of a stricter separation between religion and public life. To these more recent immigrants, strict separatism was the only way to avoid the evil effects of either America's historic cultural Protestantism or the more active promotion of "Christian America" that both proto-fundamentalist and proto-modernist Protestants advocated from the 1880s onward.[43] Thus, for many vocal Jews it was advantageous to seek alliances with all who opposed any form of Christianity in the public schools, in legal practice, or in observance of weekly or annual holy days, however irreligious such allies might be, since this strategy was thought to preserve the most space for Jews. Although this strict separatist position has been most widely associated with American Jews in the twentieth century, modern representatives of the earlier position continue to explore how Jews might support a public place for religion without going back to the informal establishment of Protestant Christianity. Complaints by noted Jewish thinker Will Herberg about the thinness of American public life stripped of religion and the campaign by Orthodox Lubavitchers in the state of New York for government support for private Jewish education have been important examples of this dissenting position.[44]

43. For discussion of these groupings, see Chapter Seven.

44. Will Herberg, *Protestant, Catholic, Jew: An Essay in American Religious Sociology* (Garden City, NY: Anchor Doubleday, 1960); Barbara J. Redman, "Strange Bedfellows: Lubavitcher Hasidim and Conservative Christians," *Journal of Church and State* 34 (Summer 1992): 521-48. Another Jewish group making similar efforts is discussed in Jonathan Boyarin, "Circumscribing Constitutional Identities in Kiryas Joel," *Yale Law Journal* 106 (March 1997): 1537-70.

Modern Judicial Innovations

From the mid-twentieth century, important changes in American jurisprudence have significantly altered the way in which the separation of
church and state is practiced. The first important judicial move was the
application of the Fourteenth Amendment of the Constitution to the
religious provisions of the First Amendment. The Fourteenth Amendment had been passed after the Civil War in 1868 with the intent of
guaranteeing civil rights to freed slaves. This Amendment prohibited
the states from making or enforcing "any law which shall abridge the
privileges or immunities of citizens of the United States" and further
restrained them from denying any of their citizens "life, liberty, or
property, without due process of law." In 1940 the U.S. Supreme Court
ruled that by the application of this Fourteenth Amendment, the First
Amendment's prohibition of a religious establishment and its guaran-
tee of religious "free exercise" must apply to state laws as well.[45]

The second key ruling came in 1947, in a case concerning a New Jersey law providing bus transportation for students in private, religious
schools as well as for students in public schools. Although the court
upheld the law, it also made an extreme claim about the implications of
the First Amendment. In a judgment overlooking 150 years of American practice, the Court used a phrase that Thomas Jefferson once wrote
in a private letter to say that the Constitution had erected "a wall of
separation between church and state."[46]

With these two judgments opening the door, the American courts
began vigorously to adjudicate many aspects of religion and public life
that had hitherto been left mostly to the individual states. Some of the
judgments expanded what it could mean to practice religion freely, as
in a case from 1972 *(Wisconsin v. Yoder)* that exempted the Amish (a sec-

---

45. For a thorough discussion, see Witte, "The Essential Rights and Liberties of Religion," pp. 410-11.

46. For the whole judgment, along with dissent, see Wilson and Drakeman, *Church
and State,* pp. 200-205. An energetic debate over whether Jefferson was merely making a
political statement for the moment or was attempting to set out a principle for all time
is found in James H. Hutson et al., "Thomas Jefferson's Letter to the Danbury Baptists:
A Controversy Rejoined," *William & Mary Quarterly* 56 (Oct. 1999): 775-824.

tarian offshoot from the Mennonites) from the public school laws of the state of Wisconsin. Other judgments expanded the new meaning of non-establishment to exclude the recitation of prayers (1962) and readings from the Bible (1963) from all of the nation's public schools, regardless of local sentiments. Many contested cases have also been adjudicated, but quite inconsistently, concerning the public display of religious symbols, the activities of government-sponsored chaplains, and the use of prayer at public gatherings. The expanded activity of the Supreme Court since the 1940s has broadened the meaning of religious freedom for some Americans, but the national intrusion into long-accepted local practices has also troubled others. Since the early 1990s, judicial opinion has swung back slightly toward earlier American tradition. With nominees of conservative presidents Ronald Reagan (1981-1989) and George Bush (1989-1993) leading the way, a little more space has been opened for religious practices in the public square. The announcement by President George W. Bush in early 2001 that his administration would channel federal money to social agencies organized by religious groups was a move in the same direction. Predictably, it won praise from those who championed "accommodation" between church and state, but fierce protests from those who insisted on "separation." As in nineteenth-century clashes between Protestants and non-Protestants, disputants in the second half of the twentieth century found it easier to agree on the wisdom of the First Amendment than on what it actually entails.

The separation of church and state has remained an important feature of American religious life to this day. As a rule, the churches still rely on voluntary societies to accomplish religious and moral purposes. Of course the boundaries between religious influence (which has always been accepted under the Constitution) and the effort to establish a religion (which is prohibited) have always been contested. Modern debate over abortion on demand that was legalized by the Supreme Court in 1973 is a good case in point. Opponents of liberalized abortion laws consider their arguments legitimate moral persuasion; defenders of those laws look upon religiously based arguments against abortion as illegitimate. What seems to opponents to be only the promotion of a religious point of view looks to defenders like a church establishment. Debates of this kind remain a persistent legacy of the effort begun in the early history of the United States to abandon principles of European establishment in favor of American "freedoms."

✑ CHAPTER FIVE

The High Tide of Protestantism, 1830-1865

The period from 1830 to 1865 was decisive for the history of Christianity in North America because of two major changes. First, the decade of the 1830s witnessed a series of turning points for the country's white Protestant majority that exerted a long-term impact on the activities and influence of those Protestants. Second, the end of the Civil War in 1865 introduced broader trends among non-white and non-Protestant Christians, as well as powerful national forces that decisively altered the religious history of the United States. Put in other terms, the generation after about 1830 saw a change in the direction of the United States' most visible Protestants, while in the next generation a change in the direction of the United States had far-reaching effects on all of the churches. In between these generations occurred the American Civil War (1861-1865), whose origin and effects were also intimately connected with the course of Christianity in the United States.

The Redirection and Limits of Revivalism

Textbooks on all aspects of American history usually treat the Civil War of 1861 to 1865 as the dividing point of their narratives. For the history of Christianity, however, there is considerable reason to regard the decade beginning in 1830 as a more important time of transition.[1] For the century from about 1740 to about 1840, the revivals promoted by evangelical Protestants were not only the most important feature of American religious life; they were also, after the events that formed the new nation, the most important public happenings of any kind. Revivalism would long continue as a potent force — for example, the lay-led "businessmen's revival" of 1857-1858 drew hundreds of thousands into the churches.[2] But for the reasons surveyed in the following paragraphs, revivalism after the decade of the 1830s was as much a fragmenting as a cohesive force; it could no longer dominate the public perception of morality, as had been the case from the 1790s into the 1820s; and the spirituality it promoted turned more toward private rather than public expressions. These changes in the course of revivalism, moreover, coincided with greatly expanded immigration, which brought many more Roman Catholics to the United States. They also took place alongside a rapid rise of African American denominations. White Protestants retained great strength, but, relative to other Christian movements, their power would wane during the last two-thirds of the century.

The Changing Course of Charles G. Finney

A physical change in location by the leading revivalist of the national period provided an important symbol for these developments. Charles G. Finney (1792-1875) was trained as a lawyer, but then in 1821 experienced a dramatic religious conversion that immediately redirected his energies to preaching.[3] As he put it, Finney received "a re-

---

1. This account follows the picture outlined in James D. Bratt, "The Reorientation of American Protestantism, 1835-1845," *Church History* 67 (March 1998): 52-82.

2. See Kathryn Teresa Long, *The Revival of 1857-58: Interpreting an American Religious Awakening* (New York: Oxford University Press, 1998).

3. See especially Charles E. Hambrick-Stowe, *Charles G. Finney and the Spirit of American Evangelicalism* (Grand Rapids: Eerdmans, 1996); *The Memoirs of Charles G. Finney,* ed. Garth M. Roselle and Richard A. G. Dupuis (Grand Rapids: Zondervan, 1989); and Keith Hardman, *Charles Grandison Finney, 1792-1875* (Syracuse, NY: Syracuse University Press, 1987).

tainer from the Lord Jesus Christ to plead his cause." He first read theology with a Presbyterian minister, but from the start he displayed a lack of concern for formal theological traditions that characterized his entire career. He began preaching in such small towns of upstate New York as Evans Mills, Antwerp, and Perch River. Soon he graduated to small cities like Troy and Utica. In 1830-1831 he orchestrated a dramatic revival in Rochester, New York, a booming city on the trade-rich Erie Canal.[4] Then he took his message to the great cities of the Eastern seacoast, Boston, New York, and Philadelphia. His greatest successes came in upstate New York, but wherever he preached, his earnest appeal for conversion and ardent demands for moral purity created a stir.

The symbolic change of location occurred in 1835 when, after serving briefly as a minister in New York City, Finney moved to Oberlin College in Ohio, which became his headquarters for the rest of his life. Oberlin, a new college close to the country's Western frontier, had been founded by Congregational evangelicals who wanted to usher in the millennium. It was ardently revivalistic; it was also in the vanguard of social reform. Oberlin admitted both women and African Americans at a time when almost no other American institution of higher education did so, and it was a leader in the fight against slavery. Its supporters thought its strategic location on the opening frontier would give it broad national influence.

Oberlin remained a hotbed of revivalism and social reform for most of the rest of the century. In many ways, it became the embodiment of Finney's revivalism, and it was his revivalistic practices that decisively shaped the course of American Protestant evangelicalism. Finney was a wholehearted advocate of "new measures," many of them taken over from the Methodists.[5] He encouraged women to speak publicly at his meetings, he urged people who were sorry for their sins and who wanted to be converted to gather at an "anxious bench" and pray for divine grace, and he often held "protracted meetings" that lasted for

4. See Paul E. Johnson, *A Shopkeeper's Millennium: Society and Revivals in Rochester, New York, 1815-1837* (New York: Hill & Wang, 1978).

5. See Richard Carwardine, "The Second Great Awakening in the Urban Centers: An Examination of Methodism and the 'New Measures,'" *Journal of American History* 59 (1972): 327-40.

weeks or even months at a time. These innovations were bitterly opposed by leaders of the older churches. Some of Finney's opponents also worried about the great stress he placed on the ability of individuals to turn to God as an exercise of their own willpower without divine assistance. Surely, they thought, this was carrying self-reliance too far. He was also criticized for urging converts to become active social reformers against drunkenness, slavery, luxurious eating, mistreatment of the mentally ill, and the Masonic Movement. But Finney and his associates overcame this opposition. His charisma as a speaker — with a clear penetrating gaze, a vigorous speaking voice, and a relentlessly logical style — made him every bit as influential as the era's great politicians. Even more, his willingness to adjust historic patterns of Protestant faith and practice in order to reach the new towns and cities of an expanding nation made him the representative figure of his age.

But the great national transformation Oberlin's founders sought, which led them to recruit Finney as its leading teacher, and which Finney himself preached, did not take place. The evangelical movement was beginning to fragment. In the 1840s and 1850s Finney became increasingly concerned that the call to conversion was being overwhelmed by efforts to reform society. His own preaching increasingly stressed "Christian perfection" — a transformation of inner life — rather than the transformation of American society.

The move to Oberlin was, thus, symbolic of an outer transformation and an inner transformation. It represented a move away from the national centers of commerce, publications, and culture toward a social margin. It also could stand for a theological shift in which inward spiritual progress began to be separated from Christian efforts to shape the entire society.

The Holiness of Phoebe Palmer

Another important factor in promoting new forms of inward spirituality was the work of Phoebe Worrall Palmer (1807-1874).[6] During her

---

6. See Thomas C. Oden, ed., *Phoebe Palmer: Selected Writings* (New York: Paulist,

early adult years, Palmer, as a faithful Methodist, earnestly pursued John Wesley's outline for a perfected Christian life. She also experienced the traumatic death of three of her children. Beginning in 1835 she conducted a "Tuesday Meeting for the Promotion of Holiness" in the New York City home of her sister, Sarah Worrall Lankford. At that gathering she encouraged guests to talk of their experience with God, and she outlined her own idea of "entire sanctification," or of perfect consecration to God. Especially after a memorable religious experience on July 26, 1837, when Palmer reported a special manifestation of the Holy Spirit's indwelling power, she became a dynamic proponent of what would become know as "holiness" or, in other circles, "the higher Christian life."

Phoebe Palmer observed many of the conventions of the nineteenth century about public activity for women; she even published several of her books anonymously. But this diffidence was not a restraint. She contributed many essays to periodicals, such as the *Christian Advocate and Journal;* she instructed many people of high estate and low in her understanding of godliness; and she participated in more than three hundred revival meetings in the United States, Canada, and the British Isles. Sales of several of her books ran into the hundreds of thousands. Expositions like *The Way of Holiness* (1845) set out her views on the power of the Holy Spirit. *The Promise of the Father* (1859) forthrightly defended women's right to preach on the basis of biblical passages like Joel 2:28 ("your sons and daughters will prophesy"). Her emphasis upon the Holy Spirit as a source of spiritual illumination and power also anticipated the spread of Holiness denominations, like the Church of the Nazarene, that occurred toward the end of the nineteenth century.[7] In the long run, it helped pave the way for the Pentecostal movement of the twentieth century.

Cultivation of inward spirituality did not mean that Phoebe Palmer abandoned the world. In fact, she participated in urban reform movements, such as a project to bring housing, education, work, and

---

1988); and Charles Edward White, *The Beauty of Holiness: Phoebe Palmer as Theologian, Revivalist, Feminist, and Humanitarian* (Grand Rapids: Francis Asbury Press, 1986).

7. Melvin Easterday Dieter, *The Holiness Revival of the Nineteenth Century* (Metuchen, NJ: Scarecrow, 1980).

regular religious services to the Five Points district, one of New York City's worst slums. At the same time, the long-term effect of her emphasis on "holiness" was to tip the balance of Christian ideals toward inner spirituality and away from full-blown engagement with the structures, institutions, and events of the developing American society. Her spiritual experiences in the mid-1830s that coincided with Finney's removal to the Ohio frontier stood for a re-orientation in the driving forces of American public life.

Other aspects of Protestant existence were changing as Finney and Palmer made these theological and geographical moves. During the 1830s and on into the next decade, at least three other important circumstances testified to the perils engendered by the very successes of revivalistic Protestantism.

Protestant Fragmentation

First was the fragmentation of the evangelical Protestant phalanx. The unleashing of ordinary individuals, who for Christian and democratic reasons were urged to think and act for themselves, produced tremendous expansionary energy in the churches, but it also fueled an ecclesiastical centrifuge. To empower ordinary people meant that some of the people so empowered might act in ways not conforming to inherited standards of faith and practice. Spokesmen for evangelical Protestantism urged people to take control of their lives into their own hands. But when individuals like William Miller and Joseph Smith did so, traditional Protestant leaders were far from pleased. The secret of the power behind the evangelical surge during the first generation of the new nation's history was also the secret behind the fragmentation of evangelicalism in the generation after 1830.

The movements led by Miller and Smith illustrated that fragmentation. Miller (1782-1849) was a self-educated farmer from upstate New York whose life illustrates the ability of ordinary people to shape the course of religious history.[8] From his own vigorous study of Scrip-

8. See Ruth Alden Doan, *The Miller Heresy, Millennialism, and American Culture* (Phila-

ture, Miller concluded that the return of Christ and the end of the world as foretold in the Bible would take place sometime around 1843. In these calculations, Miller recapitulated older apocalyptic exegesis, but he also put to use the American fascination with science that was so important in the early nineteenth century. Soon he was joined by an energetic publicist, Joseph V. Himes, whose skill at propagating Miller's message showed how well he was attuned to the times. The churches and religious movements that flourished in the early United States all were adept at publicity, at exploiting the printing press and the newspaper, in getting their message out to the people at large.

The combination of Miller's message and Himes' skill with the media led to a popular phenomenon. Himes and his associates distributed over five million pieces of literature publicizing Miller's conclusions, including several versions of a spectacular chart that outlined the whole history of the world as the fulfillment of biblical prophecies. Thousands waited expectantly on March 21, 1843, for the return of Christ, and then on October 22, 1844, as the result of Miller's new calculations. The enduring legacy of what might look like a frivolous movement was the creation of several individual denominations after the "Disappointment," as the failure of Christ to return on the second of those dates was called. Of those denominations, the most important was the Seventh-day Adventists, who were formed under the leadership of Ellen White (1827-1915).[9] White and her associates concluded that Christ had indeed returned as Miller predicted, but that the return was a spiritual passage of Christ into the presence of the Father. Under her leadership, this group practiced Saturday worship; it also was a pioneer in several dietary practices, such as the preparation of grains as cold cereals, that have had a major impact beyond the religious sphere. The history of the Seventh-day Adventists is also of note because, especially in the second half of the twentieth century, it has gradually moved closer to the practices and beliefs of more traditional evangelical Protestant churches.

---

delphia: Temple University Press, 1987); and Ronald L. Numbers and Jonathan M. Butler, eds., *The Disappointed: Millerism and Millenarianism in the Nineteenth Century* (Bloomington: Indiana University Press, 1987).

9. See Ronald L. Numbers, *Prophetess of Health: A Study of Ellen G. White*, expanded ed. (Knoxville: University of Tennessee Press, 1992).

The most remarkable example of a new religious movement grow-ing out of the fertile soil of early American freedom was the Church of Jesus Christ of Latter-day Saints (or Mormons) founded by Joseph Smith (1805-1844).[10] Smith grew up in a religious family, but one in which his mother, Lucy Mack Smith, became disillusioned with the in-compatible claims of evangelical Protestant sects that competed for ad-herents in New England, where the family originated, as well as in New York state, to which the family moved. Beginning in the 1820s, her son began to report a series of angelic visions that culminated in his discov-ery of the *Book of Mormon* that, in the English translation Smith eventu-ally produced, detailed God's special dealings with prehistoric settlers in America and long-lost tribes of Israel. Smith published the *Book of Mormon* in 1830 to great opposition. At first to a few, and then to much larger numbers, however, what Smith considered a new revelation from God seemed to be precisely the sure word that was lacking in the ca-cophony created by America's multiplicity of religions.

Smith and his followers moved first to Kirtland, Ohio, and then to western Illinois, where Smith was killed by a mob incensed by his auto-cratic politics. Under the direction of Smith's successor, Brigham Young, the Mormons made a heroic migration of about 1100 miles to the basin of the Great Salt Lake in present-day Utah.[11] The trip, made on foot and by wagon train, gave Mormons the free space to set up a refuge in which they could manage their own social and political lives as well as establish the new religion.

Mormonism represents a new religious movement, based as it is on Smith's account of a new revelation. But it is also a movement that, es-pecially throughout the twentieth century, has made more and more of its Christian connections. Mormons, for example, honor the Christian Scriptures, but regard the *Book of Mormon* as an additional revelation.[12]

10. See Richard L. Bushman, *Joseph Smith and the Beginning of Mormonism* (Urbana: University of Illinois Press, 1984); and Jan Shipps, *Mormonism: The Story of a New Religious Tradition* (Urbana: University of Illinois Press, 1985).

11. See Leonard J. Arrington, *Brigham Young: American Moses* (Urbana: University of Illinois Press, 1986).

12. See Philip L. Barlow, *Mormons and the Bible* (New York: Oxford University Press, 1991).

Under the leadership of Joseph Smith, the church illustrated the great space available in the early American republic for religious innovation. Under Brigham Young and his successors, the Mormons have demonstrated how an American-based religious movement can spread out to influence the world. At the end of the twentieth century, the Mormons numbered about 10 million members, with more than half of them living outside the United States in 155 different countries.[13]

The Conversion of the South

A different sort of fragmentation occurred when revivalistic Protestants gained the kind of success in Southern society that they had earlier achieved in many areas of the North. That Southern expansion, in turn, very much affected another important change of direction visible in the 1830s: the faltering of earlier evangelical Protestant visions of social reform.

The spread of revivalistic evangelicalism in the white population of the South was the product of long, arduous labor. That success eventually strengthened the North-South divisions that led to the Civil War, and it contributed directly to the evangelicals' greatest failure in social reform. But on its own terms, it was also a triumph. Among Southern whites, evangelical Protestantism had to overcome a very strong competing culture of honor. This culture of honor featured the display of self, manly competition, sensitivity to insult, and a great fondness for the duel. It was the product of a Cavalier origin, a republican defense of freedom, uncertainties of tobacco farming, and the heightened consciousness of social divisions brought about by the slave system.[14]

Lower-class Baptists and Methodists provided the opening wedge for active Protestantism in the South. In the 1770s and 1780s, members of the Episcopalian gentry sometimes disrupted the church services of

---

13. See Richard N. Ostling and Joan K. Ostling, *Mormon America* (New York: Harper Collins, 1999).

14. See Bertram Wyatt-Brown, *Southern Honor: Ethics and Behavior in the Old South* (New York: Oxford University Press, 1982).

these lowly evangelicals as an affront to their dignity. Gradually, however, the religion of the powerless became the religion of the powerful. Evangelical Protestant preaching seems to have been especially fruitful among middle- and upper-class Southern women. They found the message of forgiveness and consolation in Christ particularly meaningful in situations that often mixed the rough realities of slave agriculture with the refined aspirations of genteel society. By the 1820s and 1830s, there was a capable corps of Methodist, Baptist, Episcopalian, and Presbyterian ministers in the South's urban centers. They exerted a socially conservative but firmly Christian influence on Southern opinion-makers. By the 1830s and 1840s, the biblical religion of evangelical Protestantism had become the most important value system in the region.[15]

But even as they succeeded in winning converts, Southern evangelical leaders also set the stage for a moral crisis. The spread of revivalism among a slaveholding people in the South was bound to conflict with the aspirations of Northern evangelicals who felt that Christianity demanded the extermination of slavery. Intra-Protestant disputes over slavery were, however, only the most important of several signs of weakness in the great evangelical vision of social reform.

The Failure of Reform

The social promise of revivalism was that converting individuals could transform society; social reform inspired by biblical holiness would grow naturally from the actions of the converted. In the first decades of the nineteenth century, this formula seemed to be working. The voluntary societies effectively channeled the religious energies of the converted into the doing of good for the whole society. In the 1830s, however, the dream of a moral Christian society, transformed outwardly by the voluntary efforts of the inwardly converted, began to collapse.

Slavery was the major problem, but another significant failure con-

15. See Donald G. Mathews, *Religion in the Old South* (Chicago: University of Chicago Press, 1977); and Robert M. Calhoon, *Evangelicals and Conservatives in the Early South, 1740-1861* (Columbia: University of South Carolina Press, 1988).

cerned the fate of the Cherokee Indians. In general, white relations with Native Americans in the early national period continued the abysmal record of colonial days. But with the Cherokee of northern Georgia, eastern Tennessee, and western North Carolina, the positive effects of personal and social conversion seemed for a while to overcome the legacy of dispossession.[16] A peace treaty with the new United States government in 1794 stimulated a cultural revival among the Cherokee, and also opened the way for white missionaries to begin their work. While the Cherokee built roads, organized politically, rendered their language in writing, and began to print their own books and newspapers, they also welcomed the missionaries. A slow but steady acceptance of the Christian faith followed, as did also an eagerness to accept American political institutions and follow American patterns of industrious self-reliance.

During the administration of President Andrew Jackson (1829-1837), however, the evangelism and Americanization of the Cherokee both received a fatal blow. After the discovery of gold in northern Georgia about the time of Jackson's election in 1828, the lust of white settlers for Cherokee land increased. The result was a forced removal of the Cherokee from Georgia to the West. Despite a favorable judgment by the United States Supreme Court in 1832, President Jackson refused to protect the property or personal rights of the Indians. Massive white incursion onto Indian lands continued. In 1838 federal troops placed fifteen thousand Cherokee in detention, and soon thereafter the Cherokee agreed to take the long, often fatal journey to wasted territory across the Mississippi River in the Oklahoma Territory. By 1844 almost all Indians had been removed beyond the Mississippi.

The missionaries, who had come to the Native Americans as bearers of American civilization as well as of Christianity, now confronted a terrible dilemma. They now were forced to watch their country, supposedly the embodiment of Christian civilization, turn violently against a people that had accepted their message. Many of the missionaries caved

16. See William G. McLoughlin, *Cherokee Renascence in the New Republic* (Princeton: Princeton University Press, 1986); and McLoughlin, *The Cherokees and Christianity, 1794-1870* (Atlanta: University of Georgia Press, 1994).

in to the pressure and agreed to the removal. But others protested vigorously, even to the point of civil disobedience. Samuel Worcester and Elizur Butler went to jail rather than obey a Georgia state law demanding that whites leave Cherokee land. The Northern Baptists Evan Jones and his son John B. Jones stood up for Cherokee rights in the Southeast and then journeyed with the outcasts to Oklahoma, where they continued the work of evangelization and education.[17] The ministers they trained formed the backbone of a sturdy network of Cherokee Baptist churches that eventually developed in the new tribal lands. But missionary support for the Cherokee was not enough. The brutal removal went on. The United States, bearing the gifts of Christian faith and democratic politics, destroyed a tribal people working hard to accept those very gifts.

The tragedy of slavery was even greater. Protestantism had very much to do with strengthening the moral purpose of all major groups caught up in the dilemma; most importantly, the early decades of the new United States witnessed a dramatic rise in African American churches.[18] The same period saw strong white evangelical support for abolition.[19] But it also witnessed a great strengthening of Protestantism in the South, where soon the Scriptures were used to support the slave system.

Into the 1830s, it seemed possible that the application of conversionist Protestant energy could bring a peaceable end to the slave system.[20] That goal had in fact been reached in Britain, where, after intensive efforts sustained largely by Protestant evangelicals, Parliament in 1833 abolished slavery in the British empire by providing compensa-

---

17. See William G. McLoughlin, *Champions of the Cherokee: Evan and John B. Jones* (Princeton: Princeton University Press, 1990).

18. See Albert J. Raboteau, *Slave Religion: The "Invisible Institution in the Antebellum South* (New York: Oxford University Press, 1978); and Sylvia R. Frey and Betty Wood, *Come Shouting to Zion: African American Protestantism in the American South and British Caribbean to 1830* (Chapel Hill: University of North Carolina Press, 1998), pp. 149-81.

19. See Donald G. Mathews, *Slavery and Methodism: A Chapter in American Morality, 1780-1845* (Princeton: Princeton University Press, 1965).

20. For a general picture, see Ronald G. Walters, *American Reformers, 1815-1860* (New York: Hill & Wang, 1978).

tion to slave holders in the West Indies as the price for liberating their slaves. In the United States, northern abolitionist evangelicals repeatedly affirmed their belief that, if only the power of the gospel could be unleashed, slavery would soon be over. In 1835, Charles Finney stated this case with his characteristic energy: "It is the church that mainly supports this sin [of slavery]. . . . Let Christians of all denominations meekly but firmly come forth, and pronounce their verdict, let them clear their communions, and wash their hands of this thing; let them give forth and write on the head and front of this great abomination, SIN! and in three years, a public sentiment would be formed that would carry all before it, and there would not be a shackled slave, nor a bristling, cruel slave driver in this land."[21]

Finney was wrong: in fact, the tide was running against abolition. As the nation's slave population continued to grow as fast as its total population throughout the 1830s, the Protestant-driven abolitionist movement enjoyed its greatest visibility but also suffered a series of reversals. A convert in one of Finney's early revivals, Theodore Dwight Weld, published the decade's most compelling assaults on the system with his books *The Bible Against Slavery* (1837) and *Slavery As It Is* (1839). In addition, by the middle years of the decade, anti-slave societies existed in over five hundred local communities (almost all in the North). Despite a strong anti-slavery movement, however, pro-slavery was becoming even stronger. In 1831 rebellions by slaves in Jamaica and Virginia, the latter led by lay preacher Nat Turner, motivated the slave states to impose harsher laws for regulating the system. These laws, in some cases, included restrictions on slave religious activities. In the middle years of the decade, the American Colonization Society, which promoted the settlement of freed slaves in Africa, suffered a debilitating internal schism. As an indication of mounting dissatisfaction with abolition, acts of violence increased. One of the more publicized of these events occurred in 1837, when a New England–born abolitionist, Elijah P. Lovejoy, was slain by a mob in Alton, Illinois, that had been angered by Lovejoy's promotion of abolition in his

21. Charles G. Finney, *Lectures on Revivals of Religion,* ed. William G. McLoughlin (1835; reprint, Cambridge: Harvard University Press, 1960), p. 302.

newspaper.[22] Growing strength in pro-slavery forces was matched by growing weakness among the abolitionists. In 1839-1840 the American Anti-Slavery Society, the most powerful voluntary association of its kind, broke apart when leaders could not agree on whether to add campaigns for women's rights to the battle against slavery.

Most destructively, the major Protestant denominations experienced schisms over their inability to adjudicate differences over slavery. The question of how actively to promote abolition was in the background when the main body of American Presbyterians divided in 1837. But in North-South divisions among the Methodists and Baptists in 1844, slavery was front and center.[23]

With the Baptists and the Methodists, who had spearheaded evangelical Protestant expansion in the early republic, now divided North and South, with the initiative for abolition passing out of the hands of religious leaders into the hands of politicians, and with more and more Southern Protestants using the Scriptures to defend the slave system, evangelicals had lost all chance for "converting" the national society. Revivalistic Protestantism of the kind that had flourished so dramatically from the days of Whitefield to the era of Finney would remain the largest and most religiously active segment of the Christian movement in the United States. But the dream of converting the nation was rapidly passing away.

For about forty years, from 1795 to 1835, America's white evangelical Protestants had been an expanding religious force, the strongest shaper of manners and morals in the country, and a major influence on public events. After the mid-1830s, political circumstances and social forces reversed the equation and began to exert more influence on the churches than the churches did on the nation.

22. See Paul Simon, *Freedom's Champion: Elijah Lovejoy* (Carbondale: Southern Illinois University Press, 1994).

23. See C. C. Goen, *Broken Churches, Broken Nation: Denominational Schisms and the Coming of the Civil War* (Macon, GA: Mercer University Press, 1985).

The Civil War as a Religious Event

During the 1840s and 1850s, the nation's fragmented churches were unable to halt the drift toward war.[24] In fact, one of the main reasons political positions hardened in the 1850s was the religious support provided by Christians for the North and for the South. Many abolitionists felt that the Bible demanded the immediate end of slavery. Many slaveholders felt that the Bible's defense of slavery was the key to preserving a Christian social order and resisting the mad scramble for money that Southerners saw as dominating the North. Many cautious Bible believers in all regions of the country were predisposed against immediate abolition by their belief that the Bible had ordained the very kind of stable social order that the Constitution (with its compromises on slavery) gave to the United States. Religious and political convictions were linked more closely than ever before or since in the history of the United States.

The Civil War, as a consequence, was a religious war.[25] On both sides, believers claimed that their cause was ordained by God. Representatives on both sides quoted the Bible against each other. In the end, the armies of the North were triumphant, but even after the shooting stopped, few Americans conceded any ideological points to their foes. Opponents of slavery thought they were well rid of the system. Moderates North and South worried about the social disruption brought on by the war. Southern blacks rejoiced at freedom but faced a very uncertain future. Southern whites refused to admit they were wrong.[26] This strife over the war, among Protestants in particular, revealed further the weaknesses that had begun to surface earlier in the 1830s.

24. A splendid account, broader than its title suggests, is Richard J. Carwardine, *Evangelicals and Politics in Antebellum America* (New Haven: Yale University Press, 1993).

25. See James W. Silver, *Confederate Morale and Church Propaganda* (New York: Norton, 1967); James H. Moorhead, *American Apocalypse: Yankee Protestants and the Civil War, 1860-1869* (New Haven: Yale University Press, 1978); Gardiner H. Shattuck, Jr., *A Shield and Hiding Place: The Religious Life of the Civil War Armies* (Macon, GA: Mercer University Press, 1987); and especially Randall Miller, Harry S. Stout, and Charles R. Wilson, eds., *Religion and the American Civil War* (New York: Oxford University Press, 1998).

26. See Charles Reagan Wilson, *Baptized in Blood: The Religion of the Lost Cause, 1865-1920* (Athens: University of Georgia Press, 1980).

After the war, the shape of American religion changed rapidly, for a number of reasons outlined in the next chapter. But one of the reasons for rapid religious change can be found in the Civil War itself. Inasmuch as the war stimulated large-scale industrialization, the creation of large bureaucracies, and the movement of people from farms to cities, it undercut the small-town and rural ways of life in which Protestant values had been most securely rooted.

In addition, because the war itself had been so intensely religious, with especially Protestants on both sides claiming the sanction of God for their efforts, the aftermath of the war almost inevitably led to a letdown. In the victorious North, concern for fighting slavery gave way to concern for inner spirituality at the same time that increasing Protestant energy was being expended on simply coping with rapid industrial and urban change. In addition, victory over the South did not bring the purified Christian republic that a few leaders, such as theologian Horace Bushnell of Hartford, Connecticut, or preacher Henry Ward Beecher of Brooklyn, New York, had foreseen.[27]

In the defeated South, the Protestant denominations grew stronger, but at a price. In the wake of the war's economic and cultural devastation, religion offered profound consolation. Yet part of what it meant for such religion to shore up a defeated people was to sanction the sins of racism that almost no one in the country, North or South, seemed willing to challenge. So it was that in the South, most white Protestant churches actively or passively supported a racially segregated society and a system withholding civil rights from the African American population.

The Civil War may also have done grave damage to hereditary confidence in the Bible. The Scriptures were a major prop for both sides in the war, but the way in which the Bible was put to use established a troubling precedent. The fact that the Bible could be used by each side to support its own cause, and its own cause alone, led some people to

---

27. On the war's undercutting of traditional religion, see George M. Fredrickson, *The Inner Civil War: Northern Intellectuals and the Crisis of the Union* (New York: Harper & Row, 1965); and Anne C. Rose, *Victorian America and the Civil War* (New York: Cambridge University Press, 1992).

wonder if reliance on the Bible was not just a smokescreen for expressing local prejudice. There was no question that the Bible was useful in
defining the conflict on both sides. Early on, for example, a Southern
minister interpreted 2 Chronicles 6:34-35 (Solomon's prayer for success in battle for Israel) as an analysis of Abraham Lincoln's role in the
current crisis: "eleven tribes sought to go forth in peace from the house
of political bondage, but the heart of our modern Pharaoh is hardened,
that he will not let Israel go."[28] In the North, one of the more than four
hundred sermons published after Lincoln's assassination was an exposition of 2 Samuel 18:32, where David learns about the treacherous
slaying of his son Absalom. After the minister examined the text, he
concluded that no one "will be able to separate in thought the murder
of the president from [Confederate President] Jefferson Davis' persistent effort to murder the Union."[29] Such interpretations trivialized the
Scriptures. They may also have had something to do with rising academic attitudes that were only just beginning to question earlier rever-
ence for the Bible. If the Bible could be used to say anything, then
maybe it was better to consider it an ordinary human book rather than
the revealed Word of God.

The Civil War also affected religious life by the way in which it
opened the West for settlement. So long as there was contention over
whether new western states could admit slaves or not, settlement was
delayed as well as uncertain. But with the ending of slavery and the extension of federal power from the Great Plains to the West Coast, the
great western region of the country was now a target for religious outreach as well. Protestants found that the influence they had exerted
east of the Mississippi simply did not exist in the West. Even before
Protestants began missionary efforts in the region, a large Hispanic
Catholic population already existed in the Southwest, Mormon settlements had spread over Utah and Idaho, Indian reservations (with a
mixture of indigenous and Christian faiths) were in place, immigrants
from Asia who sometimes brought Eastern faiths to America were en-

---

28. Benjamin M. Palmer, *National Responsibility Before God* (New Orleans, 1861), p. 5.
29. Henry A. Nelson, *The Divinely Prepared Ruler, and the Fit End of Treason* (Springfield, IL, 1865), p. 32.

tering the region, and resistance to traditional religion of all kinds was widespread. The American West would become home to many vigorous Christian groups, but none of them dominated their sub-regions to the same extent that different forms of Protestantism continued to dominate some of the sub-regions of the South and Midwest well into the next century.

The public visibility of the white Protestant denominations has often led to the assumption that they long dominated American Christian history without a serious rival. Methodists, Baptists, Presbyterians, Congregationalists, Episcopalians, and the German and Dutch Reformed have indeed always played an important role in American Christian history. But their importance can be exaggerated. Even in the nineteenth century, when white Protestant influence was at its height, other Christian movements were developing in numbers, regional influence, and intrinsic religious interest to rival the white Protestants. To some of those other movements we turn in the next chapter.

CHAPTER SIX

A New Christian Pluralism, 1865-1906

B y the second half of the nineteenth century, organized Protestantism in the United States included a large African American com-
ponent. The Roman Catholic presence in America was growing with
great speed because of immigration, which was also establishing the
first transplantations of Eastern Orthodoxy. The presence of these new
groups gave the history of Christianity in America a diversity and complexity that has only increased throughout the twentieth century. During the four decades after the Civil War, white Protestant attempts to
deal with new urban and industrial conditions also showed that older
strands of American Christianity retained considerable vitality as well.

The Emergence of African American Churches

From difficult beginnings and hard-won gains in the Revolutionary
and early national periods, African American churches enjoyed a period
of remarkable growth after the Civil War. As they did so, they ended for-
ever the idea that Protestantism in America meant only white Protestants. The necessary preparation for this postwar experience of the
black churches had been underway for two generations.[1]

1. See Sylvia R. Frey and Betty Wood, *Come Shouting to Zion: African American Protes-*

From the 1770s African Americans began to join Christian churches in large numbers. At first most Christian blacks were formally attached to white congregations, even though their own informal meetings often provided the profoundest support for their religion. A few African Americans, like Lemuel Haynes of Connecticut, were even ordained for service in largely white New England congregations.[2]

The earliest and most important denomination organized by blacks for blacks was the African Methodist Episcopal Church. Its founder, Richard Allen (1760-1831), was born a slave and was converted by Methodists at the age of seventeen while working on a Delaware plantation.[3] He began to preach immediately, first to his family, then to his master, and then to whites and blacks throughout the region. Allen taught himself to read and write, and after much labor purchased his own freedom. After working at several trades, he finally arrived in Philadelphia at the age of twenty-six, and immediately began preaching to fellow African Americans as often as four or five times a day. Along with other African Americans, Allen regularly attended St. George's Methodist Church.

Then a distressing incident, probably occurring in 1787, drove blacks away from St. George's. While Allen's friend Absalom Jones was kneeling to pray during a Sunday service, white trustees forced Jones to his feet and tried to move him out of an area reserved for whites. In response, Jones, Allen, and the other blacks left the church. About the same time Allen and Jones founded the Free African Society, America's first self-help voluntary association that provided aid and spiritual encouragement to Philadelphia's African American community. It soon became a model for other black societies devoted to religious concerns.

After years of struggle and much opposition from whites, Allen succeeded in establishing the Bethel Church for Negro Methodists in 1793. He himself was ordained in 1799 as a Methodist deacon. Despite

tantism in the American South and British Caribbean to 1830 (Chapel Hill: University of North Carolina Press, 1998), pp. 63-148.

2. See John Saillant, "Lemuel Haynes' Black Republicanism and the American Republican Tradition, 1775-1820," *Journal of the Early Republic* 14 (1994): 293-324.

3. See Carol V. R. George, *Segregated Sabbaths: Richard Allen and the Emergence of Independent Black Churches, 1760-1840* (New York: Oxford University Press, 1973).

sustained resistance from some of Allen's white colleagues, in 1814 the African Americans succeeded in organizing their own denomination, the African Methodist Episcopal Church (Bethel). Allen became its first bishop in 1816 and served the growing body as its respected leader until his death in 1831.

Even though white Methodists often made things difficult, Methodism provided just the right combination of evangelical zeal and cooperative discipline. As Allen put it, "the plain and simple gospel [of the Methodists] suits best for any people, for the unlearned can understand, and the learned are sure to understand."[4]

By the time of Allen's death, other Northern blacks had also begun to organize churches for themselves, as local congregations of Methodist, Baptists, and Presbyterians were established in all major urban areas. By 1822 a black Episcopal association and two other Methodist denominations had joined the African Methodist Episcopal (AME) Church as independent organizations. Black Baptists, like their white counterparts, stressed congregational autonomy and so were slower to organize. But after many years of cooperation with white Baptist mission agencies, blacks established in 1845 the African Baptist Missionary Society.

By the 1820s, African American churches and denominations were venturing outward in a number of ways. They were sending missionaries to Liberia, Sierra Leone, and Haiti.[5] Black ministers were also becoming important leaders of the abolitionist movement. Although African American denominations, like their white counterparts, ordained only men, at least some black women, such as Richard Allen's associate Jarena Lee, did work as lay preachers. In 1827 Lee traveled over two thousand miles and preached on 180 different occasions.[6]

---

4. *The Life Experiences and Gospel Labors of the Rt. Rev. Richard Allen . . . Written by Himself* (reprinted, Nashville: Abingdon, 1960), p. 29.

5. For sources, see Sylvia M. Jacobs, *Black American Missionaries in Africa: A Selected Bibliography* (New York: Greenwood, 1980); for how these missionary ventures later developed, see James T. Campbell, *Songs of Zion: The African Methodist Episcopal Church in the United States and South Africa* (Chapel Hill: University of North Carolina Press, 1998).

6. See *Religious Experience and Journal of Mrs. Jarena Lee, Giving an Account of Her Call to Preach the Gospel* (Philadelphia, 1849); reprinted in *Spiritual Narratives*, Schomburg Library of Nineteenth-Century Black Women Writers (New York: Oxford University Press, 1988).

In the slave South, there were significantly fewer chances to organize churches and voluntary societies, yet such institutions did come into existence.[7] Despite the notorious "slave codes" that in some states prohibited meetings and made it illegal to teach slaves to read, Christianity made some progress. Some masters encouraged their slaves to attend church with them. Others permitted supervised religious meetings on the plantation. Still others gave grudging approval to the work of white missionaries. But even where owners forbade religious meetings, slaves were often able to meet in secret for prayer, exhortation, and preaching from fellow blacks. As it emerged, African American Christianity was a singular blend of African, European, and American elements, which made for both continuity and discontinuity with the white churches.

At meetings and on many other occasions, singing was an all-important part of African American existence.[8] Songs and hymns recounting the biblical stories of Abraham, David, Daniel, and Jesus were sung fervently. These songs offered hope for the age to come and encouragement to keep going in the present. Where possible, these songs were also acted out, often in the "shout," a counterclockwise, circular dance that recalled African ritual. After the Civil War, some of these songs were written down and their music transcribed. They became the basis of the "spiritual," America's greatest contribution to worldwide Christian hymnody.

Christianity could be a source of comfort to slaves that reconciled them to their fate in bondage, but it could also fuel rebellion. In one form or another, whether through biblical stories, images, or eschatological hopes, Christian faith contributed to major slave revolts under Gabriel Prosser in Richmond, Virginia (1800), Denmark Vesey in Charleston, South Carolina (1822), and Nat Turner in Virginia (1831). Much more commonly, Christianity emboldened slaves to disobey masters in order to meet together for worship and song, to work hard

7. A key book that includes much on slave religious activity is Eugene D. Genovese, *Roll, Jordan, Roll: The World the Slaves Made* (New York: Pantheon, 1974).

8. See James Weldon Johnson, ed., *The Book of American Negro Spirituals* (New York: Viking, 1925); and Dena J. Epstein, *Sinful Tunes and Spirituals: Black Folk Music to the Civil War* (Urbana: University of Illinois Press, 1977).

with an eye toward freedom at least for coming generations, and even to escape. In this determination to find freedom — in Christ and in this world — Southern African Americans shared the commitments of their Northern counterparts, where leaders in the church were also leaders in the struggle against slavery.

One of the most important of the black abolitionists, Frederick Douglass (1817?-1895), was also a sharp-spoken critic of the kind of Christianity that tolerated racial slavery.[9] Douglass was born in Maryland as the son of an unknown white man and a slave mother. After a childhood of cruelty and neglect, he was taken to Baltimore as a house slave. There he learned to read and write and, after several abortive attempts, managed to escape to the North on September 3, 1838. As a powerful speaker, writer, and editor, he often attacked ways in which religion was used to support the slave system. His autobiography, first published in 1845, made the charge explicit: "I love the pure, peaceable, and impartial Christianity of Christ: I therefore hate the corrupt, slave holding, women-whipping, cradle-plundering, partial and hypocritical Christianity of this land. . . . The warm defender of the sacredness of the family relation is the same that scatters whole families, — sundering husbands and wives, parents and children, sisters and brothers, — leaving the hut vacant, and the hearth desolate. . . . Revivals of religion and revivals in the slave-trade go hand in hand together."[10]

Emancipation from slavery by no means brought legal equality, economic freedom, or educational opportunity. But it did bring more space for creating and managing churches, and these opportunities did not go to waste. In fact, the end of the Civil War saw a burst of institutional creativity among African American Protestants. Some of that creativity stemmed directly from the ending of slavery, while some built upon antebellum foundations.

Black denominations that existed in the North before the war soon extended their work into the South. In this work the Methodists were

9. See David W. Blight, *Frederick Douglass' Civil War: Keeping Faith in Jubilee* (Baton Rouge: Louisiana State University Press, 1989).

10. *Narrative of the Life of Frederick Douglass, An American Slave: Written by Himself* (published 1845), in *Frederick Douglass: Autobiographies,* ed. Henry Louis Gates, Jr. (New York: Library of America, 1994), pp. 97-98.

in the lead. One of the most memorable religious moments was the dramatic return of Daniel Alexander Payne to Charleston, South Carolina.[11] Payne had been born to free black parents in Charleston, where in 1829 he established a school for fellow African Americans. In 1835 the state legislature forced it to close and, in effect, drove Payne away as well. In the North, Payne attended the Lutheran Theological Seminary in Gettysburg, Pennsylvania. Eventually he became a minister and then a very active bishop in the AME church. In 1863 he was named president of Wilberforce University in Ohio. When the war ended, he returned to Charleston to organize congregations of his denomination and a South Carolina Conference. Payne's example was soon followed by other African American denominations.

Even more important may have been the new churches founded by the liberated slaves themselves. In the five years after 1865, former slaves founded the Colored Methodist Episcopal Church and the Colored Cumberland Presbyterian Church as bodies separated from white oversight. Numerous Baptist associations also sprang up in the former slave states, which led eventually to the creation of state conventions and then, finally, to the National Baptist Convention in 1895. The two groups that emerged from this body after a split in 1907 (the National Baptist Convention U.S.A., Incorporated, and the National Baptist Convention of America, Inc.) are still two of the largest denominations of black Christians in the United States.

Emancipation also allowed for the formation of many independent African American churches. These congregations took root at first primarily in rural areas, but after the start of the twentieth century, independent Baptist or Pentecostal congregations were found increasingly in cities, North and South. These churches often sprang into existence through the dedicated work of a single individual, family, or kin network. Even more than among American whites, where a great number of independent congregations have always existed, self-standing, independent, often small churches have been a mainstay of black religious experience in America.

11. See Daniel Alexander Payne, *Recollections of Seventy Years* (ca. 1895; reprint, New York: Arno, 1969).

It would be a mistake, however, to think that a single black Protestant faith existed, for in fact there were significant differences in how African Americans pursued the practice of Christianity. A comparison between two important leaders who flourished in the generation after slavery illustrates the range of those differences.

Booker T. Washington (1865-1915) is known today as an educational pioneer who was willing to work within the boundaries set by white society.[12] That willingness has been praised as a tactical stroke of genius, but also condemned as an unforgivable accommodation to injustice. Washington, a lifelong Baptist, was trained at Hampton Normal and Agricultural Institute in Virginia, the first school established by the abolitionist American Missionary Association. Throughout his life, and especially as the founder of the Tuskegee Institute in Alabama, Washington exhibited the Christian moral earnestness he had learned at Hampton. In a famous speech in Atlanta in 1895, he urged blacks to win their way in a white society through self-discipline, moral constancy, and diligence in farming and the mechanical trades. This speech has been criticized for conceding too much to the injustices of the time. Yet Washington was not offering self-restraint or Christian faith as a substitute for justice. Indeed, three years after the Atlanta speech, he attacked what he called "sentimental Christianity, which banks everything in the future and nothing in the present." He characterized such faith as "the curse of the race." Yet Washington's vision of progress was accommodating. He asked blacks to bear with injustice, to tolerate wrongs, and to proceed patiently along the path toward freedom. He defined the object of Christian faith as getting "the inner life, the heart right, and we shall then become strong where we have been weak, wise where we have been foolish."

Bishop Henry McNeal Turner (1834-1915) pursued another way. When he became disillusioned with inner religion only, he appealed for a faith working simultaneously towards spiritual and social freedom. During Reconstruction Turner worked in Georgia both to establish the AME church and to create a government for all citizens. When Recon-

12. See Louis R. Harlan, *Booker T. Washington*, 2 vols. (New York: Oxford University Press, 1972, 1983).

struction, the original political effort to include blacks in Southern political life, failed and blacks were ousted from Georgia politics, he returned to the church full-time. Yet McNeal did not lose his political
vision; rather, he became the leading black voice against repressive decisions by the Supreme Court, and he took up the call for African colonization. His bold claim in 1896 that "God is a Negro" was meant to
shock both whites and blacks into pursuing consistency between inner
religious belief and justice in society. As he developed this theme,
Turner did not mince words: "as long as we remain among the whites,
the Negro will believe that the devil is black and that he (the Negro) fa-
vors the devil, and that God is white and that he (the Negro) bears no
resemblance to Him, and the effect of such a sentiment is contemptu-
ous and degrading."[13] Unlike Booker T. Washington, who ended his
years as a widely respected figure, Bishop Turner died in Canada an em-
bittered observer of black life in his native country.

Probably more typical than either explicit accommodation or explicit confrontation among African Americans was personal religious
action. The wide-ranging career of Amanda Berry Smith (1837-1915)
was a remarkable instance of such a path.[14] In 1880 Amanda Berry
Smith toured India, and then worked as a missionary in Liberia.
Shortly after the end of the Civil War, she had been instructed in holiness teachings at Phoebe Palmer's Tuesday meetings in New York City.
Later, through connections with the AME church and as an independent itinerant, she preached holiness at camp meetings in the Atlantic
states, in England, and during her time in India and Liberia. After returning to America she moved close to Chicago, where she set up the
Amanda Smith Industrial Orphan Home. For Amanda Smith and
many other African American Christian leaders, outreach to the disadvantaged was a natural extension of evangelistic preaching.

By the start of the twentieth century, the number of local African
American churches testified to the energy that had gone into religious

13. "God Is a Negro" (1898), in *Respect Black: The Writings and Speeches of Henry
McNeal Turner*, ed. Edwin S. Redkey (New York: Arno, 1971), pp. 176-77.

14. *An Autobiography: The Story of the Lord's Dealing with Mrs. Amanda Smith, the Colored
Evangelist* (Chicago, 1893), reprinted in *Spiritual Narratives*, Schomburg Library of Nineteenth-Century Black Women Writers (New York: Oxford University Press, 1988).

mobilization over the previous half-century. A fairly thorough census of religious bodies by the United States government in 1906 showed that about 17 percent of the nation's approximately 212,000 local churches were African American. (In 1906 African Americans made up not quite 11% of the nation's population of 83 million.) More than a third of the nation's 55,000 Baptist churches were African American, as were about a fourth of the 65,000 Methodist churches. The largest African American Baptist and Methodist denominations were among the nation's largest denominations of any kind.[15] Church formation could not by itself overcome the residual racism of American society, but it revealed a remarkable story of Christianization from the era of Richard Allen to the era of Amanda Smith.

The Rise of American Roman Catholicism

The rise of Roman Catholicism in an America dominated by Protestants was almost as important for the history of Christianity as the emergence of the African American churches. At the time of the nation's founding in 1776, there were only 25,000 Catholics (one percent of the population) served by only 23 priests. The religious census of 1906 found that 130 years later the number of communicant Catholics stood at over 12 million (14% of the population) served by over 15,000 clergy in nearly 12,000 church buildings. The transformation suggested by these numbers was twofold. They reflected multiple migrations of an array of European ethnic Catholic traditions exported from the Old World and then amalgamated further in creating a new national church in the United States. They represented as well the many adjustments required to adapt traditional Catholic positions on authority, ecclesiastical procedures, and the maintenance of church order to the democratic, individualistic, and liberal culture of the United States.[16]

15. *Bureau of the Census Special Reports: Religious Bodies, 1906* (Washington, D.C.: Government Printing Office, 1910), p. 538.

16. For outstanding general accounts, see James Hennesey, S.J., *American Catholics: A History of the Roman Catholic Community in the United States* (New York: Oxford University

The movement of peoples that brought 40 million immigrants to the United States between 1800 and 1920 dramatically affected the churches as well as every other aspect of American society. About one-fourth of these immigrants were Roman Catholics. Protestants migrating to the United States faced a difficult adjustment, since the languages, ethnic customs, and particular church practices of German and Scandinavian Lutherans or pietists and Reformed from throughout Europe created barriers between themselves and America's English-stock majority churches. But Protestant immigrants also escaped most of the hostility that could be directed against Catholics and at least in some places found a relatively cordial welcome.

For Catholics, a full range of problems accompanied the opportunities of the New World. In the forefront of these difficulties was widespread suspicion among Protestants of the Catholic church. For a few years during the American Revolution, a political alliance with France eased some of the anti-Catholic feeling that had built up over the long history of eighteenth-century English-French warfare. But by the start of the next century, the surge of Protestant revivalism provoked a resurgence of anti-Catholicism.[17] One of the driving forces behind the spread of Protestant influence by means of revival and voluntary agencies was Congregationalist minister Lyman Beecher (1775-1863), who worked tirelessly in New England and then Ohio to invigorate the Protestant churches. Throughout his career Beecher was also a firm enemy of Roman Catholicism. That opposition took shape in 1835 in a much-reprinted tract called *A Plea for the West* that spotlighted the Roman Catholic Church as the greatest danger to the expansion of both American freedom and true Christianity.

Protestant-fueled opposition to Catholicism was most explosive, however, not in the sparsely settled West but in the Eastern cities that by the 1830s were becoming home to increasing numbers of Catholics. In such places, Protestant resentment sometimes spilled over into vio-

---

Press, 1981); and Jay P. Dolan, *The American Catholic Experience* (Garden City, NY: Doubleday, 1985).

17. See Ray Allen Billington, *The Protestant Crusade, 1800-1860* (New York: Macmillan, 1938).

lence. In 1834 a Boston mob burned the Ursuline Convent in nearby Charlestown.[18] The mob was enraged by (unfounded) stories that young girls were being held there against their will. Ten years later, disputes over labor questions in Philadelphia led to Protestant-Catholic clashes in the suburbs of Kensington and Southwark. In 1840 the Irish-born Catholic Bishop of New York, John Hughes, asked the city's Public School Society to provide money for Catholic schools to balance its support for Protestant-run establishments. The quarrel that resulted flared close to violence and earned Hughes the nickname "Dagger John" for the vigorous steps he took to defend Roman Catholic churches with weapons in New York City.[19]

The antebellum climax of anti-Catholicism was the formation of a political movement, the American Party. Its members were called "Know Nothings" because they refused to divulge information about their organization. Know Nothings felt that immigrants, especially Roman Catholics, were damaging America's Anglo-Saxon stock and subverting American liberties by maintaining loyalties to a despotic foreign power — that is, the pope. In 1854 the American Party elected seventy-five members to the United States House of Representatives, but its influence quickly declined in the rapid political changes that led to the Civil War. The next year (1855), construction on the Washington Monument in the nation's capital was halted when outraged Know Nothings discovered that Pope Pius IX had donated a marble stone for use in the monument. Later flare-ups of extreme, even violent, opposition would continue to appear for many decades. Such anti-Catholicism did not characterize all Protestants in all places. But it did indicate that many Protestants thought that they, and no one else, owned America.

The internal religious difficulty for an immigrant church was the strain created by the very traumas of immigration. In 1855 a German priest in Wisconsin wrote back to his sponsors in Vienna: "All the resolutions made in Europe dissolve as soon as one feels the breezes of the

18. See Wilfred J. Bisson, *Countdown to Violence: The Charlestown Convent Riot of 1834* (New York: Garland, 1989).

19. See Richard Shaw, *"Dagger John": The Unquiet Life and Times of Archbishop John Hughes of New York* (New York: Paulist, 1977).

American coastline, [and] every tie, including the one with God, must be retied here and must undergo the American 'Probatum est' before it can be said that it is secure."[20] Securing the American seal of approval was rarely an easy matter.

As the tide of immigration grew — averaging 140,000 annually in the 1840s, 525,000 per year in the 1880s, and over 800,000 annually in the first decade of the twentieth century — the strain on the Catholic church grew as well. Much of the strain came in the multiplication of national sources of immigration. In the first half of the nineteenth century, burgeoning numbers of Irish and German Catholics joined concentrations of French Catholics in Louisiana and Hispanic Catholics in the Southwest. In the second half of the century, large numbers were added from Poland, Lithuania, Hungary, Croatia, Czechoslovakia, and Italy. Great sacrifices by local communities built churches; dedicated priests, lay brothers, and nuns staffed the churches, even as they oversaw the development of schools, insurance societies, youth organizations, newspapers, and the other accouterments of civilization. Growing numbers of bishops and archbishops also negotiated differences between European expectations and American realities, Vatican guidelines and American practice, and especially among different groups of ethnic Catholics.[21]

These intra-Catholic contentions, which often posed the sharpest challenges to the church's hierarchy, were mostly a product of timing. The surges of Irish and German immigrants from the 1840s at first had to make do with the bishops from English and French stock. When enough time had passed for the maturation of a hierarchy filled with Germans and the Irish, many of the immigrant parishes were concerned about the absence of Polish, Lithuanian, or Italian bishops. Later that same problem would affect black and Hispanic regions, for the church secured bishops from these ethnic groups only a generation

20. Quoted in Philip Gleason, *Keeping the Faith: American Catholicism Past and Present* (Notre Dame: University of Notre Dame Press, 1987), p. 44.

21. For historical accounts from the beginning and end of the twentieth century, see Gerald Shaughnessy, *Has the Immigrant Kept the Faith?* (New York: Macmillan, 1925); and John McGreevy, *Parish Boundaries: The Catholic Encounter with Race in the Twentieth-Century Urban North* (Chicago: University of Chicago, 1996).

or so after substantial constituencies existed. This general situation led to many complaints about lack of sensitivity to immigrant conditions, but the system also had welcome compensations. Even if recruitment did not move speedily, the hierarchy sooner or later was opened to representatives of ethnic communities. Ethnic parishes were constructed, with or without the active support of the hierarchy, where religious and social nurture eased the traumas of migration. The organization of parishes, and of ecclesiastical thinking, around ethnic differences proved to be an unusually helpful way of maintaining the centrality of the church for uprooted populations. Moreover, as the decades passed and urban ethnic communities spilled out into the suburbs, the American church was able to draw on the varied strengths of ethnic communities in some of its unified programs, showing that the ethnic organization of the church could function as a way station on the path toward eventual cooperation, as well as a memory of the immigrants' ancestral, European faith.

The story of the Catholic church in America is a story of rapid numerical growth fueled by immigration, but it is also a story of cultural indigenization. As bishops and other church leaders struggled to preserve the faith by ministering to the special needs of immigrants, some also took in hand the business of accommodating with America. Part of the work of John Carroll, as the first Catholic bishop, was to reassure his fellow citizens that the Catholic church could make a positive contribution to American societies. The second generation of American bishops included leaders like Irish-born John England (1786-1842), the first Catholic bishop of Charleston, South Carolina, who carried Carroll's arguments further.[22] England found it an easy matter to transfer the support for civil and religious liberty that he had developed in Ireland to his duties in the New World. When, for example, England wrote a constitution for his diocese in the 1830s, he phrased it in such a way as to control the republican instincts alive in his churches, but he also emphasized compatibilities between historic Catholicism and American democracy. As an example of the latter, England addressed directly American Protestant charges that no church owing allegiance to the pope could

22. See Chapter Four, note 19.

ever be truly loyal to the United States: "We do not believe that by virtue of this spiritual or ecclesiastical authority, the Pope hath any power or right to interfere with the allegiance that we owe to our state; nor to interfere in or with the concerns of the civil policy or the temporal government thereof, or of the United States of America."[23]

Catholic attention to the particular needs of the United States also contributed to the development of a New World church. Elizabeth Ann Seton (1776-1821) was one of the exemplary early leaders in such efforts.[24] Elizabeth Seton was born an Episcopalian, but converted to Catholicism shortly before her thirtieth birthday. Partly in response to intense opposition to her conversion from her own New York family, she moved to Baltimore, where, with the help of French Sulpician fathers, she opened a school for girls. From this initial venture eventually emerged a new order, the Sisters of Charity, who gave themselves to education as well as the care of orphans. "Mother" Seton, who in 1975 became the first person born in the United States to be made a saint by the Catholic church, was an early leader of what became a mass movement of nuns and brothers. By 1900 over 40,000 Catholic sisters were active in a wide variety of service to church and society, especially as teachers in Catholic parochial schools.

Formal organization of the church also advanced during the nineteenth century. In 1829 the first provincial council of the American church was held in Baltimore. This body of bishops met triennially until 1852. The first plenary council drew together six archbishops and twenty-eight bishops to confer over the business of the American church. By the third plenary council in 1884, the number of archbishops and bishops had grown to seventy-two, and at this meeting the construction and maintenance of parochial schools was the prime matter for discussion. Within little more than half a century, the American church not only had grown into a sophisticated institution, but also had gained the confidence and the wealth to construct its own educational system.

23. Patrick W. Carey, ed., *American Catholic Religious Thought* (New York: Paulist, 1987), p. 81.

24. Ellin Kelly and Annabelle Melville, eds., *Elizabeth Seton: Selected Writings* (New York: Paulist, 1987).

Other adjustments to the New World required mediation between ancient church practice and habits of American democracy. Throughout the national period, a continuing set of controversies beset the church over the question of property ownership. Trustees of local congregations often desired to follow the practice of American Protestant churches and vest ownership of churches and other ecclesiastical property in themselves. John Carroll and his fellow bishops stood firm for the hereditary European custom of ownership vested in the hierarchy. In an American environment enthusiastic for the "rights of the common man," it took more than fifty years, and some intense local struggles, to bring American Catholics in line with historic Catholic practice.[25]

Later in the century, a dispute erupted with even greater potential for alienating the American church from worldwide Catholicism. It has been called the "Americanist" crisis since it featured efforts by the Vatican to ensure that the democratic and republican habits of the United States did not lead American Catholics astray.[26] The origin of this dispute was the growing belief among conservative-to-moderate European Catholics that leaders of the American church were going too far in approving the liberal principles that defined American freedoms. The flashpoint was the publication in 1897 of a French translation of a biography of Isaac Hecker (1819-1888). Hecker in his early life had been an advocate of advanced liberal values who, then, however, converted to Catholicism. He became the founder of the Paulist Order and a dynamo of activity on behalf of the church. His biographer, Walter Elliott, praised Hecker's efforts at reaching out as far as possible to his fellow Americans. A complication in the dispute was a serious debate within the American hierarchy between those who favored as much accommodation to American ways as possible (later called the "Americanists") and conservatives who wanted to do more to protect American Catholics from the corrosion of democracy. In the middle of this American dispute was a third group of largely German bishops, who were conser-

---

25. Patrick W. Carey, *People, Priests, and Prelates: Ecclesiastical Democracy and the Tensions of Trusteeism* (Notre Dame, IN: University of Notre Dame Press, 1987).

26. See R. Scott Appleby, *"Church and Age Unite": The Modernist Impulse in American Catholicism* (Notre Dame, IN: University of Notre Dame Press, 1992).

vative in part for reasons of doctrine but more out of a desire to preserve the German language and German ecclesiastical customs in their churches.[27]

The upshot of the dispute was a pair of papal documents directed to the American church. In 1895 Pope Leo XIII issued an encyclical, *Longinqua Oceani,* which praised the Americans for their great efforts, but warned them about setting up American standards of the separation of church and state as the universal norm for the church. This letter was followed in 1899 by an encyclical, *Testem Benevolentiae,* which condemned "Americanism" by name as the mistaken desire for the church to conform to the shape of American culture, especially by introducing greater personal liberty in ecclesiastical affairs. In the United States, conservative leaders such as the Archbishop of New York, Michael Corrigan, were gratified. On the other side, James Cardinal Gibbons, Archbishop of Baltimore, and John Ireland, the bishop of St. Paul, Minnesota, were unruffled; they agreed that it was wrong to change the church's faith and avowed that no teaching that the pope condemned was permitted in the American church.

The results of this controversy were not clear-cut. American Catholics were duly cautioned about moving too fast in the paths of democracy and religious liberty, but no one suffered disciplinary action. The Catholic University of America, which had opened its doors in Washington, D.C., only in 1889, was directed in a somewhat more conservative path, but it remained a center of learning and considerable influence. The historical value of the incident was to show the delicacy that was needed to steer the Catholic church between its ancient Old World traditions and its opportunities for expansion in the New World.

In Chapter Eleven, we return to consider the course of Catholic higher education in the twentieth century, in another effort to chart the fate of European standards in a New World environment. Here it is possible to conclude that the nineteenth-century success of the Catholic church in the United States might be regarded as a surprise. The church largely overcame difficulties of sustaining many immigrant

---

27. See Philip Gleason, *The Conservative Reformers: German-American Catholics and the Social Order* (Notre Dame, IN: University of Notre Dame Press, 1968).

communities. Antagonism from America's Protestant majority never became crippling. American political liberalism strained Catholic traditionalism but did not overcome it. By the early twentieth century, a church that many Americans had once despised and feared had become the largest denomination in the country and had begun to win at least a measure of respect. So strikingly successful were Catholic efforts in the New World that some modern students see the American climate as better for the church than the traditions of Europe. This is the judgment of, among others, Michael Zöller, a German sociologist and historian in his 1999 book on the American Catholic church: The church "has prospered more in the climate of a religiously neutral republic that is friendly to religion than in so-called Catholic countries where it has been both privileged and persecuted."[28]

Protestant Responses to a New America

The growth of Roman Catholicism was part of a new America that emerged after the Civil War. The change that perhaps reveals the most about the Protestant situation can be seen in a simple statistic: in 1870, 9.9 million Americans lived in towns and cities with populations of 2,500 or more; by 1930 that number had risen to 69 million. The cities were places of employment for immigrants from Europe as well as vast numbers leaving farms and rural villages. The cities held concentrations of Catholics, but also of Jews, and even those without religion. They were places to make one's fortune. They were also places where social services often broke down, where incredible deprivation lurked just beyond the boundaries of prosperity, and where rootlessness and alienation were ways of life. The shift in population to the cities did not mean that revivalistic, evangelical, voluntaristic Protestantism passed away, but it did mean that considerable adjustment was required for the new environment. Growing commercial pressure, greater access to higher education, and more opportunities for contact with representa-

28. Michael Zöller, *Washington and Rome: Catholicism in the United States* (Notre Dame, IN: University of Notre Dame Press, 1999), p. 243.

tives of different religions and ethnic groups all worked to undermine the Protestant character of the national religion. Space in the cities for other kinds of Christianity and for simple inattention to the faith stimulated an evermore obvious religious pluralism.

That same pluralism was more evident also in the intellectual life of the country, especially as manifest in its colleges and universities. The changes brought about by the intellectual challenges of the late nineteenth century are treated in Chapter Nine below, but at this point it is useful to note that the cities were also the places where this intellectual change was most obvious.

One response of Protestants was to take into the new urban areas the kind of revivalism that had achieved such wonders in previous generations. No one performed that task more effectively in the last third of the nineteenth century than Dwight Lyman Moody (1837-1899).[29] After moving from his native New England to Chicago shortly before the Civil War, Moody took an active part in the work of the Young Men's Christian Association, one of the many voluntary associations founded as a result of the antebellum revivals. Moody assisted eagerly with efforts to found Sunday Schools, distribute Christian literature, and bring a general Christian influence to the growing metropolis on Lake Michigan. In 1873 he enlisted the musician and songleader Ira Sankey (1840-1908) to accompany him on a modestly conceived preaching tour of Great Britain. When the meetings proved unexpectedly successful, Moody and Sankey become instant celebrities on both sides of the Atlantic.

Moody and Sankey returned to the States in 1875, where they found themselves in demand everywhere. For the next quarter century, Moody, often joined by Sankey, was the nation's most respected religious figure. As a layman, he preached a message that fit the character of his age. He was not intense like Charles Finney, his famous predecessor, nor did he engage in the theatrical antics of Billy Sunday, his best-known successor. Rather, Moody tried to talk in a plainspoken style to

29. See James F. Findlay, *Dwight L. Moody: American Evangelist, 1837-1899* (Chicago: University of Chicago Press, 1969); and Lyle W. Dorsett, *A Passion for Souls: The Life of D. L. Moody* (Chicago: Moody Press, 1997).

audiences about God and the need for a Savior. He dressed like a conventional businessman and spoke with reassuring calm. Moody summarized his basic Christian message as the "three R's": Ruin by Sin, Redemption by Christ, and Regeneration by the Holy Ghost. He did not expound learned theology, nor did he promote sophisticated formulas for Christian action in society. Instead, he emphasized powerful themes of Christian sentiment. These were the themes that Ira Sankey evoked with hymns like "The Ninety and Nine" — which drew on the biblical parable of the shepherd who left all of his sheep (the ninety and nine) in the fold while he went looking for the one who was lost. Moody was not callous to the needs of society, but increasingly his focus was on the soul. In his most famous statement about his own work, Moody said, "I look upon this world as a wrecked vessel. God has given me a lifeboat and said to me, 'Moody, save all you can.'"[30]

Moody's personal influence was extended through the important institutions he founded. These included a Bible training center for lay workers in Chicago (later the Moody Bible Institute) and a summer missions conferences held near his home in Northfield, Massachusetts. From these meetings came the founding, in 1876, of the Student Volunteer Movement, a great effort that encouraged thousands of students to seek "the evangelization of the world in this generation." Moody's solution to the problems of America's growing cities was primarily preaching. Indeed, a full range of Protestants addressed themselves to the solution of social problems as a specifically religious duty.

The most widespread Protestant attempts to reform American society were based on principles of private action and personal responsibility, but many older churches, as well as newer bodies, also developed special programs attempting to meet the special needs of the day. One of the most successful of the newer bodies was the Salvation Army.[31] The Army had been founded in London in the 1860s by William and

---

30. For theological discussion, see Stanley N. Gundry, *Love Them In: The Proclamation Theology of D. L. Moody* (Chicago: Moody Press, 1976).

31. See Edward H. McKinley, *Marching to Glory: The History of the Salvation Army in the United States, 1880-1992,* 2nd ed. (Grand Rapids: Eerdmans, 1995); and Diane Winston, *Red-Hot and Righteous: The Urban Religion of the Salvation Army* (Cambridge: Harvard University Press, 1999).

Catherine Booth in order to provide Christian witness and social service to the urban poor neglected by other churches. Its brass bands, its willingness to use popular entertainment to attract a crowd, and its combination of spiritual and social activities made a deep impression in Britain. William's daughter Evangeline (1865-1950) eventually came to head up the work of the Army in the United States, where she promoted the same range of activities that her parents had advanced in England — provision of food, shelter, and medical assistance; vocational training, elementary schooling, and internships in manufacturing and farming; and visits to prisons, legal aid for the indigent, and inexpensive coal in the winter. By 1904 the Army had over nine hundred stations, or corps, in the United States. It was (and remains) the most comprehensive Protestant urban outreach ever attempted.

Better known at the time, however, was a broader, more informal movement to address urban challenges called the Social Gospel. It existed as a loosely organized force from about 1880 to the start of the Great Depression in 1929. Its leaders attempted a Christian response to the rapid social changes of the period by emphasizing the need to make large-scale structural changes in society.

The strong link in the American revival tradition between personal holiness and social reform contributed greatly to the Social Gospel.[32] So also did a newer concern for the scientific study of social problems. An important early leader of the Social Gospel was Washington Gladden (1836-1918), a Congregationalist minister in Springfield, Massachusetts, and Columbus, Ohio.[33] While in Massachusetts he published *Working People and Their Employers* (1876), an appeal for fairness toward labor. Gladden's Ohio congregation included mine owners whose workers struck twice in the mid-1880s for better wages and working conditions. His belief in the justice of their demands led Gladden to appeal more insistently for the rights of labor and the application of the Golden Rule to industrial organization.

---

32. See Robert T. Handy, ed., *The Social Gospel* (New York: Oxford University Press, 1966); and Charles H. Hopkins and Ronald C. White, *The Social Gospel* (Philadelphia: Temple University Press, 1976).

33. See Jacob H. Dorn, *Washington Gladden: Prophet of the Social Gospel* (Columbus: Ohio State University Press, 1967).

The most important exponent of the Social Gospel was Walter Rauschenbusch (1861-1918), a German-American Baptist.[34] He worked for ten years in New York City's "Hell's Kitchen" before becoming a professor of church history at Rochester Seminary in upstate New York. Rauschenbusch's firsthand experiences with industrial exploitation and governmental indifference to workers made him a convinced critic of the established order. His friendship with New York City socialists like Henry George encouraged him to propose new models for the organization of society. But Rauschenbusch's main concern was to search the Scriptures for a message regarding the troubles of industrial society. The results were published in 1907 as *Christianity and the Social Crisis,* a work that drew on the Old Testament prophets as well as on New Testament warnings about the dangers of money.

The Social Gospel is often associated with more liberal trends in theology. Gladden, for example, popularized more liberal views of the Bible. Rauschenbusch was thoroughly realistic about the sinful character of human nature, but he also reinterpreted some traditionally supernatural elements of Christian doctrine. With the Salvation Army and many local efforts scattered from coast to coast, leaders of the Social Gospel were trying to solve an American dilemma — how to adapt the Protestant tradition of an earlier rural America to the changing demands of a newly industrial society.

Social concern of a different sort drove large-scale efforts to control the production and use of alcoholic beverages. The various temperance and prohibition movements may now appear somewhat quixotic, but they were the direct successors of antebellum movements like the fight against slavery. Just as Protestants had labored to win freedom for the slaves, so after the Civil War many of them exerted great efforts to free the nation from slavery to alcohol. In that effort they were joined by some of the leading "Americanist" Catholics, especially Archbishop John Ireland of St. Paul.

One of the most successful reform agencies in all of American his-

---

34. See Paul M. Minus, *Walter Rauschenbusch: American Reformer* (New York: Macmillan, 1988); and Winthrop Hudson, ed., *Walter Rauschenbusch: Selected Writings* (New York: Paulist, 1984).

tory was the Women's Christian Temperance Union (WCTU), a voluntary agency that flourished under the able leadership of Frances Willard (1839-1898).[35] In the course of her very active public career, Willard, a Methodist, promoted innovative strategies for preserving the domestic values of Victorian America. She urged prohibitionists to broaden their concern to take on the general protection of the family. She was a colleague of Dwight L. Moody, for whom she helped to organize women's ministries in conjunction with his urban revivals. She also broadened her activities to Europe, where she helped to establish a formidable British counterpart to the WCTU. As she grew older, Willard also grew more interested in the efforts of Christian socialists to repair the defects of industrial society. She was a persistent advocate of women's right to preach, although her denomination, the Methodist Episcopal Church, did not ordain women. More than any leader of her age, she succeeded in mobilizing women for the causes of domestic purification and personal order that the temperance crusade represented.

The events of World War I heightened fears of social disorder in America and paved the way for a prohibition amendment to the Constitution.[36] Growing fears about the effects of drink on the unsavory elements in American society together with a belief that the evils of drink had inspired the crimes of the Kaiser's Germany motivated the passage of the Eighteenth Amendment to the Constitution in 1919. The war had shown how fragile civilization was and seemed to spotlight the need for more strenuous measures toward social discipline. Americans shared this view with many Europeans, who also successfully promoted various temperance measures in their own countries.

Prohibition did bring improvements in the nation's health and welfare, but it did not create anything like the utopia its promoters had foreseen. If the results of national Prohibition did not meet its lofty goals, however, the movement still illustrated the lingering power of the nation's public Protestants — generally evangelical, almost all

---

35. See Ruth Bordin, *Frances Willard* (Chapel Hill: University of North Carolina Press, 1986).

36. See Norman H. Clark, *Deliver Us from Evil: An Interpretation of American Prohibition* (New York: Norton, 1976).

white, largely of British background — to translate their moral vision into the law of the land.

The prohibition movement, however, could be considered the last gasp of Protestant hegemony. The rapid strengthening of African American churches, Roman Catholicism, Judaism, and still other religious forces new to the United States also made it more and more anachronistic to speak of an America dominated by the descendants of the Puritans. Unanticipated effects of the Civil War, failure with respect to the newly emancipated slave population, large-scale industrial development, and a series of changes in the universities — all these undermined Protestant cultural dominance.

The end of that dominance, however, certainly did not mean universal decline in the fate of Christianity in the United States. As the next chapters show, a splintered Protestantism allowed room for many forms of renewal. Moreover, beyond the boundaries of the white, English-stock Protestant churches that were declining relative to their earlier power were fresh signs of life from other Christian movements. The twentieth century lacks the coherence of America's earlier Christian history, and there are certainly dimensions of the story that constitute decline. But alongside decline were many signs of vitality and hope. Sorting out the complexities of that story is the task of the next two chapters.

CHAPTER SEVEN

Divisions, Renewal, Fragmentation, Acculturation, 1906-1960

The years 1906 and 1960 have special meaning for a history of Christianity in the United States. The former witnessed the beginnings of the Pentecostal movement, which over the course of the twentieth century became a dramatic religious force throughout the whole world. The latter witnessed the election of a Roman Catholic, John F. Kennedy, as president of the United States, an election that testified to the acceptance of Catholics as full partners in the nation's political and social life. In between these two events, the Christian story involved a further fragmentation of Protestantism, but also a considerable renewal in some Protestant subgroups. American participation in two world wars, a depression, and the economic boom after the Second World War substantially affected the course of the churches as well. Before trying to chart the effects of those events, this chapter considers at some length the main divisions that existed within twentieth-century American Christianity, several of which emerged only in the first years of this era.

Orthodoxy

The swelling tides of immigration from Southern and Eastern Europe were responsible for bringing members of the oldest Christian communions to the New World. Russian and Ukrainian immigration became significant in the mid-1880s, and Greek immigration in the earliest years of the new century. Their numbers included many Eastern Orthodox Christians.[1] Russian Orthodox monks had been active from as early as the 1790s in what is now Alaska; during the nineteenth century, this early work had broadened somewhat to small Orthodox communities on the western coast of the United States.[2] In 1905 Tikhon Bellavin (1865-1925), the Russian Orthodox bishop in North America, transferred his see from San Francisco to New York in order to minister more effectively to newer centers of Orthodox settlement. In 1907 Tikhon convened the first All-American Council of the Orthodox churches and, by so doing, took the first small step toward cooperation among the many ethnic Orthodox churches that eventually came to America. That process moved very slowly in subsequent decades. In 1960 a Standing Conference of Canonical Bishops was founded to improve dialogue among the Orthodox churches, which by that time included Byelorussian, Albanian, Romanian, Serbian, Egyptian, Bulgarian, and Syrian groups as well as Russians, Ukrainians, and Greeks. But for most of the twentieth century, the Orthodox existed in the United States and Canada as distinct ethnic immigrant communities. Especially the Russian churches have suffered from schisms in the mother country occasioned by communist rule, but almost all of the Orthodox churches in America have been disrupted by a combination of Old World quarrels transported to America and fresh disputes begun on this side of the Atlantic involving questions of jurisdiction, language, and national identity.

Only late in the century did some of the Orthodox churches begin to work directly at adapting their ancient creeds, liturgies, and iconic practices to the American environment. The largest of the Russian immigrant churches is now known as the Orthodox Church in America. With leading American-born theologians such as Thomas Hopko

---

1. For a general account of the American story, see Thomas E. FitzGerald, *The Orthodox Church,* Denominations in America Series (Westport, CT: Greenwood, 1995).

2. See Michael Olekas, ed., *Alaskan Missionary Spirituality* (New York: Paulist Press, 1987).

(b. 1939) joining such prominent émigré theologians as Georges Florovosky (1883-1979), Alexander Schmemann (1921-1983), and John Meyendorff (1926-1992), this branch of Orthodoxy is establishing a distinct American presence.[3] Toward the end of the twentieth century, Orthodoxy became increasingly attractive to some American Christians who concluded that America's Catholic and Protestant churches were too much the captive of rationalism, liberalism, and individualism. Examples of this newfound appeal included a number of staff members of Campus Crusade for Christ, an evangelical youth movement, who in the 1980s joined the Antiochean Orthodox Church, as well as the distinguished historian of theology, Jaroslav Pelikan, who in 1998 departed from his life-long Lutheranism to join the Orthodox church.

Orthodoxy is still an exotic exception in the United States. But the constituency of the Orthodox churches is large nevertheless, with 3 to 4 million at least nominally attached, and the appeal of Orthodoxy to disillusioned adherents of Western churches remains surprisingly strong. If the American environment helps the ethnic Orthodox churches to cooperate among themselves and to draw from deep historical resources a carefully defined alternative to traditional American church practice, the twenty-first century could witness a blossoming of this ancient form of Christianity in an unexpected new setting.

Roman Catholicism

During the twentieth century, American Roman Catholicism became what the Orthodoxy of the next century might become — a Christian tradition grounded in the Old World that has matured into a church at home in America. The relative decline in European immigration occasioned by the First World War and then by restrictive legislation during the 1920s accelerated a process of acculturation that for many Catholics was already well underway before the turn of the century. Over the

3. For indications, see Bradley Nassif, ed., *New Perspectives on Historical Theology: Essays in Memory of John Meyendorff* (Grand Rapids: Eerdmans, 1996).

course of the twentieth century Roman Catholicism in the United States came to appear less and less as a mélange of immigrant churches and more and more a cohesive American church. To be sure, the marks of European ethnic origin have by no means vanished, and the surge of Hispanic immigration after World War II (from the Philippines, Costa Rica, and Central America, as well as Mexico) has preserved the immigrant character of large parts of the church. Yet as a whole it has become increasingly at home with its American character.

In an interesting turn of events, several of the movements that in the decades before the Second Vatican Council (1962-1965) testified to Catholic maturity in the New World involved significant critiques of American secularism, individualism, and unchecked capitalism. These movements were possible only in a church that had overcome the traumas of migration and was now able to support active engagement with American social and intellectual culture. Among the most important of those movements were the emergence of a Neo-Thomist intellectual program, a significant liturgical revival, and vital social action known as the Catholic Worker Movement.

The modern revival of Thomism was signaled by Pope Leo XIII's encyclical, *Aeterni patris,* in 1879.[4] Americans were late in appropriating the energies of Neo-Thomism, but by the 1920s it was flourishing as an active philosophical and theological enterprise in many parts of the American church. This revival of Thomism took several forms: a fairly mechanical commentary on the works of Thomas Aquinas; a more creative appropriation of Thomas for modern circumstances inspired by the work of Jacques Maritain and Etienne Gilson, French thinkers who both taught at the University of Toronto in the pre-war years; and, after World War II, a transcendental form that linked aspects of twentieth-century idealist philosophy to Thomism as promoted by the German Jesuit Karl Rahner and the Canadian Jesuit Bernard Lonergan. What each of the forms shared was a confidence in human reason as a gift of

---

4. For introduction and representative samples, see Patrick W. Carey, ed., *American Catholic Religious Thought* (New York: Paulist, 1987), pp. 46-61, 253-302; and for the kind of works popular in America, see A. C. Pegis, ed., *A Gilson Reader* (Garden City, NY: Image, 1957).

God, the centrality of God for human understanding of truth, the appropriateness of faith as a foundation for reason, and the importance of organized church practice for modern intellectual life.

The appropriation of Neo-Thomism gave American Catholics a great deal of confidence as they emerged from the straitened circumstances of immigrant life. It inspired the establishment of several notable journals in philosophy and theology; it provided a self-confident standpoint for evaluating the events and circumstances of the rapidly changing twentieth century; it offered a rationale for the rapidly expanding bureaucracies of the church; it supported liturgical renewal and at least some aspects of the Catholic Worker Movement; and it gave such leading Jesuit intellectuals as John Courtney Murray and Gustave Weigel a platform for effective theological creativity. In Murray's case, it meant a singularly Catholic defense of civil liberty and the modern separation of church and state that would eventually exert a considerable influence at the Second Vatican Council. In Weigel's case, it meant pioneering efforts at ecumenical dialogue with other Christians in the decades before the Second Vatican Council made such dialogue *de rigueur.*

The liturgical renewal also drew on European sources, but again put them to use self-consciously in an American setting. The central ideal of this movement was of the church as the mystical body of Christ. As promoted by such leaders as Virgil Michel, O.S.B., of St. John's Abbey in Minnesota, concentration on the mystical body aimed at restoring vitality to personal and parish spiritual life, reviving the participation of the laity, and undergirding a sense of organic solidarity in the church.[5]

When taken beyond the bounds of the church, that sense of organic solidarity was also a spark for the Catholic Worker Movement that developed in the 1930s under the lay leadership of Peter Maurin (1877-1949) and Dorothy Day (1897-1980).[6] Day, the inspiring force

---

5. For example, Virgil George Michel, *The Liturgy of the Church: According to the Roman Rite* (New York: Macmillan, 1939).

6. See Mel Piehl, *Breaking Bread: The Catholic Worker and the Origin of Catholic Radicalism in America* (Philadelphia: Temple University Press, 1982); and William D. Miller, *Dorothy Day* (San Francisco: Harper & Row, 1982).

behind the movement, was one of the most important figures in recent American religious history. After a tempestuous adolescence, an abortion, and a common-law marriage, Day was converted to Catholicism and embarked on a life of social engagement. Maurin, an immigrant to the United States from France by way of Canada, brought to the movement insights from continental Christian personalism, which stressed the responsibility of individual believers to express personal holiness through personal sacrifice on behalf of others. Through their newspaper, the *Catholic Worker,* and through a network of "Houses of Hospitality," Day, Maurin, and their associates fed the hungry, housed the homeless, defended orphans, and intervened for those without work. Because of her outspoken criticism of warfare, capitalism, racism, and American involvement in Vietnam, Day and the Catholic Worker Movement were often regarded with suspicion by many in the Catholic hierarchy. But due in large part to her ability to link these social positions with her commitment to traditional Catholic dogma and liturgy, the respect with which she was regarded grew steadily. At the time of her death, she was hailed by her admirers as the most important American Catholic of the century.

Neo-Thomism, liturgical renewal, and the Catholic Worker movement all exerted their greatest influence in the generation before the opening of the Vatican Council in 1962. Later observers have highlighted many defects of these movements, from a lack of engagement with the twentieth century's liveliest intellectuals to a romantic idealization of the poor. It is also true that each of these movements was occasionally hamstrung by church bureaucrats more interested in strengthening personal fiefdoms than in promoting creative Christian activity; and their existence failed to touch many of the Catholic faithful. Nonetheless, they provided evidence not only of the religious vitality of twentieth-century American Catholicism but also for the ability of the American church to move beyond strategies of preservation that had dominated its life for the century before World War I.

Protestant Division and Renewal

The picture of a unified, dominant American Protestantism has never actually applied in the realities of American history. Before the start of the twentieth century, however, there was at least a measure of truth to the image; after the turn of the century, it became increasingly clear that Protestantism was more a very rough general category for non-Catholic Christians than a cohesive religious force. At the start of the century, two opposing factions — modernists and fundamentalists — began to diverge as they provided dramatically different responses to the era's intellectual and social pressures. The noise of their conflict made it difficult at the time to observe that a substantial body of what might be called "moderate inclusivists" remained unaligned with either extreme, carrying on instead some of the proprietary tasks of the nineteenth-century Protestant mainstream. Beyond the well-publicized fundamentalist-modernist conflict and the activities of the moderate mainline Protestants, two other important movements of Protestant piety proved important. One was the holiness movement guided by nineteenth-century spiritual mentors such as Phoebe Palmer. The other was Pentecostalism, which grew in part from the holiness movement, but with a difference that meant a very great deal in later decades. Finally, it is important to note that the modern self-described "evangelical" movement was emerging from fundamentalism by the late 1930s and early 1940s, and that African-American Protestant churches were undergoing both crises of organization and expansion of vision during roughly the first half of the twentieth century. Alongside the emergence of Orthodoxy and vigorous developments within Roman Catholicism, these Protestant groupings — modernists, fundamentalists, the moderate mainline, the holiness movement, Pentecostals, evangelicals, and black Protestants — defined the American Christian landscape for most of the twentieth century.

Modernists were Protestants who felt it was important to adjust Christianity to the new norms that had come to define progressive culture by the late nineteenth century.[7] They believed that God was best

---

7. See William R. Hutchison, *The Modernist Impulse in American Protestantism* (Cambridge: Harvard University Press, 1976).

understood as immanent, a force working within human society and within human nature. Modernism won its most important victories in centers of higher learning. Arthur Cushman McGiffert (1861-1933), who taught at Union Seminary in New York, spoke for many of the early modernists. He had studied theology in Germany and used the new approaches he learned there to stress three things: the model of the life of Christ, the need for a scientific approach to history, and the priority of social ethics. The Apostle Paul was a villain for McGiffert, since he held that Paul promoted teachings that undercut the peace-loving consciousness of God marking the life of Jesus. Christianity through the ages, McGiffert held, was distorted by overemphasizing the divinity of Christ and by stressing the institutions of the formal churches.

The University of Chicago was home to the most influential promoters of a modernist Christianity. Shailer Mathews (1863-1941) was a key leader at Chicago as well as the author of a widely used book, *The Faith of Modernism* (1924).[8] It proposed ways to reinterpret traditional Christian teaching that Mathews felt honored those traditions while bringing them up to date. Mathews looked to Christianity to provide a moral basis for pacifying the strife in modern society. He did not think that holding rigidly to Christian formulas of the past was at all helpful. In opposition to the conservative theological movements of his time, Mathews once wrote scornfully, "The world . . . needs faith in the divine presence in human affairs and is told it must accept the virgin birth of Jesus Christ."

Modernism has had a long-lasting influence on the academic study of religion; the desire of leading modernists to recast Christian teaching into generic religious language played a large role in the early promotion of religion as a formal subject of university study.[9] Modernism had a less direct impact on the Protestant churches at large, even though the general sense that Christian teaching needed to be re-stated for modern audiences has been widely accepted among many twenti-

8. See Shailer Mathews, *New Faith for Old: An Autobiography* (New York: Macmillan, 1936).

9. D. G. Hart, *The University Gets Religion: Religious Studies in American Higher Education* (Baltimore: Johns Hopkins University Press, 1999).

eth-century Protestants. Ironically, the greatest impact of modernists may have been to energize their polar opposites, the fundamentalists, in defense of traditional Christianity.

Fundamentalists represented a counterpart to modernists.[10] A few of them were also academics who tried to defend a traditional view of the faith through intellectual means. For example, Presbyterian scholar J. Gresham Machen (1881-1937) published a major polemic in 1923 entitled *Christianity and Liberalism*. His case was that the theological changes proposed by such modernists as McGiffert and Mathews changed the inherited faith so radically as to make it a new religion. With such arguments, Machen won the respect of such secular intellectuals as H. L. Mencken and Walter Lippmann, but he did not win over the modernists.[11]

Most fundamentalists, however, responded to modernist theology through populist counterattack. They mostly favored vigorous preaching, stem-winding debate, and popular writing aimed at moving the heart more than swaying the mind. A new theology came to the fore to assist these efforts, one that seemed designed for desperate times. That new theology was premillennial dispensationalism, which, figuratively speaking, dug in its heels at every point against the new ideas of the era.[12] This theology divided the teaching of the Bible into separate divisions — or dispensations — in each of which God was said to act from common principles but with different purposes. Prophecy was very important in dispensationalism, especially the effort to perceive the divine plan for the end of time. As dispensationalists interpreted Scripture, Christ would return before establishing a thousand-year reign of peace and righteousness called the millennium (hence a "premillennial" return).

10. See George M. Marsden, *Fundamentalism and American Culture: The Shaping of Twentieth-Century Evangelicalism, 1870-1925* (New York: Oxford University Press, 1980); and Joel A. Carpenter, ed., *Fundamentalism in American Religion, 1880-1945*, 45 vols. (New York: Garland, 1988).

11. See D. G. Hart, *Defending the Faith: J. Gresham Machen and the Crisis of Conservative Protestantism in America* (Baltimore: Johns Hopkins University Press, 1994).

12. See Ernest R. Sandeen, *The Roots of Fundamentalism: British and American Millenarianism, 1800-1930* (Chicago: University of Chicago Press, 1970).

Major conferences examining the Bible's teachings on end times took place in the late 1880s. These meetings became opportunities to disseminate the new dispensational emphasis. The new emphasis on the end times was partly a fresh presentation of traditional Christian teaching on the return of Christ; it probably was also a defensive reaction to the realization that American culture was slipping away from traditional Protestant control.[13] Not all the premillennialists at these conferences or among later Protestants were dispensationalists, for dispensationalists stressed more literal interpretations of the Bible and sharper divisions between periods of history than did other Protestants who shared their conservative attitude toward the Bible.

The most influential formulation of dispensational teaching appeared in 1909, when Oxford University Press published a Bible annotated by C. I. Scofield (1843-1921). Scofield, a lawyer before becoming a Congregational minister, intended this edition of the Scriptures to serve as a portable guide for missionaries more than as a polished theological system. But the thick web of notes and annotations in which the biblical text was embedded served as a fairly complete theology. As a multimillion-copy bestseller, the impact of the Scofield Reference Bible (published in a revised edition in 1967) has extended well beyond the early centers of dispensationalism to influence a wide spectrum of conservative Protestants around the world. Dispensationalism, with its great stress on biblical prophecy, has remained a potent force in American religious life.[14] The best-selling book of any sort published in the United States in the decade of the 1970s was a popular dispensational description of the end of the world, *The Late Great Planet Earth,* by Hal Lindsey.

At the start of the twentieth century, dispensational theology fueled what came to be known as a fundamentalist reaction to both modernism and the perceived decline of western Christian civilization. From 1910 to 1915 a series of booklets were published under the title

---

13. See Douglas Frank, *Less Than Conquerors: How Evangelicals Entered the Twentieth Century* (Grand Rapids: Eerdmans, 1986).

14. See Paul S. Boyer, *When Time Shall Be No More: Prophecy Belief in Modern American Culture* (Cambridge: Harvard University Press, 1992).

The Fundamentals: A Testimony to the Truth, reasserting traditional Protestant theology. Among the fundamentals defended in these tracts were the reality of the Bible as the inspired Word of God, the incarnation of Jesus Christ as the Son of God in real human flesh, the substitutionary atonement of Christ on the cross as God's way of redeeming sinners, and the reality of a literal second coming of Christ to the earth at the end of the age.

It took the cultural trauma of World War I to galvanize a defense of such convictions into a full-fledged ecclesiastical battle. Conflict centered among Northern Presbyterians and Baptists, although there were ripples of conflict in many other denominations. The term "fundamentalist" was coined by a Baptist editor in 1920 to designate those who wanted to defend the traditional, supernatural convictions of Christianity against modern attempts to reinterpret them. Fundamentalists were far from the only theological conservatives among Protestants, but in many of the ethnic denominations and among many groups more concerned about pious life than correct doctrine, there was never the same sense of alarm.

On May 22, 1922, the liberal minister Harry Emerson Fosdick preached and then published a striking sermon entitled "Shall the Fundamentalists Win?" His opinion was that they should not. Fundamentalists rose up fiercely to show why they should. The result was a full decade of acrimonious theological strife that led to turmoil among the Baptists and Presbyterians, the creation of several new denominations whose members left the older churches for being too liberal, and a general increase of confusion in the churches.

Fundamentalists lost the ecclesiastical battles of the 1920s; the Northern Presbyterian and Baptist churches remained under the control of inclusive moderates. A series of well-publicized conflicts also undercut fundamentalist standing in the broader culture. Especially important for the later image of fundamentalism, although it took many years for the image to develop, was the 1925 trial in Tennessee of a young science teacher found guilty of teaching evolution in violation of a state statute. This trial became important because it was eventually taken to stand for the heroic defense of free inquiry and scientific progress, represented by the noted agnostic attorney Clarence Darrow, against the bigoted obscurantism of a petty-minded fundamentalism, represented by the populist lay Presbyterian William Jennings Bryan. Although the reality of what actually went on in Dayton, Tennessee, at the trial of John Scopes was quite different from this picture, by the mid-1930s it had come to stand for the intellectual suicide of the fundamentalist movement.[15]

Fundamentalism was never as dead as it appeared in the aftermath of the Scopes trial.[16] But by the time fundamentalists re-emerged into the public eye in the 1970s and 1980s, the term had narrowed in meaning. In recent decades it has stood not so much for a general defense of traditional principles of Protestantism, but for a particular combination of biblical interpretations based on premillennial dispensationalism with attitudes and practices of nineteenth-century populist revivalism.[17]

The *inclusive moderates of the mainstream,* in effect, rejected both modernist and fundamentalist alternatives.[18] Most Protestants among the more traditional and often wealthier Congregationalists, Presbyterians, Methodists, Episcopalians, Disciples of Christ, Baptists in the North, and eventually among several Lutheran synods continued a course more closely modeled after the leading Protestants of the nineteenth century than either of the factions on the wings. These moderates retained more or less traditional Christian beliefs, and so were more theologically conservative than the modernists, but in the interests of maintaining the cohesion of their denominations they also abjured the polemics of the fundamentalists. These Protestants are sometimes

15. See Edward J. Larson, *Summer for the Gods: The Scopes Trial and America's Continuing Debate over Science and Religion* (New York: Basic Books, 1997).

16. See Joel A. Carpenter, "Fundamentalist Institutions and the Rise of Evangelical Protestantism, 1929-1942," *Church History* 49 (March 1980): 62-75.

17. See David Beale, *In Pursuit of Purity: American Fundamentalism Since 1850* (Greenville, SC: Unusual Publications, 1986); and Jerry Falwell with Ed Dobson, *The Fundamentalist Phenomenon* (Garden City, NY: Doubleday, 1981).

18. See Bradley J. Longfield, *The Presbyterian Controversy: Fundamentalists, Modernists, and Moderates* (New York: Oxford University Press, 1991); Martin E. Marty, *Modern American Religion*, vol. 2: *The Noise of Conflict, 1919-1941* (Chicago: University of Chicago Press, 1991), pp. 155-214; and the helpful context provided by William R. Hutchison, ed., *Between the Times: The Travail of the Protestant Establishment in America, 1900-1960* (New York: Cambridge University Press, 1989).

called "mainstream" or "mainline" because of their continuity with the previous century. Their proprietary interests can be seen in the many efforts they sponsored in the twentieth century to continue to act as the nation's unofficial religious establishment.

These moderates, for example, were the driving force in founding the Federal Council of Churches of Christ (1908) and also the National Council of Churches, which succeeded the Federal Council in 1950 as the most visible inter-church association in the United States. They included the leading missionary statesmen of the first half of the century, such as John R. Mott (1865-1955) of the YMCA and the Presbyterian Robert Speer (1867-1947). During this same period, they were the most visible Protestant academics in the country's leading universities and divinity schools, and they were the ones most likely to embrace the neo-orthodox theology (or "theology of crisis") of Karl Barth and Emil Brunner. From their ranks came, and to their ranks spoke, the most influential public theologian of the 1930s and 1940s, Reinhold Niebuhr of Union Theological Seminary in New York.[19] Their centrality in the culture is suggested by the fact that the Federal and then National Councils of Churches were the primary sponsors of the first widely accepted revision of the revered King James Version of the Bible, and by the fact that, when this Revised Standard Version was finished in 1952, a committee of the National Council held a special ceremony to present the first published copy to President Harry Truman.

The accomplishments of moderate mainline Protestants became increasingly difficult to highlight as the twentieth century wore on. Although many within mainline churches retained traditional Christian beliefs, the traumas of the early fundamentalist-modernist battles made these churches generally more frightened of fundamentalist precisionism than modernist heresy. Especially after World War II, almost all of the mainline churches softened earlier doctrinal standards or allowed ministers to hold them as historical guidelines rather than expressions of their living faith. In the intellectual arena, moderate instincts for inclusion prevented the mainline churches from excluding modern ideas or advocates from their educational institutions, which

19. See Richard Wightman Fox, *Reinhold Niebuhr* (New York: Pantheon, 1985).

began to lose their Christian character in the 1940s and 1950s.[20] As noted in the next chapter, when the social disruption in the 1960s came, these moderate churches rapidly lost whatever mainline position they once had enjoyed.

Holiness churches have always existed on the margins of public visibility in the United States, and so have never enjoyed the influence nor undergone the decay that marked the mainline moderate Protestants. "Holiness" is a term used by many Christian traditions, but as the designation of a particular expression of revivalistic Protestantism it emerged in the nineteenth century as a way of designating the emphasis on holy living that had been a major theme of Methodists such as Phoebe Palmer and revivalists such as Charles Finney.[21] In the mid-nineteenth century, the renewed emphasis on holiness took many forms. Among Methodists, ecclesiastical separations occurred throughout the nineteenth century when dissident groups such as the Free Methodists (established 1860) and Wesleyan Methodists (established 1843) felt that John Wesley's teaching on Christian perfection was being neglected.[22] The National Campmeeting Association for the Promotion of Christian Holiness, which was formed in 1867, promoted holiness themes among a mostly Methodist constituency.

Toward the end of the nineteenth century, a resurgence of concern for the doctrines and practices of holiness led to significant breakaway movements from the main Methodist bodies. Methodists who continued to promote the possibility of entire sanctification and who looked for a distinct second work of grace after conversion sponsored a variety of camp meetings, mission initiatives, orphanages, and independent churches. Under the leadership of Daniel Sidney Warner, the denomination now known as the Church of God, Anderson, Indiana, broke from

---

20. See George M. Marsden, *The Soul of the American University: From Protestant Establishment to Established Nonbelief* (New York: Oxford University Press, 1994); and James Tunstead Burtchaell, *The Dying of the Light: The Disengagement of Colleges and Universities from Their Christian Churches* (Grand Rapids: Eerdmans, 1998).

21. See Donald W. Dayton, ed., *The Higher Christian Life: Sources for the Study of the Holiness, Pentecostal and Keswick Movements*, 48 vols. (New York: Garland, 1984).

22. In 1968, the Wesleyan Methodists joined with the Pilgrim Holiness Church to become the Wesleyan Church.

the main denomination in 1881. Phineas F. Bresee (1838-1916), who had been a Methodist minister, was the first of the holiness advocates to use the name Church of the Nazarene when in 1895 he organized an independent congregation in Los Angeles. Others who emphasized the direct work of the Holy Spirit organized the Pentecostal Church of the Nazarene in 1907. After absorbing other groups with similar aims and after dropping the name "Pentecostal" in 1919 (Nazarenes do not practice speaking in tongues), the Church of the Nazarene became a leading institutional proponent of distinctive holiness teachings.

The characteristic phrases of the holiness movement extended far beyond individual denominations. These phrases spoke of a search for a deeper spirituality — the desire "to lay all on the altar," to be "clay in the potter's hands," to experience a "deeper work of grace," a "closer walk" with Christ, the "baptism of the Holy Ghost," "a higher life," "victorious living," or "overcoming power." Among those of Baptist or Presbyterian background, the holiness emphasis did not usually mean the search for a separate experience after conversion. But the desire for inner peace and a tangible experience of God drew a wide circle of American Protestants to such teachings. Summer conferences, networks of holiness periodicals, and classic books such as Hannah Whitall Smith's *The Christian's Secret of a Happy Life* (1875) created networks with the power of denominations.

In the course of the twentieth century, there was much intermingling of holiness emphases with fundamentalism and even moderate mainstream Protestantism. Holiness emphases have also been exported around the world by several different varieties of American missionaries. The most important legacy of the holiness movement, however, was probably its laying of the groundwork for the beginnings of Pentecostalism.

Pentecostalism has become the fastest growing, most diverse form of Christianity in the world.[23] Even more than the holiness movement,

---

23. See David Martin, *Tongues of Fire: The Explosion of Protestantism in Latin America* (Oxford: Blackwell, 1990); and Edith L. Blumhofer, Russell P. Spittler, and Grant A. Wacker, eds., *Pentecostal Currents in American Protestantism* (Urbana: University of Illinois Press, 1999).

Pentecostalism began as a movement of personal piety. Early Pentecostals did not usually participate in large-scale denominational activities and they mostly shunned systematic contact with the broader world.

The cradle of this new Christian movement was an abandoned Methodist church at 312 Azusa Street in the industrial section of Los Angeles. In 1906 William J. Seymour (1870-1922), a mild-mannered black holiness preacher, founded the Apostolic Faith Gospel Mission on that location. Soon Seymour's emphasis on the work of the Holy Spirit was a local sensation. Before coming to Los Angeles, Seymour had been guided by the ministry of Charles Fox Parham (1873-1929), who in turn was influenced by teachings on the importance of the Holy Spirit in his own Methodist and holiness upbringing. At small Bible schools in Kansas and Texas, Parham taught that a baptism of "the Holy Ghost and fire" should be expected among those who had been converted and who had gone onward to perfect holiness. With many in the Methodist and holiness traditions at the end of the nineteenth century, he placed a stronger emphasis generally on the gifts of the Spirit, including the gift of healing. Parham was a pioneer in teaching that a special sign of the Holy Spirit's baptism would be "speaking with other tongues."

Speaking in tongues would become the most visible mark of Pentecostalism. It is a practice based on New Testament passages such as Acts 2:4, where listeners at Pentecost heard the disciples of Jesus speaking in their own languages. It also draws on the Apostle Paul's discussion in the First Epistle to the Corinthians about "speaking in a tongue," which referred to a kind of ecstatic spiritual speech. For modern Pentecostals, speaking in tongues is a definite sign of the baptism of the Holy Spirit, although almost all modern tongues speaking is ecstatic speech rather than utterances in other languages.

The revival that began on Azusa Street in 1906 was marked by fervent prayer, speaking in tongues, earnest new hymns, and healing of the sick.[24] One of its most prominent features was the full participation of women in public activities. In an America that still took racial

24. Grant Wacker, *Heaven Below: Early Pentecostals and American Culture* (Cambridge: Harvard University Press, 2001).

barriers for granted, Azusa Street was also remarkable for the striking way that blacks and Hispanics joined whites in the nightly meetings. Soon the Azusa Street chapel became a mecca for thousands of visitors from around the world, who often went back to their homelands proclaiming the need for a special post-conversion baptism of the Holy Spirit. From a number of new alliances, networks of periodicals, and circuits of preachers and faith-healers, the Assemblies of God, established in 1914, emerged as the most important Pentecostal denomination among European Americans.[25] At the end of the century, there were nearly twelve thousand Assemblies of God congregations in the United States ministering to nearly 2.5 million adherents; indigenous churches begun by Assemblies of God missionaries outside the United States multiplied the outreach of the denomination several times over.

For African Americans, Pentecostalism opened up types of worship, singing, and spiritual exercises similar to what had been practiced in their churches before.[26] A number of largely African American denominations soon took shape as distinctly Pentecostal groups. The Church of God in Christ, which has become the largest of these bodies, was organized in Memphis in 1897 by C. H. Mason (1866-1961) and Charles Price Jones (1865-1949). For some time, they had been urging their Baptist churches to seek an experience of God's holiness after being converted. Later, after Mason journeyed to Azusa Street, he accepted the Pentecostal expression of special gifts of the Holy Spirit, which led to a split with Jones and his followers, who rejected speaking in tongues. Jones, whose hymns were widely reprinted in holiness and Pentecostal hymnbooks, and his supporters became known as the Church of Christ (Holiness) U.S.A.

Under the leadership of Mason, which resembled the earlier work of Francis Asbury among the Methodists, the Church of God in Christ expanded into most parts of the United States and to many places over-

---

25. See Edith Blumhofer, *Restoring the Faith: The Assemblies of God, Pentecostalism, and American Culture* (Urbana: University of Illinois Press, 1993).

26. See Cheryl J. Sanders, *Saints in Exile: The Holiness-Pentecostal Experience in African American Religion and Culture* (New York: Oxford University Press, 1996).

seas. Mason was a firm leader but was also widely recognized for the spirituality of his own life. He also took pains to maintain fruitful contacts with largely white Pentecostal bodies.

Denominational concerns were not priorities in the early years of the Pentecostal movement. Later observers have noted that Pentecostalism spread most rapidly among self-disciplined, often mobile folk of the middle and lower-middle classes. But an ardent desire for the unmediated experience of the Holy Spirit was a still more common characteristic of those who became Pentecostals. Observers at the time linked Azusa Street with the great Welsh Revival of 1904 and 1905 and the "Latter Rain" movement that had pockets of influence throughout the United States. Today it symbolizes the inaugural dynamism of the fastest growing Christian movement in the world.

Evangelical is another widely-shared word in Christian history that has assumed a new meaning in the United States during recent decades.[27] Sometimes the word is used broadly to mean all non-modernist Protestants, or all Protestants who retain a belief in the Bible as the revealed word of God, who share their Christian faith, and who trust in Christ alone for their salvation. Used historically, it can be applied more precisely to a movement within fundamentalism but also bridging over into mainline, holiness, and Pentecostal churches that sought in the 1930s and 1940s to move beyond the constraints of polemical fundamentalism.[28] The founding of the National Association of Evangelicals in 1942 signaled an early stage of the movement. These "neo-evangelicals," as they called themselves at first, wanted to position themselves between a recently founded fundamentalist association, the International Council of Christian Churches, and the mainline Federal Council of Churches. Its leaders wanted to affirm doctrinal fundamentals, but to do so with a more sophisticated hermeneutic, with greater attention

27. Difficulties in defining this term are addressed in the introduction and postscript to *Evangelicalism: Comparative Studies of Popular Protestantism in North America, The British Isles, and Beyond, 1700-1990,* ed. Mark A. Noll, David W. Bebbington, and George A. Rawlyk (New York: Oxford University Press, 1994); and in Mark A. Noll, *American Evangelical Christianity: An Introduction* (Oxford: Blackwell, 2001).

28. See especially Joel A. Carpenter, *Revive Us Again: The Reawakening of American Fundamentalism* (New York: Oxford University Press, 1997).

to modern intellectual life, and with heightened responses to matters of social reform.

Leaders of this neo-evangelical movement were mostly drawn from the softer side of fundamentalism. They included Charles E. Fuller (1887-1969), host of a phenomenally popular radio program broadcast from California in the 1930s and 1940s called "The Old Fashioned Revival Hour." In 1947 Fuller joined with Harold John Ockenga (1905-1985), pastor of the historic Park Street Congregational Church in Boston, to found the Fuller Theological Seminary in Pasadena, California, which rapidly became an institutional leader of the movement.[29] In its early days, Fuller Seminary recruited a bright young faculty of ex-fundamentalists such as Edward John Carnell (1919-1967), who came to the seminary after earning doctorates at Harvard and Boston University, and converts without church backgrounds such as Carl F. H. Henry (b. 1913), who in 1956 became the founding editor of *Christianity Today*, a magazine that has served as a guide and clearinghouse for modern evangelicalism.

Evangelist Billy Graham (b. 1918) lent his growing prestige to this movement, and it, in turn, followed Graham as he left behind many of the shibboleths of fundamentalism in his career as an itinerant evangelist.[30] It was also assisted by some members of mainline churches as well as by members of ethnic churches that had heretofore not involved themselves in broader American affairs. Prominent among these churches was the largely Dutch Christian Reformed Church, which had nurtured a tradition of confessional Christian learning and produced several publishers, notably the Wm. B. Eerdmans Publishing Company, that became the major early promoters of books by individuals like E. J. Carnell and Carl Henry.

Since the 1950s, the evangelicals associated with Billy Graham and publications like *Christianity Today* have been joined by a wide variety of individuals and groups for a wide variety of projects. Periodic internal

29. See George M. Marsden, *Reforming Fundamentalism: Fuller Seminary and the New Evangelicalism* (Grand Rapids: Eerdmans, 1987).

30. The best biographical treatment is William C. Martin, *A Prophet with Honor: The Billy Graham Story* (New York: William Morrow, 1991).

debates on questions of doctrine — for example, on how closely to observe nineteenth-century or fundamentalist formulations defining the truthfulness of the Bible — reveal the movement's internal diversity, as does also the wide number of denominations where individuals are found who are willing to describe themselves as "evangelicals."

As with several of the other Protestant sub-groupings, "evangelical" does not establish hard and fast boundaries. Thus, some mainline and African-American Protestants use the term for themselves, and some individuals or groups whom others regard as "evangelical" do not use the term for themselves. (This happens most with such bodies as the Southern Baptists or the Lutheran Church — Missouri Synod that are conservative in theology, often conservative in political and social views, but do not promote the kind of interdenominational cooperation that is common among self-described "evangelicals.") When used with care, however, the term is a useful designation for a strand of twentieth-century American Protestants who retain some of the positions of their nineteenth-century predecessors, but who have adjusted those positions in the face of twentieth-century circumstances differently than fundamentalists or mainline moderates.

African-American Protestants underwent considerable expansion and diversification in the decades after 1900.[31] During and after the First World War, a great migration began from the rural South to the cities of the North that eventually drew hundreds of thousands of African Americans into new ecclesiastical, as well as social, environments.[32] In both the South and the North, the older black denominations continued to link a large number of churches and to provide educational, publishing, and missionary connections as well. These included especially the African Methodist Episcopal Church, the African Methodist Episcopal Zion Church, the Christian Methodist Episcopal Church, the National Baptist Convention, U.S.A., Incorporated, and a denomination that broke away from the National Convention in 1915 in a dis-

---

31. A full survey is C. Eric Lincoln and Lawrence H. Mamiya, *The Black Church in the African American Experience* (Durham, NC: Duke University Press, 1990).

32. See Milton C. Sernett, *Bound for the Promised Land: African American Religion and the Great Migration* (Durham, NC: Duke University Press, 1997).

pute over ownership of publications, the National Baptist Convention of America (unincorporated).

By the 1920s, churches from these older denominational clusters were being joined in great numbers by holiness and Pentecostal churches. As we have seen, within a few years of the Azusa Street revival, several black denominations were in existence among Pentecostals, with the Church of God in Christ joined by the Pentecostal Assemblies of the World, a "oneness" denomination that baptized in the name of Jesus alone and that denied traditional understandings of the Trinity. In addition, numerous independent churches founded in urban storefronts often embraced holiness or Pentecostal practices. Increasing numbers of African Americans also entered the Catholic church. In 1886 Augustus Tolton had become the first American of pure African descent to be ordained as a priest, and in the following years conventions and separate publications began to minister directly to the considerable body of black Catholics.

Besides Christian movements, the urban migration also spurred the formation of many other religious organizations, including the Nation of Islam (the Black Muslims) and several groups of Black Jews. Charles ("Sweet Daddy") Grace's United House of Prayer for All People began to flourish in the 1920s with a message linking some Pentecostal practices to Daddy Grace's miraculous powers of healing. Father Divine's Peace Mission Movement, which affirmed the divinity of its founder, established shelters and other relief centers in several northern urban centers.

Because they were over-represented in the lower socio-economic strata, black church members suffered even more dislocation from the Great Depression of the 1930s than their white counterparts. In the more traditional Christian groups, the Depression and America's entry into the Second World War stimulated greater interest in support for civil rights even as it prompted an expansion of church-based social services. After the war, educational opportunities opened slightly for some leaders and future leaders of black churches, such as the Rev. Dr. Martin Luther King, Jr.; this opening made possible the accumulation of spiritual resources — traditional Christian beliefs, elements of contemporary liberal theology, and such non-Western resources as the pacifism of Mahatma Gandhi — that in the 1950s and 1960s would coalesce in the Civil Rights Movement.

In the transition from a primarily rural and Southern setting to a national distribution, African American churches sometimes flourished, sometimes struggled to survive, and sometimes lost members to secular substitutes for religion. Their place in the broader American picture, however, grew in importance as the churches continued their often silent witness to the anomaly of a supposedly Christian nation with a supposedly freedom-loving society that continued to subject an entire body of its citizens to systematic racial discrimination.

Events

Against a religious landscape defined by the existence of these multiple forms of Christianity, the often traumatic events of the century usually involved religious developments as well.

- With the exception of some Quakers, Mennonites, other traditional pacifists, and some Pentecostals, most church leaders gave their vigorous support to the First World War.[33] Fundamentalists accused modernists of promoting the evolutionary theory and the higher criticism of Scripture that they thought had corrupted Germany; modernists responded by accusing fundamentalists of being so preoccupied with the second coming of Christ that they were slacking off in their support of the war effort.
- For Roman Catholics, the First World War offered an opportunity to form an ongoing national bureaucracy. The National Catholic War Council was formed in August 1917 to oversee chaplains in the military and promote a wide range of other activities. After the war, it became the National Catholic Welfare Council, a national agency that continues to this day.
- During the 1920s, several religious groups and entrepreneurial

33. See John F. Piper, *The American Churches in World War I* (Athens: Ohio University Press, 1985).

leaders were quick to exploit the development of radio. Among the pioneers of religious broadcasting who used the medium most effectively were Paul Rader (1879-1938), a moderate, missionary-minded fundamentalist, and Aimee Semple McPherson (1890-1944), a Pentecostal evangelist who founded the Church of the Foursquare Gospel.[34]

- The Depression years of the 1930s witnessed a proliferation of extremist groups. On the Right, the "radio priest," Charles Coughlin (1891-1979), gained many followers through his attacks on President Roosevelt. Coughlin was joined by several other individuals who combined elements of traditional Christianity with apocalyptic denunciations of Roosevelt's New Deal policies.[35] On the Left, a few leaders in the mainstream Protestant churches followed their disillusionment with Western capitalism toward the embrace of various forms of socialism, with Harry F. Ward, a socialist and professor at Union Seminary in New York, the most conspicuous.[36]

- The tangled political-ethical-economic debates of the 1930s resulted in specifically religious outcomes for several noteworthy individuals. During this decade, for example, Joy Davidman, who later wrote books of biblical exposition and became the wife of the British apologist C. S. Lewis, and the Jewish theologian and social commentator, Will Herberg, both began their journeys away from Marx toward traditional faith in God.

- During the Depression, mainline Protestant churches generally had a difficult time.[37] But for fundamentalist, holiness, Pentecostal, African American, and the new-evangelical churches and organizations, it was a time of expansion. The Southern Baptist Convention, the holiness Church of the Nazarene, the Pentecostal Assemblies of God, and the main black Baptist denominations all

34. See Edith Blumhofer, *Aimee Semple McPherson: Everybody's Sister* (Grand Rapids: Eerdmans, 1993).

35. See Leo P. Ribuffo, *The Old Christian Right: The Protestant Far Right from the Great Depression to the Cold War* (Philadelphia: Temple University Press, 1983).

36. See Marty, *Modern American Religion,* vol. 2, *1919-1941,* pp. 293-97.

37. See Robert T. Handy, "The American Religious Depression, 1925-1935," *Church History* 29 (March 1960): 3-16.

grew rapidly during this period. With over twelve thousand members, the Olivet Baptist Church in Chicago, a leader in the National Baptist Convention of the U.S.A., Incorporated, was in the 1930s the largest Protestant church in the country.

- The Second World War enlisted the support of most of the churches, but the crusading, apocalyptic zeal that had fueled religious support of the First World War was largely absent.[38]
- The end of the Second World War inaugurated an economic boom in the United States, fueled especially by the expansion of the suburbs around major cities and a massive increase in the production of automobiles. Most major Protestant denominations as well as the Catholic church benefited from these conditions, as they were able to construct more church buildings than in any other comparable period in the nation's history.
- The postwar economic boom coincided, however, with the Cold War and a period of fervid rhetoric describing the evils of godless Communism in contrast with the virtues of the West's divinely inspired liberties. Soviet suppression of the 1956 Hungarian Revolution and the launching of Sputnik in 1957 fueled American fears and also provided the backdrop to a flourishing industry of books, speakers, and movies predicting the end of the world in the terms defined by fundamentalist interpretations of scriptural prophecy. The linking of American values with the freedom of Western democracy and a generic Christian faith led to what scholars eventually called an "American civil religion."[39]
- The Supreme Court's decree in 1954 ending the racial segregation of American schools was one of the sparks for the large-scale Civil Rights Movement that affected more and more areas of the country over the next two decades. Central in the promotion of that movement were such African American Christian groups as the

---

38. See Gerald L. Sittser, *A Cautious Patriotism: The American Churches and the Second World War* (Chapel Hill: University of North Carolina Press, 1997).

39. See Robert N. Bellah, "Civil Religion in America," *Daedelus* 96 (Winter 1967): 1-21; Russell E. Richey and Donald G. Jones, eds., *American Civil Religion* (San Francisco: Harper & Row, 1974); and James A. Mathisen, "Twenty Years After Bellah: Whatever Happened to American Civil Religion?" *Sociological Analysis* 50 (1989): 129-46.

Southern Christian Leadership Conference, often aided by a few Roman Catholics and mainstream Protestants as well.

- In 1960 the election of a youthful Catholic, John F. Kennedy, as president marked a breakthrough in Catholic-Protestant relations. In a highly publicized speech during his presidential campaign, Kennedy reassured a largely Protestant audience in Houston, Texas, that his Catholic faith was fully compatible with American traditions concerning the separation of church and state. Much disillusionment of several kinds followed in the decade of the 1960s, but the politics of Catholic-Protestant antagonism were now largely a thing of the past.

During the first half of the twentieth century, the fragmentation of Protestantism meant that the nation's historically most potent religious force became a declining influence in the nation as a whole. It is important to note, however, that decline did not take place in all locations, and that in fact the strength of various Christian churches or movements grew appreciably in certain sectors of American society in these years. Nevertheless, in general the twentieth century marked the beginning of a new phase in the history of Christianity in the United States. The growing strength of non-Protestant forms of Christianity and non-Christian religions broadened the United States' already extensive religious pluralism. Secularizing pressures from cycles of economic bust and boom, the general expansion of the national government through two major wars and under all administrations, and the neglect of religion in the nation's colleges and universities also worked against the forces of traditional religion.[40] Compared to most European nations, however, the breadth and depth of Christian energies remained surprisingly strong. From a position of relative strength, American Christian churches and agencies were well-positioned to exert significant, if never dominant, influence in the recent history of the United States.

---

40. Treatment of the growing role of government is only one of the outstanding features of Robert W. Wuthnow, *The Restructuring of American Religion: Society and Faith Since World War II* (Princeton: Princeton University Press, 1988).

CHAPTER EIGHT

The Recent Past, 1960-2000

The tumultuous events, political standoffs, and changing cultural circumstances in America's most recent decades have also affected the churches. The assassinations of political leaders (John Kennedy in 1963, Robert Kennedy and Martin Luther King, Jr., in 1968), controversy over United States involvement in the Vietnam War, the sexual revolution of the 1960s and 1970s, the appearance of feminism as an ideological and practical force, computerization and the revolution in communications, radical movements of deconstruction in the universities and countervailing reactions upholding the objectivity of science — all these and more have influenced American Christian understandings of faith, structuring of churches, and approaches to daily life.

A good case could be made, however, that for the history of Christianity, such upheavals in the broader culture have not been the most important matters, but have rather provided a context for deeper, more permanent Christian developments. Of course, all contemporary history must by nature be exceedingly speculative, but by keeping Christian events and circumstances in the forefront, it is possible to examine recent American decades for their place in the general history of Christianity.

The Diversity of Churches and Christian Organizations

The place to begin consideration of recent history is the staggering degree of organizational Christian diversity within the United States. The institutional inventiveness that has always distinguished Christianity in America has only become more remarkable in recent decades.

Even to grasp the outlines of that diversity is a formidable task. Within the United States are to be found, for example, twenty-two separate Orthodox churches that register their existence with national clearinghouses, and there are probably several more that do not.[1] Among Protestants, institutional creativity is almost beyond accounting. In the *Encyclopedia of American Religions* (5th edition, 1996), J. Gordon Melton lists ten different "families" of Protestants, some of which have many sub-families as well. When Melton counted the number of individual Christian communions, he found that there were 19 separate Presbyterian denominations, 32 Lutheran, 36 Methodist, 37 Episcopal or Anglican, 60 Baptist, and 241 Pentecostal. Even if a few of these denominations are little more than a single congregation, and even though Melton included Canadian denominations in his lists, the number of such groupings is staggering nevertheless.

For Catholics, the hierarchical structures linking the faithful to Rome cannot mask the profusion of theological, racial, educational, ideological, social, linguistic, and cultural sub-groups within its single church. Many commentators have made the point that, because of internal differences over the course of Catholicism since the Second Vatican Council and because of fissures remaining from an earlier ethnic history, the Catholic church now has almost as many sub-divisions, interest groups, lobbies, and shades of opinions as can be found in the wide divergence of Protestantism. American Catholics remain united by their common Roman identification, but some of them think Pope John Paul II has been a disaster for the church, while others think he has been the greatest pope of modern times; many blithely disregard the church's dogma prohibiting artificial birth control, while others

---

1. Eileen W. Linder, ed., *2000 Yearbook of American and Canadian Churches* (Nashville: Abingdon, for the National Council of Churches, 2000).

support it; some regard Vatican II as a charter for liberalization, while others think it enlivened the traditions of the church; some insist on changing historic Catholic guidelines on the celibacy of priests and ordination of only men to the priesthood, while others defend these traditions as essential to the very being of the church; some consider the essence of Catholic practice to be service to the poor, while others think of devotion to the Virgin Mary or charismatic life in the Holy Spirit or faithful obedience to the hierarchy in the same light; some think the National Council of Catholic Bishops must assert more independence from Rome, while others think it has already gone too far. Catholicism, in other words, now contributes to the diversity of American Christianity almost as actively as do America's Protestants.

Moreover, diversity among Protestant denominations and within the Catholic church only begins to tell the story of America's Christian pluralism. Within the borders of the United States exist also a bewildering array of newer sectarian movements. Some of these movements, such as the Church of Jesus Christ of Latter-day Saints (Mormons), have increasingly taken on church-like status and functions. Others such as the Jehovah's Witnesses remain closer to their original sectarian character, but with nearly one million members they constitute an important factor in American religion. Still other once-sectarian groups such as the Seventh-day Adventists or the Worldwide Church of God have in recent decades come to emphasize more their commonality with historic evangelical Protestantism and less the distinctives of their founding.[2]

But even a roster of denominations and denomination-like groups only begins to chart the full measure of diversity; it is necessary also to take account of what the British sociologist David Martin has called "the buzzing complex of voluntary organizations" found in the United States to complete the picture.[3] Among Protestants, there have always

---

2. See Kenneth R. Samples, "The Recent Truth about Seventh-Day Adventists," *Christianity Today,* 5 Feb. 1990, pp. 18-21; Doug LeBlanc, "The Worldwide Church of God: Resurrected into Orthodoxy," *Christian Research Journal,* Winter 1996, pp. 6-7, 44-45.

3. David Martin, *Tongues of Fire: The Explosion of Protestantism in Latin America* (Oxford: Blackwell, 1990), p. 206. This important book explains why America's important earlier forms of Protestantism (Puritanism and Methodism) did not transport easily to Latin America, but why Pentecostalism is doing so with a vengeance.

existed more associations, groups, and societies outside the churches than churches. The effects of the Second World War in putting millions of people into new places, new occupations, and new associations, combined with the postwar economic boom, all only multiplied the quantity of such groups. A sampling of some important voluntary groups of the last few decades suggests the range of such bodies in which Protestants have played a large role. The Southern Christian Leadership Conference spearheaded the Civil Rights Movement of the 1950s and 1960s. The Christian Coalition has been a promoter of conservative politics since the early 1990s. The Concerned Women for America and Women's Aglow Fellowship link women together in promoting traditional family causes.[4] Bread for the World tries to alleviate hunger around the world. Clergy and Laity Concerned protested the United States involvement in the Vietnam War. Promise Keepers attempts to revitalize spirituality among men. An enumeration of these groups only scratches the surface.

Again, it is also easy to underestimate the amount of Catholic voluntary organization. Although Catholic associations usually are connected to the church's official hierarchy in some way, their vitality comes in large part from their partaking of the standard American penchant for nearly limitless creation of special-purpose organizations. Thus a recent Catholic almanac could list 26 "secular institutes" constituted by laypersons to achieve specific religious goals; 11 third-order lay religious groups; 237 colleges and universities; 1,408 secondary schools; 7,772 primary schools; about 570 facilities for retired and aged persons; 250 facilities for the disabled; 250 houses of retreat and renewal; 11 youth organizations with programs for individual parishes; 650 Catholic newspapers, magazines, and newsletters; 24 programs or services in television, radio, and communications; about 200 miscellaneous associations such as the Canon Law Society of America, the Catholic Medical Association, the Hungarian Catholic League of America, or the National Catholic Conference of Airport Chaplains; and many hospitals, centers for treating substance abuse, homes for unwed mothers, programs to rehabilitate criminals, and other service agen-

4. On Aglow, see Marie R. Griffith, *God's Daughters: Evangelical Women and the Power of Submission* (Berkeley: University of California Press, 1997).

cies.[5] Even with the hierarchical connections sustained for many of these societies, it is obvious that Catholics have become quite thoroughly American in their ability to form specialized societies for specific religious and secular purposes.

The extent of American Christian diversity means that it is almost impossible to predict the theological, social, or political consequence of nominal religious adherence. A recent study by historian Charles Marsh of the dramatic civil rights confrontations of 1964 in the state of Mississippi provides a clear illustration of that reality. Marsh found that all of the major participants were Protestants, and yet extraordinarily different kinds of Protestants. They included Fannie Lou Hamer, an African American leader of the Mississippi Freedom Democratic party, who once was sustained by thoughts of Jesus as she was being savagely beaten in the Winona, Mississippi, city jail. But they also included Sam Bowers, Imperial Wizard of the White Knights of the Ku Klux Klan, who saw himself defending the sovereignty of God and the resurrection of Jesus Christ in his conspiracy to murder three civil rights workers. The other principals were not as extreme, but they too illustrated the very diverse paths that Christian allegiance took in this one situation and that it regularly takes in other American settings.[6]

Contemporary Culture and the Christian Churches

Developments in recent American history that bear directly on the churches include new understandings of gender and sexuality, new responses to the class and racial divisions of American society, and new initiatives in politics. Each of these matters has been the subject of extensive literature and each deserves at least capsule summarization in an account of the recent past.

---

5. *1998 Catholic Almanac* (Huntington, IN: Our Sunday Visitor, 1998).

6. Charles Marsh, *God's Long Summer: Stories of Faith and Civil Rights* (Princeton: Princeton University Press, 1997).

Gender and Sexuality

The Second World War expanded the number of women working in the marketplace, and ideological explorations of later decades have kept women's concerns in the forefront of public religious discussion.[7] Changing sexual mores in the wider culture have put several kinds of pressures on the churches. Considerable sentiment exists within the Catholic church in favor of clerical marriage and the ordination of women as priests. These pressures exist alongside a steady decline in religious vocations among both men and women. In the decade from 1987 to 1997, for example, while the number of Catholic adherents rose in the United States from about 50 million to over 61 million, the number of active priests declined from 53,382 to 48,097, the number of lay brothers dropped from over 7,000 to slightly more than 6,000, and the number of sisters declined from over 112,000 to under 88,000.[8]

All of the churches, Catholic and Protestant, have been forced to deal with the presence of homosexuals in their communions. The most liberal Protestant bodies have accepted homosexual practice to one degree or another, most mainline Protestant churches have drawn the line at accepting the ordination of homosexuals, while conservative Protestant denominations have echoed official Catholic and Orthodox positions in continuing to label homosexual practice a deviation, or a sin, even while most have gone on record affirming the civil rights of homosexuals.

For all communions, dealing with increased numbers of divorces, cases of marital infidelity, and new medical possibilities for conception

---

7. For only a sample, see Elizabeth Schüssler Fiorenza, *In Memory of Her: A Feminist Theological Reconstruction of Christian Origins* (New York: Crossroad, 1983); Anne E. Carr, *Transforming Grace: Christian Tradition and Women's Experience* (San Francisco: Harper & Row, 1988); Mary Stewart Van Leeuwen, et al., *After Eden: The Challenge of Gender Reconciliation* (Grand Rapids: Eerdmans, 1993); Rosemary Skinner Keller and Rosemary Radford Ruether, eds., *In Our Own Voices: Four Centuries of American Women's Religious Writing* (San Francisco: Harper & Row, 1995); and Christel Manning, *God Gave Us the Right: Conservative Catholic, Evangelical Protestant, and Orthodox Jewish Women Grapple with Feminism* (New Brunswick, NJ: Rutgers University Press, 1999).

8. *1998 Catholic Almanac*, p. 435.

and birth control have strained traditions of moral casuistry that had mostly developed within traditional contexts of European and American ethical reasoning.

Among all communions there have also been increased opportunities for leadership by women, although the shape of that leadership varies greatly depending on the theological and ecclesiastical practices of the different groups.[9] Throughout American history, women have made up a majority of the members in most churches. But only in the twentieth century did women begin widely to assume places of leadership in churches and religious agencies. Many of the more conservative Protestant bodies continue to limit the pastorate to men, but even these churches have developed new tasks for women, such as leading Bible studies. For conservatives, liberals, and those in between, the huge industry of religious publishing depends very heavily on women as authors, editors, and readers. Most mainline Protestant denominations as well as many Holiness and Pentecostal bodies now encourage the ordination of women as pastors.

The opening of pastoral ranks to Protestant women has obviously had a great impact on the women who become ministers. It has meant significant changes in the emphases of denominational publishing, ideals of pastoral care, and the role of ministers in society. It has also altered the shape of theological education: as late as 1980, the proportion of women students in theological institutes was barely one in five; by 1998 it was more than one in three.[10] It has also given issues traditionally associated with women a higher visibility in the churches. Concern for nurture alongside conversion, for teaching focused on life transitions alongside teaching focused on permanent doctrine, for a stress on relationships alongside action — these are some of the spiritual trends associated with the growing public place of women in religious life in general.

9. See Paula D. Nesbitt, *Feminization of the Clergy in America: Occupational and Organizational Perspectives* (New York: Oxford University Press, 1997); and Mark Chaves, *Ordaining Women: Culture and Conflict in Religious Organizations* (Cambridge: Harvard University Press, 1997).

10. *2000 Yearbook,* p. 363.

Urban Action

Where cultural changes associated with gender and sexuality have been the center of extensive debate in the churches, the stagnation of American cities — with problems compounded by racial, economic, and criminal realities — has, regrettably, received less attention.[11] The economic and social problems of American urban areas have made life as difficult for the churches as for other mediating institutions of civil society. But in many of the country's largest cities, active Catholic, Protestant, and sectarian churches sustain a vigorous religious life. The churches are also the providers of significant support for education, health care, job placement, and housing. Earlier in the twentieth century, the Catholic church was a major factor in questions of urban reform and renewal. Its ranks included progressive voices calling for racial integration, proactive consideration of the poor, and a wide range of other social relief, but also stalwart ethnic communities that struggled to maintain their own homogeneity, their own schools, their own churches, and their hard-won urban identities.[12]

Catholic involvement in American urban life remains extensive, especially through parochial systems that in many cities provide the best education of any kind available to disadvantaged populations. In recent decades, creative Protestant leaders have also made a difference. The Deliverance Temple in northwest Philadelphia, for example, ministers to several thousand African American Pentecostals through the teaching of the Rev. Ben Smith, but also through a shopping center, a large Bible school, and several other local enterprises. The Iglesia Cristiana Juan 3:16 in the Bronx is the mother church of Puerto Rican Pentecostalism in the United States. It takes its name and its broad mandate from a well-known biblical passage, John 3:16 ("For God so

---

11. See Kendig Brubaker Cully and F. Nile Harper, eds., *Will the Church Lose the City?* (New York: World, 1969); Alice Shabecoff, *Rebuilding Our Communities* (Monrovia, CA: World Vision, 1992); John M. Perkins, ed., *Restoring At-Risk Communities: Doing It Together and Doing It Right* (Grand Rapids: Baker, 1995); and Helene Slessarev, *The Betrayal of the Urban Poor* (Philadelphia: Temple University Press, 1997).

12. See especially John T. McGreevy, *Parish Boundaries: The Catholic Encounter with Race in the Twentieth-Century Urban North* (Chicago: University of Chicago Press, 1996).

loved the world that he gave his one and only Son, that whoever believes in him shall not perish but have eternal life"). Under the leadership of the Rev. Ricardo Tañón it has engaged in many local ministries and also directed many of its members to further study and service in a wide variety of churches and religious agencies. The Mount Zion Missionary Baptist Church of Los Angeles is likewise involved in feeding the hungry and developing the community in addition to featuring the fiery evangelical preaching of the Rev. E. V. Hill. Some of the dynamics involved in such churches are revealed in what appear to be the odd combination of Rev. Hill's loyalties. He was a strong supporter of the politically conservative Republican presidents Ronald Reagan and George Bush (which was unusual for African American leaders), but he also helped raise money for the presidential campaigns of Jesse Jackson, a liberal African American Democrat, and he was asked by the mayor of Los Angeles to assist interracial understanding after the 1993 urban riots. These churches and many more like them face great difficulties in America's cities, but they are making a difference.

Politics

Religion has always played a political role in America. The politicization of modern American religion began in the special circumstances of the 1950s, when the dynamics of the Cold War led many white Protestants and quite a few Catholics to become ardent supporters of the American status quo.[13] But the most influential political movement with religious support was the Civil Rights Movement. The Rev. Martin Luther King, Jr. (1929-1968), the most visible spokesman of that movement, drew his power, insights, rhetoric, and images from his black Baptist heritage combined with an appeal to the unrealized potential of American ideals.[14] King's ability to draw on sophisticated philosophy, the pacifist so-

---

13. See Patrick Allitt, *Catholic Intellectuals and Conservative Politics in America, 1950-1985* (Ithaca, NY: Cornell University Press, 1993); and Richard V. Pierard, *The Unequal Yoke: Evangelical Christianity and Political Conservatism* (Philadelphia: Lippincott, 1970).

14. Taylor Branch, *Parting the Waters: America in the King Years, 1954-1963* (New York:

cial theory of Mahatma Gandhi, a deep familiarity with Scripture, and the preaching traditions of African American churches made him an extraordinarily powerful force. He exasperated many moderates and conservatives, who distrusted his push for civil rights and his eventual opposition to the Vietnam War. Yet he also became an inspiration to millions in the United States and abroad for his willingness to seek social reform aggressively, but in a spirit of Christian charity. The strongest supporters for the civil rights goals for which King strove were the black churches, which eventually also recruited a few notable allies from Catholic and mainline Protestant churches.

The next stage in the integration of religion and politics was both illustrated and accelerated by the presidency of Jimmy Carter (1977-1981).[15] When Carter was campaigning for president on the Democratic ticket in 1976, it became obvious that his private life as a Baptist Sunday School teacher in Plains, Georgia, connected at many points with his politics. The way Carter brought religion more visibly into public view did not necessarily please his fellow Southern Baptists, but it was an unmistakable aspect of his presidency from 1977 to 1981. As a reader of Reinhold Niebuhr, as a president willing to explore the moral implications of public policy, as a Christian who did not try to hide the importance of his own conversion experience — in all these ways Carter brought religion and politics into closer public contact than they had been since the era of Woodrow Wilson and William Jennings Bryan at the start of the century. After leaving the White House, Carter continued a course that stressed moral action, traveling around the world to monitor democratic elections and supporting publicly the work of Habitat for Humanity in providing housing for the urban poor. In these ways he expanded the practical effects of what had begun years before in his Sunday school.

Following on from the heightened moral sensitivities raised in the 1960s by the Civil Rights Movement and the Vietnam War, and in the 1970s by the example of President Carter, the last quarter of the century

---

Simon & Schuster, 1988); Branch, *Pillar of Fire: America in the King Years, 1963-1965* (New York: Simon & Schuster, 1998); and *The Papers of Martin Luther King, Jr.*, ed. Clayborne Carson (Berkeley: University of California Press, 1992-).

15. A good overview is provided by Garry Wills, *Under God: Religion and American Politics* (New York: Simon & Schuster, 1990).

was filled with Christian efforts at shaping public life. If the results of such linkages often appear contradictory, it is a testimony to the breadth of viewpoints found among the nation's churches. The best-publicized efforts have come from the political and theological Right.[16] But there have been other religious visions as well. The nomination of Sen. Joseph Lieberman, an Orthodox Jew, as the Democrats' Vice Presidential candidate in 2000 opened the way to a fuller consideration of religious positions from all points of view. One of the prominent spokesmen of the Left who continues to insist on the importance of religion is the academic and commentator Cornel West (b. 1953). As a philosopher, activist, and social critic holding various posts at Yale, Princeton, and Harvard, West has argued that a combination of Christianity and Marxism is necessary to overcome the United States' stubborn retention of oppressive white racism. His book *Prophecy Deliverance! An Afro-American Revolutionary Christianity* (1982), was a major statement of how he thought biblical themes of liberation complemented radical proposals for reform.

From the other side of the political universe, the efforts of Jerry Falwell (b. 1933) played an important role in forming the ethos of the political New Christian Right.[17] In 1956 Falwell founded the Thomas Road Baptist Church in Lynchburg, Virginia, which then grew to become a very large church and the home base for a wide range of religious and political activities. In his sermons, radio and television programs, and many books, Falwell has argued that biblical religion supports conservative political action. In 1979 Falwell founded the Moral Majority as a public lobby to advance such views. It disbanded ten years later, but not before making a major impact in linking the religion of many evangelical and fundamentalist white Protestants to the conservative goals of the Republican Party. Falwell's general course has

16. See Robert Liebman and Robert Wuthnow, eds., *The New Christian Right: Mobilization and Legitimization* (Hawthorne, NY: Aldine, 1983); Richard John Neuhaus and Michael Cromartie, eds., *Piety and Politics: Evangelicals and Fundamentalists Confront the World* (Washington, D.C.: Ethics and Public Policy Center, 1987); and John C. Green, James Guth, Lyman Kellstedt, and Corwin Smidt, *Religion and the Culture Wars: Dispatches from the Front* (Lanham, MD: Rowman & Littlefield, 1996).

17. On Falwell and similar leaders, see Clyde Wilcox, *God's Warriors: The Christian Right in Twentieth-Century America* (Baltimore: Johns Hopkins University Press, 1992).

been followed by popular broadcaster Pat Robertson (b. 1930), who combines Southern Baptist and Pentecostal emphases. Robertson's campaign for president in 1988 was not successful, but it did succeed in politicizing some Pentecostals, charismatics, fundamentalists, and evangelicals who had previously been politically inactive. Robertson's later establishment of a political action organization called the Christian Coalition has extended those efforts.

The great publicity bestowed upon Falwell, Robertson, the Moral Majority, and the Christian Coalition has been due to the strategic alliance that Christian conservatives have established with political conservatives in the Republican Party. This coalition has benefited from, and also promoted, America's general swing to the Right since the mid-1970s. It has definitely had an influence in drawing more white Protestants in a conservative political direction. In the presidential election of 2000, white evangelical Protestants who regularly attend church gave 84% of their vote to Republican candidate George W. Bush, and these votes constituted almost exactly one-third of Bush's total vote.[18]

It would, however, badly distort the reality of recent American history to conclude that American Christianity as a whole has moved *en bloc* to the Right. Some conservative Protestants join many Catholics and mainline Protestants in maintaining the long predilection of American church bodies for the political center, and a few from each of those groups continue to argue for the fit between liberal politics and Christianity. Even more importantly, masses of American Christians, especially some of those most active in the churches, retain a pietist uneasiness with politics as a whole and continue the long American religious tradition of avoiding the political sphere.

Christian History in America

Developments in the American churches that are probably more directly germane to the world history of Christianity are certainly connected to

18. See James L. Guth, John C. Green, Corwin E. Smidt, and Lyman A. Kellstedt, "Partisan Religion: Analyzing the 2000 Election," *Christian Century*, Mar. 21-28, 2001, pp. 18-20.

recent developments in the broader culture, but their importance may also be construed in more directly ecclesiastical or religious terms. They include new levels of Catholic-Protestant interaction, growing strength for new ethnic churches, major shifts in the number of adherents to various American churches, and a broadening circle of influence radiating out from the Pentecostal and charismatic movements.

Catholics and Protestants

The Second Vatican Council (1962-65) had an almost immediate impact on the often-strained relationship between Catholics and Protestants.[19] In the wake of the Council, Catholics initiated formal dialogues with several Protestant bodies as well as with the Orthodox. Some of these dialogues have produced documents pointing to remarkable convergences of Catholic and Protestant convictions, though most regularly report honestly on outstanding differences. Perhaps the most significant was the Lutheran-Catholic statement of 1983 that outlined a basic agreement on the meaning of justification by faith.[20] While noting a range of still unresolved issues, the discussants were able to affirm agreement that God's grace redeems sinners apart from human works of righteousness (thus affirming a main Protestant conviction since the time of the Reformation), but also that justified believers naturally perform good works as a result of their justification (thus allaying the Catholic fear that Protestant theology cut the root of moral behavior). This document in turn spurred action toward the joint statement on justification approved by the Vatican and the Lutheran World Federation in October 1999.

Many other formal and informal connections now exist between these two ancient Christian antagonists. Although staunch traditionalists in both camps urge caution about giving in too rapidly to ecumeni-

19. See Mark A. Noll, *American Evangelical Christianity: An Introduction* (Oxford: Blackwell, 2001), Chapter Seven, "Roman Catholics."

20. "U.S. Lutheran-Roman Catholic Dialogue: Justification by Faith," *Origins: NC Documentary Service,* Oct. 6, 1983, pp. 277-304. The text with discussion was also published by Augsburg Press of Minneapolis.

cal goodwill, the number and pace of Protestant-Catholic exchanges are both increasing.[21] Quite apart from what leaders say, inter-confessional activities are now widespread among the laity from both sides. The pro-life movement opposing liberal abortion practices is a thoroughly ecumenical enterprise involving Catholics, Protestants, Mormons, and also some Jews. Spiritual reading has long since crossed the ecumenical Rubicon, with popular Catholic authors such as Henri Nouwen read widely among Protestants, popular Protestants such as Eugene Peterson read widely among Catholics, and the Anglican savant C. S. Lewis read widely by Catholics and Protestants alike.

The New Ethnics

What might be called "ethnic churches" have become an ever-larger part of the Christian story. Where identifiable religious forms inherited from Britain and Northern Europe have faded into more general American patterns, African Americans have retained distinctive religious practices. In addition, Asian Americans and Hispanics have recently become increasingly important in the overall Christian picture.

Hispanics still remain largely identified with the Catholic church, but also reflect the profound changes of recent years. The American Catholic hierarchy concentrates much energy on reaching and encouraging the Catholic Hispanic population, in part because of long-existing practices of nominal participation and in part because of recent inroads by Protestants, especially Pentecostals. Predictions vary, but all observers see Hispanics becoming a larger, perhaps even a majority, presence in the American church over the next half-century.[22]

The activities and goals of Hispanic Catholics in the United States naturally reflect broader developments in Latin America. The assemblies of Latin American bishops at Medellín, Columbia, in 1968 and in

21. See, for example, Charles Colson and Richard John Neuhaus, eds., "Evangelicals and Catholics Together," *First Things* 43 (May 1994): 15-22.

22. Jay P. Dolan and Allan Figueroa Deck S.J., eds., *Hispanic Catholic Culture in the United States: Issues and Concerns* (Notre Dame: University of Notre Dame Press, 1994).

Puebla, Mexico, in 1979, focused Catholic energies on the crying needs of Latin America's poor. Neither Pope Paul VI nor Pope John Paul II favored Marxist solutions to the burgeoning urban poverty of Latin America, but both encouraged the church to act aggressively in bringing the gospel as well as material assistance to those in need. Such themes have resonated as well in areas of the United States with strong Hispanic populations. In the manner of earlier generations of Catholic immigrants, Hispanic Catholics are also finding ways of incorporating their ancestral traditions of devotion and festival in an American setting.[23]

Protestantism among American Hispanics has been given a tremendous boost by the Pentecostal movement. Hispanics took part in the earliest Pentecostal moments of Azusa Street, and as early as 1916, Puerto Ricans who had received the gift of tongues returned to their native land to establish a Pentecostal presence there. In the last quarter of the century, Pentecostal Hispanic churches have been among the fastest-growing churches in North America. Unlike the Presbyterians and Methodists, who hesitated to establish Spanish-speaking districts, Pentecostal denominations such as the Assemblies of God have regularly followed this practice, with the result that Hispanic sections of Pentecostal denominations flourish in California, Texas, the Southwest, and some northern urban centers.

The recent immigration of Asians is also working its effects on the American churches. Identification with Christianity is linked with immigration to the United States, with the result that almost all Asian-American populations (Korean, Chinese, Japanese, Vietnamese, Thai, and others) have a higher percentage of Christian allegiance than populations in the Asian lands. Korean Americans have been especially active in forming churches on the West Coast and in several major cities of the North, although Koreans, with all other Asian American Christian groups, face the very difficult problem of keeping their American-born young people satisfied with combined Asian and American religious practice. This so-called "1.5 generation" problem has affected all other immigrant communities as well, but has a particular effect

23. See, for example, Thomas A. Tweed, *Our Lady of the Exile: Diasporic Religion at a Cuban Catholic Shrine in Miami* (New York: Oxford University Press, 1997).

where Christian allegiance has been so strong among the immigrating cohorts.[24]

Shifting Ecclesiastical Strengths

Definite shifts have also been taking place in denominational adherence. Previously marginal groups have become larger and more important, while previously central denominations have moved toward the margins. The 1930s marked the beginning of the relative decline of the older, mainline Protestant churches. The public turmoil of the 1960s accelerated that decline. In general, the older, proprietary bodies that had done so much to shape American life in the nineteenth century struggled to adjust.[25] For some the difficulty seemed to be a top-heavy bureaucracy trying to run churches like corporations. For others controversy over beliefs seemed to impede vigorous action. The colleges and seminaries of these older, mostly Northern bodies were the centers of a generally liberal theology. That theology stressed human capacities more than traditional views of God's loving power. It tended to accent what humans could do for themselves in this life instead of how religion prepared people for heaven. Sometimes it waffled in providing moral guidelines for church members. To the extent that such beliefs prevailed in the older denominations, or were even thought to prevail, the churches lost credibility with some of their constituents and failed to recruit new members. By contrast, denominations that stressed traditional beliefs about the supernatural power of God and the reliability of the Bible, or that featured the newer Pentecostal emphases on the immediate action of the Holy Spirit, continued to expand.

24. See R. Stephen Warner and Judith G. Witner, eds., *Gatherings in Diaspora: Religious Communities and the New Immigration* (Philadelphia: Temple University Press, 1998).

25. See Ward Clark Roof and William McKinney, *American Mainline Religion* (New Brunswick, NJ: Rutgers University Press, 1987); John M. Mulder, Louis B. Weeks, and Milton J Coalter, eds., *The Presbyterian Presence: The Twentieth-Century Experience,* 6 vols. (Louisville, KY: Westminster/John Knox, 1990-1992); and Wade Clark Roof, *Spiritual Marketplace: Baby Boomers and the Remaking of American Religion* (Princeton: Princeton University Press, 1999).

Specific numbers provide some help in charting these changes.[26] The steady growth of the Catholic church has made it overwhelmingly the most important Christian denomination in the country. Where the national population grew 102% between 1940 and 1997, the number of Catholic adherents grew 188%. With over 62 million adherents in 1998, the Catholic church in the United States is larger than the total population of either the United Kingdom or France. Even if a large proportion of that Catholic population is nominal, the remainder constitutes a huge, vital force. At least some polling in the 1990s suggests that over half of American Catholics practice their faith with some consistency.

The greatest contrast to Catholic growth is mainline Protestant losses. Since 1960 (to 1997), and taking account also of denominational mergers of intervening years, the Presbyterian Church (USA) has suffered a net decline of about 500,000; the Episcopal Church a decline of 700,000; the United Church of Christ (which incorporates most of the Congregationalists) a decline of 800,000; the Disciples of Christ a decline of 900,000; and the United Methodist Church a decline of over two million members. It must be kept in mind that these are large denominations, so that, for example, the Methodists still enjoy over eight million members, and the others enjoy the adherence of from one to three million each. But the declines are still substantial.

The older ethnic churches — such as the Evangelical Lutheran Church in America, the Lutheran Church — Missouri Synod, the Wisconsin Evangelical Lutheran Synod, the Mennonite Church, the Christian Reformed Church, or the Baptist General Conference with its Swedish roots — have fared somewhat better, with some growing substantially after the Second World War. But the growth rate for such denominations has lagged considerably behind the growth rate of the national population at least since 1960.

The Protestant bodies whose rates of growth in recent decades have exceeded general population increases — sometimes far exceeded — are nearly all characterized by such labels as Bible-believing, born again, conservative, evangelical, fundamentalist, holiness, Pentecostal, or

---

26. A listing of Canadian and American denominations, along with current estimates of membership, is provided in Appendix A.

restorationist.[27] They include the Assemblies of God, the Christian and Missionary Alliance, the Church of God in Christ, the Seventh-day Adventists, the Church of the Nazarene, the Salvation Army, the Baptist Bible Fellowship International, the Churches of Christ, and several more. To provide comparisons with the older mainline churches, the Assemblies of God grew from 1960 to 1997 by nearly two million members, the black Pentecostal Church of God in Christ by at least that many millions, the Church of God (Cleveland, Tennessee) by about 600,000, the Seventh-day Adventists by nearly 500,000, and the Church of the Nazarene by about 300,000. During that same period, the Church of Jesus Christ of Latter-Day Saints (Mormons) added a net of 3.3 million members.

The largest Protestant denomination, the Southern Baptist Convention, underwent a bruising internal struggle during the 1970s and 1980s between a conservative faction seeking to reaffirm more staunchly supernaturalistic theology and more traditional social programs against a moderate faction that resembled the inclusive mainline Protestants of a previous generation.[28] It is indicative of more general trends among Protestants that the conservatives won that internal struggle, and that the Southern Baptist Convention, from 1960 to 1997, grew by nearly 6 million members and at a pace nearly 50 percent higher than the rate of national population growth.

Within the mix of Protestant churches, adherents of what might be called the new ethnic churches make up an increasingly large share. In 1996, the Gallup Poll reported that 58 percent of American adults identified themselves as Protestants (or about 110 million out of the country's approximately 190 million people over the age of 20). Of the Protestants, about one-sixth are African Americans. As noted, the number of Asian American and Hispanic Protestants is each into the millions.

Increasingly sophisticated procedures in survey research have

27. For a tour, see Randall Balmer, *Mine Eyes Have Seen the Glory: A Journey into the Evangelical Subculture in America,* 3rd ed. (New York: Oxford University Press, 2000).

28. See Bill Leonard, *God's Last and Only Hope: The Fragmentation of the Southern Baptist Convention* (Grand Rapids: Eerdmans, 1990); and Nancy Tatom Ammerman, *Baptist Battles: Social Change and Religious Conflict in the Southern Baptist Convention* (New Brunswick, NJ: Rutgers University Press, 1990).

helped researchers to conclude that about one in four Americans (or 25 percent) are now affiliated with a church from this network of conservative Protestant churches (that is, fundamentalist, evangelical, holiness, or Pentecostal). Not quite one in six (around 15 percent) are affiliated with the older denominations that used to be called the Protestant mainline.[29]

These denominational shifts seem to indicate that churches providing relatively clear boundaries for belief and practice, relatively sharp affirmation of the supernatural, and relatively more demands on their members have done better in modern America than those that have not.[30] It is important, however, to stress that such differences are only relative. Newer, more conservative denominations often develop their own in-grown preoccupations, while congregations and agencies of the older churches often retain great vigor of worship, teaching, and social service in many localities.

Broader Pentecostal-Charismatic Influences

Large-scale trends in denominational adherence tell something about the state of modern religion. Even more revealing are the many movements of reform and renewal that have emerged in a bewildering variety over the last decades.

Almost all Protestant denominations and large sections of the Catholic church have witnessed significant movements of spiritual renewal since the 1960s. For many of the traditional bodies, as well as many of the new, this development has led to fresh thought about the weekly worship service. Most of the denominations issued new hymnbooks in the last quarter of the century, and there have been serious efforts at liturgical reform guided by more thorough study of the Christian past.

29. See Lyman Kellstedt and John C. Green, "The Mismeasure of Evangelicals," *Books & Culture: A Christian Review,* Jan.-Feb. 1996, pp. 14-15.

30. On this subject, an important discussion was sparked by Dean M. Kelley, *Why Conservative Churches Are Growing* (New York: Harper & Row, 1972).

Far and away the most important changes in the regular worship services have been due to the broadening influence of Pentecostals and charismatics. The Pentecostal churches expanded very rapidly after the beginning of the century. But in those early decades, Pentecostal concentration on the special work of the Holy Spirit made them distinctive, even odd. Now, however, Pentecostal themes and Pentecostal leaders have joined the mainstream. The Assemblies of God, a majority white denomination with considerable strength among Hispanics and Korean Americans, enrolls about 2.5 million members, and so is as big as or bigger than the denominations descended from the first major Protestant churches in America, the Episcopalians and the Congregationalists. Its pastors and leaders play an increasingly large role outside their own denomination. The largely black Church of God in Christ is about twice as large as the Assemblies of God, which makes it, after the National Baptist Convention, U.S.A., Incorporated, the largest of the predominately African American denominations. There are also many smaller denominations of "classical Pentecostals," which emphasize the present-day work of the Holy Spirit in healing, ecstatic worship, and the gift of tongues.

Pentecostal worship has traditionally been exuberant, spontaneous, and subjective. In the early decades of the movement, a great quantity of new hymns appeared as expression of the heightened emotions resulting from direct contact with the Spirit. But Pentecostal patterns of worship and religious practice began to have a broader impact on the wider religious world only after World War II. One factor in the increasing prominence of Pentecostalism was the rise in public meetings for healing. Evangelists William Branham (1909-1965) and Oral Roberts (b. 1918) were the figures best known in that "healing revival," but there were many others as well. These preachers, all from Pentecostal backgrounds, fanned out over especially the South, Southwest, and West to promote the healing of physical ills by a special work of the Holy Spirit.[31]

The second, even more important development was the beginning of the charismatic movement in the late 1950s. This movement promoted some of the emphases of classical Pentecostalism, but it pro-

---

31. See David Edwin Harrell, Jr., *All Things Are Possible: The Healing and Charismatic Revivals in Modern America* (Bloomington: Indiana University Press, 1975).

moted them in typical American fashion by presenting a kind of spiritual smorgasbord to sample as individuals chose. Charismatic emphases included a stress on personal conversion, physical healing, speaking in tongues, participation in small group fellowships, and freshly written songs — but always as a range of open possibilities rather than formal requirements. Charismatic (in the other sense of the term) leaders have also played a major role in the charismatic (in the religious sense of the term) movement.

Charismatic renewal has taken many forms. It has provided a bridge of common associations, songs, and attitudes between Pentecostals and non-Pentecostals. The charismatic movement also entered the Catholic church, where it continues to exert a persistent influence. More often it took shape in such parachurch organizations as the Full Gospel Business Men's Fellowship, International, founded as a nondenominational association by Demos Sharkarian in California in 1952.

Somewhat later associations of churches drew on the emphases of the charismatic movement, including a network of Calvary Chapels under the leadership of Chuck Smith. Smith in 1965 became the minister of a small independent congregation in Costa Mesa, California, and immediately opened the church door to "hippies" and others with countercultural affinities. Through a mix of informality, soft rock music, biblical exposition, and the standard charismatic options, the Calvary Chapel network has grown to include six hundred chapels around the world. A similar story can be told about the Association of Vineyard Churches, which was connected to Smith's Calvary Chapel in its early days. Under the leadership of John Wimber, this California-based evangelical movement stressed divine healing and promoted nontraditional forms of worship. It has grown to over three hundred congregations with more than 100,000 members, many outside of the United States. More generally, charismatic influences spread into almost all of the established Protestant denominations as well as the Roman Catholic Church.[32]

32. A fine book dealing mostly with the Calvary Chapel and Vineyard movements is Donald E. Miller, *Reinventing American Protestantism: Christianity in the New Millennium* (Berkeley: University of California Press, 1997).

Effects of charismatic influence include greater concern for specific acts of the Holy Spirit, but even more a general turn toward subjective spirituality, even in churches where specific Pentecostal teachings are unknown. The great changes in church music that began to take place in the 1960s were almost all related to charismatic influences. Many congregations and fellowships began to sing newly written choruses and scripture texts set to catchy melodies. By the 1980s, church musicians were exploiting a full range of pop, folk, and even rock styles as settings for this new wave of song. The increasingly common practice of singing with a combination of guitar, drums, and synthesizer has begun to push aside the organ as the instrument of choice in many Protestant and some Catholic churches. Songs projected by an overhead onto a screen have supplemented or replaced the hymnbook in many places. The same set of religious forces has provided the foundation for a multimillion-dollar industry of contemporary Christian music. This industry has made stars out of individuals such as Amy Grant and groups such as D. C. Talk.

A focal point for charismatic renewal was provided in the 1990s by well-publicized experiences at two local churches. In early 1994 at a Vineyard Fellowship that met near Toronto's international airport, a series of nightly meetings began that featured what adherents considered special manifestations of the Holy Spirit. Those attending participated in "holy laughter" and many were "slain in the Spirit" (falling backwards into a prostrate position during a time of concentrated spiritual release). Soon people were coming from all around the world, including many places in the United States, to experience this "Toronto Blessing."[33]

A somewhat different series of meetings began in June 1995 at the Brownsville Assembly of God in Pensacola, Florida. Although this congregation was part of a classical Pentecostal denomination, its revival meetings featured a traditional evangelical emphasis on repentance from sin, faith in Christ, and resolution to live a godly life. Under the direction of pastor John Kilpatrick and evangelist Steve Hill, the meet-

---

33. See James Beverley, *Holy Laughter and the Toronto Blessing* (Grand Rapids: Zondervan, 1995).

ings were held four nights a week and often lasted into the early hours of the next day. Charismatic music and Pentecostal phenomena were standard features. By September 1997, cumulative attendance had reached 1.7 million.[34] These dramatic manifestations of intense religion in Toronto and Pensacola were both a reprise of previous American revivals and an adjustment of traditional revivalism to the sensibilities of the late twentieth century.

A development related to the charismatic movement, or at least to the relaxed institutional framework in which charismatic emphases flourish, is the rise of "megachurches." Megachurches are spiritual shopping malls designed intentionally to provide religious resources for people caught in the tense circumstances of modern life. The model for such congregations is the Willow Creek Community Church in South Barrington, Illinois. It began in 1975 with services in a rented movie theater as an outreach for youth and their parents. The purpose of its leaders, including founding pastor Bill Hybels, is explained on its colorful Web page on the Internet: "to build a church that would speak the language of our modern culture and encourage non-believers to investigate Christianity at their own pace, free from the traditional trappings of religion that tend to chase them away."[35] The Willow Creek founders took an extensive survey to find out what kept people away from church and discovered that incessant appeals for money and practices unconnected to life during the rest of the week were the main culprits. From the start, Willow Creek avoided churchy language and sought professional standards of music and drama. It also offered specialized services to such segments of its audience as the unmarried or divorced, mothers, the unemployed, and dozens of special interest groups. Within a year, weekly attendance was over a thousand, and by the mid-1990s as many as fifteen thousand were attending weekend services on its 127-acre "campus." The Willow Creek church building, complete with its 750-seat atrium/food court, is hard to distinguish from the upscale corporate headquarters sprinkled throughout the northwest suburbs of Chicago.

34. Steve Rabey, "Pensacola Outpouring Keeps Gushing," *Christianity Today*, March 3, 1997, pp. 54-57.
35. www.willowcreek.org

The church is non-traditional in almost all its forms, but it — and at least some of its many imitators — has provided a meaningful religious message to suburbanites of the Baby Boom generation and their children, many of whom find themselves stranded by prosperity, mobility, and the American elixir of self-determination.[36]

Critics of the charismatic movement, the megachurches, and other Protestant adaptations to modern sensibilities are not shy about expressing their disapproval.[37] They charge that charismatic worship focuses on the self and not on God. They see the megachurches as catering to the transitory, felt needs of a pleasure-driven population. They hold that modern innovations obscure the realities of human sinfulness and the holiness of God and so make it impossible to grasp the true character of divine grace.

Contemporary debate over these modern innovations resembles earlier controversies between Puritans and the English state church, Methodists and the original American church establishments, Protestant modernists and their opponents at the end of the nineteenth century, and Pentecostals and their critics early in the twentieth century. The debates are important because they address the twin but sometimes competing strengths of American Christianity: connections with the historic Christian faith and a drive to regain adherents to that faith within the world's most liberal and most democratic culture.

It is still too early to say what the larger significance of the Pentecostal and charismatic renewal movements means. What happens in the rest of the world makes a difference; many of the fastest growing forms of Christianity in Africa, China, Korea, India, and Latin America are Pentecostal or charismatic in some fashion. It may even not be far-fetched to say that the last third of the twentieth century has been the age in America of charismatic spirituality, just as the colonial period was dominated by Puritan spirituality, Methodist spirituality exerted a

36. See G. A. Pritchard, *Willow Creek Seeker Services: Evaluating a New Way of Doing Church* (Grand Rapids: Baker Books, 1996).

37. The most substantial theological critique is found in the work of David F. Wells, for example, *No Place for Truth; or, Whatever Happened to Evangelical Theology?* (Grand Rapids: Eerdmans, 1993), and *Losing Our Virtue: Why the Church Must Recover Its Moral Vision* (Grand Rapids: Eerdmans, 1998).

very wide influence during most of the nineteenth century, and the first two-thirds of the twentieth century were dominated by forms of Baptist and mainline spirituality.

Recent events are difficult to place in proper perspective, and historical interpretations are not reliable for predicting the future. The tremendous diversity of the American churches makes all generalizations suspect. Yet at the start of the twenty-first century, it seems likely that a few prominent trends will continue to influence the shape of Christian faith in America for the future. The number of Roman Catholics will continue to rise, and the Catholic presence will be more heavily influenced by its Hispanic components. Free-flowing Pentecostal and charismatic styles will go on spreading their influence far beyond the explicitly Pentecostal churches. The most important Christian schisms will increasingly follow theological-ideological lines rather than denominational lines. Especially as the historic Catholic-Protestant chasm continues to narrow, Christians will be linked to fellow believers from other denominations according to shared convictions; the result is likely to be even further erosion of the importance of denominations as such in American Christian life. These predictions are plausible extrapolations from recent history, but the future will, of course, tell its own story.

CHAPTER NINE

Theology

A s with every other aspect of American religious life, the writing of Christian theology has been decisively influenced by the American context. Foreign visitors, even when sympathetic, have repeatedly noted the ways that American life has affected Christian patterns of thought. In a book on religion in America published in 1975, Claude-Jean Bertrand, who has written widely on the English-speaking world, gave much credit to the churches for making the United States unique among the nations of the world: "it is the only one in history which has mixed all the major ethnic groups and built the strongest power on the globe without falling under the boot of a tyrant or of a military caste." At the same time, Bertrand was not completely impressed, for his research caused him to ask troubling questions about habits of American religious reflection: "The laxity, the syncretism, the utilitarianism, the secularization, the nationalization of the church — are these compatible with a genuine faith and transcendent realities? In the absence of profound thinking, of a tragic sense, and of mystic ecstasy, has not America destroyed religion from the inside?"[1] Similarly, the German theologian Dietrich Ritschl, after considerable travel in America and elsewhere in the English-speaking world, had nothing but praise for the

---

1. Claude-Jean Bertrand, *Les Eglises aux Etats-Unis* (Paris: Presses Universitaires de France, 1975), pp. 125-26.

zeal with which Americans founded and maintained institutions of re-ligious higher learning, "often with astounding sacrifices and marvel-ous vision." At the same time, Ritschl was not impressed by American efforts in theology: "The practical effects of mixing a misconceived pragmatism with the certainty inspired by the optimism of the Enlight-enment that they know and possess the truth of the gospel are still to-day only too blatant." Moreover, there was need for self-criticism, espe-cially for asking "why twentieth-century America still maintains an astonishingly unbroken connection to the ideals of the eighteenth cen-tury which cannot possibly solve the problems of the second half of our century."[2]

Whether such criticisms and similar critiques made by American insiders about the character of American Christian thinking[3] are en-tirely fair, they point to the fact that observers of Christian theology in America regularly look to the environment as an explanation for weak-nesses. That instinct is sound. The history of Christian theology in America has been profoundly affected by the distinctly American cir-cumstances in which it has taken place. This chapter cannot offer a full history, but it can highlight four of the most important ways in which the American environment has shaped the thought of the Christian churches: first, by imprinting a colonial character on much of that thought; second, by exaggerating the role of science for theology; third, by expanding opportunities for populist theological innovation; and fourth, by stimulating important mediations between classical theo-logical traditions and the American churches. Comment on these mat-ters leads naturally to several examples of American Christian theology that, however much they may have arisen in American circumstances, still offer potential value for communities elsewhere in the world.

---

2. Dietrich Ritschl, *Theologie in den neuen Welt* (Munich: Chr. Kaiser Verlag, 1981), pp. 19, 23-24.

3. For example, John Tracy Ellis, *American Catholics and the Intellectual Life* (Chicago: Heritage Foundation, 1956); and Mark A. Noll, *The Scandal of the Evangelical Mind* (Grand Rapids: Eerdmans, 1994).

American Theology as Colonial

Nowhere has America's status as a colony of Europe been more evident than in its formal Christian theology. The United States has become a world leader economically and the key nation in western politics; it sets world standards in several sports and is also the prime disseminator of popular culture. Yet in realms of Christian thought, colonial patterns have been very difficult to break. The colonial situation is visible in an institutional way among Roman Catholics and the Orthodox, but prevails just as strongly among Protestants.

Catholic theologians in America have, with a few exceptions to be noted later, been mostly content to follow the guidance of European intellectual life. The American promotion of Neo-Thomism from roughly 1870 to 1960 is the most important example of dependence on cues from the Vatican and European theologians. The Americanism crisis at the end of the nineteenth century amounted to a reminder for Catholics in the United States not to stray too far into indigenous theologizing. In the twentieth century, American Catholics, again with a few exceptions, have done better at popularizing the work of Jacques Maritain, Etienne Gilson, Karl Rahner, Hans Urs von Balthasar, Hans Küng, and other prominent European theologians than in promoting their own ideas.

Much the same situation has prevailed among the Orthodox, with the major difference that the European theology influential among American Orthodoxy has appeared in the person of refugees as well as through the medium of European books. As noted in the previous chapter, a distinguished line of Russian theologians — especially Alexander Schmemann, Georges Florovosky, and John Meyendorff — has been crucial for giving theological direction to twentieth-century American Orthodoxy.

To notice that theological inspiration for American Catholics and the Orthodox has come mostly from Europe is not necessarily to make a value judgment. In fact, strong arguments can be made that the greatest contribution of Catholics to the general writing of theology in America has been the fidelity to tradition represented by the influence of European theology and theologians. The American desire for novelty and the American eagerness to subject all theological inheritances to the standards of popular culture can be detrimental to theological integrity. However, if European-based theology is, by many judgments, simply superior to comparable American efforts and therefore worthy of emulation in the United States, it reinforces the impression of America as still a colony deferring to the insights of the Old World.

Among Protestants, European theology has exerted the same kind of influence, although diffused in many more directions. During the nineteenth century, careful reading of European authors became an inspiration for what has appeared to later observers to be some of the most interesting theology of the century. Thus Horace Bushnell (1802-1876) began to adjust New England Calvinism in the direction of modern romanticism by heeding insights from Germany's Friedrich Schleiermacher and, even more, from England's Samuel Taylor Coleridge. Similarly, the German Reformed theologian John W. Nevin (1803-1886) proposed a theology stressing the importance of the historic church and the sacraments in part because he was influenced by the German "mediating theologies" of Isaak Dorner and J. A. W. Neander.[4] Later in the century, the works of Albrecht Ritschl, Adolf Harnack, and Ernst Troeltsch were perhaps even more important for progressive or modernist theologians in the mainline Protestant denominations.[5] In the twentieth century, the influence of neo-orthodox theology, especially from Emil Brunner and Karl Barth, has probably been more important in university-level theological considerations than the work of any American.[6] The one exception, but an exception that supports the generalization, is Paul Tillich (1886-1965), who in America did gain a wide following with his analysis of *kairos* moments when the divine breaks into the temporal. But Tillich's American reputation was enhanced greatly by his status as an immigrant from Germany. In the latter decades of the twen-

---

4. See William DiPuccio, *The Interior Sense of Scripture: The Sacred Hermeneutics of John W. Nevin* (Macon, GA: Mercer University Press, 1998).

5. See William R. Hutchison, *The Modernist Impulse in American Protestantism* (Cambridge: Harvard University Press, 1976).

6. See Dennis Voskuil, "America Encounters Karl Barth, 1919-1939," *Fides et Historia* 12 (Spring 1980): 61-74.

tieth century, themes from the liberation theologians of Latin America were influential among American Catholics and, to a lesser degree, among Protestants.[7]

For the formal study of Scripture, it is only a slight exaggeration to suggest that a history of biblical scholarship in America since about 1850 could be written as a competition between German and British influences. That is, American biblical scholarship has been divided between those who are strong on deductions from first principles, open to influences from hermeneutical theory, and tending toward theological liberalism (that is, the German influence) and those who emphasize a chaste empiricism, express confidence in the possibilities of historical research, and tend toward a defense of orthodoxy (that is, the British influence).[8]

Popular theology has been fueled by a host of American writers, but even in this domain the influence of Europe is great. In the nineteenth century, works by the Scottish minister-scholar Thomas Chalmers (1780-1847) were read widely, as were European books on the life of Jesus, books growing out of England's high-church Anglican Oxford Movement, and books doing battle on the Bible.[9] In the second half of the twentieth century, a good case could be made that the German Roman Catholic Hans Küng (b. 1928) and the Anglican evangelical John R. W. Stott (b. 1921) have been among America's most influential popular religious authors. The pattern of significant modern influence from overseas was well established by England's G. K. Chesterton (1874-1936) earlier in the century. That pattern has certainly continued, as the tremendous American fascination with the re-

---

7. See Donald G. Musto, *Liberation Theologies: A Research Guide* (New York: Garland, 1991); and Mar Peter-Raoul et al., eds., *Yearning to Be Free: Liberation Theologies in the United States* (Maryknoll, NY: Orbis, 1990).

8. See Mark A. Noll, *Between Faith and Criticism: Evangelicals, Scholarship, and the Bible in America,* expanded ed. (Grand Rapids: Baker, 1991).

9. See Mark A. Noll, "Thomas Chalmers in America (1830-1917)," *Church History* 66 (Dec. 1997): 762-77; Daniel L. Pals, *The Victorian "Lives" of Jesus* (San Antonio, TX: Trinity University Press, 1982); and Diana Hochstedt Butler, *Standing Against the Whirlwind: Evangelical Episcopalians in Nineteenth-Century America* (New York: Oxford University Press, 1995), pp. 93-135.

ligious writings of Oxford don C. S. Lewis (1898-1963) testifies so powerfully.[10]

It is important to repeat that noting America's status as a theological colony of Europe is not a value judgment. Books imported from Europe have, for the most part, served American audiences very well. The point worth making is as much cultural as theological: during a period when American products, expectations, and political values have exerted an immense influence on the rest of the world, in the domain of formal theology the United States remains as much acted upon as acting.

The Unusual Importance of Science for Theology

Science — or at least a popular perception of the authority of science — has played an unusually important role in American theology. The dynamics of the American Revolution cast into doubt all forms of traditional authority inherited from Europe, including the authority of historic churches and ecclesiastical traditions. In realms of intellectual discourse, principles of the moderate Scottish Enlightenment associated with Francis Hutcheson (1694-1746) and Thomas Reid (1710-1796) provided American thinkers with apparently secure intellectual foundations for reconstructing theology and the churches without the need to rely on tradition.[11] These Enlightenment principles included a strong Baconian appeal to empiricism, a belief that the human mind could be studied objectively as natural philosophers studied the material world, a great respect for the science of Sir Isaac Newton as the best way to secure any sort of knowledge, and a great confidence in reasoned discourse for establishing intellectual first principles. Armed with these weapons, a generation of American Christian thinkers diligently employed rational apologetics, natural theology, and common-sense interpretation of the Bible to defend Christianity and to reconstitute

10. In 1998, the year of Lewis' centennial, it was estimated that at least 50 million copies of his books were in print, with the United States certainly the greatest contributor to that publishing phenomenon.

11. See especially Henry F. May, *The Enlightenment in America* (New York: Oxford University Press, 1976).

the churches.[12] For them, scientific reasoning replaced Europe's traditional props for the churches. Their number included college leaders like Congregationalist Timothy Dwight of Yale (president 1795-1817), Unitarian Henry Ware, Sr., of Harvard (professor of divinity, 1805-1845), Presbyterian Samuel Stanhope Smith at Princeton (president, 1794-1812), and, somewhat later, Baptist Francis Wayland of Brown University (president, 1827-1855).[13] Energetic frontier organizers like Alexander Campbell of the Churches of Christ may have been even more influential in promoting commonsense reasoning as a substitute for church tradition.[14] One of the most important reasons for the success of Protestantism in the period between 1790 and 1865 was the skill with which these leaders convinced other Americans that Christianity met the highest standards of modern scientific discourse. Church traditions, inherited ecclesiastical practices, and the dictates of bishops who had never faced a popular election might lead the church astray, but the pure voice of scientific reason would not.

With this background, it should not be surprising that a defining era in theological history came in the generation after 1860, when more and more Americans began to view science not as the handmaiden for theology but as an autonomous power in itself. The publication in 1859 of Charles Darwin's *Origin of Species* posed a particular

12. This connection has been thoroughly explored in a series of outstanding books, including Theodore Dwight Bozeman, *Protestants in an Age of Science: The Baconian Ideal and Antebellum American Religious Thought* (Chapel Hill: University of North Carolina Press, 1977); Herbert Hovenkamp, *Science and Religion in America, 1800-1860* (Philadelphia: University of Pennsylvania Press, 1978); E. Brooks Holifield, *The Gentlemen Theologians: American Theology in Southern Culture, 1795-1860* (Durham, NC: Duke University Press, 1978); and Walter H. Conser, Jr., *God and the Natural World: Religion and Science in Antebellum America* (Columbia: University of South Carolina Press, 1993).

13. See Daniel Walker Howe, *The Unitarian Conscience: Harvard Moral Philosophy, 1805-1861* (Cambridge: Harvard University Press, 1970); and Mark A. Noll, *Princeton and the Republic, 1768-1822: The Search for a Christian Enlightenment in the Era of Samuel Stanhope Smith* (Princeton: Princeton University Press, 1989).

14. See Richard T. Hughes and C. Leonard Allen, *Illusions of Innocence: Protestant Primitivism in America, 1630-1875* (Chicago: University of Chicago Press, 1988); and Richard T. Hughes, *Reviving the Ancient Faith: The Story of Churches of Christ in America* (Grand Rapids: Eerdmans, 1996), pp. 1-134.

challenge.[15] Darwin seemed to embody rigorous, critical thought of the sort highly esteemed by American church leaders. But Darwin's science did not celebrate God's design of the natural world, as these leaders had done. Rather, he proposed that randomness, not God, provided the basic mechanism for understanding the natural world.

The problem was not evolution as such, since many Protestants felt it was possible to show how God could have used evolutionary processes to bring the world into existence. Benjamin B. Warfield (1851-1921) of Princeton Theological Seminary enjoyed a reputation as one of the country's most conservative theologians; he was, for example, known as a fierce defender of the idea that the Bible was "inerrant," or absolutely truthful in all of its statements if interpreted correctly. Yet Warfield also felt that this view of the Bible could be adjusted to theories of evolution accounting for the development of life, including even human beings.[16]

The problem was rather that evolution as a grand scientific scheme was being used increasingly to undermine, rather than to support, traditional views of God and his design of the world. In prominent universities, such leaders as the educational theorist and public philosopher John Dewey (1859-1952) simply dropped the earlier American effort to demonstrate the harmony of science and Scripture. Other leaders of American universities in the last third of the century acted even more aggressively. Andrew Dickson White, the founding president of Cornell University, vowed that his institution would "afford an asylum for Science — where truth shall be sought for truth's sake, where it shall not be the main purpose of the Faculty to stretch or cut sciences exactly to fit 'Revealed Religion'."[17] It was not so much that university intellectuals were giving up the idea of a deity, but that for at least some influential voices, the deity was now defined as scientific method.

15. See James R. Moore, *The Post-Darwinian Controversies . . . 1870-1900* (New York: Cambridge University Press, 1979); and Jon H. Roberts, *Darwin and the Divine in America: Protestant Intellectuals and Organic Evolution, 1859-1900* (Madison: University of Wisconsin Press, 1988).

16. See David N. Livingstone and Mark A. Noll, eds., *B. B. Warfield: Evolution, Science and Scripture — Selected Writings* (Grand Rapids: Baker, 2000).

17. White was also the author of the widely read *A History of the Warfare of Science and Theology in Christendom,* originally published in 1896.

The new learning, in other words, disrupted the settled relationship between Protestantism and the nation's intellectual life. It began the process that eventually ended Protestant control of higher education.[18] It opened the door to secular interpretations of life. It opened up a possibility that had barely existed in America before the last third of the century: the willingness of some intellectuals to publicly question the existence of God.[19]

A parallel challenge in the same era concerned the Scriptures. Much of the new scholarship from the European continent seemed to undermine the confidence most American Protestants had placed in the truthfulness of the Bible. A rapid increase in knowledge about the ancient world was one of the factors that led some scholars to look on Christianity as merely one of the many similar religions of the ancient Near East. An increased willingness to view historical writing as a product of the historian's worldview led other academics to question some or all of the stories of miracles in the Bible. Advances in the study of ancient texts convinced still more scholars that much of the Bible was actually composed, or at least collected, many centuries later than traditional views had held.

The critical factor in the new approaches to Scripture was, however, the more general religious climate. For many scholars, confidence in the ability of scientific research to reveal new truths replaced confidence in the older understanding of the Bible. Scripture was being transformed from an authority supported by scientific investigation into a human document interpreted by the scientific authority of advanced scholarship.

In the twentieth century, the central role of science in broader theological considerations was illustrated by strife over "creation science."[20] "Creation science" is the theory, made popular by a long line of effective speakers and authors, that a literal interpretation of the cosmological sections of the book of Genesis provides guidance for a modern sci-

---

18. See George M. Marsden, *The Soul of the American University: From Protestant Establishment to Established Nonbelief* (New York: Oxford University Press, 1994).

19. See James Turner, *Without God, Without Creed: The Origins of Unbelief in America* (Baltimore: Johns Hopkins University Press, 1985).

20. See Ronald L. Numbers, *The Creationists* (New York: Knopf, 1992).

entific understanding of the world. "Creationists" also contend that if scientists approached the physical world objectively, they would be able to demonstrate the recent creation of the earth in such a way as to support a literal interpretation of the Genesis account. Discussion of the merits of this case has almost always been overshadowed by intense public struggle aimed at enlisting the prestige of science on behalf of traditional religion or on behalf of progressive secular opinion. The result has been a much greater salience in America concerning evolution and "creation science" than in any other Western society. The main historical reason is a heritage in which scientific procedures and conclusions have taken on an outsized importance because of the absence of other normative authorities used to defend the truthfulness of religious claims. Monarchies, history, and tradition may lead people astray, but not — so Americans tend to think — science.

Populist Theological Innovation

If a particular set of American conditions has exaggerated the role of science in theology, similar conditions have opened the door to many opportunities for popular theological innovation. Without a national state church, with few widely revered theological traditions, with no centralized scheme of national education, with all of the denominations compelled to enter into vigorous popular competition for adherents, with innovations in communications implemented by ordinary people, and with significant amounts of wealth widely distributed and available for establishing colleges, publishing houses, newspapers, and other means of disseminating ideas, the United States has been a very fertile medium for popular theologies.

In the early decades of the United States, for example, the growing influence of Methodist theology arose directly from the ability of Francis Asbury and his itinerating colleagues to exploit the open spaces of America to establish Methodist cells, circuits, publishing networks, and churches. The dominant theology of the colonial period had been Calvinistic, with a strong emphasis on God's control over the path that sinners took from the self to God. George Whitefield innovated in many things, but in his theology he held resolutely to Calvinism. For Whitefield, humans responded to God's initiatives, rather than originated the move to God themselves. The Methodists, as Arminians, shared many convictions with the Calvinists — belief in the holy Trinity, belief in the Bible as a revelation from God, belief that God redeemed sinners by his grace, but they differed in maintaining a stronger sense of human capability. Methodists believed that people had been given freedom by God to choose for or against the offer of salvation. With their founder John Wesley they also held that faithful exercise of the will could move a person toward a position of Christian "perfection" (or an end to willful sin after conversion). Because of the rapid proliferation of Methodism in the United States, these emphases on human capability and the possibility of a higher form of Christian life after conversion enjoyed wider currency than anywhere else in the Western world.

Several of the other most important theologians and theological movements of the nineteenth and twentieth century also developed "from below," from the circles of ordinary people who, if usually not beneficiaries of formal education, nonetheless mastered popular organs of communication, understood popular religious psychology, and were themselves gripped by a powerful religious vision. For example, Phoebe Palmer's account of "holiness unto the Lord" was not fortified by the intellectual resources that had already been present in antebellum America, but her teaching had a greater effect on later generations than the work of any contemporary academic theologian. The same can be said of Charles Finney, although his scholarly aspirations went higher than Palmer's, as indicated by the publication of his *Lectures on Systematic Theology* in 1846. Yet the considerable influence exerted by the common-sense Arminianism of this work, and the much greater influence of his *Lectures on Revivals of Religion* (1835), lay in their power to compel the thinking of the ordinary laity.

The same kind of widespread theological influence has been exerted by two contrasting popular theological systems of the late nineteenth and early twentieth century: dispensational premillennialism and Pentecostalism. The two are joined in their great debt to the English Bible as popularly studied and preached, but are in many other ways quite different. Dispensationalism, the theology that drove the fundamentalist movement and that lies behind such widespread modern American phenomena as the "creation science" movement, offers a rational account of the interlocking character of biblical propositions, especially those concerning the Second Coming of Christ.[21] It grew out of classical Calvinism, but as modified by the nineteenth-century founders of the Plymouth Brethren, especially John Nelson Darby (1800-1882), who in 1827 resigned his position as an Anglican rector in order to take up an influential ministry of travel and preaching. For the Plymouth Brethren, the modern world was marked by a precipitous falling away from God. Their response was to abandon formally organized churches and to place hope in a dispersed invisible church made up of God's faithful remnant. Dispensational theology never caught on at America's elite universities or seminaries, but it was a huge popular success that drove the activities of conference speakers, lay theological institutes, prophecy conferences, popular magazines, and the publication of thousands of books. Its confidence in both the literal meaning of Scripture and in the ability of lay people to understand the Bible fitted it perfectly to traditional patterns of American Protestant life.

Pentecostalism has been the affective counterpart to dispensationalism. Based on intense longing for the "latter rain" of revival in the Holy Spirit prophesied in Joel 2:23, the movement identified the gift of tongues as the sign of the infilling of the Holy Spirit. Again, academically respectable theology was never a key to the movement, but a powerful message brought by gifted ordinary speakers to eager ordinary audiences was. The pragmatic success of the movement in giving hope to a wide spectrum of society, in providing psychological stability in the midst of day-to-day vicissitudes, and in offering the gratification of direct communion with God the Holy Spirit stimulated its dramatic expansion in the United States and around the world. Neither dispensationalism nor Pentecostalism has ever appeared respectable in academic environs, but each has attracted far more adherents and driven far more practical religious activity than any academically respectable theology of the twentieth century.

---

21. See Timothy P. Weber, *Living in the Shadow of the Second Coming: American Premillennialism, 1875-1982* (Chicago: University of Chicago Press, 1987).

A similar process has empowered a host of more sectarian movements in American history. The Church of Jesus Christ of Latter-day Saints (Mormons), Seventh-day Adventism, Christian Science, the Jehovah's Witnesses, and the World Wide Church of God are only some of the many religious movements that have sprung up in the short history of the United States. All of these movements possess clarity of theological vision, often elaborated in surprising detail to treat questions of epistemology, metaphysics, and ethical casuistry, as well as central religious concerns. Their claims of special revelation — usually to the group's founder — makes them unacceptable to the broad range of Christian churches. But their dynamism in promoting those claims have made them powerful religious forces. Sometimes, as with the Mormons in Utah and Idaho, they have become the dominant religion in a single region. More generally, they have existed on the margin of society, but with great attraction for hundreds of thousands of ordinary Americans.

America's populist theologies have never become a force in elite educational institutions, but they have triumphed among the American people at large. Several of these popular American theologies have also meant a great deal in Latin America, Africa, and the Far East, as waves of religious influence spread out alongside American economic and cultural influence.

Mediations of Classical Theology

As a parallel to populist theological innovation, much of the best formal theology in American history might be called elite popularization. This is theology that embodies high academic standards, is written in dialogue with major theological voices in the United States and Europe, and has been read with appreciation by significant ecclesiastical communities. If this kind of theology does not gain widespread attention from secular intellectuals and remains important mostly to those who share the theologian's intellectual and religious perspective, this kind of academically mediated theology has provided effective theological anchorage for many religious communities.

The nineteenth century was the great period for such work.[22] Trinitarian New England Congregationalists during the Revolutionary period, led by Joseph Bellamy (1719-1790) and Samuel Hopkins (1721-1803), showed how historic Calvinism could be broadened to accommodate Revolutionary notions of law and moral responsibility.[23] In the next theological generation, a broader range of New England theologians made further adjustments to the Puritan tradition in an effort to offer their communities theological self-understanding in an era of rapid cultural change. The most important of these theologians was Nathaniel William Taylor (1786-1858) of the Yale Divinity School, who adjusted Calvinist tradition to meet the need for a theology of revivalism. The Unitarian William Ellery Channing (1780-1842) made even more changes in Calvinism's historic views of human nature and of Christ as divine, but also communicated his views very effectively to the increasingly wealthy upper classes of New England. In the middle decades of the nineteenth century, several theologians propounded other versions of Calvinism and so contributed to the general sway of a Reformed perspective as the dominant religious discourse until late in the century. From Princeton Theological Seminary, Charles Hodge (1797-1878) gained a powerful reputation for thorough, often polemical, exposition of a historic Calvinist theology. The Christocentric New York Presbyterian Henry Boynton Smith (1815-1877) drew more directly on European mediating theologies, but shared many of Hodge's concerns. R. L. Dabney (1820-1898) and James Henley Thornwell (1812-1862) were Southern Presbyterians whose defense of slavery damaged their later reputations, but in their day they provided a wide range of Southerners with expert tutelage in traditional Reformed thought. John Williamson Nevin was joined by the Swiss-born, German-educated Philip Schaff (1819-1893) as the leading theologians at the German Reformed Seminary in Mercersburg, Pennsylvania. Because Nevin and Schaff made greater use of European organic theology, featured the sacra-

---

22. For a general account, see Bruce Kuklick, *Churchmen and Philosophers: From Jonathan Edwards to John Dewey* (New Haven: Yale University Press, 1985).

23. See Mark Valeri, *Law and Providence in Joseph Bellamy's New England: The Origins of the New Divinity in Revolutionary America* (New York: Oxford University Press, 1994).

ments prominently, and explored the development of theology over the centuries, they won increased attention as parallel themes became more important in twentieth-century academic theology.

Later in the century, still others offered their respective ecclesiastical communities reliable guidance in negotiating between traditional viewpoints and contemporary American issues. Among Presbyterians, the conservative Benjamin Breckinridge Warfield (1851-1921) and the moderately liberal Charles A. Briggs (1841-1913) shared an ability to master vast quantities of exegetical, historical, and theological materials in making their arguments. White Baptists, whose growth was continuing at a rapid pace, enjoyed the services of several distinguished theologians. In the North, A. H. Strong (1836-1921) adapted a cautious account of evolution to his moderately Calvinist views. In the South, the distinguished educator and leader of the Southern Baptist Convention E. Y. Mullins (1860-1928) combined a romantic sense of human dependence on God with an effective restatement of conservative Protestant principles.

Few of these respected theologians exerted much influence overseas. One exception was Charles Hodge, who was read in Canada, Scotland, and Northern Ireland, but only among his fellow Presbyterians. Otherwise, the influence of these worthy theologians was mostly restricted to their individual ecclesiastical communities.

In the twentieth century, the evolution of formal theology in the nation's universities and elite seminaries had the ironic effect of strengthening its academic respectability while weakening its appeal among the public. Yet several individuals carried on the earlier tradition of mediating the discourse of elite religious thinking to specific Christian communities. One of the first women to participate in this once almost exclusively male activity was Georgia Harkness (1891-1974), who effectively blended philosophical personalism and neo-orthodox elements into her own Methodist tradition. Her fellow Methodist Albert Outler (1908-1989) enlisted intensive study of Patristics and of John Wesley to serve the same purposes. For the neo-evangelicals who arose out of Northern fundamentalism in the 1930s and 1940s, Carl F. H. Henry (b. 1913) provided an able exposition of moderately rational Reformed perspectives in his wide-ranging work as editor and author.

In the American environment, it is tempting to neglect the contribution of these mediating theologians. More obviously influential in the public at large have been the popularizers; more influential in the twentieth-century university have been the elite religious thinkers who write for their academic peers. But the extensive number, intellectual stability, and ecclesiastical service of the mediating theologians make them a significant American phenomenon. It could even be that the large quantity and sturdy quality of such mediating theology constitutes a distinctly American response to the churches' need for reliable religious guidelines in the flux of constant social change.

Lasting Theological Contributions

Finally, one further question must be asked: if so much of American theological history is explainable in terms of the American environment, are there individual theologians or schools of theology that deserve to receive recognition in wider Christian circles beyond the borders of the United States? Almost certainly there have been such theologians and theologies. For some, the contribution arises from the nature of engagement with the American environment; for others, the contribution comes from more traditional engagement with the West's broader theological traditions.

American experience has been the cradle for a long line of African-American pastors, preachers, and reformers. More than any other Christian group in American history, blacks have lived under the cross. The result from the early nineteenth century through the end of the twentieth has been a series of significant religious thinkers who have seen more clearly than most of their white contemporaries the contradictions of Christianity that, along with the openings for Christianity, have characterized American society. The founder of the African Methodist Episcopal Church, Richard Allen, expertly exploited the Methodism of John Wesley and Francis Asbury in preaching a message attuned to the status of slaves and freed blacks. One of his successors as guiding bishop of that church, Daniel Alexander Payne, put the traumas of enslavement, emancipation, and reconstruction to excellent theological use through his sermons and writings in the middle decades of the nineteenth century. As we have seen, the abolitionist Frederick Douglass became adept at contrasting the Christianity of the whip with the Christianity of Christ. The tradition of black Christian theology merged with a wide range of twentieth-century religious influences in the life of Martin Luther King, Jr. to prepare one of the most public and most moving Christian voices of the post–World War II era.

A different kind of marginalization — not racial but ecclesiastical — has shaped the theological efforts of American Roman Catholics. Many Catholics have worked at the task of adjusting their rich Christian tradition to American experience, but only a few have carried out the task of adjustment so as to maintain the tradition while also being heard in circles beyond the American church. In the nineteenth century, the Catholic convert Orestes Brownson demonstrated in scores of books and hundreds of articles the vitality that a distinctly Catholic voice could maintain in an American culture otherwise directed by its Protestant origins.[24] Two twentieth-century examples of theological creativity are Dorothy Day and John Courtney Murray. Day took the integral Thomism she learned from Peter Maurin and made it a potent vehicle for ministry to the poor, advocacy for peace, and challenge to religious nominalism, as well as for an attractive liturgical and theological conservatism. Murray's immersion in the neo-scholastic revival took him in a different direction. By arguing carefully, over a period of decades, for the essential compatibility between Catholic theology and American practices of religious liberty, Murray convinced Americans that the Catholic church could enhance citizenship while at the same time convincing Catholics around the world to promote religious liberty. Murray's thinking played an important role in the Second Vatican Council's "Declaration on Religious Freedom" (*Dignitatis Humanae*, 1965).[25]

American circumstances have also created other situations prompting creative theology, especially in relation to tumultuous social condi-

---

24. See Patrick W. Carey, ed., *Orestes Brownson: Selected Writings* (New York: Paulist Press, 1991).

25. See especially John Courtney Murray, S.J., *We Hold These Truths: Catholic Reflections on the American Proposition* (New York: Sheed and Ward, 1960).

tions. Experience as a pastor in a rapidly industrializing section of New York City led the German-trained minister Walter Rauschenbusch to construct principles for a "Social Gospel" that have been studied elsewhere in the world when similar conditions have prevailed.[26] After the Second World War, the emergence of Anabaptist churches from linguistic and sectarian isolation allowed several theologians from Mennonite, Church of the Brethren, and Brethren in Christ backgrounds to engage circumstances of American public life with especially creative reasoning from the Anabaptist tradition. Among these have been John Howard Yoder (1927-1997), who argued forcefully for Jesus as a model of the non-resistance all believers should follow, and Ronald Sider (b. 1939), who has appealed for Western Christians to make a biblical identification with the poor.[27]

African-American theologians, Roman Catholic theologians, and theologians of social conditions have never been central for academic theology in America. Speaking from positions from outside the mainstream of American Christianity, these theologians have often offered fresh interpretations of the Christian faith and insightful applications of that faith in the American context. Their status as outsiders to the academy may explain why their work has sometimes been read more widely outside the United States than within.

Since the development of the modern research university, a significant number of academics have appeared whose intellectual agendas have been shaped by Christian concerns. An outstanding early example was the Harvard psychologist and philosopher William James (1842-1910) who, though far from orthodox, nonetheless wrote so well about such subjects as conversion that his works have affected religious psychology abroad as well as in the United States. During the second half of the twentieth century, intellectuals in the broader academy sometimes have presented more forceful interpretations of Christian foundations than have the theologians. As an example, the sociologist Peter

26. See Winthrop S. Hudson, ed., *Walter Rauschenbusch: Selected Writings* (New York: Paulist Press, 1984).

27. As examples, John Howard Yoder, *The Politics of Jesus: Vicit Agnus Noster* (Grand Rapids: Eerdmans, 1972); Ronald J. Sider, *Rich Christians in an Age of Hunger*, 3rd ed. (Dallas, TX: Word, 1990).

Berger (b. 1929) of Boston University has expertly charted the difficulties of conventional liberalism and simultaneously explored possibilities for meaningful transcendence in a world shaped by secular conventions of thought.[28] In addition, a full cohort of Christian philosophers has emerged since the 1960s who have both rejuvenated older traditions of religious reasoning and inspired a wide circle of academics to attempt to think about their subjects from Christian principles. Their number has included the British-born Roman Catholic Alasdair McIntyre; several representatives of the Dutch American Christian Reformed Church, including Alvin Plantinga and Nicholas Wolterstorff; the Episcopalians Marilyn Adams, William Alston, and Eleonore Stump; and the Presbyterian Robert Adams.[29] In fact, the present-day contingent of Christian philosophers may be offering the most consistently powerful encouragement for Christian reasoning found anywhere in America at the beginning of the twenty-first century.

A very different kind of contribution to worldwide Christian theology is also being provided by American Pentecostalism, a movement that began and has grown remarkably in the United States. The theological contribution of Pentecostalism is as yet more latent than actual, since Pentecostals have never stressed the intellectual disciplines of traditional theology. What Pentecostalism provides to rapidly growing circles of believers around the world (perhaps as many as 500 or 600 million) is precisely the sense of fresh experience with God that historically has nurtured powerful theology. Of all Christian movements in the United States during the twentieth century, Pentecostalism may be the most important for theological development in the twenty-first century.

It is unlikely, with perhaps a few exceptions, that the works of any

---

28. As examples, Peter L. Berger, *A Rumor of Angels: Modern Society and the Rediscovery of the Supernatural,* expanded ed. (New York: Anchor, 1990); and Berger, *A Far Glory: The Quest for Faith in an Age of Credulity* (New York: Anchor, 1993).

29. To this list should also be added the Canadian Catholic philosopher of Hegel and the modern self, Charles Taylor. *Faith and Philosophy,* the journal of the Society of Christian Philosophers, contains a series of accounts on the founding of the society in vol. 15 (April 1998): 141-59. See also Kelly Clark, ed., *Philosophers Who Believe* (Downers Grove, IL: InterVarsity Press, 1993); and Thomas V. Morris, ed., *God and the Philosophers* (New York: Oxford University Press, 1994).

individual American theologian will ever be studied the way, for example, the works of Friedrich Schleiermacher, Pope Leo XIII, or Karl Barth have been studied in so many places throughout the twentieth century. One of the exceptions might be Reinhold Niebuhr.[30] From his base at Union Theological Seminary in New York, and through the tumults of the Depression and the Second World War, Niebuhr provided an unusual degree of sober theological reflection to both the mainline Protestant churches and some of the nation's premier intellectuals. The key to Niebuhr's thought was his dialectical reasoning about the human situation: humanity was sinful and capable of sainthood, subject to history and social forces but also shaper of history and society, egotistical but capable of living for others. In the Bible, and especially in the example of Christ, Niebuhr found the sort of power growing out of powerlessness that was a consistent leitmotif. As a testimony to his influence, the South African Christian novelist Alan Paton said that Niebuhr was the most "enthralling" speaker he had ever heard.[31]

An even more likely candidate for serious theological study outside the United States is Jonathan Edwards (1703-1758), the colonial New England Calvinist who is almost universally recognized as America's most compelling theologian. The remarkable recovery of interest in Edwards was spurred first by secular scholars during the 1930s, especially Perry Miller, one of the century's most powerful historians.[32] The study of Edwards was then stimulated by the general recovery of Puritan history. That recovery has led to a great boom in Edwards studies since the 1960s.[33] This burgeoning interest in Edwards grows out of the subtle

30. See Robert McAfee Brown, ed., *The Essential Reinhold Niebuhr* (New Haven: Yale University Press, 1986).

31. Alan Paton, *Towards the Mountain: An Autobiography* (New York: Charles Scribner's Sons, 1977), p. 259.

32. See Perry G. Miller, *Jonathan Edwards* (New York: W. Sloane, 1949).

33. See M. X. Lesser, *Jonathan Edwards: A Reference Guide* (Boston: G. K. Hall, 1981); Lesser, *Jonathan Edwards: An Annotated Bibliography* (Westport, CT: Greenwood, 1994); Nathan O. Hatch and Harry S. Stout, eds., *Jonathan Edwards and the American Experience* (New York: Oxford University Press, 1988); Stephen J. Stein, ed., *Jonathan Edwards's Writings: Text, Context, Interpretation* (Bloomington: University of Indiana Press, 1996); and Sang Hyun Lee and Allen C. Guelzo, eds., *Edwards in Our Time* (Grand Rapids: Eerdmans,

combination of strengths in his thought, which is marked by creative fidelity to traditional orthodox Calvinism, thorough immersion in the Scriptures, and unusually perceptive engagement with his era's great intellectual problems. The twentieth-century recovery of Edwards has also been fueled, at least in part, by a recognition that the matters about which he thought so well have become cruxes for main developments in Western thought since his time — for example, the shape of human agency, the nature of the physical world, and the adjudication of allegiances competing within the individual person.

Although Edwards' writings on revival kept his name alive during the nineteenth century, his more demanding studies in metaphysical theology and religious psychology were largely dismissed in the nineteenth century by proponents of the age's very popular faculty psychology.[34] At the end of that century and the start of the next, Edwards' reputation suffered another setback among theological modernists, who found his view of God too demanding and his view of human nature too pessimistic. For their part, fundamentalists neglected Edwards because of his consistent intellectual rigor, despite the fact that they mirrored, at least indirectly, some of Edwards' own convictions. The rise of neo-orthodox theology, the profitable use made of Edwards by such major figures as H. Richard Niebuhr,[35] and the growing realization of Edwards' massive engagement with the thought of his age among religious and cultural historians contributed to the striking renaissance in Edwards scholarship.

Edwards wrote the works now studied so intently during his pastorate from 1726 to 1750 at Northampton in central Massachusetts, then at an outpost on the frontier at Stockbridge, Massachusetts, from 1750 to shortly before his death in 1758. Ironically, this most widely re-

---

1999). The most important stimulus to study of Edwards, however, has been the critical edition of his works from Yale University Press; that edition began in 1957 and is now nearing 20 volumes; its general editors have been Perry Miller, John E. Smith, and Harry S. Stout.

34. See Joseph A. Conforti, *Jonathan Edwards, Religious Tradition, and American Culture* (Chapel Hill: University of North Carolina Press, 1995).

35. See especially H. Richard Niebuhr, *The Kingdom of God in America* (Chicago: Willett, Clark, 1937).

spected theologian was dismissed from his Northampton pulpit for insisting that parents follow his theological conclusions on questions concerning participation in the Lord's Supper and the presentation of infants for baptism.[36] Edwards died just as he was taking up a new post as president of the Presbyterian College of New Jersey (later Princeton University).

Edwards' theological writing ranged broadly over theology proper, theological metaphysics, ethics, religious psychology, and the person. His vision penetrated as deep as his reach was broad. In constant engagement with both Scriptural sources and modern learning, he proposed a God-centered conception of the universe that incorporated many findings of modern thinkers. Thus he read with appreciation Sir Isaac Newton on gravity and the natural world, John Locke on perception, and the ethicists Francis Hutcheson and the Earl of Shaftesbury on the affections as basic for moral reasoning. Yet in all cases, Edwards also critiqued these important thinkers in the effort to reconceptualize their contributions in classical Calvinist terms.[37] He postulated God's will as an ongoing cause of the physical universe in order to counteract materialist conclusions drawn from Newton. He undermined Locke's empiricism with a counterargument asserting a theocentric idealism. And while accepting voluntaristic ethics, he reversed Hutcheson and Shaftesbury by insisting that God's grace was the essential foundation for genuine virtue.[38]

Edwards' writings, which aimed at discriminating genuine from false aspects of the colonial Great Awakening, have never been out of print, but his metaphysical theology and his theocentric ethics found

36. The best account of this event is the introduction by David D. Hall, ed., *The Works of Jonathan Edwards*, vol. 12: *Ecclesiastical Writings* (New Haven: Yale University Press, 1994).

37. See especially Norman S. Fiering, *Jonathan Edwards's Moral Thought and Its British Context* (Chapel Hill: University of North Carolina Press, 1981); and Paul Ramsey, ed., *The Works of Jonathan Edwards*, vol. 8: *Ethical Writings* (New Haven: Yale University Press, 1989).

38. Fine studies are presented by Harold Simonson, *Jonathan Edwards: Theologian of the Heart* (Grand Rapids: Eerdmans, 1974); and Sang Hyun Lee, *The Philosophical Theology of Jonathan Edwards* (Princeton: Princeton University Press, 1988).

few adherents. Even the recent recovery of interest in Edwards is marked more by respect than imitation. But that respect is wide and deep, and it is growing. The ultimate reason for such respect is that the skill with which he engaged the great minds of his age was matched by devotion to divine revelation and his own profound articulation of the Augustinian tradition.

As with all other aspects of the history of Christianity in North America, there is no single storyline for American theology. Many kinds of popular theology have competed with many varieties of formal theology, and with each other as well. The great space of America has allowed Christian groups to live in isolation and so to develop their theologies in isolation. With a few individuals, such as Jonathan Edwards, and a few movements, such as Pentecostalism, Christian theology from America has the potential for world-historical significance. Mostly, however, theology in America has served, and often served with considerable integrity, the needs of local groups and individual ecclesiastical traditions. It is not so much in thinking as in acting that American Christians have affected the world.

CHAPTER TEN

In the Shadow of the United States —
Canada and Mexico

E ven a cursory glance at Canada and Mexico is useful for a fuller history of Christianity in North America. Both of these modern nations are themselves firmly rooted in European history, as is the United States. Both have witnessed the same combination of local development and absorption of non-European influences that made the history of the United States different from Europe. Again like the United States, both also have experienced the effects of vigorous Christian activity throughout their histories, and both strikingly illustrate the dialectical give-and-take of ecclesiastical influence on society and social influence upon the churches.

Beyond these general ways in which the Christian histories of the three North American nations resemble each other, however, there are also immense differences. Because the situation is usually not framed this way, it is useful to enumerate a few of those differences from a Mexican angle.[1]

The religious history of Mexico was stamped at its outset by the kind of comprehensive Roman Catholicism characteristic of Southern

---

1. Examples of important comparative studies are David Martin, *Tongues of Fire: The Explosion of Protestantism in Latin America* (Oxford: Blackwell, 1990); and Edward Norman, *Christianity in the Southern Hemisphere: The Churches in Latin America and South Africa* (Oxford: Clarendon, 1981).

European regimes of the late Renaissance and the Catholic Counter-Reformation. Canada, by contrast, developed under the necessity of accommodating in one nation a traditional Old World society with church and state linked together organically (Quebec) along with English-language societies influenced by both British Protestant paternalism and the American separation of church and state. For its part, the United States carried Reformed Protestant tendencies toward voluntary action and democratic polity to their logical conclusions (and sometimes beyond).

The European Christianity brought to Mexico attempted to absorb the native Indian population. In Canada and the United States, by contrast, native populations were mostly shunted aside, if they were not wiped out altogether, by European diseases, loss of land, and warfare. Canadian Christian outreach to native populations achieved somewhat more positive results than in the United States, but not by much.[2]

In all three societies, race has been an ever-present social factor. But Mexican history does not match the American experience (black-white-Hispanic-other ethnicities) or the Canadian (French-English-other ethnicities). Rather, in Mexico, three kinds of "lower" orders (Indians, mestizos [mixed race Indians and Spanish], and blacks) have been incorporated into a larger society dominated by two kinds of "superior" orders (Spanish and American-born descendants of the Spanish, or Creoles).

The tensions dominating the modern history of Christianity in Mexico are those characteristic of Roman Catholic Europe; they feature the clash between anti-clerical liberal rationalism and ultramontane Catholic conservatism. In the United States, the tensions are mostly the result of differences over how best to apply modern liberalism to church and society. In Canada a mixture of patrician conservatism and democratic liberalism has dominated religious history.

A Protestantism with enduring institutions did not exist in Mexico

---

2. Compare Henry Warner Bowden, *American Indians and Christian Missions: Studies in Cultural Conflict* (Chicago: University of Chicago Press, 1985); and John Webster Grant, *Moon of Wintertime: Missionaries and the Indians of Canada in Encounter Since 1534* (Toronto: University of Toronto Press, 1984).

before the mid-nineteenth century; it was then only a small factor during the next century; at the end of the twentieth century, though the number of Protestant adherents and the diversity of Protestant churches are both growing rapidly, Protestants play only a small role in public life.[3] In the United States and English-speaking Canada, by contrast, Catholics learned to survive as a minority, while the Catholic majority in Quebec has always had to take account of the surrounding Protestant dominance of the United States and English Canada.

The consequence of these systemic differences is that the histories of Christianity in Mexico and Canada have been quite different from each other and from the United States. These differences also arise from the character of cross-border interaction. The religious border between the United States and Mexico was defined by the antagonism that existed in the sixteenth and seventeenth centuries between the Iberian Catholic Hapsburg monarchs and the English Protestant Tudor monarchs. The border between the United States and Canada was defined by the strife between Catholic France and Protestant Britain in the eighteenth century. Yet after Britain, with its Protestant institutions, completed the conquest of Canada, it set the stage for a much freer religious exchange between the United States and Canada than has existed between the United States and Mexico. The one exception to that generalization is the fairly recent flow of migration from Mexico to the United States, which also builds a bridge between the religious histories (Protestant as well as Catholic) of the two countries.[4]

The Christian histories of Canada and the United States share more commonalities than either does with Mexico. Where the organic, society-wide Catholicism of traditional Quebec does resemble some aspects of Mexican Catholicism, until after the Second World War Quebec enjoyed a much more tranquil history of Catholic dominance than did Mexico. It is also symbolic of New World differences that, while

3. See Jean Pierre Bastian, *Protestantismo y Sociedad en México* (Mexico City: Casa Unida de Publicaciones, 1983); and Lindy Scott, *Salt of the Earth: A Socio-Political History of Mexico City Evangelical Protestants, 1964-1991* (Mexico City: Editorial Kyrios, 1991).

4. The outstanding treatment to date of that development is Jay P. Dolan and Gilberto M. Hinojosa, eds., *Mexican Americans and the Catholic Church, 1900-1965* (Notre Dame: University of Notre Dame Press, 1994).

France and Spain are separated by only a single mountain range, in North America New France and New Spain were divided by the English colonies that became a sprawling continental nation.

A single brief chapter cannot do justice to the Christian history of either Canada or Mexico, much less to the range of useful comparisons possible for either with the United States.[5] By returning to questions of religion and politics or church and state, however, it is possible to show that American patterns were not the only New World expressions of Christianity. First, a narrative of church-state relations in Mexico sheds even stronger light on distinctives of American experience. Second, a more thematic account of religion and politics in Canada is useful for illuminating the same subject in the United States.

Mexico

The Colonial Period

The first period of Mexican church-state relationships witnessed a wholesale translation of traditional Catholicism to the New World. Catholicism in New Spain (which included modern Mexico, most of Central America, and the western third of the modern United States) was almost completely insulated from Protestantism as a religious or civil force. Hence in New Spain there existed almost no pressure toward religious pluralism, nor any sympathy for the voluntarism, political liber-

---

5. For Canadian-American comparisons, there has been a gratifying surge of recent attention: see, for example, Robert T. Handy, "Protestant Patterns in Canada and the United States," in *In the Great Tradition*, ed. J. D. Ban and Paul R. Dekar (Valley Forge, PA: Judson, 1982); Phyllis D. Airhart, "'As Canadian as Possible Under the Circumstances': Reflections on the Study of Protestantism in North America," in *New Directions in American Religious History*, ed. Harry S. Stout and D. G. Hart (New York: Oxford University Press, 1998); William Westfall, "Voices from the Attic: The Canadian Border and the Writing of American Religious History," in *Retelling U.S. Religious History*, ed. Thomas A. Tweed (Berkeley: University of California Press, 1997); and Mark A. Noll, *A History of Christianity in the United States and Canada* (Grand Rapids: Eerdmans, 1992), pp. 545-50 and passim.

alism, democracy, and the free market found in Protestant regions of Europe and North America.[6]

The first two generations of Spanish missionaries were intense, self-sacrificing, and successful — at least in the sense of incorporating native populations into the church, and establishing networks of dioceses and archdioceses, educational institutions, publishing ventures, and the general apparatus of a European state church. To be sure, much syncretism occurred in mixtures of native Indian religion and the new Catholicism, but the conversion of the Indian population to Catholicism was undertaken early and remains to this day a prime feature of religious life in Mexico.

Significantly, the power to nominate bishops in the New World was granted by the papacy to the monarchs of Spain and Portugal, which resulted in Latin America witnessing the greatest control ever granted by the papacy to secular sovereigns. This *Patronato Real* remained a linchpin of cultural conservatism in New Spain; the precedents it established for church-state cooperation have been almost impossible to break even long after the end of the Spanish Empire.[7]

The most enduring legacy of that early missionary Catholicism has been devotion to Our Lady of Guadalupe. According to tradition, on December 9 and December 12, 1531, the Virgin Mary appeared to the Indian peasant Juan Diego at Tepeyac, outside of Mexico City. Devotion to the Virgin of Guadalupe eventually became one of the defining aspects of Mexican spirituality, but that devotion is also sometimes cited as an example of Latin American syncretism, since elements from the worship of the Aztec Earth Goddess Tonantzin, which was carried out near the shrine to the Virgin, were taken up into this Marian devo-

---

6. Helpful orientation to Mexican religious history for North American audiences is provided in *The New Catholic Encyclopedia*, s.v. "Miguel Hidalgo y Costilla," "Mexico," "Colonial Mexico," "Modern Mexico," "Patronato Real," and related subjects; Lino Gómez Canedo, "Religion in the Spanish Empire," *Scribner's Encyclopedia*, vol. 1, pp. 187-200; and Edwin E. Sylvest, Jr., "Religion in Hispanic America since the Era of Independence," *Scribner's Encyclopedia*, vol. 1, pp. 201-22.

7. See J. Lloyd Mecham, "The Church in Colonial Spanish America," in *Colonial Hispanic America*, ed. A. Curtis Wilgus (Washington, D.C.: George Washington University Press, 1936), pp. 200-39.

tion. In May 1990, during his second visit to Mexico, Pope John Paul II beatified Juan Diego in a new Basilica of Our Lady of Guadalupe. Over ten million people visit the Basilica each year.

For modern purposes, the other most notable contribution of Catholicism in New Spain was the work of Bartolomé de Las Casas, the first European to offer a systematic theological and legal defense of the Native American Indians, as noted in Chapter Two.

The First Revolution

A second period of Mexican church-state relations ensued in the early nineteenth century, when the Napoleonic Wars undercut the rule of Spain over its vast New World colonial empire. In this period, Mexican efforts at promoting political liberalization coexisted alongside an ambiguous place for the Catholic church.

In 1810 turbulence in Spain led to corresponding turbulence in New Spain. On the question of whether to seek independence, the Catholic clergy were divided, with the higher clergy (mostly Spanish by birth) opposed to revolution, but many of the lower clergy (mostly Creoles) behind the push for independence. On September 16 of that year, a Creole priest, Father Miguel Hidalgo y Costilla, issued the "Grito de Dolores" (An Appeal from the town of Dolores, but also a "cry of sorrows"), which instigated armed rebellion. Hidalgo, who was influenced by Enlightenment values, called for Mexican independence in the name of Our Lady of Guadalupe and of Jesus Christ. September 16 is now celebrated as Mexican Independence Day. When Hidalgo was executed the next year, his work was taken up by another priest, the mestizo José María Morelos, who inspired widespread support but who soon met the same fate as Father Hidalgo.

It was indicative of the conservative character of New Spain that, for leading this political movement, Hidalgo and Morelos were accused of fomenting Lutheran heresy, they were stripped of their clerical offices, and they became the last two individuals condemned to death by the Mexican Inquisition, which had been established in 1571.

Despite the suppression of the two revolutionary priests, agitation for independence continued. In early 1821, several factions supporting the revolution united under the leadership of a Creole general, Agustin de Iturbide. Iturbide was a convinced political liberal but also a loyal adherent of the Catholic Church. He set out his vision for Mexico in his *Plan de Iguala,* which contained three main provisions: (1) the preservation of Roman Catholicism, (2) independence from Spain, and (3) equality of Europeans and Creoles in government. The army of these Three Guarantees successfully occupied Mexico City in September 1821, and the church hierarchy, which originally opposed independence, supported Iturbide because his program did not contain the anti-clerical elements that had by this time arisen in Spain.

There followed, however, several decades of turmoil in which the difficulties of accommodating a conservative state church in a liberal polity fueled uncertainty. The basic clash was between the ideal of Catholicism as an effective agent of social cohesion for this racially and regionally diverse nation and an ideology of republicanism that drove successive generations of liberals to seek greater separation between church and state. It did not help matters that the United States, with its entwined commitments to republicanism and Protestantism, exerted pressure on Mexico's trade, land, and national security.

Mexico's early independent governments continued to offer many of the same privileges to the Catholic church that it had enjoyed under the old regime. When a constitutional congress was convened in February 1822, for example, the clergy were well represented, and official business began with a mass and an oath by the delegates to support the Catholic church. The constitution of 1824 contained the explicit statement that "The religion of the Mexican nation is and shall be perpetually the Roman Catholic Apostolic. The nation will protect it by wise and just laws and prohibits the exercise of any other."[8] A successor constitution of 1843 once again declared Roman Catholicism to be the exclusive national religion.

Yet these formal professions of loyalty to Catholic tradition were also attended by significant strain. Iturbide, who ruled briefly as the

8. J. Lloyd Mecham, *Church and State in Latin America: A History of Politico-Ecclesiastical Relations,* rev. ed. (Chapel Hill: University of North Carolina Press, 1966), pp. 343-44.

Emperor Agustin I, was a self-styled champion of the church, but he was deposed in 1823, and none of Mexico's succeeding strong men were as supportive. A particular tension was the *Patronato Real,* which the new constitutional governments sought to exercise for themselves as replacements for the Spanish monarchs. That arrangement, however, generated great opposition in the Vatican with, for example, Pope Leo XII in 1824 writing to the clergy of Latin America to urge them to support the deposed king of Spain. Tension between Rome and the new independent government of Mexico led to a period in the late 1820s when all bishoprics in the country were vacated and to another episode in 1833 when a new liberal government confiscated the property and funds of the missions, turned parishes over to secular clergy, ceased collecting tithes for the church, repealed laws compelling the fulfillment of religious vows, assumed authority to make appointments to ecclesiastical posts, and forbade political activity by priests. An immediate outcry by the clergy led to popular opposition that in turn caused many of these measures to be overturned. Only in 1836 did the Vatican then recognize the independence of Mexico.

The inability of Mexican political liberals, despite persistent efforts, to wean Indian and large portions of the rest of the population from all-encompassing loyalty to the church remained a central theme of the nation's life. That loyalty was expressed fiercely by conservative leader Lucas Alamán, in a famous letter to the chief of state in 1853: "First and foremost is the need to preserve the Catholic religion, because we believe in it and because even if we did not hold it to be divine, we consider it to be the only common bond that links all Mexicans when all the others have been broken; it is the only thing capable of sustaining the Spanish-American race and of delivering it from the great dangers to which it is exposed. We also consider it necessary to maintain the ceremonial splendour of the Church, as well as its temporal properties, and to settle everything relating to ecclesiastical administration with the Pope."[9] These sentiments, modified only slightly, have never passed away.

9. Edwin Williamson, *The Penguin History of Latin America* (London: Penguin, 1992), p. 242.

The 1846-1848 war with the United States affected the church only indirectly. The expansionary policies of the American government had encouraged an independence movement in Texas during the 1830s; in the 1840s, they led to armed conflict. American intervention contributed to Mexico's tangled political history, which witnessed rapid changes of government, local resistance to national authority, and much conflict among the Spanish and Creole elites. The United States conquest of California and other territory in the American southwest, for which a $15 million indemnity was paid, was and remains a stinging blow to Mexican national pride.

The American war was also important for the ongoing struggle concerning the place of religion in Mexican society. At one point early in the war the liberal chief of state Gómez Farías proposed confiscating Roman Catholic property to finance the conflict. This proposal, however, became counterproductive when it led to a clergy-inspired revolt by part of the Mexican army.

War with the United States also stimulated a vestigial Protestant presence in the country. During the colonial era, the Mexican Inquisition had dealt sternly with stray Dutch, English, or German Protestants who washed up on the shores of New Spain. But independence opened up at least a little space for Protestants. In the mid-1820s, the American Bible Society began efforts at Scripture distribution. These efforts were strengthened in 1827 by the arrival in Mexico of James Thomson, agent of the British and Foreign Bible Society. When Thomson was forced out of the country in 1830, the ex-priest and editor José María Luis Mora took up his work. Mora's career underscored connections between Protestantism and political liberalism; he not only distributed Bibles in Spanish and several Indian languages, but he also promoted freedom of conscience in his magazine *El Observador de la Republica Mexicana*, became a political advisor to Gómez Farías, and in 1832 authored a study on the relationship between church and state that later became a blueprint for the nationalization of church property.

American Protestant mission agencies began to take a greater interest in Mexico during and after the crisis over Texas and in the buildup to the Mexican War. In 1839 the *Annual Report of the Board of Foreign Missions* for the Presbyterian Church in the United States explored the desirability of expanding its efforts southward from Texas. Then during the war the United States sent both Protestant and Catholic chaplains with its army, and colporteurs of the American Bible Society accompanied the troops. American newspaper accounts also inspired individual missionary efforts among the Mexicans. In 1852 a Presbyterian laywoman, Melinda Rankin, opened a school for Mexicans in Brownsville, Texas, while awaiting an opportunity to enter Mexico as a Protestant missionary. Fourteen years later she moved to Monterrey and formed a Presbyterian church, which two years later called a pastor.

In a situation similar to that of the United States, Mexico was witnessing an elective affinity between Protestantism and political liberalism. Unlike the United States, in Mexico that affinity was always contested by the overwhelming presence of an organic Catholic tradition.

La Reforma

The next stage of church-state developments in Mexico began in the 1850s during a period identified by the reforming efforts of Benito Juárez (1806-1872). While Minister of Justice and Ecclesiastical Affairs in 1855, this future president issued a decree known as the *Ley Juárez* that limited the jurisdiction of ecclesiastical and military courts. The army and the church united to protest. But for a time, liberal sentiment prevailed. The next year the government issued the *Ley Lerdo*. It stipulated that churches must dispose of all property not used directly for purposes of worship. The stated intent of this law was to make holders of large properties sell to the middle and lower classes and so encourage economic growth through the distribution of real property. Government leaders also hoped that stripping the church of real estate would weaken its political power. Prior to the Reform, the church may have owned over a third of the land in Mexico, and it controlled agricultural activity through heavy mortgages.

A new constitution in 1857 enacted several provisions restricting the church and failed to reaffirm Roman Catholicism as Mexico's sole official religion. Implicitly this meant the legalization of Protestantism. In response, church leaders threatened government officials with excommunication. A few Catholic clergy, however, sided with the government. From this group eventually emerged a dissident Catholic church, encouraged by then-President Juárez, that eventually established a relationship with the Episcopal Church in the United States. Popular support for the official Catholic church remained very strong, and the split-away church never became large, although it did serve as a source for key leaders among later Protestant churches.

In December 1857 a military-clerical alliance, under the leadership of General Felix Zuloaga, declared war on the government of the new Constitution. This alliance called for the restoration of church lands, income, juridical privileges, and official recognition of Catholicism as the sole religion of Mexico; it also appealed for the establishment of a monarchy or European protectorate in place of the 1857 Constitution. Three years of civil war (the War of the Reform) followed. The fact that this civil conflict took place on the eve of the American Civil War and with the same prominence of religion as displayed in the American War reveals a measure of similarity in the religious histories of the two nations. The great difference separating them is shown by the fact that religion figured in the American Civil War as part of the struggle to define a "Christian republicanism," while in Mexico it concerned a struggle over whether a European system of church-state integration should be restored.

During the War of the Reform, Juárez's government instituted the most extreme anti-clericalism Mexico had yet seen. All church property was nationalized, religious communities were suppressed, a civil registration for births, marriages, and deaths was established, divorce was legalized, and cemeteries were secularized. The government also announced both a complete separation of church and state and official recognition of freedom of religion. As if to ensure that no one misread his intentions, in 1861 Juárez expelled Luigi Clementi, Rome's first apostolic delegate to Mexico.

To shore up the *ancien régime*, France, Britain, and Spain invaded Mexico. Soon the Spanish and British gave way and the European intervention became solely the affair of France, which wanted to secure payment of debts owed its citizens and to expand the empire of Napoleon III. The French action was supported by the church hierarchy, which saw the restoration of European rule as a way to regaining its own power. In 1864 the French invaders installed Maximilian, Archduke of Austria, as emperor of Mexico. Maximilian, a personable and relatively liberal thinker, failed to reach an agreement with the Vatican, since Rome demanded a fuller restoration of power than Maximilian was willing to grant. This Thermidorean reaction soon failed. When the French, preparing for war with Prussia, withdrew their troops from Mexico in 1867, guerrillas fighting under Juárez quickly regained control, deposed Maximilian, and then put him to death.

In the wake of war, Mexico's formal constitution reaffirmed the liberal provisions of the 1857 Constitution, and even added sections confirming the separation of church and state, declaring marriage a civil contract, making monastic vows illegal, and prohibiting religious organizations from acquiring real estate. As so often in Mexican history, however, official statement and actual practice diverged. Under the long-term presidency of the dictator José de la Cruz Porfirio Díaz (1877-1910), restrictions against the church were not enforced.

As might be expected, a governmental turn against state-church Roman Catholicism also opened the doors to Protestant expansion. In 1872 President Juárez went out of his way to encourage Mexico's minuscule number of Protestants. He could even say, "the future happiness and prosperity of my nation depend on the development of Protestantism. . . . I could wish that Protestantism would become Mexican by conquering the Indians; they need a religion which will compel them to read and not to spend their savings on candles for the saints."[10]

During the Juárez period, several Protestant denominations planted seeds for further growth, including the first Lutheran congregation, organized by German-speaking immigrants (1861), an independent church in Monterrey with Baptist principles (1864), and the Presbyterian church of Melinda Rankin (1868). In the 1870s, Protestant mission boards from the United States began sending missionaries. The Society of Friends, Northern and Southern Presbyterians, Northern and Southern Methodists, American Baptists, and Southern Baptists were among the groups that established a presence at this time. By

10. Scott, *Salt of the Earth,* pp. 29-30.

1883 twelve American mission boards were sponsoring 85 missionaries in 264 missionary congregations.

Over the last third of the century, Protestant educational efforts bore some likeness to what Catholics were attempting in the United States. On both sides of the border, the often-beleaguered religious minorities were mobilizing to create schools as a way of preserving their young for the minority faith. The major difference, however, was that the Protestant schools of Mexico welcomed children who were not from Protestant families and regarded them in general as a vehicle for evangelization. During the Porfirio Díaz years, Protestants established over six hundred schools and a number of teacher-training institutes to prepare graduates for teaching in those schools. As for American Roman Catholics, separate schooling became for Protestants in Mexico an ideal way of advancing a larger religious cause. But again in this instance, results over time were different. In the United States, Catholic education underwent a century or more of expansion and enrichment while receiving virtually no recognition from the nation's mainstream cultural establishments. By contrast, during the Mexican Revolution of 1910 and following, Protestant educators received the highest national recognition when leaders of new governments turned to Protestants for a number of critical educational tasks, but the Mexican Protestant schools did not survive the revolutionary period. They went into oblivion alongside Catholic educational efforts when in 1934 the education provision (Article 3) of the 1917 Constitution was changed from mandating "secular (that is, lay) education" to requiring "socialist education."[11]

Despite considerable governmental approval for Protestant activities in this period, resistance to Protestants could still be severe. William Butler, founder and director of the Methodist mission in Mexico, estimated that between 1873 and 1892 at least fifty-eight persons were murdered for belonging to Protestant churches. Other Protestants ex-

---

11. Lindy Scott, "The Political Significance of the Protestant Presence in Latin America: A Case Study from Mexico," *Transformation: An International Evangelical Dialogue on Mission and Ethics* 12 (Jan.-Mar. 1995): 28-33, with discussion of education on pp. 29-30.

perienced less extreme harassment, such as social ostracism and difficulty in finding work or carrying on business.

The Second Revolution

At the end of President Porfirio Díaz's tenure, the inability to hand over power peacefully created tumult that led to revolution. Several factions, including powerful *caudillos* in Northern Mexico (led by Alvaro Obregón), the former bandit Pancho Villa in the North, and the leader of southern Indians, Emiliano Zapata, worked to overthrow the inherited government. Attitudes toward religion varied greatly among both revolutionaries and supporters of the old government; Zapata, for example, encouraged his Indian followers in their Catholicism and occasionally made use of Protestants to write revolutionary documents, and one of the important northern generals, Pascual Orozco, was an active Congregationalist. But in general, the violent anti-clericalism of most northern *caudillos* and the stiff resistance of the Catholic church to liberalizing reforms created more strain between church and state over the next quarter century than had ever before existed in Mexican history.

A complicated series of coups, wars, reprisals, and revolts finally led in 1917 to the ratification of a new revolutionary constitution. This document recognized freedom of conscience and freedom in the practice of religion (Article 24), but put restrictions on the functioning of religious bodies. Free practice of religion was limited to indoor services in government-owned buildings. Religious ministry could be regulated by the state, with local authorities having the power to set a maximum number of clergy. Churches were given no legal standing. Ministers were disenfranchised and could not participate in politics (Article 130). Churches lost all property rights, while the state controlled all property held by churches (Article 27). Religious associations and clergy were prohibited from engaging in education (Article 3), and the establishment of monastic orders was forbidden (Article 5). Moreover, only native Mexicans were permitted to be ministers.

The draconian anti-clericalism of these measures remained mostly a dead letter for the next nine years, but then in 1926 President Calles began to enforce them. In response, Archbishop Mora y del Rio announced that the church did not accept Articles 3, 5, 27, and 130 of the Constitution and would fight against them, whereupon the Mexican government ordered the arrest and deportation of all foreign priests. In April, when Archbishop Mora y del Rio was arraigned on a charge of inciting revolt, he offered this defense: "We have aided no revolution. We have plotted no revolution, but we do claim that the Catholics of Mexico have the right to fight for their rights by peaceful means first and with arms in an extremity."[12] He and five other church leaders were immediately deported to the United States. In July the Mexican bishops issued a letter suspending all religious services requiring priests, in protest of the "anti-religious laws of the Constitution." War followed.

The intermittent Cristero War of 1926-1929 was extraordinarily violent, with thousands of casualties and much destruction of property. It saw Catholic citizens engage in protests, riots, and armed violence against the government, while most of the much smaller Protestant community maintained its support for the Revolutionary government. A much-publicized act of violence was the assassination of a president-elect in 1928 by a zealous Catholic acting independently of church leaders or organizations. President Calles blamed the assassination on "direct clerical action."

Finally in 1929 a compromise was reached between the church and the state, which led to the resumption of formal services and the return of exiled bishops, priests, and religious. Nonetheless, tensions remained high. In 1931 most of the Mexican states passed legislation that severely restricted the number of priests allowed to work in their jurisdictions, and a few of the states suspended public services altogether. In October 1932, Pope Pius XI issued an encyclical to the archbishops and bishops of Mexico in which he called for continued protests against the government's effort at destroying the Catholic church. Less than two years later, the government responded by amending the Constitution to specify that all education should be socialist in orientation. Religious organizations were prohibited from operating any schools — even seminaries for the training of ministers. Mexican semi-

---

12. Mecham, *Church and State,* p. 400.

naries were forced underground, and some Mexican priests went to the United States to pursue their education. Protestants submitted to the law and closed mission schools, but Catholics protested that the socialist education in the public schools was antireligious. Bishops issued pastoral letters warning parents that it was a mortal sin to allow their children to remain in schools teaching socialism. Teachers in some states were required to make "Ideological Declarations," stating, "I am an atheist, an irreconcilable enemy of the Catholic, Apostolic, Roman religion, [and] I will endeavor to destroy it. . . ."[13] The next year (1935) all buildings used for the administration, propaganda, or teaching of religion were nationalized, including private homes used for religious services and illegal private schools, and distribution of religious literature by mail was prohibited. By the end of 1935 there were fewer than five hundred Catholic priests serving the whole nation, of which fewer than two hundred were legally registered with the government. Seven states lacked either Catholic or Protestant clergy. These parlous circumstances set the stage for one of the great English-language novels of the twentieth century, Graham Greene's *The Power and the Glory* (1940), the story of an outlaw priest who, despite many personal flaws, remained faithful to his ecclesiastical vocation. The great contrast to the religious history of the United States can be seen in the fact that, despite these extraordinary anti-clerical steps, the mass of Mexicans retained their loyalty to the Catholic church.

The revolutionary years also witnessed important developments among Protestants.[14] In 1914 Pentecostalism was introduced by Mexicans returning from the United States. The indigenous *Iglesia Apostólica* thus became the first of a surge of Pentecostal groups that, since mid-century, have become far and away the dominant form of Protestantism in Mexico. By the early 1990s there were several Pentecostal denominations, each with over 100,000 adherents.

During the early years of the Revolution, many American Protestant missionaries pulled back to the United States. In 1914 and

13. Mecham, *Church and State,* p. 407.

14. See, for a general picture, Deborah J. Baldwin, *Protestants and the Mexican Revolution: Missionaries, Ministers, and Social Change* (Urbana: University of Illinois Press, 1990).

following years they held a series of meetings in Cincinnati, Ohio, in order to reduce competition among denominations in Mexico. These meetings produced an ironic result: members of the Mexican Protestant churches resented being dictated to by the missionaries acting without their consultation from a base in the United States and began to chart more of an independent course for themselves.

Gradual Accommodation

The most recent phase of Mexican church-state developments began with the presidency of Lázaro Cárdenas in 1934. Although he was a dedicated socialist, Cárdenas declared that it was not the place of the government to promote the kind of antireligious campaigns that only created resistance and retarded the economic revival so necessary for the health of Mexico. While the anti-clerical constitution remained in place, government hostility toward the Catholic church relaxed considerably. For its part, the Catholic church also turned aside from the path of overt confrontation. In 1937 Pope Pius XI issued the encyclical, *On the Religious Situation in Mexico,* that urged Mexican clergy to be involved in social service and to concern themselves with the conditions of the poor, lest they "become prey of de-Christianizing propaganda." The encyclical emphasized the advantage of a peaceful program of Catholic action rather than violence as a way of defending Catholic rights.

Cárdenas also went out of his way to promote several Protestant ventures. He was an especially close friend of William Cameron Townsend, founder of the Wycliffe Bible Translators, an evangelical mission agency attempting to translate the Scriptures into indigenous tongues. Wycliffe's sacrificial labor on behalf of the indigenous peoples linked its efforts with Cárdenas' concern to better the lot of the Indians.[15]

In the 1940s, the constitution's clause requiring socialistic education was revoked and Catholic parochial schools were re-established,

---

15. See William Svelmoe, "The General and the Gringo: W. Cameron Townsend as Lázaro Cárdenas's Man in America," in *Distant Seeds, American Harvest: The Missionary Impulse in United States History,* ed. Grant Wacker and Daniel Bays (forthcoming).

though the earlier flourishing of Protestant schools did not revive. Also during this decade the Catholic church sponsored new missionary ventures in several places including the Yucatan peninsula, where priests had been excluded for more than a century. Protestant missionary efforts also increased in this period, with non-denominational evangelical mission boards sending recruits to work alongside the older denominational bodies.

In recent decades, the increasing flow of goods, services, and personnel across the Mexican–United States border has had important religious implications. In 1973 the Catholic church in the United States began issuing its pastoral letters in both English and Spanish as a recognition of the growing role of its Mexican and other Hispanic Catholics. A number of Protestant bodies, mostly the non-Pentecostals, also draw on missionary and financial support from the United States. The rapid growth of Pentecostal churches among the Indians in the South of Mexico has prompted occasional acts of violence from the loyal Catholic population.

In the 1990s, complicated political, economic, and diplomatic developments also worked their effects on the churches. The long-ruling PRI (Institutional Revolutionary Party) was increasingly challenged by dissenting political forces and the tumults of international markets. After a contested election in 1988, the newly elected PRI President, Carlos Salinas de Gotari, received a show of support from both the Catholic hierarchy and the United States government. Those actions may have contributed to Mexican approval of the free trade agreement with the United States and Canada (NAFTA) as well as to significant changes in the nation's laws with respect to the churches. Salinas broke precedent by inviting the papal nuncio and the Archbishop of Mexico City to his first presidential address. He also traveled to the Vatican, and he provided a warm welcome for Pope John Paul II's Mexican visits of 1990 and 1992. In addition Salinas reached out to several Protestant denominations and leaders. In January 1992, he revoked by presidential decree the anti-clerical provisions of the 1917 constitution, so that churches enjoyed legal status and the right to own property, clergy and other religious workers from abroad were again welcomed, and the clergy were given the right to vote and to be exempt from taxes.

At the end of the 1990s, rebellion of Indian groups in the South of Mexico, continued financial stress, the growth of Mexico City to incredible size (nearing 20 million people), and the triumph of dissident political parties in some state and local elections combined to create uneasy conditions. Catholic renewal was advancing through *comunidades eclesiales de base* that featured the themes of liberation theology, as well as through expanding work of conservative movements such as Opus Dei. The number of Protestants continued to grow, in some areas rapidly, although Protestants were only beginning to find much of a voice in public affairs, with the most notable Protestant participation in the state of Chiapas.[16] The election in July 2000 of Vicente Fox as Mexican president, the first non-PRI president and the first practicing Catholic in that office for over eighty years, will doubtless change the shape of the future.

This rapid survey is enough to show that Mexico's religious history is very different from the religious history of the United States. Liberal democracy has never dominated Mexico as it has the United States, which means that the place for American forms of Protestantism is much smaller. The persistence of Catholic loyalties among the vast majority of the population is especially remarkable in light of the many efforts by governments and secular elites to break that hold. Even with rapid gains among Protestant Pentecostals in recent years, eighty to ninety percent of Mexico's nearly one hundred million people continue to identify with the Catholic church. The shape of Mexico's Christian history makes especially clear how much Christianity in the United States depends upon not just its European origin but the strikingly Protestant character of that origin.

Canada

With a history that shares much with that of the United States, Canada, like its much more populous neighbor, has also experienced close connections between religion and politics, though neither in the same way nor for the same reasons. Canada's modern history began in the

16. See Scott, *Salt of the Earth*, pp. 121-40.

early seventeenth century with French settlements in what is now Quebec. By contrast to the United States, Catholicism was politically important from the first. The corporate conception of civic life that characterizes Roman Catholic societies has exerted an especially strong influence in Quebec, even in recent decades when levels of religious practice in that province have fallen dramatically.[17]

The Catholic factor loomed large in almost all major Canadian political developments until recent times. After the Treaty of Paris (1763), when Britain took control of Quebec, British success at accommodating the province's Catholic establishment prepared the way for Catholic loyalty to the crown during the American Revolution.[18] When patriots invaded Canada in 1775, Bishop Briand of Quebec labeled support for the Americans "heresy," and most of his fellow Catholics took the message to heart.

The tragic career of Louis Riel, who twice attempted to set up quasi-independent governments for the *métis* (mixed bloods of French-Canadian and Indian parentage) in the prairie province of Manitoba, also involved religion in several ways.[19] When Riel was executed in 1885 following his second failed rebellion, it fueled bitter conflict between Protestants eager to extend a British religious hegemony and French-speaking Catholics who felt Riel had been wronged. Ill will generated by the Riel episode came to an end only when Wilfrid Laurier, the Liberal Party's candidate in the 1896 national election, successfully assuaged the wounded sensibilities of both sides. It is worth noting that Laurier, a Catholic from Quebec who won widespread affection from all regions of Canada during his lengthy tenure (1896-1911), became his nation's prime minister more than three decades before a Catholic was even nominated for president by a major political party in the United States and more than six decades before a Catholic (John F. Kennedy) was elected to that office.

17. For context, see Yvon Desrosiers, ed., *Religion et Culture au Québec* (Montreal: Fides, 1986).

18. See George A. Rawlyk, ed., *Revolution Rejected, 1775-1776* (Toronto: Prentice Hall, 1986).

19. See Thomas Flanagan, *Louis "David" Riel: Prophet of the New World*, rev. ed. (Toronto: University of Toronto Press, 1996).

Even with the easing of Catholic-Protestant antagonism over the last half-century, Catholicism still makes a difference in Canadian electoral politics. In the mid-1980s, political scientists found that Catholic-Protestant differences explained more electoral variance than any other social structural trait and that these differences were not simply a reflection of Anglophone-Francophone differences.[20] In the Quebec referendum for provincial independence in 1995, active Francophone Catholics were much less likely to vote in favor of sovereignty than were nominally Catholic or secular Québeçois.

Rejecting Revolution

In contrast to American society, religion has played an important role in the persistent Canadian rejections of revolution as a means of altering the political system and of liberalism as the sole norm for political life. Catholic gratitude for the Quebec Act of 1774, which secured civil rights to Canadian Catholics that their co-religionists in Britain did not gain until 1829, helps explain Quebec's rejection of American pleas to join the War for Independence. In the Atlantic Maritime provinces, a much smaller, more Protestant population also refused to join the patriot cause. In that case, at least part of the reason was the apolitical pietism fostered by Henry Alline and other leaders of the revivalistic "New Light Stir" that began about the same time as the war.[21]

The greatest stimulus to the creation of an anti-American Canadian nationalism, however, was the War of 1812 between the United States and Britain, a war which neither side desired and whose resolution merely underscored the status quo. When undermanned militia and British regulars repelled the attacks of American troops in the Niagara peninsula and on the Great Lakes in 1813 and 1814, Canadian

20. Richard Johnston, "The Reproduction of the Religious Cleavage in Canadian Elections," *Canadian Journal of Political Science/Revue Canadienne de Science Politique* 18 (March 1985): 99-114.

21. See Maurice Armstrong, *The Great Awakening in Nova Scotia, 1776-1809* (Hartford: American Society of Church History, 1948); and George A. Rawlyk, ed., *Henry Alline: Selected Writings* (New York: Paulist Press, 1987).

ministers hailed God's providential rescue of his people from tyranny with the same assurance that Americans had employed after their struggle against Britain a generation before. Loyalty to the king and trust in God constituted the Canadian "Shield of Achilles" that frustrated the despotic plans of what Canadians regarded as the American democratic mob.[22]

The rejection of revolution, commemorated by the descendants of the 50,000 Loyalists who eventually settled in the Maritime provinces and Ontario and sealed decisively by the War of 1812, encouraged a spirit that several scholars, most famously Seymour Martin Lipset, have described as the critical element in Canadian politics.[23] Though the individualism, free market advocacy, and democratic principles that have meant so much in the United States are not absent in Canada, liberalism there has always been balanced by corporate visions of the Left and the Right, and often with significant religious support. For example, the fundamentalist preacher William "Bible Bill" Aberhart (1878-1943) embodied populist and communitarian principles in Alberta's Social Credit Party, which he led to power in the 1930s.[24] A Baptist minister and contemporary of Aberhart, Tommy Douglas (1904-1986), exploited principles from the Social Gospel in organizing the Cooperative Commonwealth Federation in the prairies during the same Depression years.[25] That movement eventually was transformed into the New Democratic Party, Canada's socialist alternative to the Liberal and Progressive Conservative parties. It has come to power in several provinces at various times since the 1960s. The redoubtable Christian philosopher George Parkin Grant (1918-1988) was only the most forceful of several prominent spokespersons in the 1950s and

22. As an example of that Loyalism by a prominent Methodist minister and educator, see Egerton Ryerson, *The Loyalists of America and Their Times . . . 1620 to 1816* (New York: Haskell House, 1970; originally 1880).

23. Seymour Martin Lipset, *Continental Divide: The Values and Institutions of the United States and Canada* (New York: Routledge, 1990).

24. See David R. Elliott and Iris Miller, *Bible Bill: A Biography of William Aberhart* (Edmonton, Alberta: Reidmore, 1987).

25. See Doris French Shackleton, *Tommy Douglas* (Toronto: McClelland and Stewart, 1975).

1960s for a kind of statist conservatism that excoriated Canada's drift into American economic, political, and intellectual orbits.[26]

Catholic corporatism as well as several varieties of Protestant Loyalism have together encouraged a different approach to questions of church and state than developed in the United States. The Catholic establishment in Quebec, where the school systems, hospitals, and labor organizations were once exclusively ecclesiastical enterprises, has given way only since the end of the Second World War. In the Maritime provinces and Ontario, the Anglican and Presbyterian churches never received quite the governmental support that their established counterparts enjoyed in England and Scotland, but direct forms of aid to the churches did not end until the Clergy Reserves (land set aside for the use of the churches) were secularized in 1854. Even after that contentious event, indirect government support continued for many religious agencies. Denominational colleges, for instance, were folded into several of the major provincial universities, so that to this day a few such colleges exist as components of the universities. In addition, varying kinds of aid are still provided to at least some church-organized primary and secondary schools in every Canadian province. As late as 1997, the Newfoundland school system was still operated on a denominational basis (but with proposals moving forward to set up a "public system" for the first time).

Canadian-U.S. Differences

Canadian distinctives are suggested by other differences with the United States. Sunday closing laws, for example, continue to be enforced more widely in Canada than in the United States. As an indication of corporatist concepts of government, the Canadian Radio-television and Telecommunications Commission puts much stricter restrictions on independent religious broadcasters than exist in the United States. For yet

---

26. See George Parkin Grant, *Lament for a Nation: The Defeat of Canadian Nationalism* (Toronto: McClelland and Stewart, 1965); and William Christian, *George Grant* (Toronto: University of Toronto Press, 1993).

another contrast, the religious views of major political leaders are much less subject to public scrutiny than has become customary in the United States. Thus, the religious allegiance of leading politicians has never been a major factor in political campaigns, whether for Alexander Mackenzie (1874-78) and John G. Diefenbaker (1957-63), who were practicing Baptists; John Turner (1984), a serious Catholic; William Lyon Mackenzie King (1921-30, 1935-48), a Presbyterian and spiritualist (who took part in séances in which he spoke with his long-dead dog and mother); Pierre Elliott Trudeau (1968-79, 1980-84) and Brian Mulroney (1984-94), nominal Catholics; or John A. Macdonald (1867-74, 1878-91), a casual Presbyterian who late in life established a close connection with the evangelists H. T. Crossley and John E. Hunter. In recent years, the evangelical connections of Stockwell Day and Preston Manning, heads of the Canadian Alliance and one of its constituent groups (the western, protest Reform Party), have made a stir in Canadian public life, but nothing on the scale of American preoccupation with the New Christian Right. Manning is the son of Edward Manning, who succeeded William Aberhart as both Social Credit premier of Alberta and preacher for a radio Bible class.[27]

One of the most important reasons for structural differences in religion and politics between the two nations arises from the varied proportions of religious adherence. A major cross-border survey by the Angus Reid Group in October 1996 revealed that about the same proportion of the populations adhere to mainline churches (15 percent in the U.S., 16 percent in Canada), but in the United States a much higher proportion adhere to conservative Protestant churches (26 percent to 10 percent) as well as to black Protestant churches (9 percent to less than 1 percent). By contrast, a higher proportion of Canadians were adherents to the Roman Catholic Church (26 percent to 20 percent) and a much higher proportion were secular or only nominal in religious attachments (40 percent to 20 percent). The fact that each of these large blocks is constituted differently in the two countries — with,

27. This account follows George A. Rawlyk, "Politics, Religion, and the Canadian Experience: A Preliminary Probe," in *Religion and American Politics*, ed. Mark A. Noll (New York: Oxford University Press, 1990), pp. 253-77.

for example, the Mennonites and Dutch Reformed relatively more important in Canada and conservative Protestants and Baptists more important in the United States — also helps to explain different religious tendencies.

At the same time, however, contrasts between Canada and the United States on questions of religion and politics are intriguing precisely because they coexist with so many similarities between the two nations. Those similarities include an active evangelical voluntarism that in the nineteenth century (outside of Quebec) came close to establishing an informal Protestant hegemony in Canada.[28] Part of Canada's dominant nineteenth-century Protestant culture was a propensity to use biblical imagery for the aspirations of Canadian nationalism that also mirrored practices south of the border. When the Dominion of Canada was formed in 1867, it seemed only natural for the Methodist Leonard Tilley of New Brunswick to apply the words of Psalm 72:8 to his country ("He shall have dominion also from sea to sea").[29] Again like the United States, Canada had a dismal record of Protestant-Catholic violence in the nineteenth century, fueled sometimes by Catholic resentment of Protestant missionaries and sometimes by demonstrations of the Irish Protestant Orange Order.

In the immediate past, social scientific research has provided another way of comparing Canada and the United States. In both countries, there seems to be a "God's party" vote associated with politically conservative movements, but that association is considerably stronger in the U.S. than in Canada. Where in the United States 72 percent of self-identified fundamentalists and evangelicals who regularly attend church voted for the Republican presidential candidate in 1992, only 41 percent of church-attending adherents to conservative Protestant denominations voted for the Reform Party in Canada's 1993 Parliamentary election. The Angus Reid poll of October 1996 showed that on

28. See the especially fine study by John Webster Grant, *A Profusion of Spires: Religion in Nineteenth-Century Ontario* (Toronto: University of Toronto Press, 1988).

29. See Preston Jones, "The Bible and Protestant British North American Identity in the Early 1860s," *American Review of Canadian Studies* (Winter 1999): 651-67; and Jones, "'His Dominion'? Varieties of Protestant Commentary on the Confederation of Canada," *Fides et Historia* 32 (Summer/Fall 2000): 83-88.

some issues, Canadians and Americans are virtually the same — for example, in percentages of respondents who take a religiously motivated stance on abortion or who report that their clergy speak out on social issues. However, Americans are considerably more likely than Canadians (by at least ten percentage points) to say that Christian values should influence politics, to express confidence in organized religion, to belong to a church or a religious group, to say that Christians should get involved in politics to protect their values, and to affirm that religion is important for political thinking. By contrast, Canadians are more likely (again, by at least ten percentage points) to say that churches and religious organizations should be required to pay taxes, to express confidence in the news media, and to vote for a self-described atheist running for high political office.[30] Such polling results suggest that processes of secularization have moved more rapidly in Canada than in the United States. They suggest as well that, although Canadians and Americans share many social attitudes and experiences, historical differences in approaching questions of religion and politics continue to exist.

These snapshots from the Christian histories of Mexico and Canada demonstrate how valuable comparative perspectives can be. They show that in the transportation of Christianity from Europe to the New World many results were possible. These results depended on what the immigrants did in North America, the physical geography in which they attempted to establish churches, their interaction with the indigenous inhabitants, and the European inheritances they carried with them to the New World. Above all, the critical factor for the development of Christianity in North America has been whether it took place in Mexico, Canada, or the United States.

30. For further details on these comparisons, see Mark A. Noll, "Religion in the United States and Canada," *Crux* 34:4 (Dec. 1998): 13-25.

CHAPTER ELEVEN

The Fate of European Traditions — Lutherans, Roman Catholics

A comparison of religious developments in the United States, Canada, and Mexico draws attention to issues concerning the transplanting of Europe's Christianity into the New World; considering how historic European traditions have fared in the environment of United States history raises the same issues in different form. The story is, of course, different for each branch of European Christianity with an American offshoot. The same is true for the passage of non-Christian religions to North America. The openness of the United States to Jewish immigration, for example, has created unprecedented opportunities for Jewish scholarship, literature, and theological self-consciousness, even as it has raised concerns about whether assimilation to American ways threatens historic Jewish patterns of faith, practice, and identity.[1] Large-scale immigration to the United States during the latter decades of the twentieth century by Muslims (mostly from the Middle East) and by representatives of such Asian religions as Hinduism and Buddhism also reveals similar contrasts.[2]

1. For outstanding samples of a flourishing literature, see Naomi W. Cohen, *Jews in Christian America* (New York: Oxford University Press, 1992); Jonathan D. Sarna and David G. Dalin, *Religion and State in the American Jewish Experience* (Notre Dame, IN: University of Notre Dame Press, 1997); and Elliott Abrams, *Faith or Fear: How Jews Can Survive in a Christian America* (New York: Free Press, 1997).

2. For examples, see Yvonne Yazbeck Haddad, ed., *The Muslims of America* (New York:

The United States provides unprecedented opportunities for such groups, but almost all of them experience uncertainty in the midst of success. The worrisome question for the future is almost always the same — whether America's liberal, democratic, commercial, mobile, and individualistic values inevitably erode the particular structures of inherited religious tradition.

In the history of Christianity, myriad communities of European immigrants have felt similar pressures to conform to broad patterns of American life, although these pressures have been felt differently in different places. The pressures have also increased steadily over time as modern forms of transportation, communication, business, entertainment, and education pull once-isolated localities into the national culture. Yet since the seventeenth century the environmental push toward democratic polity, an acceptance of religious pluralism, a stress on individual self-determination, and a preference for innovation over tradition has operated in roughly the same way.

The push was felt, for example, by early Dutch settlers along the Hudson River in modern New York whose attempts to establish feudal enclaves, undertaken with the tacit support of the Dutch Reformed church, eventually failed, but only after more than a century.[3] By contrast, the several groups of French Huguenots who came to the American colonies after the Revocation of the Edict of Nantes in 1685 assimilated quite rapidly.[4] In the eighteenth century, German settlers were able to keep alive Old World cultural patterns, including religion, but only as long as the use of the German language kept them relatively isolated.[5] Again by contrast, settlers from Scotland and from Scotland by

Oxford University Press, 1991); Thomas Tweed, *The American Encounter with Buddhism* (Bloomington: Indiana University Press, 1992); Charles S. Prebisch and Kenneth K. Tanaka, eds., *The Faces of Buddhism in America* (Berkeley: University of California Press, 1998).

3. See Randall H. Balmer, *A Perfect Babel of Confusion: Dutch Religion and English Culture in the Middle Colonies* (New York: Oxford University Press, 1989).

4. See Jon Butler, *The Huguenots in America* (Cambridge: Harvard University Press, 1983).

5. See A. G. Roeber, *Palatines, Liberty, and Prosperity: German Lutherans in Colonial British America* (Baltimore: Johns Hopkins University Press, 1993).

way of Ireland almost from the moment of their arrival fueled the growth of the Presbyterians, an English-language denomination; but whether as Presbyterians or not, the Scots and Scots-Irish embraced broader American values fairly rapidly.[6] During the nineteenth century, assimilation of European religious groups operated at a variable pace depending upon whether the size of the migrating group was large or small, whether immigrants moved into cities or the more isolated Midwestern plains, whether or not a continuing supply of immigrants kept alive the European language, and if the surrounding population of Americans welcomed or rejected the newcomers. Mennonites who came from Russia and the outskirts of the Austrian empire, as well as German and Scandinavian Lutherans and members of free churches who settled in the Upper Midwest, tended to preserve Old World habits longer than the Protestants from Germany, Hungary, Britain, and Scandinavia who settled in the cities.[7] Each of the major stands of Catholic immigration — in rough order, English, French, Irish, German, Italian, Polish, Czech, Slovenian, and more recently Hispanic and Vietnamese — contained multiple patterns of ethnic identification and American assimilation.[8] Because the migration of the Orthodox came later and from cultures further removed from America's Anglo-Saxon traditions, assimilation for Greek, Russian, Ukrainian, Syrian, Armenian, Lebanese, Romanian, and Serbian Orthodox has not proceeded rapidly. In addition, because of the strongly holistic character of Orthodox Old World cultures, assimilation to American ways has probably meant leaving the ancestral church more frequently than for either Protestant or Catholic streams of immigration.

Among the vast array of immigrant religious communities have been found many different responses to the environmental pressures of American life. The patterns discussed in Chapter One are representative of countless individual cases, each of which is important for its

6. See the chapter "The Presbyterian Church," in James G. Leyburn, *The Scots-Irish: A Social History* (Chapel Hill: University of North Carolina Press, 1962), pp. 273-95.

7. See Theron F. Schlabach, ed., *The Mennonite Experience in America,* 4 vols. (Scottdale, PA: Herald, 1985-1996).

8. See, for example, Paula M. Kane, *Separatism and Subculture: Boston Catholics, 1900-1920* (Chapel Hill: University of North Carolina Press, 1994).

own circle of adherents, but also as a factor in the broader, more complex American mosaic.

Of many possible accounts of the opportunities and perils of Americanization for inherited European religious traditions, two of the most interesting (and also best documented) concern the fate of Lutheran confessional theology and Roman Catholic higher education. These narrower themes only begin to hint at the broader meaning of Christian life in America for even these two large, diverse families of Christians. Moreover, the patterns observable in the American histories of Lutheran confessionalism and Catholic higher education are not necessarily typical of other religious traditions transplanted to America. Yet because they so clearly display the vicissitudes of faith traditions adjusting to the American context, they are unusually useful as heuristic accounts.

Lutheran Confessionalism

The history of Lutheran theology in America is a story with several remarkable twists.[9] After early, ineffective efforts at settlement by Swedes in Delaware early in the seventeenth century, the story of Lutheran churches in America really begins with organizing efforts by Henry Melchior Muhlenberg (1711-1789). Muhlenberg, who had been sent from the pietist center of Halle to provide guidance for the German Lutheran immigrants in colonial Pennsylvania, quickly established himself as a forceful leader, blending orthodox and pietist emphases in strengthening the new immigrant churches. As the Lutheran settlers learned English and took on other American characteristics, their theology — quite naturally, it seemed — began to assume an American cast.[10]

---

9. A good introduction, with full bibliography, is provided by Christa R. Klein, "Lutheranism," *Scribner's Encyclopedia,* vol. 1, pp. 431-450.

10. For helpful treatment concerning complexities of assimilation between Muhlenberg and Schmucker, see A. G. Roeber, "J. H. C. Helmuth, Evangelical Charity, and the Public Sphere in Pennsylvania, 1793-1800," *Pennsylvania Magazine of History and Biography* 121 (1997): 77-100.

Americanization continued in the next generation, especially under the direction of Samuel Simon Schmucker (1799-1873), a graduate of the Presbyterian Princeton Seminary who worked throughout his life for causes that he felt would benefit both Lutherans and other Protestants in the United States.[11] It was Schmucker's conviction that New World Lutherans could profitably link characteristics of American Protestantism with traditional European convictions. From these convictions, he worked on behalf of the General Synod of Lutheran churches (formed in 1820), became a mainstay at Gettysburg Lutheran Seminary, and pledged himself to fight rationalism and religious indifference with the Augsburg Confession and Luther's Small Catechism. At the same time, Schmucker's concerns moved beyond narrow definitions of traditional Lutheran faith and practice. He supported revivalism. He favored the development of interdenominational agencies, such as the Sunday School movement, to spread Christianity and to improve national morality. He spoke out on American national issues, expressing fears, for example, concerning immigrants and Roman Catholics. He also was a founder of the American branch of the interdenominational Evangelical Alliance (1846), and he prepared an address for the 1873 New York meeting of the Alliance as almost the last act of his life.

The social pressure of Americanization became apparent when Schmucker risked antagonizing traditional Lutherans by moving to modify the historic Augsburg Confession. To Schmucker, it was Lutheran enough to agree that "the fundamental doctrines of the Word of God are taught in a manner substantially correct in the doctrinal articles of the Augsburg Confession."[12] If he held on to this much of the Old World heritage, Schmucker concluded, it would be appropriate to modify selected elements of his Lutheran theological heritage. Spe-

---

11. For general accounts, see Paul P. Kuenning, *The Rise and Fall of American Lutheran Pietism: The Rejection of an Activist Heritage* (Macon, GA: Mercer University Press, 1988); Leigh D. Jordahl, "Samuel Simon Schmucker and American Lutheranism," *Encounters with Luther*, vol. 2, ed. Eric W. Gritsch (Gettysburg, PA: Institute for Luther Studies, 1982), pp. 101-19; and Vergilius Ferm, *The Crisis in American Lutheran Theology: A Study of the Issue Between American Lutheranism and Old Lutheranism* (New York: Century, 1927).

12. Quoted in Theodore G. Tappert, ed., "Introduction," *Lutheran Confessional Theology in America, 1840-1880* (New York: Oxford University Press, 1972), p. 24.

cifically, Schmucker was willing to question the real presence of Christ's body in the Lord's Supper, to reject private confession, to wonder if baptism really brought regeneration, and (in keeping with American, "Puritan" opinions) to desire a much stricter observance of Sunday. As he proposed these modifications, Schmucker still thought of himself as a good Lutheran. But others did not.

Schmucker's point of view came close to prevailing until about the mid-nineteenth century. Then, however, the growing numbers of immigrants from Germany and Scandinavia and a revival of interest in the roots of the Reformation combined to lessen his influence. Schmucker's books, such as *A Fraternal Appeal to the American Churches* (1838), pleased his friends, but more recently arriving immigrants and other conservatives worried about adding modern American convictions to traditionally Lutheran beliefs. The anonymous *Definite Synodical Platform* of 1855, which proposed a revision of the Augsburg Confession along lines favored by Schmucker, precipitated a clash of interests that eventually led to the mobilization of "European" Lutheranism against the trends favored by Schmucker.

Support for preserving European Lutheran theology was provided by a flood of immigration from Germany, which included many Lutherans, and from Scandinavia, where state-church Lutheranism in some way touched almost all immigrants. Numbers tell part of the story, with about 3.5 million Germans arriving in the United States in the period 1860-1900, and about 1.5 million from Scandinavia over the same period — and then another million from each region over the next four decades.[13]

In the struggle between "American" and "European" Lutherans, defenders of old ways also enjoyed capable leaders. One of these was the American-born Charles Porterfield Krauth (1823-1883), whose book *The Conservative Reformation and Its Theology* (1871) provided a forthright rationale for maintaining strict Old World standards, even in the confines of the New World. For Krauth, a belief in the general correctness of the Augsburg Confession was not enough. The confession instead

---

13. *Historical Statistics of the United States: Colonial Times to 1957* (Washington, D.C.: U.S. Bureau of the Census, 1960), pp. 58-59.

needed to be affirmed in its details, for it was "the greatest work, regarded in its historical relations, in which pure religion has been sustained by human hands. . . . It is our shield and our sword, our ensign
and our arming, the constitution of our state, the life of our body, the
germ of our being."[14]

Additional defense of Old World Lutheranism came from Carl
Ferdinand Wilhelm Walther (1811-1887), a native of Saxony who mi-
grated to the United States in 1838.[15] Walther was every bit as active as
an American revivalist, but it would have been an insult to tell him so,
since he put so much stock in preserving European Lutheran orthodoxy. Walther pastored a church in St. Louis, helped start a training institute for ministerial candidates, founded a publishing house, a newspaper, and a theological journal, and worked to unite several different
Lutheran synods. He became president of the German Evangelical Lutheran Synod of Missouri, Ohio, and Other States (forerunner of the
modern Lutheran Church — Missouri Synod), and was a leading figure
in the Evangelical Lutheran Synodical Conference of North America established in 1872. Although Walther leaned toward congregationalism
and proclaimed such high views of God's grace that he was called a
"crypto-Calvinist," he agreed with Krauth that the Lutherans' main
task in the New World was to maintain Old World distinctiveness
rather than adjust to American ways. Walther therefore insisted that
ministers, as a condition of their service, affirm "that without any exception the doctrinal contents of the confessions of our church are in
complete agreement with the Holy Scriptures and are not in conflict
with the same in any point, whether a major or a secondary point. Ac-
cordingly, [the minister] declares that he heartily believes the contents
of the confessions to be divine truth and that he intends to preach it
without adulteration."[16]

14. Charles Porterfield Krauth, "The Conservative Reformation and Its Confessions," in Tappert, *Lutheran Confessional Theology*, pp. 50-51.

15. A fine overview of his work is provided in the six-volume set of English translations edited by August R. Suelflow, *Selected Writings of C. F. W. Walther* (St. Louis: Concordia, 1981).

16. C. F. W. Walther, "The Kind of Confessional Subscription Required," in
Tappert, *Lutheran Confessional Theology*, p. 56.

Following Krauth, Walther, and like-minded confessionalists, American Lutheran theology turned back toward Europe and away from the path of Schmucker. With other ethnic Protestants such as the Dutch Reformed, some of the Lutherans also established their own system of private schools, at a time when most other American Protestants were becoming stronger supporters of public education. In sum, American Lutherans rejected what Schmucker had thought was a pious form of Americanized Lutheranism, but what his detractors concluded was only a mildly Lutheranized form of American pietism. Lutherans would not re-establish extensive connections to the wider world of American religion until after World War II.

Very different interpretations of the transition from Schmucker to Krauth and Walther are possible. When one considers the contribution Lutherans might have made to American religion more generally, this reversal was unfortunate. Because it took place, Lutherans lost influence among the public at large, promoted a parochial spirit, strengthened their dependency on the memory of Europe, and rejected the lessons of an active, hundred-year tradition of negotiating a livable compromise between Old World traditions and New World realities.

From another angle, however, it was fortunate for the fate of a distinctive Lutheranism in America that this reversal took place. By not following Schmucker's path into nineteenth-century American Protestantism, Lutherans avoided the troubles that lay only a few years in the future at the time of Schmucker's death in 1873. Schmucker had hoped that Lutherans could join nineteenth-century evangelical culture and, by so joining, make a distinctively Lutheran contribution to an expanding Protestant force. But the force that Schmucker so much wanted Lutherans to share was, even as he appeared before the 1873 meeting of the Evangelical Alliance, beginning to decline.

As we have seen, soon after Schmucker's death an enervating threefold division took place in the Protestant mainstream. In response to new social and intellectual challenges, some heirs of nineteenth-century evangelicalism, who would soon be called modernists, moved with the times, conceded the hegemony of the new sciences, and sought a new alliance between modernized faith and the American way of life. Others, the later fundamentalists, made a more complicated response.

They moved both with and against the times — with, by adopting the new applied technologies of mass media and public marketing, and against, by resisting the evolution of old doctrines demanded by the new era. They too attempted to preserve a Protestant America, but with its old content as well as its old form. By far the majority of Protestants vacillated in the middle, nostalgic for the vanishing harmonies of society, mind, and religion. They were unsettled by the tendency of new ways to dismiss traditional Christian convictions, but also unwilling to decide for either the modernist or fundamentalist construction of true religion.

The reversal of Lutherans from an Americanizing course to a separatist course meant that they were spared this disruption of the evangelical Protestantism that Schmucker had so admired. From the perspective of American history in general, however, Lutherans had entered into a desert sojourn, as they once again became a relatively isolated religious tradition. From the perspective of the history of Christianity, this situation did mean that when the Lutherans re-emerged after World War II, they retained at least some of the distinctively Lutheran theology that the nineteenth-century traditionalists had hoped to preserve.

After Lutherans began to re-engage the larger American culture in the second half of the twentieth century, however, it was not entirely clear that these Lutheran theological distinctives were going to be preserved. The largest Lutheran denomination, the Evangelical Lutheran Church in America (ELCA), with over five million members in 1997, was the result of countless mergers between separate ethnic denominations over the course of the twentieth century. Its very existence, therefore, is a signpost to the weakening of ethnic identity, since the mergers that contributed to this denomination took place only after ties with Europe faded and English replaced the German, Swedish, Norwegian, Danish, and Finnish languages in worship services. The critical question for the history of theology is whether the ELCA's movement beyond ethnic, linguistically separated identities necessarily entailed also a loss of Lutheran theological distinctives. At least one study — on the social pronouncements in the 1960s and 1970s of one of the denominations that merged to form the ELCA — suggests that these Lutherans were responding to American society in ways quite similar to those of the mainline Protestant denominations.[17] That is, they were reacting to American events in the mildly liberal fashion that had come to characterize denominations associated with the National Council of Churches. Lutheran distinctives, such as Martin Luther's two-kingdom theology or Luther's effort to maintain a theology of the cross, were largely absent. In the decades of the 1990s, moreover, the issues most hotly debated in the ELCA concerned proposals for the ordination of practicing homosexuals and other progressive sexual matters — in other words, the very issues that have drawn a great deal of attention in other mainline Protestant denominations. The Austrian-born sociologist Peter Berger takes a dim view of the modern ELCA; in fact, Berger feels that the ELCA's theological position has become so watered-down that Berger, a life-long Lutheran, describes himself now as "ecclesiastical homeless."[18] In such an interpretation of the Lutheran theological tradition in America, the conclusion is that nineteenth-century conservative Lutherans preserved something distinctive about their theological inheritance from Europe only to sacrifice it in the late twentieth century to mainline Protestant conventions of the day.

A similar account is possible for the other main Lutheran tradition in America, the Lutheran Church — Missouri Synod, with over three million members. In the 1970s, this denomination was torn by internal dissension sparked by the desire of seminary teachers and other church leaders to employ some of the methods of biblical scholarship and some of the assumptions about modern learning that had become standard in the universities and many of the mainline Protestant denominations.[19] In this dispute, however, the Missouri Synod moved opposite the ELCA. It reaffirmed conservative positions on the inerrancy of the Bible, the reservation of the ordained ministry to men only,

17. Christa R. Klein with Christian D. von Dehsen, *Politics and Policy: The Genesis and Theology of Social Statements in the Lutheran Church in America* (Minneapolis: Fortress, 1989).

18. Peter L. Berger, "Reflections of an Ecclesiastical Expatriate," *Christian Century*, Oct. 24, 1990, p. 969.

19. See John H. Tietjen, *Memoirs in Exile: Confessional Hope and Institutional Conflict* (Minneapolis: Fortress, 1990); and Bryan V. Hillis, *Can Two Walk Together Unless They Be Agreed? American Religious Schisms in the 1970s* (Brooklyn, NY: Carlson, 1991).

and firm rejection of modern sexual ethics. The Missouri Synod also included many leaders who looked kindly on creation science, conservative politics, and other traits of recent American fundamentalism. Some observers thought these decisions by the Missouri Synod were influenced more by American fundamentalism than by historic Lutheranism.

It would be possible, therefore, for a student of Lutheran theology to conclude that American Lutherans turned aside from Samuel Schmucker's American modifications of Lutheranism in the nineteenth century only to yield to Americanizing pressures in the twentieth century, with the ELCA becoming less and less distinguishable from older mainline Protestant denominations and the Missouri Synod taking on the colors of American fundamentalism.

Such a judgment could be premature. Considerable interest in distinctly Lutheran theological traditions remains alive in the ELCA.[20] There is also a long tradition in the Missouri Synod of sharing tactical positions with American fundamentalists while preserving a distinctive Lutheran identity.[21] Clearly, however, the decisions that faced the generation of Schmucker, Krauth, and Walther are still confronting American Lutherans in the twenty-first century. Pressures to Americanize can take several forms, but they seem to be ever-present. Lutherans took steps to resist that pressure in the nineteenth century; whether they are willing to do so again in the twenty-first century — especially since historical study shows so clearly the isolation that resulted from that earlier choice — remains an open question.

Roman Catholic Intellectual Life

Another important story containing dramatic turning points is the history of Roman Catholic higher education in the United States.[22] As

---

20. See the periodicals *Lutheran Forum* and *Pro Ecclesia.*

21. See Milton L. Rudnick, *Fundamentalism and the Missouri Synod: A Historical Study of Their Interaction and Mutual Influence* (St. Louis: Concordia, 1966).

22. This account depends very heavily on Philip Gleason, *Contending with Modernity:*

with the story of Lutheran theology, Catholic educational efforts in colleges and universities reveal much about both possibilities and perils for European Christian traditions in the New World. The story is important for many reasons, not least because foreign observers have singled out educational efforts as among the greatest triumphs of Catholic history in America. Thus German sociologist and historian Michael Zöller has written, "American Catholicism's success story is most clearly mirrored in its schools and universities, and therefore they also serve as a showpiece of the American church."[23]

During the first two-thirds of the nineteenth century, American Catholics struggled to create educational institutions that would support the broader life of the church. In a few American regions, Catholics simply took part in the rising American expansion of public education. More often, however, the Protestant character of that education, including higher education, was so heavy-handed that Catholics attempted to set up alternative systems on their own. The Third Plenary Council at Baltimore in 1884 encouraged American Catholics to make the necessary sacrifices to create an alternative, separate system.

Catholic higher education began to come into its own in the last third of the nineteenth century. Numerous tactical adjustments (for example, recording courses by credit hours or abandoning an integrated prep school–university curriculum for the common American divide between high school and college) brought the form of Catholic higher education into line with usual American patterns. But the key development was a new ideological vision. How that vision came to be implemented raises the issue of acculturation, for the same dynamic that gave Catholic higher education its great impetus also attempted to preserve American Catholics from Americanization.

American Catholic higher education, in other words, became a successful enterprise as part of the process by which the Vatican warned American Catholics away from the evils of "Americanism." As we have

---

Catholic Higher Education in the Twentieth Century (New York: Oxford University Press, 1995). See also Neil G. McCluskey, S.J., ed., *The Catholic University: A Modern Appraisal* (Notre Dame, IN: University of Notre Dame Press, 1970).

23. Michael Zöller, *Washington and Rome: Catholicism in American Culture* (Notre Dame, IN: University of Notre Dame Press, 1999), p. 235.

seen in Chapter Six, an 1899 letter from Pope Leo XIII, *Testem Benevo-lentiae,* condemned a shadowy collection of traits denominated "Ameri-canism." In particular the letter attacked the notion that Catholicism needed to conform to American ideals of liberty and individual auton-omy. In a famous response, Archbishop James Gibbons said that he too opposed such errors, but that they were not found in America. Nonethe-less, this "Americanist" controversy led to much greater caution among American Catholics in their engagement with American cultural norms.

Shortly thereafter a second papal document pushed American Catholics further in the same direction. This was the 1907 encyclical *Pascendi Dominici Gregis* from Pius X, with its wholesale condemnation of "modernism." Although aimed mostly at Continental and British thinkers who were following paths marked out by such Protestant lib-erals as Albrecht Ritschl and Adolf von Harnack, Pius X's sweeping con-demnation of modern intellectual conventions insured that Catholic institutions in America would keep their distance from intellectual cur-rents in the American academy at large.

Pressure from the Vatican had a positive as well as a negative goal. At the same time that Leo XIII and Pius X were warning the faithful away from modernism, including "Americanism," they and their suc-cessors were mounting a strenuous campaign to promote the work of Thomas Aquinas as an intellectual anchor for Catholic intellectual life. So it was that just as American Catholics were setting about the task of refurbishing their colleges and universities, they received explicit papal guidance about what they should fear and what they should foster in the life of the mind.

The result of this papal guidance was a flourishing of American Catholic higher education from the late nineteenth century into the 1950s and 1960s. While conforming outwardly to the conventions of American educational practice, Catholic educators created their own world where the ideas of Thomas Aquinas and his modern proponents took the central place that various secular theories were coming to en-joy in the American university world as a whole.[24]

24. For that other story, see Laurence R. Veysey, *The Emergence of the American Univer-sity* (Chicago: University of Chicago Press, 1969), pp. 121-79.

Evaluating the quality of the separated Catholic higher education is a difficult matter. Positively assessed, the Catholic colleges and universities enjoyed a vigorous *raison d'être* that arose out of the heart of their religion. The center of neo-Thomist education was its confidence that the right use of reason would lead the fair-minded thinker very close to what God had revealed to the church through the Scriptures and the apostolic traditions guarded by the church's hierarchy. What made Neoscholasticism so profoundly important in the first sixty years of the twentieth century, however, was not just its sense of intellectual depth and adventure, but also its many links to social action, missionary service, and liturgical renewal. The teaching of theology — or of Thomistic philosophy that carried manifest theological implications — was being carried on in self-conscious connection with a revival of liturgy and a renewed concentration on a practical theology of the Mystical Body that joined together study of this world, contemplation of the person of Christ, and commitment to the work of the church.

A short-hand indication of the power of the neo-Thomist synthesis is to note that it undergirded not only the social radicalism of Dorothy Day and the Catholic Worker Movement, but also the popular apologetics of Bishop Fulton Sheen, as well as the profound reflections of John Courtney Murray, S.J., on church and state in the modern world. More prosaically, this neo-Thomism inspired a network of innovative social initiatives known as "Catholic Action," an imposing empire of Catholic popular magazines, academic journals, educational societies, and a vigorous intellectual elite. The only movements of comparable intellectual power in American religious history are the Puritanism of the seventeenth century and the brief outburst of theological creativity among Reformed theologians in the two decades before the Civil War (including, with all their differences, Horace Bushnell, Robert Lewis Dabney, Charles Hodge, C. W. Nevin, E. A. Park, H. B. Smith, and James H. Thornwell). But both of those earlier Protestant movements were much more narrowly theological than neo-Thomism between the wars, and both had the advantage Neoscholasticism lacked of flowing along with historic currents in American culture rather than resisting them. The only Protestant system currently at work in twentieth-century America that can even approach the intellectual depth, breadth, and sanctity of neo-Thomism is the Dutch-American cultivation of the Calvinist theology of the Dutch activist and politician Abraham Kuyper (1837-1920).[25] But Kuyperianism in America has never come close to the scope, energy, and achievements of neo-Thomism in its heyday.

Quite apart from comparisons, the Catholic revival testifies to remarkable strengths when observed in itself. Even if its highest ideals were never fully realized and partially realized only among a few of its adherents, those ideals possessed great integrity. Philip Gleason, the leading historian of Catholic education, summarizes the neo-Thomist revival in these terms: "To learn more of God and God's creation was not merely to be called to apostolic action; it was to be drawn more powerfully to God as the object of contemplation, of worship, of prayer, of devotion, of the soul's desire for spiritual fulfillment. . . . The God-centeredness that was integral to Thomism, and the affective reactions it aroused, help us to understand how the philosophical dimensions of the Catholic revival — which seems, in retrospect, so often dry and mechanical — nourished, and was in turn nourished by, the literary, aesthetic, and even mystical dimensions of the revival."[26] An intellectual system with these goals fits very well with a Christian perspective on the world, grounded as it is in creation, incarnation, and redemption — in the realities of sin and grace.

At the same time, a more negative evaluation can be made of America's separated system of Catholic higher education. For one thing, the action of the Vatican at the turn of the century in restraining American Catholic engagement with broader American culture might be construed as oppressive. The cumulative effect of *Testem Benevolentiae* and *Pascendi* was to short-circuit self-conscious consideration of how Catholics should best relate to the national culture. Intellectual passivity was the result in wide stretches of the church. Positive interaction with America's broader intellectual culture did not begin for decades.[27]

25. For learned commentary as well as the texts, see James A. Bratt, ed., *Abraham Kuyper: A Centennial Reader* (Grand Rapids: Eerdmans, 1998).

26. Gleason, *Contending with Modernity*, p. 122.

27. For the negative assessment, see Gleason, *Contending with Modernity*, pp. 12-16.

Considered neutrally, the Catholic intellectual revival can also be viewed as simply a way of buying time. Neo-Thomism dominated the world of Catholic higher education from about 1900 to about 1960, which was exactly the time when the largely immigrant church was being transformed economically, socially, and politically into a much more American body. From this perspective, the Catholic intellectual revival seems to be a way of letting intellectual matters simply coast in order to preserve energy for the practical tasks of learning to get along in English, constructing church and school buildings, becoming financially established, and beginning to internalize American cultural mores.

Finally, it must count against this system of education that, when the Second Vatican Council and altered social conditions combined to create the shockwaves of the 1960s, the whole edifice of neo-Thomist education collapsed. The synthesis unraveled for a combination of factors — the impact of World War II (which brought Catholic colleges and universities the benefits and bane of government assistance), growing pressure to conform to broader secularizing patterns in American higher education, criticism of neo-Thomism from within the church itself, the unanticipated effects of the Second Vatican Council, the movement of once-immigrant Catholic communities to the prosperous suburbs, and the culture shocks of the 1960s.

Since the 1960s, American Catholic higher education has continued to grow in numbers and financial strength, but its intellectual unity has vanished. At major Catholic universities such as Boston College, Georgetown in Washington, D.C., Notre Dame in Indiana, and at several Loyola Universities run by the Jesuits (in Baltimore, Chicago, Los Angeles, and elsewhere), major debates have occurred on just what a "Catholic education" is supposed to mean in the modern intellectual world.[28] These debates have only intensified in response to *Ex corde ecclesiae*, a document prepared in the mid-1990s by the Vatican and the American bishops aimed at securing the orthodoxy of Catholic theologians at Catholic universities. Following the path of earlier Protestant

---

28. For such debates over the course of one year at the University of Notre Dame in Indiana, see Keith Coyne, *Domers: A Year at Notre Dame* (New York: Viking, 1995).

modernism, extreme voices on the Left want to reduce Catholicism to a thin ethical wash that hardly affects the day-to-day operations of the university. Along the lines of earlier Protestant fundamentalism, extreme voices on the Right call for a reintroduction of a womb-to-tomb cocoon dominated by militant Catholic ideals. The great majority of Catholic educators are in the middle, desiring meaningful retention of genuinely Catholic identity but also wanting to fit into the broader worlds of contemporary American intellectual life.[29]

Efforts to assess this complex intellectual history are made even more difficult by noting that scholars trained in the sectarian neo-Thomism of the Catholic intellectual revival drew on principles of that system to call it into question during the years surrounding Vatican II. In 1955 leading Catholic historian John Tracy Ellis criticized American Roman Catholics for their intellectual failings.[30] That critique played more of a role in dismantling the entire Neoscholastic system than Ellis intended, but it is also true that Ellis' critique owed as much to the high ideals of Neoscholasticism as it did to his internalization of standards from elite American universities. Long-term president of the University of Notre Dame Theodore Hesburgh played a large role in pushing for more independence from papal control for Catholic institutions. But the prodigies of intellectual midwifery that Hesburgh accomplished in transforming Notre Dame from a regional university with a local intellectual reputation into a wide-ranging research institution with an international academic reputation were not conceivable apart from his nurturing in the Neoscholastic revival.[31] In the most poignant example, when after World War II John Courtney Murray's opinions on questions of church and state displeased his Jesuit superiors in the United States and the Vatican, he was ordered to stop writing on these subjects, a proscription he obeyed. Yet in retrospect it is clear that

29. For a solid discussion, see David J. O'Brien, *From the Heart of the American Church: Catholic Higher Education in America* (Maryknoll, NY: Orbis, 1994).

30. John Tracy Ellis, *American Catholics and the Intellectual Life* (Chicago: Heritage Foundation, 1956).

31. See Michael O'Brien, *Hesburgh: A Biography* (Washington, D.C.: Catholic University of America Press, 1998); and Theodore M. Hesburgh, ed., *The Challenge and Promise of a Catholic University* (Notre Dame, IN: University of Notre Dame Press, 1994).

Murray's path-breaking insights into how deeply-rooted religious convictions could flourish in a democratic polity sprang directly from certain balancing features of the Thomism in which he was trained. To put the matter provocatively, the penetrating *Catholic* intelligence of John Courtney Murray is difficult to imagine outside of a church marked by both the intellectual genius and the cultural narrowness of American Roman Catholicism in the period 1900-1960.

As a case study in the Americanization of a European Christian inheritance, the story of Catholic higher education is most instructive. Like the Lutheran theologians discussed in this chapter, Catholic educators also pulled back from embracing American ways. But the succeeding period of isolation, though it produced a remarkable flourishing, did not last. Now, again like the Lutherans, Catholics face a decision on how best to maintain the vitality of an inherited faith in an America that offers many opportunities for religious growth and expression, but that also has always acted powerfully to conform European immigrant faiths to the norms of liberal democracy and sectarian individualism. The task would seem to require steering between the Scylla of assimilation without tradition and the Charybdis of tradition without assimilation.

CHAPTER TWELVE

Day-to-Day Christian
Spirituality and the Bible

The shape of day-to-day religious life for ordinary believers is difficult to recover historically. Not only is there immense diversity
within a region as large as North America and in a period as long as the
centuries since European settlement; there are also huge problems of
research constituted by the fact that most people do not record their
quotidian practices and beliefs. Despite these difficulties, however, the
study of religion in America has benefited from several decades of concentrated attention to the ordinary lives of ordinary Americans in their
ordinary circumstances. This kind of study has made it possible to say a
great deal about the experiential quality of day-to-day religious lives
throughout American history.[1]

For the history of Christianity, the study of day-to-day life has
brought to light some patterns that largely replicate European practices, but it has also examined behavior that distinguishes the North
American history of Christianity from patterns prevailing in Europe. In
the former category, which will be treated briefly here, are the following: American tendencies to intermingle the formal and ecclesiastical
aspects of Christianity with populist practices often described as super-
stitious or magical; American habits of ethical seriousness deriving as

---

1. A recent volume exploring these dimensions is David D. Hall, ed., *Lived Religion in
America: Toward a History of Practice* (Princeton: Princeton University Press, 1997).

much from the ethos of religious traditions as from their formal dogmatic structures; American propensities for fleshing out religious sentiments and loyalties in a panoply of popular material forms; American
practices of spiritual reading that freely combine an interest in elite literature with a taste for populist authors; and consistent use of a
"canon" of Protestant hymnody as an expression of dynamic lay theology. On the other hand, two features of Christian life that probably reflect more direct influence from the American context, and which will
be treated at greater length here, are the importance of conversion for
individual religious life and the centrality of the Bible in the religious
practices of the civilization.

Formal Religion and Magic

Keith Thomas's magisterial study *Religion and the Decline of Magic* (1971)
defined a process that has been at work throughout the Western world
since the Middle Ages whereby formal religious teachings edge aside local magical practices as elite religious authority becomes more important for the churches and as scientific assumptions spread eventually
through more levels of society. But as Thomas documents, and a wide
range of religious historians have shown for Europe and America, that
transition from magic to religion is almost never complete. Recent history for religion in North America has shown, for example, that even
the Puritans, where formal adherence to Calvinist theology was always
a defining foundation of existence, tolerated and even encouraged
dreams, portents, special providences, and a number of other "wonders" alongside their formal dogmatic structures.[2] Outside of New England, the difference between formal religion and lay magical practices
was, at least for much of the population, even harder to discern.[3] In the
nineteenth century, the spread of literacy and the explosion of print

---

2. David D. Hall, *Worlds of Wonder, Days of Judgment: Popular Religious Belief in Early
New England* (New York: Knopf, 1989).

3. Jon Butler, *Awash in a Sea of Faith: Christianizing the American People* (Cambridge:
Harvard University Press, 1990), pp. 67-97.

worked to increase both the power of denominational leaders in defining the disciplined character of true religion and the spread of popular religious practices that to outsiders seemed as magical as ever. For example, the great antislavery reformer Frederick Douglass underwent an experience of evangelical conversion, but also retained a good luck charm from his days as a slave.[4] At the same time, alternative lay-led practices such as phrenology, mesmerism, Christian Science, and spiritualism mixed together generous components from both scientific and magical approaches to the world.[5] During the twentieth century — supposedly the great age of scientific rationality — various magic-like alternatives have flourished in America, whether astrology, New Age religions of bewildering variety, or cultures of personal therapy that function like formal religious institutions.[6] In continuing to exploit magic or magic-like practices alongside the formal religions, Americans show that they are much more like religious practitioners elsewhere than different from them.

Ethical Seriousness

Throughout American history, the public visibility of the Christian religion has always been high, and Christian religious influence has been brought to bear in many different ways. Some of these manifestations of influence have involved prominent public practices, whether dignified worship services in stately churches and cathedrals or the enthusiastic liturgies of revivalism, modern Pentecostalism, and Catholic street festivals. Christianity has also been brought to bear through a huge range of publications, from ephemeral tracts to weighty tomes

4. Will Coleman, "Roots of Black Theology: Frederick Augustus Douglass, 1818-1895," in *Makers of Christian Theology in America,* ed. Mark G. Toulouse and James O. Duke (Nashville: Abingdon, 1997), p. 254.

5. See R. Laurance Moore, *In Search of White Crows: Spiritualism, Parapsychology, and American Culture* (New York: Oxford University Press, 1977).

6. See Catherine L. Albanese, *Nature Religion in America: From the Algonkian Indians to the New Age* (Chicago: University of Chicago, 1990); and Albanese, ed., *American Spiritualities: A Reader* (Bloomington: University of Indiana Press, 2000).

and every possible genre in between. In every American era there have also existed multiple influences exerted by Christian groups or traditions in what might be called ethical tone. The overwhelming characteristic of this ethical influence is seriousness, but a seriousness expressed in several different ways.

Puritanism, for example, was always as much an ethos, an approach to life, as it was a formal body of doctrine.[7] Nineteenth-century revivalists embodied an ethical sense that has been labeled immediatist, ultraist, and perfectionist.[8] More generally, nineteenth-century Northern evangelical Protestant culture embodied strong principles of what has been called diligent personal responsibility, or "discipline."[9] Toward the end of the nineteenth century, the sense of proprietary solicitude for America as a civilization reached its peak among mainline Protestants.[10] Twentieth-century fundamentalists both promoted spiritual revival and embodied a revivalistic approach to life itself.[11] Pentecostals have been marked by an abandoned approach to spirituality as much as by a particular set of doctrines.[12] Each strand of ethnic Catholicism has also communicated a singular combination of religious, domestic, filiopietistic, and international sentiment.[13] In recent de-

7. Despite legitimate scruples raised about details of his interpretation, no one caught that tone better than Perry G. Miller in such books as *The New England Mind,* 2 vols. (1939, 1953), and *Errand into the Wilderness* (Cambridge: Harvard University Press, 1956).

8. This theme is developed in Mark A. Noll, *One Nation Under God? Christian Faith and Political Action in America* (San Francisco: Harper & Row, 1988), pp. 105-44.

9. For expert explanation of that word, see Daniel Walker Howe, "The Evangelical Movement and Political Culture in the North during the Second Party System," *Journal of American History* 77 (March 1991): 1216-39.

10. That sense is described with special clarity in George M. Marsden, *The Soul of the American University: From Protestant Establishment to Established Nonbelief* (New York: Oxford University Press, 1994).

11. See Joel A. Carpenter, *Revive Us Again: The Reawakening of American Fundamentalism* (New York: Oxford University Press, 1997).

12. See Edith L. Blumhofer, ed., *"Pentecost in My Soul": Explorations in the Meaning of Pentecostal Experience in the Assemblies of God* (Springfield, MO: Gospel Publishing House, 1989).

13. See Philip Gleason, *Speaking of Diversity: Language and Ethnicity in Twentieth-Century America* (Baltimore: Johns Hopkins University Press, 1992).

cades, a post–Vatican II Catholicism has joined together great concentration on lay ecclesiastical involvement, new concern for world issues, and fresh interest in catechizing the young and newly converted. African American churches have also fostered distinctive ethical styles, sometimes featuring an outlet for emotions, at other times stressing the spiritual meaning of day-to-day tasks, and at still others exhibiting a "worldly spirituality" (or "spiritual worldliness") in which sacred-secular distinctions simply melt away. Mennonite communities have encouraged an earnestness about the environment along with concern to offer practical assistance to those in need.[14] Mainline Protestants display what has been called "Golden Rule Christianity," a non-ideological approach to life that stresses doing good.[15]

In all of these examples, and more that could be enumerated, there is an ethical expression to Christian faith that grows more from shared community practices and subtly promoted ideals than it does from formal theology or liturgy. Novels offer clear examples of these forms of ethical seriousness, including Harriet Beecher Stowe's *Old Town Folks* (1869) for nineteenth-century evangelical Protestants, Charles Sheldon's *In His Steps* (1897) for turn-of-the-century moderate Protestant liberals, Shirley Nelson's *The Last Year of the War* (1978) for twentieth-century fundamentalists, Ralph McInerny's mystery stories featuring Father Roger Dowling that showcase Catholicism in tension between emphases from before and emphases after the Second Vatican Council, or James Baldwin's *Go Tell It on the Mountain* (1953) for an African American urban setting in the mid-twentieth century. The presence of these various forms of ethical seriousness points out the importance of local religious traditions in the spaciousness of the United States. It also points out the importance of religion not so much as formal creeds, codes, or catechisms, but as expectations of how best to approach life in general.

The ethical seriousness promoted by religious communities has of-

14. See Calvin W. Redekop, *Mennonite Society* (Baltimore: Johns Hopkins University Press, 1989).

15. See especially Nancy T. Ammerman, "Golden Rule Christianity: Lived Religion in the American Mainstream," in Hall, *Lived Religion*, pp. 196-216.

ten featured values, judgments, or habits of reflection strikingly at odds with what seem to be the chief "American" values of a period. For example, many religious traditions foster a respect for community that contradicts the individualism of broader American social values, or a respect for in-group traditions that contradicts the abandonment of history so evident in the presentations of the popular media. In these ways, ethical traditions growing out of specific religious communities resemble similar patterns in Europe, with the main difference being the multiplicity of such groups in America's variegated religious landscape.

Material Christianity

Leaders of Reformed Protestantism of the sort that has been very important in American Christian history reacted to what they perceived as Roman Catholic error by stressing the distinction between true spirituality and wrong-headed materiality. In an ironic parallel, Catholic leaders in many parts of the world since the Reformation have worked hard to control lay-led devotional movements connected with appearances of the Virgin Mary, statues that weep or speak, and populist religious festivals linked to indigenous cultures. Believers in the United States, whether Protestant or Catholic, resemble their fellows elsewhere in the world by ignoring such scruples and investing a huge range of common-place material objects with religious significance.[16]

Among American Protestants, sacred objects have played a large role in practical Christianity since the very first settlers. The Puritans of New England, for example, exerted great energy in cleansing their worship and church government from everything that smacked of "Romish idolatry." Thus were banished statues, stained glass, organs, pictures, communion tables, kneeling benches, candles, and much else that had been customary in the Anglican worship of the Old World. Yet the Puritans made at least one exception in their effort to purge wor-

---

16. This section is particularly indebted to the exceptional book by Colleen McDannell, *Material Christianity: Religion and Popular Culture in America* (New Haven: Yale University Press, 1995).

ship from decadent materiality: from the earliest days in New England they provided a pulpit cushion, often elegantly woven with elaborate tassels, as a resting place for the Scriptures. The exception proved how hard it was to disengage material and spiritual realms.

Later Protestants embraced an ever-expanding realm of goods that, in one way or another, used ordinary material objects to express spiritual values. The Victorian nineteenth century was the great age of the decorative family Bible whose massive size, graphic illustrations, blank pages for recording family births, deaths, and marriages, and considerable expense testified to the intersection of religious and domestic values. In the last two centuries, Protestants have been avid producers and consumers of cemetery headstones, religious games for children, religious art, and (in more recent decades) bumper stickers, refrigerator magnets, and t-shirts imprinted with religious messages. A widely reproduced print by Warner Sallman called the "Head of Christ," which was first produced in 1941, has been distributed by the hundreds of millions of copies in the United States and around the world.[17]

Catholics in America have followed a parallel path, but have also incorporated into American practice religious uses of material objects with roots in Europe. During the high tide of immigration and afterwards, celebratory street festivals often enlisted much more enthusiastic support for Catholic icons and Catholic practices than the church's ordinary labors.[18] Pictures of the Sacred Heart and other icons related to Catholic teaching have been produced in great numbers. Sacred objects related to the intercession of St. Jude also enjoy a considerable popularity.[19] A particularly interesting European connection is illustrated by the attraction among American Catholics of the shrine in Lourdes, France; consecrated water from Lourdes was a special inspiration for the construction of the main church at the University of Notre Dame in Indiana and also for the replica Lourdes grotto on that campus dedicated

17. See David Morgan, ed., *Icons of American Protestantism: The Art of Warner Sallman* (New Haven: Yale University Press, 1996).

18. As an example, see Robert A. Orsi, *The Madonna of 115th Street: Faith and Community in Italian Harlem, 1888-1950* (New Haven: Yale University Press, 1985).

19. See Robert A. Orsi, *Thank You, St. Jude: Women's Devotion to the Patron Saint of Hopeless Causes* (New Haven: Yale University Press, 1996).

to the Blessed Virgin. By refusing to maintain the clergy's fastidious distinctions between what in the material realm is holy and what is not, American believers have simply continued attitudes, and even practices, that extend as widely as the Christian faith itself has extended.

Spiritual Reading

Inner spirituality is much harder to describe than outward lives of individual action or the activities of churches, denominations, and religious associations. Nonetheless, from what Americans have read (or at least purchased to read), it is possible to gain hints about attractive ideals of Christian spirituality. Once again, the reading habits of American Christians are probably not too different from those of their counterparts in Europe, except perhaps in the unusually wide range of style, taste, and emphasis in that reading.

Americans have sustained a huge appetite for devotional spiritual reading. Among the Puritans and many of their successors, printed sermons were a mainstay of Christian reading.[20] In the nineteenth century, countless editions of the diary of David Brainerd were snapped up. As edited by Jonathan Edwards, Brainerd's intense introspection while a missionary to the Delaware Indians in the 1740s became a model of religious seriousness for many. It has remained in print to this day.[21] Other diaries, letters, and memoirs from such noted leaders as George Whitefield, the eighteenth-century Quaker John Woolman, Francis Asbury, or the twentieth-century Catholic Thomas Merton have reached almost as many readers as Brainerd's famous diary.

In the nineteenth century, basic statements of Christian belief by notable theologians, but aimed at popular audiences, often sold incredibly well. Such volumes included *The Way of Life* (1841) from the Presbyterian leader at Princeton Theological Seminary, Charles Hodge, and

20. See Harry S. Stout, *The New England Soul: Preaching and Religious Culture in Colonial New England* (New York: Oxford University Press, 1986).

21. See Joseph A. Conforti, *Jonathan Edwards, Religious Tradition, and American Culture* (Chapel Hill: University of North Carolina Press, 1995), pp. 62-84.

The Faith of Our Fathers: Being a Plain Exposition and Vindication of the Church Founded by Our Lord Jesus Christ (1876) by James Cardinal Gibbons, Catholic Archbishop of Baltimore, which sold more than two million copies in more than one hundred editions during its first forty years in print. To a somewhat lesser degree, the same thing has happened in the twentieth century. J. I. Packer is a learned Anglican evangelical who relocated from his native England to Canada, but in the United States his book *Knowing God* (1973), which is strongly influenced by the spirituality of the Puritans and the original evangelicals of the eighteenth century, has sold nearly a million copies.

The list of twentieth-century American authors who have become renowned through their writing on the spiritual life is a long one. Frequently reprinted books by such authors include volumes early in the century on prayer by Walter Rauschenbusch and Harry Emerson Fosdick and on the consecrated life by A. B. Simpson. Later authors with wide readerships were the mystical evangelical A. W. Tozer (1897-1980), the Quaker Elton Trueblood (1900-1994), and the Catholic Bishop Fulton Sheen (1895-1979), who was nearly as effective a writer as a television speaker.

Spiritual writers have also broken the once formidable barriers between Protestants and Catholics. For example, books from the Anglican-become-Catholic G. K. Chesterton are read as widely by Protestants as by Catholics. More recently, Protestants have probably purchased as many books by the Catholic writers Thomas Merton and Henri Nouwen as have these authors' fellow Catholics. Of special note in cross-confessional spiritual writing is the remarkable popularity of the seventeenth-century Catholic mystical quietist Madame Guyon, whose works have been widely reprinted by Protestants in the holiness and fundamentalist traditions since the mid-nineteenth century.[22]

Spiritual reading is difficult to classify. Yet those who would understand the religious character of a people must attend to it as carefully as to the well-publicized personages and dramatic events that often monopolize the pages of the history books.

---

22. See Patricia A. Ward, "Madame Guyon and Experiential Theology in America," *Church History* 67 (Sept. 1998): 484-98.

Hymns

Generally the same can be said concerning hymnody. The hymns that Christians sing, memorize virtually without effort, and then pass on to their children are rarely the object of formal study. Despite that neglect, the most widely reprinted hymns undoubtedly offer a more accurate guide to the beliefs and spiritual aspirations of ordinary people than almost any other literature. The hymns reprinted generation after generation are important as gauges of popular spirituality for a number of reasons: they provide succinct digests of the Christian faith that stick with those who sing them more securely than most formal dogma; their emotional force carries hymns far deeper into the subconscious than almost any of the churches' official teachings or formal practices; and their association with the deepest domestic relations and strongest personal convictions gives hymns an intimacy that is rarely approached by other forms of Christian expression. In America these realities have characterized all Christian groups, but especially African American churches.[23]

There are few surprises in what study of the most popular hymns reveal. Yet that study does show that the Christian content of the most popular hymns presents the truths and the comforts of the faith with great power. While these popular hymns do not avoid doctrines of sin and human fallibility, their stress is on the hope offered to the erring by God's mercy in Christ. Examination of the most widely reprinted hymns among Protestants shows how forceful the main emphases of the classic evangelical hymns have remained. A recent study of two hundred American Protestant hymnals from the 1730s to the 1960s revealed that the three most often reprinted hymns were from eighteenth-century Britain: "All Hail the Power of Jesus' Name" by Edward Perronet (and edited by others), Charles Wesley's "Jesus, Lover of My Soul," and Isaac Watts' "Alas! and Did My Savior Bleed."[24] The strong

23. See Jon Michael Spencer, *Black Hymnody* (Knoxville: University of Tennessee Press, 1992); Michael W. Harris, *The Rise of Gospel Blues: The Music of Thomas Andrew Dorsey in the Urban Church* (New York: Oxford University Press, 1992); and James H. Cone, *The Spirituals and the Blues* (Maryknoll, N.Y.: Orbis, 1991).

24. The survey is by Stephen Marini in connection with a study of hymnody in

theme of rescue that runs through these and similarly popular hymns is often linked to themes of this-worldly activity, as in these stanzas taken, respectively, from the three most popular hymns:

> Sinners, whose love can ne'er forget
> the wormwood and the gall,
> go, spread your trophies at his feet,
> and crown him Lord of all.
> * * *
> Jesus, lover of my soul, let me to thy bosom fly,
> while the nearer waters roll, while the tempest still is high:
> hide me, O my Savior, hide, till the storm of life is past;
> safe into the haven guide, O receive my soul at last!
> * * *
> But drops of grief can ne'er repay
> the debt of love I owe;
> here, Lord, I give myself away,
> 'tis all that I can do.

The British origin of these hymns suggests that there is nothing uniquely American about the great, but often neglected, importance of hymnody for Christian communions. Nonetheless, drawing attention to that importance is one way of opening doorways to lived realities of Christian experience as they have been shared by many Americans across both time and space.

Conversion

A prominent feature of American religion that may in fact speak to a consistent difference from Europe is the emphasis on conversion. As

---

American Protestantism being conducted by the Institute for the Study of American Evangelicals at Wheaton College, Illinois; for Marini's own use of the results, see "Evangelical Hymns and Popular Belief," in *Music and the Public Sphere, 1600-1900*, ed. Peter Benes (Boston: Boston University, 1998).

with American attention to the Scriptures, conversion accounts reflect the significance of individual choice and its consequences for American Christian history. In the relative absence of powerful Christian churches exerting an all-encompassing influence across the generations, American religion is extensively shaped by the individual actions from which the religious traditions themselves have been constructed. Of course, not all Americans have dramatic conversion stories, and some Europeans certainly do. Nevertheless, accounts of conversion loom large in American religion because American religious history has reflected so actively the choices, decisions, and turning points of individuals.

Stress on conversion was naturally a prominent theme in the literature of the colonial Great Awakening, which can be dated from the publication in 1737 of Jonathan Edwards' *A Narrative of the Surprising Work of God in the Conversion of Many Hundred Souls in Northampton, and the Neighbouring Towns and Villages of the County of Hampshire, in the Province of the Massachusetts-Bay in New England*. In the nineteenth century, such leading Protestants as Charles Finney and D. L. Moody publicized their own conversion and promoted practices of revival based on those experiences. In an era dominated by such preaching, it was not surprising that conversions *from* Protestantism, especially to Catholicism, were memorable occasions. So it was that a counter-literature grew up that featured the conversion to Rome, as with Mother Ann Seton, Isaac Hecker, Orestes Brownson, and Sophia Ripley, the wife of a leading transcendentalist.[25]

The conversion narratives of the twentieth century feature both old and new themes. Some of the most interesting twentieth-century conversion stories are those of people who left Protestantism. The novel *The Flight of Peter Fromm* (1973) by the mathematician and all-around genius Martin Gardner is one of the most interesting of such examples. The novel's central character, who seems to be Gardner's alter ego, comes from a fundamentalist background to the University of Chicago in the 1930s with the intent of converting the secular pagans to Christianity, only to be converted by them to a version of their worldview.

25. See Jenny Franchot, *Roads to Rome: The Antebellum Protestant Encounter with Catholicism* (Berkeley: University of California Press, 1994).

Even more interesting conversions out of Protestantism are told by individuals who, though grateful for their Protestant beginnings, became Roman Catholics or joined an Eastern Orthodox Church. To the Catholic church have come the novelist Walker Percy from Southern Episcopalianism, the theologian and political writer Richard John Neuhaus from Lutheranism, and the literary critic Thomas Howard from Northern conservative evangelicalism.[26] Their accounts are as revealing of the Protestant worlds they left behind as of the Roman Catholic worlds they entered.

An even more intriguing tale is told by Jack Sparks, Peter Gillquist, and a substantial number of their colleagues who came of age in the evangelical youth ministry Campus Crusade for Christ.[27] Their search for a historically grounded faith eventually led them to the Antiochean Orthodox Church. This exchange of a form of Protestantism for Orthodoxy is especially intriguing. It demonstrates how important it is in America for people to determine their own religious destinies, yet since that importance is largely the product of forces connected to Protestantism, Protestant attitudes toward personal choice enabled these Protestants to move rather easily into a form of Christianity where personal choice has traditionally had a much smaller role.

Conversions *to* Protestant Christianity have continued to be a large part of America's religious history. A few of those conversions are to mainline or liberal Protestantism. The journalist John Cogley (1916-1976), who worked for many years as a Catholic journalist, left Catholicism in 1973 to join the Episcopal Church. An account of his experience written shortly before his death expressed the hope that faith in Christ could become similarly liberating for everyone, even though Cogley was not necessarily interested in having others join him as an Episcopalian.[28]

26. For broader context, see Patrick Allitt, *Catholic Converts: British and American Intellectuals Turn to Rome* (Ithaca, NY: Cornell University Press, 1997).

27. See Peter E. Gillquist, *Becoming Orthodox: A Journey to the Ancient Christian Faith* (Ben Lomond, CA: Conciliar, 1992); and for a different trajectory in the same direction, see Frederica Mathewes-Green, *Facing East: A Pilgrim's Journey into the Mysteries of Orthodoxy* (San Francisco: HarperSanFrancisco, 1997).

28. John Cogley, *A Canterbury Tale* (New York: Seabury, 1976).

More typical have been stories that follow the traditional path of evangelical Protestant conversion. The notable African American singer Ethel Waters (1900-1977), who enjoyed a long career in many venues before she began singing such spirituals as "His Eye Is on the Sparrow" at Billy Graham rallies, used several phrases to describe her conversion as a teenager that many others have echoed: "I got down on the mourner's bench. . . . And then it happened! The peace of heart and of mind, the peace I had been seeking all my life. . . . Love flooded my heart and I knew I had found God and that now and for always I would have an ally, a friend close by to strengthen me and cheer me on."[29]

The conversion of Marion G. "Pat" Robertson (b. 1930) took a somewhat different course.[30] In 1956 Robertson's turn to Christianity gave him not only personal religious faith but a calling to public activity. Although he worked initially with Southern Baptist churches, which remain ambiguous about the charismatic movement, Robertson himself embraced a charismatic form of faith. That form of religion then became the driving force behind a meteoric career. In the early 1960s Robertson purchased a small, struggling television station in Norfolk, Virginia, which he eventually built up through a popular variety show (the "700 Club") into the Christian Broadcasting Network. Other ventures into education, communications, and politics grew out of that earlier experience whereby Robertson seems to have found confidence in himself as a result of having found God.

Another conversion story with political overtones is told by Charles Colson. Colson was a well-connected, high-powered lawyer who eventually became a member of the White House staff of President Richard Nixon. Colson was implicated in activities related to the Watergate scandal of 1972, and eventually served a seven-month jail term. Before he entered prison, however, Colson's outlook on life was decisively altered through the witness of Tom Phillips, a business executive who gave Colson a copy of C. S. Lewis' *Mere Christianity,* another popular book by a British scholar that has enjoyed an immense distribution in

29. Ethel Waters, with Charles Samuels, *His Eye Is on the Sparrow: An Autobiography* (Garden City, NY: Doubleday, 1951), p. 54.

30. David Edwin Harrell, *Pat Robertson* (San Francisco: Harper & Row, 1987).

the United States. The result, after the passage of some time, was what Colson described in the title of a book he published in 1976: *Born Again*. Like many others in American history, Colson was transformed when a message about trust in Christ coincided with a crisis in his own life. In Colson's case, the change was particularly dramatic, for he went from lawyering in high places to founding a ministry called Prison Fellowship that works for the spiritual and material well-being of inmates in the United States and abroad. That movement from personal spiritual experience to outward effort at doing good is also a very common pattern in American Protestant history.

American conversion stories differ a great deal from each other. Their general prominence, however, also reveals a general religious situation in which the choices of individuals make a greater difference than for comparable religious cultures in Europe.

The Bible

The same kind of analysis helps to understand the nearly universal presence in American history of the Bible.[31] Of all ancient religious authorities carried to the New World, only the Bible was exempted from America's profound suspicion of the past. Allegiance to Scripture also merged easily with American democracy. Literacy became the only requirement for harvesting spiritual fruit from the Bible. The explosion of cheap printing in the United States' early national period meant that the means were also at hand to put the Bible, and all manner of biblical interpretations, into the hands of nearly everyone.[32] Religious tumults

31. This section draws extensively from several of my own writings: "Introduction," *The Bible in America,* ed. Nathan O. Hatch and Mark A. Noll (New York: Oxford University Press, 1982), pp. 3-18; "The Bible, American Minority Faiths, and the American Protestant Mainstream, 1860-1925," in *Minority Faiths and the American Protestant Mainstream,* ed. Jonathan Sarna (Urbana: University of Illinois Press, 1997), pp. 191-231; "The Bible in American Culture," *Scribner's Encyclopedia,* vol. 2, pp. 1075-87; and "The Bible in America," *Journal of Biblical Literature* 106 (Sept. 1987): 493-509.

32. See especially Paul C. Gutjahr, *An American Bible: A History of the Good Book in the United States, 1777-1880* (Stanford: Stanford University Press, 1999).

caused by ecclesiastical schism, traumatic national cataclysm, and extraordinary economic expansion have never directly undermined the incredibly widespread and diverse use of the Scriptures.

A few facts, arranged chronologically, suggest the breadth of the Bible's presence in American civilization:

- Before he set sail in 1492, Christopher Columbus was convinced on a reading of Scripture (specifically Isaiah 46:11) that his voyages were a result of divine prophecy.
- The first English book published in North America was *The Whole Booke of Psalmes Faithfully Translated into English Meter* (1640). Later in the colonial period, heroic efforts would be made to provide printed versions of the Bible in several Indian languages and also in German for the use of settlers from the European continent.
- During the colonial period, publication of the King James Bible had been reserved to designated British printers, but with the War for Independence, American publishers began the incredible industry of Bible publication that survives with great force to this day. Between 1777 and 1865, at least 1800 different editions of English-language Bibles were published, the overwhelming majority of them the King James Version.
- The American Bible Society, founded in 1816, was distributing over 300,000 copies of the Bible (in whole or parts) each year by 1830. Well before the close of the twentieth century, the society's total distribution of the Bible or biblical portions went past four *billion*.
- Opinions on Scripture, even by those outside the main Protestant churches, were uniformly high throughout early American history. Early American presidents John Adams, a Unitarian, and Thomas Jefferson, a Deist who thought well of Jesus, both praised the Bible, at least as they felt it should be interpreted.[33] The thorough spread of the Scriptures during the nineteenth century accounts for the fact that many of the most important political statements of the

33. See the introduction as well as Jefferson's own editorial work in Dickinson W. Adams, ed., *Jefferson's Extracts from the Gospels,* The Papers of Thomas Jefferson, Second Series (Princeton: Princeton University Press, 1983).

period — such as Abraham Lincoln's "House Divided" speech of 1858 or his Second Inaugural Address of 1865, which quotes from the Scriptures in several places — drew directly for metaphors and substance from the Bible.

- Throughout the nineteenth century, American settlers regularly named their communities after biblical places, like Zoar, Ohio (Genesis 13:10), and Mount Tirzah, North Carolina (Joshua 12:24), as well as forty-seven variations on Bethel, sixty-one on Eden, and ninety-five on Salem.[34]
- When in 1842 the Roman Catholic Bishop of Philadelphia, Francis Patrick Kenrick, petitioned city officials to allow school children of his faith to hear readings from the Douay-Rheims translation of the Bible instead of the King James Version sacred to Protestants, the city's Protestants rioted and tried to burn down Philadelphia's Catholic churches.
- In 1881, American publication of the Revised Version, produced by a blue-ribbon panel of noted biblical scholars from Britain, for the first time provided a serious alternative to the King James Version as "America's Bible." Nonetheless, throughout the nineteenth century, a huge number of foreign-language editions of the Bible were printed in the United States (for example, at least a hundred different German editions were published between 1860 and 1925). But only with the appearance of the Revised Version, which several newspapers rushed to print in its entirety, did the possibility of other English-language translations become possible.[35]
- In 1898, two traveling salesmen, John H. Nicholson and Samuel Hill, who met by chance at the Central Hotel in Boscobel, Wisconsin, discovered that they shared a love of the Scriptures. As a way of providing easy access to the Bible for people like themselves, they cooperated in founding a movement that came to be called "The Gideons." Since its founding, this lay movement has placed Bibles

34. John Leighly, "Biblical Place-Names in the United States," *Names* 27 (March 1979): 46-59.

35. See especially Peter J. Thuesen, *In Discordance with the Scriptures: American Protestant Battles over Translating the Bible* (New York: Oxford University Press, 1999).

in hotels and motels in 140 countries, passed out millions of New Testaments to school children and to men and women entering the military, and distributed Bibles in prisons, inner-city rescue missions, hospitals (in large print), airplanes, ships, and trains. In 1990 the Gideons presented their 500 millionth Bible to President George Bush.

- The celebrated Scopes Trial of 1925 in Dayton, Tennessee, which pitted the agnostic barrister Clarence Darrow against William Jennings Bryan, the populist defender of traditional American values, featured a highly polemical exchange on the interpretation of passages from the Book of Genesis.
- Hours after the murder of President Kennedy in Dallas in November 1963, his legislative liaison, Larry O'Brien, secured the slain President's own leather-bound Bible for the swearing in of Lyndon Johnson. Ironically, the Texas judge who had been recruited to swear in the new president hesitated momentarily for fear that a Bible from the Roman Catholic Kennedy might be a Catholic translation and so somehow not adequate for the job.[36]
- Two of the most popular rock-operas of the 1970s, *Jesus Christ Superstar* and *Godspell*, were based on the biblical gospels.
- During the same decade, the best-selling book in the United States of any kind (except the Bible itself) was Hal Lindsey's *The Late Great Planet Earth*, which provided a dispensational premillennial account of how current events were fulfilling prophetic passages of Scripture.
- It was a sign of Catholic support for Scripture distribution that the Sacred Heart League placed record orders with the American Bible Society for 775,000 New Testaments in 1979 and 800,000 in 1983.
- In 1990, at least seven thousand different editions of the Bible were available from hundreds of publishers in America. The KJV remained the most popular edition, but several other versions had each enjoyed cumulative distribution of over 50 million copies. These included the Revised Standard Version (in the line of KJV re-

36. William Manchester, *The Death of a President* (New York: Harper & Row, 1967), p. 324.

visions), the Living Bible paraphrase of Kenneth Taylor (which accustomed fundamentalists and conservative evangelicals to using a translation other than the KJV), and the New International Version (which exploited the opening created by the Living Bible and became the widely used translation of choice among more conservative Protestants).

However difficult it may be to define the impact of the Bible on ordinary people precisely, Scripture has always been a vital element in American popular life. From the beginning, the Bible provided themes for Americans to define themselves as a people, and then as a nation. Puritans in New England thought they were in covenant with God just like the Jews of the Old Testament. The first public political campaigns of the 1830s were modeled directly on the organized enthusiasm and passionate rhetoric of the religious revival. In the intense sectional strife leading to the Civil War, the Bible became a weapon put to use by both sides. In the South, passages such as Leviticus 25:45 ("the children of the strangers that do sojourn among you . . . they shall be your possession") defined the righteousness of the cause. In the North, favored passages, usually from the New Testament, such as Galatians 5:1 ("Stand fast . . . in the liberty wherewith Christ hath made us free"), did the same. Abraham Lincoln, in his sublime Second Inaugural Address, put the Civil War into perspective by quoting Matthew 18:7 and Psalm 19:9 and by noting that "Both [sides] read the same Bible." Biblical phrases and conceptions, particularly in the hands of such Southerners as Woodrow Wilson, Jimmy Carter, and Bill Clinton, have continued to exert a political force even in the more secular twentieth century.

If anything, the Bible has been more obviously at work in the popular culture of African-Americans than among whites.[37] Slaves made a sharp distinction between the Bible their owners preached to them and the Bible they discovered for themselves. Under slavery, stringent regulations often existed against unsupervised preaching and sometimes

---

37. See Cain Hope Felder, ed., *Stony the Road We Trod: African American Biblical Interpretation* (Minneapolis: Fortress, 1991); and Theophus Smith, *Conjuring Culture: Biblical Formation of Black America* (New York: Oxford University Press, 1994).

even against owning Bibles. But with permission or not, slaves made special efforts to hear black preachers. One slave left this striking testimony: "a yellow [light-complexioned] man preached to us. She [the slave owner] had him preach how we ought to obey our master and missy if we want to go to heaven, but when she wasn't there, he came out with straight preachin' from the Bible."[38]

Blacks sang and preached about Adam and Eve and the Fall, about "wrestlin' Jacob" who "would not let [God] go," about Moses and the Exodus from Egypt, about Daniel in the lions' den, about Jonah in the belly of the fish, about the birth of Jesus and his death and future return. Grateful blacks from Baltimore in September 1864 presented President Lincoln with a pulpit Bible bound in violet-tinted velvet, furnished in gold, with a raised design depicting the emancipation of the slaves, which cost far more than the average per capita income of white Americans. In response, Lincoln, who never joined a church, called the Bible "the best gift God has given to man." The slaves' profound embrace of Scripture created a climate for Bible reading and biblical preaching that has continued among African Americans since the Civil War.

In the popular media, Scripture has been just as omnipresent as in politics. Fiction, hymns, and poetry employing biblical themes have always made up a huge proportion of American publishing. Composers William Billings (1746-1800), John Knowles Paine (1839-1906), and many in the twentieth century like Charles Ives and Aaron Copland followed earlier precedents by writing musical settings for the psalms. Among the populace at large, the flood of sheet music, hymnals, chorus books, and gospel songs has never ebbed. In the nineteenth century, one of the most frequently reprinted sheet-music titles was "My Mother's Bible." Its first appearance (1843) evoked an emotional domestic ideal: "My mother's hands this Bible clasped,/She dying gave it me." At another level, millions of Sunday-School children have learned songs like

> The B-I-B-L-E, Yes, that's the book for me,
> I stand alone on the word of God, The B-I-B-L-E.

38. Charles V. Hamilton, *The Black Preacher in America* (New York: William Morrow, 1972), p. 39.

American writers of popular fiction have always drawn on biblical materials. Biblical allusions feature prominently in the work of authors who have become the object of critical study — Herman Melville's *Moby Dick* (which begins, "Call me Ishmael"), William Faulkner's *Absalom, Absalom!* (1936) and *Go Down Moses* (1942), and Peter De Vries's *The Blood of the Lamb* (1961), to name just a few. The American people have never been able to get enough of popular fiction inspired directly by the Bible. The first important novel of this kind was William Ware's *Julian: Or, Scenes in Judea* (1856), which described gospel events through the letters of its fictional protagonist. General Lew Wallace's *Ben Hur* (1880), which climaxed in a breathtaking chariot race, is probably the supreme example of biblical fiction. President Garfield wrote his personal thanks to Wallace from the White House, and it soon became a huge success with the public at large (in part because the pioneering mass retailer, Sears and Roebuck Company, printed up a million inexpensive copies). *Ben Hur* was also the inspiration for an immensely successful touring drama (complete with surging horses on a treadmill) and two motion pictures. Other similar books have had nearly as much success, including Henryk Sienkiewicz's *Quo Vadis?* (1896), Lloyd Douglas's *The Robe* (1942), Marjorie Holmes's *Two from Galilee* (1972), and several novels of both Taylor Caldwell and Frank G. Slaughter. One of the most unusual examples of this fiction was written first in Yiddish by a Jewish author, Sholem Asch. When published in English in 1939, *The Nazarene* won praise from Christians for its sensitive portrayal of contemporary customs at the time of Christ. Many of the blockbuster biblical novels eventually found their way to the screen; Cecil B. De Mille's *The King of Kings* from 1927 (with H. B. Warner as a diffident Jesus) and George Stevens's *The Greatest Story Ever Told* from 1965 (with Max von Sydow as a Jesus who was allowed to show traces of humor) were among the most memorable, but there have been many others.[39]

The Bible as a theme in popular communications is hardly exhausted by songs, poems, stories, and movies. In the visual arts, biblical materials have provided inspiration for German immigrants embellish-

---

39. See Peter T. Chattaway, "Jesus in the Movies," *Bible Review* 14 (Feb. 1998): 28-35, 45-46.

ing needle work with *Fraktur* print, for nineteenth-century lithographers such as Currier and Ives, for countless painters at countless levels of ability, and for a few masters acclaimed by both public and critics (like Edward Hicks who in the mid-nineteenth century painted several versions of *The Peaceable Kingdom*). Since the beginning of mass-marketed religious objects about the time of the Civil War, both Catholics and Protestants have purchased immense quantities of pictures, statues, games, children's toys, paperweights, refrigerator magnets, jewelry, t-shirts, greeting cards, calendars, and business cards decorated with biblical motifs.

Allene Stuart Phy, editor of the best book on the subject, once observed that there is often a "ludicrous discrepancy . . . between the ancient wisdom of the scriptures and the vulgarities of American popular culture."[40] But Phy also saw clearly that even these "vulgarities" show the "profound ways in which the holy books of the Jewish and Christian religions relate to [the] lives of Americans."

The heart of the biblical presence in America is religious. The Bible has been the focus of private meditations, regular reading by families, and informal study in Methodist cell groups, Catholic retreats, and a multitude of other gatherings. In addition, no one will fathom the meaning of the Bible in America who does not heed the sermon, for the sermon has been a nearly universal vehicle by which for centuries, week in and week out, biblical language, values, and culture have worked their way into the fabric of daily life.[41]

"Popular religion" remains extraordinarily difficult to define, measure, and evaluate. What even a preliminary survey shows, however, is that the great flotilla of America's formal religious history floats on a vast, ever-moving sea of popular Christian practice.

40. Allene Stuart Phy, "Introduction," *The Bible and Popular Culture in America* (Philadelphia: Fortress, 1985), p. vii.

41. Unfortunately, the sermon as a force in culture is vastly understudied. For significant exceptions, see note 20 above, and Marsha Witten, *All Is Forgiven: The Secular Message in American Protestantism* (Princeton: Princeton University Press, 1993).

AFTERWORD

In the summer of 1998, Manfred Siebald, professor of American studies at the University of Mainz, who had traveled much in the United States, was asked to explain "the country's variety of denominations" to a group of German citizens whom he was accompanying in their American travels. Siebald's assignment allowed him to do what a long line of European observers before him had done, which was to summarize in blunt, quick strokes the main features of American religious life. As with so many others who have performed this function, Siebald's outline also highlighted themes that have differentiated America's Christian history from the Christian history of Europe (and also from the Christian history of non-European parts of the world). To Siebald, six factors were most important:

- The impulse toward separatism
- The division between church and state
- Immigration
- The westward movement
- Slavery
- Revival movements

As with previous attempts by outsiders to summarize the essence of American religion, Siebald's rapid accounting was not able to communicate the complexity, diversity, and many changes over time that fuller narratives must consider. At the same time, however, it is remarkably successful at catching just the sort of essence that makes for a fitting conclusion to a book that has attempted to sketch a few of those details and some of that complexity. Visitors, in other words, may not be able to describe with perfect completeness all the trees on the ground, but they sometimes communicate a sure understanding of the forest.

So it is with a number of other European observers who have highlighted as central to the history of Christianity in America the singular combination of disestablishment and voluntarism. Alexis de Tocqueville's conclusions about religion in America, which he made after his travels in the 1830s and which have been cited earlier in this book, remain the classic example. His perceptions, however, have been shrewdly extended by European commentators of the twentieth century. Dietrich Bonhoeffer, for example, made two trips to the United States in the 1930s, one extending for nearly a year. Shortly after his second visit in 1939, and while he was becoming ever more deeply involved in the German church struggle against Hitler, Bonhoeffer wrote a perceptive essay about the Christianity he had witnessed in America. To him, one of its most prominent features was the combination of statutory freedom of religion and dynamic social involvement: "Nowhere has the principle of the separation of church and state become a matter of such general, almost dogmatic significance as in American Christianity, and nowhere, on the other hand, is the participation of the churches in the political, social, economic, and cultural events of public life so active and so influential as in the country where there is no state church."[1]

Bonhoeffer's judgment has recently been underscored in a thoughtful essay by Hartmut Lehmann, which adds an insightful comparison with German religious life. In addressing the question of why the United States has seemed to Christianize at the same time that much of Europe

---

1. Dietrich Bonhoeffer, "Protestantism Without Reformation," in *No Rusty Swords: Letters, Lectures and Notes from the Collected Works of Dietrich Bonhoeffer,* vol. 1, ed. Edwin H. Robertson, trans. Robertson and John Bowden (New York: Harper & Row, 1965), p. 105.

has de-Christianized over the last two centuries, Lehmann stressed the American combination of structural religious freedom and entrepreneurial religious activity: "In the complex processes described here as christianization and dechristianization, in the United States and Germany, differences in the legal framework were effectively reinforced by differences in the religious context. In the United States factors such as voluntarism, revivalism, and pluralism created a cultural climate that favored the growth of religion and in which religious activism could easily be related to matters of justice and social reform. In Germany, factors such as the close cooperation between state and church, the suppression of nonconformism, and the domestication of active Christian groups produced a cultural climate in which religion was tainted with conservatism and with opposition to 'progress'."[2]

The repetition in slightly different form of a similar theme is significant: When religious freedom of the sort reflected in the American Constitution was joined to voluntary religious activity rooted in revivalism — but then moving on with revivalistic zeal to religious organizations, social reforms, self-help groups for therapy, and many more community causes — the result has been religious vitality fully engaging the middle classes, large segments of the lower classes, and a significant portion of the upper classes, of a sort unknown in Europe. (An American observer is aware of continuing centers of religious vitality in Europe — for example, Poland, the Irish Republic, and Northern Ireland — but the social-religious dynamics in these regions are singular enough to suggest that explanations for American religious vitality do not apply directly in these situations.)

The continuing effects of this American pattern for the vigor of *religion* seem quite clear. At the end of the 1990s, survey researchers found that perhaps as many as 40-42 percent of Americans attended religious services once a week, two-thirds claim membership in churches or synagogues, 96-98 percent profess belief in God, and a very large proportion

---

2. Hartmut Lehmann, "The Christianization of America and the Dechristianization of Europe in the 19th and 20th Centuries," *Kirchliche Zeitgeschichte* 11 (1998): 12. A helpful response to Lehmann's essay was made by William R. Hutchison in the same volume, pp. 137-42.

tell the researchers that they hold to traditional Christian convictions. In October 1996, 69 percent of three thousand randomly-selected Americans told survey researchers from the Angus Reid Group that they "strongly agreed" that "through the life, death and resurrection of Jesus, God provided a way for the forgiveness of my sin."[3] By comparison with most countries in Europe, these numbers are astounding.

A question remains, however, about what this historical pattern of American religious vigor has meant for the health of *Christianity*. Leigh Schmidt, a historian of religion in America, has recently observed shrewdly that "Most of the things that count about Christianity cannot be counted, like the warmth or coolness of prayer, the resonance or hollowness of scriptural words, the songs or silences of the saints in heaven, the presences or absences in the sacrament."[4] On the question of how Christianity survived amidst so much religious activity, Dietrich Bonhoeffer, though he praised many particulars of American religious life, had his doubts. To Bonhoeffer, the very activity that characterized the American churches raised the question whether American Christians understood the gospel. As he put it toward the end of his essay from 1939, "American theology and the American church as a whole have never been able to understand the meaning of 'criticism' by the Word of God and all that signifies. Right to the last they do not understand that God's 'criticism' touches even religion, the Christianity of the churches and the sanctification of Christians, and that God has founded his church beyond religion and beyond ethics. . . . In American theology, Christianity is still essentially religion and ethics. But because

3. George H. Gallup, Jr., *Religion in America 1996* (Princeton: Princeton Religious Research Center, 1996); "Canada/U.S. Religion and Politics Survey," Angus Reid Group (Toronto, 1996). The Angus Reid "World Poll" in 1997 asked respondents in 33 countries whether they attended church, prayed, felt religion was important in their lives, and if they were "converted" Christians. The following are the percentages in various countries who responded positively to all four items: United States (35 percent), Italy (27 percent), Poland (22 percent), Greece (20 percent), Spain (17 percent), Canada (15 percent), Switzerland (9 percent), Ukraine (8 percent), Britain (7 percent), Germany (7 percent), Netherlands (7 percent), Norway (6 percent), Czech Republic (4 percent), Belgium (4 percent), Finland (3 percent), Sweden (3 percent), France (1 percent), Russia (1 percent).

4. Leigh E. Schmidt, "Mixed Blessings: Christianization and Secularization," *Reviews in American History* 26 (Dec. 1998): 640.

of this, the person and work of Jesus Christ must, for theology, sink into the background and in the long run remain misunderstood, because it is not recognized as the sole ground of radical judgment and radical forgiveness."[5]

Bonhoeffer did not expand upon his judgment. But he certainly could have been thinking of the historic American propensity for both Protestant conservatives and Protestant liberals to move swiftly from considering the nature of God and the work of Christ to very particular moral agendas — usually pietistic and personal for the conservatives, social and public for the liberals. He also could have instanced the tremendous achievements of American Roman Catholics in building churches, organizing schools, and establishing solid local communities, while at the same time only rarely nurturing inner spirituality of the sort found in various forms among modern European Catholics like Thérèse de Lisieux, Georges Bernanos, Simone Weil, or Hans Urs von Balthasar. Bonhoeffer's observation about the dangers to Christianity of the vigorous religion in America is worth pondering, especially since it came from one who was kindly disposed to the Christians and the churches he had come to know in his American sojourns.

Still other European observations may provide an angle of departure for responding to Bonhoeffer's query. Bonhoeffer himself noted that paths toward secularization have moved differently in the United States and Europe: "The secularization of the church on the continent of Europe arose from the misinterpretation of the reformers' distinction of the two realms; American secularization derives precisely from the imperfect distinction of the kingdoms and offices of church and state, from the enthusiastic claim of the church to universal influence in the world."[6]

The judgment that religious integrity in America is threatened more by promiscuous intermingling of church and world than by sharply defined antagonism between them has echoed in the observations of other Europeans as well. An assessment of American theology by a French observer, Klauspeter Blaser, for example, has pointed to "a continuity,

---

5. Bonhoeffer, "Protestantism Without Reformation," pp. 117-18.
6. Bonhoeffer, "Protestantism Without Reformation," p. 108.

which has never been called into question, with the ideals of the eighteenth century that makes the American climate very different from the European." Blaser meant specifically what he calls "a combination of Puritanism and the Enlightenment," which "thinks of the truth in terms of action and tangible results rather than as something metaphysical or spiritual. Thought is oriented toward the realization of the human future, which corresponds to the American dream."[7] Blaser, in other words, finds mixtures in America — for example, Puritanism and the Enlightenment — of the sort foreign to recent European history.

Manfred Siebald reaches the same conclusion, this time in his role as a literary scholar. At the end of a thorough investigation of the significant place that the parable of the prodigal son has held in American literature, Siebald concludes that some trends visible in the recent literature of the United States point distinctly to post-Christian and postmodern rejections of traditional understandings of this parable, as well as of Christianity itself. At the same time, however, he points to the work of writers like Frederick Buechner and David Jaffin who have recently put the parable freshly to use, and in ways fully continuous with traditional understandings of both biblical text and historical Christianity. In his words, "Despite all the signs of a loss of spiritual substance, theological efforts to grasp the biblical content of the parable, along with literary projects and retrievals that continue right to the present, show that the process of secularization has not been an uninterrupted and inevitable development."[8]

Together, Bonhoeffer, Blaser, and Siebald point to the fact that Christianity in America is so intermingled with democratic, voluntaristic, and innovative aspects of American society that modern European models of a traditional church opposed by elite secular intellectuals in league with the sovereign state simply do not apply. In specifically Christian terms, the American situation can be evaluated positively, as an instance of an incarnated faith carrying the message of a God incar-

---

7. Klauspeter Blaser, *Les théologies nord-américains* (Geneva: Labor et Fides, 1995), p. 14.

8. Manfred Siebald, "'Prodigal Parable': Studien zur Parable vom Verlorenen Sohn in der amerikanischen Literatur" (Habilitationsschrift, University of Mainz, 1995), p. 344.

nated in human flesh into its surrounding society. Or it can be evaluated negatively, as a peculiar instance of secularization where an anthropocentric religion of self-realization and salvation through productivity replaces a theocentric religion of divine revelation and salvation in Christ.

Outside observers help Americans see the alternative Christian paths to which the American religious situation can lead. A history of Christianity in America provides many details to illustrate how this religious situation has pointed sometimes to Christian integrity, sometimes to the ironic loss of Christian integrity. Not historical scholarship but an ability to hear the gospel and to act upon it will determine which of these paths mark the way to the future.

The Largest Denominations (as of 2000) in the United States and Canada

T his list includes churches, denominations, and Christian religious associations with over 100,000 affiliates (inclusive membership) as recorded in *The Yearbook of American and Canadian Churches 2000*, ed. Eileen W. Lindner (Nashville: Abingdon, 2000). The *Yearbook* reports figures as produced by the churches. For the historical origins of these denominations, see J. Gordon Melton, *Encyclopedia of American Religions*, 5th ed. (Detroit: Gale, 1996).

The groupings below are historical, and within the groups denominations are ranked by reported number of affiliates. In the modern era, some denominations or associations are closer in beliefs and practices to groups that do not share their historical origins than to those that do. **Canadian denominations are in bold type.** The population for the two countries in 2000 was estimated at 276,000,000 (U.S.) and 31,000,000 (Canada).[1]

1. Church statistics for Mexico are somewhat more difficult to determine. Of Mexico's population of about 97 million in 1998, roughly 80-90 percent have at least nominal affiliation with the Roman Catholic Church. Actual participation by Catholics is, however, relatively low. All observers acknowledge that Protestant and sectarian churches have been growing rapidly, with adherents of Protestant churches now estimated at between 5 and 10 percent of the national population. Among the largest of the non–Roman Catholic groups are the Church of Jesus Christ of Latter-day Saints (Mormons), with approximately 780,000 adherents, and Jehovah's Witnesses, with approxi-

Roman Catholic

Roman Catholic Church — United States	62,018,436
Roman Catholic Church — Canada	**12,498,605**

Orthodox Churches[2]

Greek Orthodox Archdiocese of North and South America	1,954,500
Orthodox Church in America	1,000,000
Orthodox Church in America — Canadian Section	**1,000,000**
Armenian Apostolic Church, Diocese of America	414,000
Greek Orthodox Metropolis of Toronto (Canada)	**350,000**
Armenian Apostolic Church of America	200,000
Coptic Orthodox Church	180,000
Ukrainian Orthodox Church of Canada	**120,000**

British background with roots in the colonial period

Southern Baptist Convention	15,729,356
The United Methodist Church	8,400,000
Presbyterian Church (U.S.A.)	3,574,959
The Episcopal Church	2,364,559
The United Church of Canada	**1,620,754**
American Baptist Churches in the U.S.A.	1,507,400
United Church of Christ	1,421,088
Anglican Church of Canada	**739,699**
Unitarian Universalist Association	214,000

---

mately 500,000 (both figures from the late 1990s as reported on http://www.adherents.com). David Barrett, *World Christian Encyclopedia* (2nd ed., New York: Oxford University Press, 2001), using figures from the mid-1990s, lists four Protestant churches with more than one-half million affiliated (the Seventh-day Adventists, the Assemblies of God, the national Presbyterian church, and the Unión de Iglesias Evangelicos Independentes), and another seven denominations with more than 100,000 affiliated.

2. Adherence counts for the Orthodox tend to reflect size of ethnic communities affiliated, however loosely, with the particular church.

Presbyterian Church in Canada	**211,812**
National Association of Free Will Baptists	210,461
Canadian Baptist Ministries	**129,055**
Religious Society of Friends (Conservative)	104,000
Christian Brethren (Plymouth Brethren)	100,000

Denominations originating on the continent of Europe

Evangelical Lutheran Church in America [Germany, Scandinavia]	5,178,225
Lutheran Church — Missouri Synod [Germany]	2,594,404
Wisconsin Evangelical Lutheran Synod [Germany]	411,295
Reformed Church in America [Holland]	295,651
The Evangelical Free Church of America [Scandinavia]	242,619
Christian Reformed Church in North America [Holland]	199,290
Evangelical Lutheran Church in Canada	**198,751**
Baptist General Conference [Sweden]	141,445
Church of the Brethren [Germany]	141,400

Primarily African American denominations with origins in the 19th century

National Baptist Convention, U.S.A., Incorporated	8,200,000
National Baptist Convention of America	3,500,000
African Methodist Episcopal Church	2,500,000
National Missionary Baptist Convention of America	2,500,000
Progressive National Baptist Convention, Inc.	2,500,000
African Methodist Episcopal Zion Church	1,252,369
Christian Methodist Episcopal Church	718,922

Restorationist churches with origins primarily in the first half of the nineteenth century

Churches of Christ	1,500,000
Christian Churches and Churches of Christ	1,070,616

Christian Church, Disciples of Christ	879,436
Seventh-day Adventist Church	839,436
International Council of Community Churches	250,000
Reorganized Church of Jesus Christ of Latter-day Saints, now known as the Community of Christ	140,245
The Christian Congregation, Inc.	117,039
International Churches of Christ	100,000

Holiness churches with origins in the second half of the nineteenth century

Church of the Nazarene	627,054
The Salvation Army	471,416
The Christian and Missionary Alliance	345,664
Church of God (Anderson, Ind.)	234,311
The Wesleyan Church	119,914

Pentecostal and charismatic denominations or associations originating in the twentieth century

The Church of God in Christ	5,499,875
Assemblies of God	2,525,812
Pentecostal Assemblies of the World	1,500,000
Church of God (Cleveland, Tenn.)	753,230
United Pentecostal Church International	500,000
Full Gospel Fellowship of Churches and Ministers International	275,200
International Church of the Foursquare Gospel	238,065
Pentecostal Assemblies of Canada	**218,782**
International Pentecostal Holiness Church	176,846
Pentecostal Church of God	104,300
Vineyard Churches	100,000

New denominations in the twentieth century arising from older British or colonial bodies

Baptist Bible Fellowship International	1,200,000
Presbyterian Church in America	279,549
American Baptist Association	275,000
Baptist Missionary Association of America	234,732
Conservative Baptist Association of America	200,000
General Association of Regular Baptist Churches	101,854

American-founded religions related to Christianity

Church of Jesus Christ of Latter-day Saints — U.S.	4,923,100
Jehovah's Witnesses — U.S.	1,040,283
Jehovah's Witnesses in Canada	**184,787**
Church of Jesus Christ of Latter-day Saints in Canada	**151,000**

Regional Variations in the United States and Canada

Foreign visitors to the United States are regularly amazed at the great number of different churches they find. Yet a few of the shrewdest visitors have also noticed that the variety of Christian churches pertains to the nation as a whole, not necessarily to each of its regions. The same situation prevails for Canada. North America's great cities do usually provide a home for many varieties, but outside the cities the churches tend to be clumped together into strong regional concentrations. It has always been that way. At the end of the colonial period in the 1770s, the new United States' largest denomination was the Congregationalists, who were located almost exclusively in New England, and the second largest was the Church of England (soon to be known as Episcopalians), which was overwhelmingly concentrated in the Southern colonies.

Strikingly different regional strengths remain to the present. In the United States' four large census areas (Northeast, South, Midwest, and West), Protestants are over-represented in the South and Midwest and under-represented in the Northeast and West. Conversely, Roman Catholics are over-represented in the Northeast and Midwest and under-represented in the South. Although the South has only slightly more than one-third of the nation's population, over one-half of African American Protestants live in that region. The number of conservative, evangelical, fundamentalist, or Pentecostal Protestants is also considerably higher in the South than in the nation as a whole. The American West is home to the largest concentration of the non-churched population. In Canada, Protestants are over-represented in the Western and Atlantic provinces, while Catholics are over-represented in Quebec.

Tables 1, 2, and 3 (on pp. 289-90) provide details on these regional differences. Their information comes from the 1996 Angus Reid cross-border survey of three thousand Americans and three thousand Canadians. For Tables 1 and 2 the following abbreviations are used:

ConProt = the conservative or evangelical Protestant denominations;

MainProt = the mainline Protestant denominations;

BlackProt = adherents to African-American churches in the United States;

Catholic = Roman Catholic adherents;

Sec/Nominal = those with no or only nominal religious attachment; and

hi = high levels of actual religious practice.

The Angus Reid survey found that of the United States populations a whole 19.9% fell into the Conservative Protestant-hi category, 9.5% into the Mainline Protestant-hi, 9.2% into the Black Protestant category, 12.9% into the Catholic-hi category, and 19.9% into the Secular/Nominal category. For Canada, 7.1% fell into the Conservative Protestant-hi category, 7.2% into the Mainline Protestant-hi category, 13.4% into the Catholic-hi category, and 40.2% into the Secular/Nominal category. These tables measure the disproportion between national population distribution and the distribution of these categories of religious affiliation.

Table 3 shows regional differences in response to the survey researchers' question about how often people attended church.

Region also makes a large difference in the distribution of individual denominations.[1] As of 1990, Baptists made up the largest sector of

---

1. The information in this paragraph comes from an extensive county-by-county enumeration of the churches that was made in 1990, as reported in Martin B. Bradley et

Table 1.   Percentage of Each Religious Tradition
in Different American Regions

	Northeast[2]	South[3]	Midwest[4]	West[5]	
U.S. population	20	35	23	22	= 100%
ConProt-hi	12	46	26	16	= 100%
MainProt-hi	19	37	28	15	= 99%
BlackProt	18	54	19	9	= 100%
Catholic-hi	28	20	29	23	= 100%
Sec/Nominal	22	28	21	29	= 100%

Table 2.   Percentage of Each Religious Tradition
in Different Canadian Regions

	B.C.	Alberta	Sask/Man	Ontario	Quebec	Atl.Prov.	
Canadian pop.	13	9	7	38	25	8	= 100%
ConProt-hi	21	14	15	30	8	12	= 100%
MainProt-hi	11	9	12	46	7	13	= 98%
Catholic-hi	6	5	5	36	38	10	= 100%
Sec/Nominal	16	10	6	37	25	6	= 100%

al., *Churches and Church Membership in the United States 1990* (Atlanta: Glenmary Research Center, 1992).

2. Maine, New Hampshire, Vermont, Massachusetts, Rhode Island, Connecticut, New York, New Jersey, and Pennsylvania.

3. Delaware, Maryland, Washington D.C., Virginia, West Virginia, North Carolina, South Carolina, Georgia, Florida, Kentucky, Tennessee, Alabama, Mississippi, Arkansas, Louisiana, Oklahoma, and Texas.

4. Michigan, Ohio, Indiana, Illinois, Wisconsin, Minnesota, Iowa, Missouri, North Dakota, South Dakota, Nebraska, and Kansas.

5. Montana, Wyoming, Idaho, Utah, Nevada, Colorado, Arizona, New Mexico, Alaska, Washington, Oregon, California, and Hawaii.

Table 3. Percentage of Canadians and Americans by Region Who Told Survey Researchers (in 1996) They Attended Church at Least Once Per Week or More

ALL UNITED STATES	39	ALL CANADA	21
Northeast	35	British Columbia	18
South	45	Alberta	19
Midwest	43	Sask/Manitoba	23
West	30	Ontario	22
		Quebec	15
		Atlantic Provinces	31

the churched population in fourteen Southern and mid-South states. In another six states of the Southwest and West, where they were outnumbered by Catholics, Baptists were the most numerous Protestant denomination. Outside of the broad southern third of the country, however, Baptists are a much smaller part of the population. In the upper Midwest, Lutherans are the most numerous Protestant body in Wisconsin, Iowa, Minnesota, North Dakota, South Dakota, Nebraska, and Montana. Methodists are especially strong in a band running from Delaware (the state with the highest concentration of Methodists in the country) through Nebraska. The main denominations of the Restorationist movement (Churches of Christ, Disciples of Christ, and Christian Churches) are likewise strong in the lower Midwest and upper South. There are also many counties scattered across the country where for specific historical reasons other individual denominations predominate. For example, Pentecostal churches make up the largest Protestant group in several counties in Washington, Oregon, and northern California; there are a few counties in South Dakota where the Episcopalians are the largest denomination (because of Episcopalian missions among the Dakota Indians); and there are a couple of counties in the Midwest where the United Church of Christ, Presbyterians, or Reformed churches predominate. Roman Catholics are strongest in New York and New England, around the shores of Lake Michigan, in the Southwest, and in the far southern portions of Texas,

Louisiana, and Florida. Tables 4 and 5 below also use data from the 1996 Angus Reid poll to show how many adherents of the various denominations live in each region of Canada and the United States. Unlike Tables 1 and 2, Tables 4 and 5 report on all who claim a denominational affiliation, regardless of the level of actual participation.

Table 4.   Percentage of population in each United States region claiming adherence to various denominations

	U.S. total	Northeast	South	Midwest	West
Roman Catholic	30	47	18	33	32
Baptist	18	7	33	13	8
Methodist	9	5	13	9	5
Lutheran	6	6	2	9	6
Nondenominational	6	4	4	5	9
Presbyterian	3	3	4	3	3
Pentecostal	2	1	2	2	2
Mormon	2	1	1	1	5
Episcopalian	2	3	3	1	1
Jewish	2	5	2	–	3

Table 5.   Percentage of population in each Canadian region claiming adherence to various denominations

	All Canada	BC	Alb	Sk/Mn	Ont	Qbc	Atl
Roman Catholic	48	23	26	29	38	83	45
United Church	13	16	19	23	17	1	5
Anglican	9	13	7	5	14	2	11
Lutheran	3	3	11	6	3	–	1
Presbyterian	3	5	1	2	6	1	2
Baptist	2	4	4	4	2	–	5
Pentecostal	2	2	3	2	2	1	7
Jewish	1	–	–	–	2	1	–
Mormon	–	1	1	–	–	–	–

CHRONOLOGY

1492	Columbus journeys to the New World with a hope that his voyage would discover "how [the Native Americans'] conversion to our Holy Faith might be undertaken."
1493	Pope Alexander VI grants Ferdinand and Isabella of Spain control of the lands Columbus explored.
1521	Conquistador Hernán Cortés besieges the Aztec capital as Martin Luther speaks at the Diet of Worms.
1523-33	Franciscan, Dominican, and Augustinian missionaries arrive in Mexico baptizing as many as ten million Indians in the first two decades of Spanish rule.
1531	A Christian Indian in Mexico, Juan Diego, according to several reports, receives a visitation from the Virgin Mary at Guadalupe.
1537	Pope Paul III issues the bull *Sublimis Deus,* which, against colonial practice, defines the Indians as fully human and fully capable of becoming Christians.
1607	English Anglicans settle in Jamestown, Virginia.
1608	The French explorer Samuel de Champlain establishes the city of Quebec.
1619	The first Africans arrive in Virginia as indentured servants.
1620, 1630	Plymouth and the Massachusetts Bay Colony, respectively, are settled by two different groups of Puritans (in 1691 they unite as the Commonwealth of Massachusetts).
1630-49	Father Jean de Brébeuf and fellow Jesuits contextualize the Christian message for the Huron Indians in what is now Ontario, Canada, before being martyred.

292

1634	George and Cecil Calvert establish the colony of Maryland as a refuge for English Roman Catholics.
1636	Roger Williams is banished from Massachusetts and soon founds the colony of Rhode Island with an unusual extension of religious freedom.
1636	The first college in the English colonies, Harvard, is formed by Massachusetts Puritans to train ministers and magistrates.
1638	Anne Hutchinson is banished from Massachusetts for her views on the freedom of God's grace.
1663	Quebec Catholics found Laval, the first university in Canada.
1673	The French Jesuit, Jacques Marquette, joins Louis Jolliet's exploration of the Mississippi River Valley for the purpose of preaching the gospel to Native Americans.
1681	Pennsylvania is established by William Penn as a Quaker colony, but open for settlement to all Christians.
1684	Francis Makemie, a Scots-Irish immigrant, establishes the first American Presbytery.
1692	Twenty Massachusetts residents are executed for witchcraft at Salem.
1707	The Philadelphia Association of Regular Baptists becomes the first Baptist organization in the New World.
1735-45	The colonial Great Awakening features George Whitefield (itinerant) and Jonathan Edwards (theologian) as central figures.
1740	George Whitefield, although a slaveowner himself, goes out of his way to preach to African Americans during his second visit to the colonies.
1763	Britain gains control of Quebec in the Treaty of Paris.
1769	The first Methodist preachers, commissioned by John Wesley, arrive in New York and Pennsylvania.
1771	Francis Asbury migrates to America and soon becomes the key figure in the establishment of an American Methodist church (1784).
1773	The first independent black church forms in Silver Bluff, South Carolina; many follow soon thereafter.
1774	The Quebec Act secures civil rights for Canadian Catholics that their co-religionists in Britain do not gain until 1829.
1776	On July 4, the thirteen American colonies declare their independence from Britain.
1784	John Carroll, the first American Catholic bishop, devotes several pages of a published work to rebutting the charge that Catholics stifle free inquiry.
1786	The Virginia legislature enacts Thomas Jefferson's Bill for Establishing Religious Freedom.
1789	The First Amendment, which guarantees the free exercise of religion

to all citizens and prohibits the establishment of any national religion, is added to the United States Constitution.

1790   A great mobilization of Protestants begins featuring the Methodists and Baptists but involving many other Protestant churches in what is sometimes called "the Second Great Awakening."

1795   Russian Orthodox monks settle in Alaska and establish the first lasting Orthodox presence in North America.

1809   Elizabeth Ann Seton, an Episcopalian-born convert to Roman Catholicism, founds the Sisters of Charity, one of the first religious orders in the United States (in 1975 "Mother" Seton becomes the first North American-born person declared a saint by the Roman Catholic Church).

1814   Richard Allen forms the first African American denomination, the African Methodist Episcopal Church.

1816   The American Bible Society is founded, emblematic of a great wave of new, mostly religious voluntary societies in the United States.

1821   Charles Finney converts to Christianity and begins work as a revivalist preacher.

1821   Mexico gains its independence from Spain.

1820s   Joseph Smith begins to see visions that culminate in the publication of *The Book of Mormon* in 1830.

1827   Harriet Livermore, a revival preacher, becomes the first American woman to preach before the United States Congress.

1827   Jarena Lee, a black female associate of Richard Allen, travels over two thousand miles and preaches on 180 different occasions.

1831   Followers of Alexander Campbell and Barton W. Stone join ranks to form the Christian Church (Disciples of Christ), from which later also come the Churches of Christ and the Christian Church.

1831-32   Alexis de Tocqueville visits North America from France and then publishes *Democracy in America* (1835, 1840), a work stressing the free nature of American religion as a key to its success.

1833   The Congregationalist Church of Massachusetts is disestablished; it is the last American denomination to retain vestiges of state support.

1834   A Boston mob burns an Ursuline convent, illustrating the strong anti-Catholicism of many American Protestants.

1835   Phoebe Palmer, a Methodist writer and speaker, begins an influential home meeting in New York City where she teaches "holiness," or entire consecration to God.

1836   Angelina Grimké publishes a widely-read abolitionist tract (her sister Sara does the same in 1838).

1837	Northern and Southern Presbyterians split over issues of church order and theology (and secondarily of whether to tolerate slavery).
1842	Immigration to the United States tops 100,000 for the first time, with almost half of the immigrants from Ireland and their presence increasing the Roman Catholic numbers in America.
1843	Thousands of followers of William Miller wait for the return of Christ on March 21 and then on October 22, 1844 as Miller prophesied (several denominations spring from the "Disappointment" when nothing happens, the most important being the Seventh-day Adventists of Ellen White).
1844	The two largest and most widespread American denominations, the Baptists and Methodists, both divide North and South over the question of slavery.
1845	Frederick Douglass, an escaped slave and himself a Christian, attacks the use of Christianity to protect slavery.
1850s	Religious arguments sharpen North-South tensions and so help prepare for the violence of the Civil War.
1852	Harriet Beecher Stowe publishes *Uncle Tom's Cabin,* a novel with many religious themes supporting its denunciation of slavery.
1854	The American (or Know Nothing) party organizes with the intent of keeping Roman Catholics and immigrants from gaining political office.
1855	An anonymous *Definite Synodical Platform* circulates among Lutherans and calls for a revision of the Augsburg Confession along lines dictated by American revivalism; rejection of this proposal indicates the growing influence of confessional Lutheranism.
1861-65	During the American Civil War there are widespread revivals among soldiers in the camps, but changes stimulated by the war undercut the influence of the country's historic Protestant churches.
1865	The United States Congress passes legislation to place the phrase "In God We Trust" on certain gold and silver coins.
1865	African American churches in the South break from white control, resulting in several new denominations.
1867	The Dominion of Canada is formed.
1868	The Fourteenth Amendment passes with the intent of guaranteeing civil rights to freed slaves.
1874	Frances Willard and associates found the Women's Christian Temperance Union.
1875	Dwight L. Moody returns from a successful revival tour in Britain and embarks upon a noteworthy career as an urban evangelist in the United States and Canada.

1880   Amanda Berry Smith, an African American, visits India; later she carries out preaching and social work in Liberia and then her native Chicago.

1880   The Salvation Army opens its work in the United States (two years later in Canada) and soon is sponsoring the most effective Protestant outreach to the continent's burgeoning cities.

1881   Immigration to the United States tops 500,000 for the first time, with Germany providing the most immigrants and the presence of Germans increasing the number of Lutherans (along with high immigrant totals from Scandinavia), Catholics, Jews, and "free thinkers" in the country.

1884   The construction and maintenance of parochial schools is the prime matter for discussion by the third plenary council of American Catholic archbishops and bishops.

1885   Josiah Strong, later secretary of the Evangelical Alliance, publishes *Our Country,* a work warning against the religious effects of immigrants, Roman Catholicism, and city life.

1886   Augustus Tolton becomes the first American of pure African descent to be ordained a Roman Catholic priest.

1886   Catholic parents in Edgerton, Wisconsin petition their local school board to stop readings from the King James Version of the Bible.

1895   Pope Leo XIII issues the encyclical *Longinqua Oceani,* followed by *Testem Benevolentiae* in 1899, addressed specifically to curb "Americanism," or excessive accommodation to democratic liberalism.

1905   Immigration to the United States tops one million for the first time, with countries of Southern and Eastern Europe accounting for most of the immigrants and their presence increasing the number of Catholics, Jews, Orthodox, and nonbelievers in the country.

1906   Black and white worshipers at a chapel on Azusa Street in Los Angeles speak in tongues and inaugurate the worldwide Pentecostal movement.

1906   A federal census reveals astounding growth in the Roman Catholic Church in the United States, reaching 12 million adherents (14 percent of the U.S. population) and over 15,000 clergy.

1907   Tikhon Bellavin, the Russian Orthodox bishop in North America, convenes the first All-American Council of Orthodox Churches.

1908   The Federal Council of Churches is formed to promote cooperative action by the older, mainline Protestant denominations.

1909   Oxford University Press publishes the Scofield Bible, the most influential publication promoting the theology of dispensational premillennialism.

1910-15	*The Fundamentals: A Testimony to Truth* are published as a way of defending traditional Christian doctrines against the new proposals of theological modernists.
1912	The publication of Walter Rauschenbusch's *Christianizing the Social Order* is the fullest statement of the Social Gospel, a movement of moderate and liberal Protestants aimed at alleviating the inhumane conditions of recently industrialized cities.
1914	World War I and legislation in Congress from the 1920s dramatically reduce the number of immigrants arriving in the United States.
1917	Mexico enacts a new constitution with many rules against religion, particularly Catholicism. When it is enforced nine years later, it sparks violence and civil war that finally results in the restoration of church privileges.
1917	The National Catholic War Council is established during World War I to oversee chaplains in the military; later it evolves into the National Catholic Welfare Council and other national Catholic organizations.
1919	Pressure from many religious groups, mostly Protestant, leads to the passage of the Eighteenth Amendment to the U.S. Constitution, which prohibits the sale or use of alcoholic beverages (the amendment is repealed in 1933).
1923	Pentecostal evangelist Aimee Semple McPherson employs the radio as one of the first in a great flood of American religious figures who exploit the same medium.
1925	At the trial of John Scopes in Dayton, Tennessee, William Jennings Bryan defends the rights of states to ban the teaching of evolution, while Clarence Darrow attacks such laws as bigoted.
1927	Dorothy Day is converted to Roman Catholicism and soon thereafter founds, with Peter Maurin, the Catholic Worker Movement.
1928	Al Smith, the Democratic governor of New York, is the first Roman Catholic nominated by a major party for president (he is defeated by the Republican Herbert Hoover, at least in part because of fear of his Catholicism).
1930s	During the Great Depression, mainline Protestant churches lose ground, but fundamentalist, holiness, Pentecostal, and African American continue to grow.
1932	The publication of Reinhold Niebuhr's *Moral Man and Immoral Society* establishes his reputation as the most influential public theologian of the period.
1933	Jacques Maritain, the French neo-Thomist, lectures for the first time in North America (Toronto) and in so doing supports Catholic engagement with Thomism in many spheres of life.

1940, 1947 Decisions of the United States Supreme Court apply to the states the Constitutional guarantees of freedom of religion that have hitherto been considered a check only on the national government.

1943 The establishment of the National Association of Evangelicals marks the desire of some Northern fundamentalists to move beyond the narrow confines of that movement.

1945 In the economic boom that follows World War II, there is also a boom in new church construction for both Protestants and Catholics.

1949 Billy Graham holds a successful evangelistic campaign in Los Angeles and soon emerges as the most visible American Protestant in the United States and abroad.

1950 The National Council of Churches is formed as a successor to the Federal Council; soon it broadens its membership to include Orthodox churches and invites Roman Catholics as observers.

1952 A copy of the new Revised Standard Version, the first translation of the Bible besides the King James Version to gain a large American following among Protestants, is presented to President Harry Truman.

1954 The Supreme Court ends the racial segregation of American schools, sparking the large-scale Civil Rights movement of the next two decades.

1950s Mainline Protestant denominations, following the earlier example of several Holiness, Wesleyan, and Pentecostal denominations, begin to ordain women to the ministry.

1960 A Standing Conference of Canonical Bishops is founded to improve dialogue among the Orthodox churches, which by this time include Byelorussian, Albanian, Romanian, Serbian, Egyptian, Bulgarian, and Syrian as well as Russian, Ukrainian, and Greek congregations.

1960 John F. Kennedy becomes the first Roman Catholic elected as president of the United States.

1962-63 The U.S. Supreme Court prohibits prayers and Bible readings as mandated activities in public schools.

1962-65 The Second Vatican Council leads to much greater Catholic/non-Catholic dialogue in all areas of North American life.

1963 Martin Luther King, Jr. delivers the climactic closing address at a massive March on Washington to promote civil rights.

1963 John F. Kennedy's assassination, followed by the assassinations of Robert Kennedy and Martin Luther King, Jr. (both 1968), adds to the feeling of crisis in a tumultuous decade.

1973 The United States Supreme Court legalizes most forms of abortion, thus laying the groundwork for the rise of the New Christian Right.

1974 An International Congress on World Evangelization is held in

Lausanne, Switzerland, connecting American evangelicals with many delegates from around the world.

1975 Willow Creek Community Church is formed outside Chicago and serves as a model for "megachurches."

1976 Jimmy Carter becomes president while not hiding his Christian convictions and attempts to put those convictions into practice throughout his time in office (1977-81).

1979 Jerry Falwell, a Baptist minister, founds the Moral Majority, the forerunner of the Christian Coalition and a general rallying point for the New Christian Right.

1980s Pentecostal Hispanic churches are recognized as being among the fastest growing in North America.

1984 The United States establishes full diplomatic relations with the Vatican.

1987-99 The American Catholic church deals with pressure for clerical marriage and the ordination of women amidst the decline in religious vocations.

1992-94 A renewed wave of conservative political activism leads to the formation of the Christian Coalition and other right-wing religious political organizations.

1995 Donald Argue (a minister of the Assemblies of God) becomes head of the National Association of Evangelicals, demonstrating the entry of Pentecostals into the mainstream of American Protestant life.

1996 A series of arson attacks strike Southern black churches (seventy-five fires in eighteen months).

1997 Promise Keepers, an evangelical men's organization, holds the largest reported religious gathering in U.S. history to promote fidelity and renewed religious commitment for husbands and fathers.

1997-99 Almost-daily revival services continue at a congregation of the Vineyard Movement outside Toronto and at the Brownsville Assemblies of God Church in Pensacola, Florida.

1997-2000 Mainline Protestant churches continue to debate whether to ordain practicing homosexuals and whether to bless same-sex unions.

2000 Federal elections in the United States, Mexico, and Canada feature heightened attention to religious questions; in the United States, Joseph Lieberman, an orthodox Jew, is nominated as the Democrats' vice-presidential candidate and speaks freely about the importance of religion for American public life.

BIBLIOGRAPHY

U nlike the chronological divisions for the chapters of this book, which reflect major eras in the *Christian* history of North America, this bibliography is arranged by the standard divisions of American political history. It is limited to only five hundred books, though of course there are many other useful volumes, as well as innumerable important articles, essays, and even reviews that illuminate the history of Christianity in North America. For study of themes and special subjects, many of the titles in the sections labeled "Orientation" and "Periods/Eras" will also be useful.

Outline

(1) ORIENTATION

(1.1) Reference

(1.1.1) Best sources for beginning research

Bradley, Martin B., et al. *Churches and Church Membership in the United States, 1990.* Glenmary Research Center, 1992.

Gaustad, Edwin Scott, and Philip L. Barlow. *New Historical Atlas of Religion in America.* Oxford, 2000.

Lippy, Charles H., and Peter W. Williams, eds. *Encyclopedia of the American Religious Experience,* 3 vols. Scribner's, 1988.

Melton, Gordon J., ed. *Encyclopedia of American Religions,* 5th ed. Gale, 1996.

New Catholic Encyclopedia, 15 vols. McGraw-Hill, 1967. Updates 1974, 1979, 1989, 1996.

Reid, Daniel G., et al., eds. *Dictionary of Christianity in America.* InterVarsity Press, 1990.

(1.1.2) Others

Barrett, David B., et al. *World Christian Encyclopedia,* 2nd ed. Oxford, 2001.

Blumhofer, Edith L., and Joel A. Carpenter, eds. *Twentieth-Century Evangelicalism: A Guide to the Sources.* Garland, 1990.

Burgess, Stanley M., and Gary M. McGee, eds. *Dictionary of Pentecostal and Charismatic Movements.* Zondervan, 1988.

Fox, Richard Wightman, and James T. Kloppenberg, eds. *A Companion to American Thought.* Blackwell, 1995.

Hill, Samuel S., ed. *Encyclopedia of Religion in the South.* Mercer, 1984.

(1.2) Collections of documents

Blumhofer, Edith L., ed. *"Pentecost in My Soul": Explorations in the Meaning of the Pentecostal Experience in the Early Assemblies of God.* Gospel Publishing, 1989.

Carpenter, Joel A., ed. *Fundamentalism in American Religion, 1880-1950,* 45 vols. Garland, 1988.

Cherry, Conrad, ed. *God's New Israel: Religious Interpretations of American Culture,* 2nd ed. North Carolina, 1998.

Dayton, Donald W., ed. *The Higher Life: Sources for the Study of Holiness, Pentecostal, and Keswick Movements,* 48 vols. Garland, 1985.

Farina, John, ed. *Sources of American Spirituality,* 20 vols. Paulist, 1984ff.

Gaustad, Edwin S., ed. *A Documentary History of Religion in America,* 2 vols., 2nd ed. Eerdmans, 1993.

Gifford, Carolyn De Swarte, ed. *Women in American Protestant Religion, 1800-1930,* 36 vols. Garland, 1987.

Keller, Rosemary Skinner, and Rosemary Radford Ruether, eds. *In Our Own Voices: Four Centuries of American Women Religious Writers.* HarperSanFrancisco, 1996.

Kuklick, Bruce, ed. *American Religious Thought of the 18th and 19th Centuries,* 32 vols. Garland, 1987.

Lundin, Roger, and Mark A. Noll, eds. *Voices from the Heart: Four Centuries of American Piety.* Eerdmans, 1987.

Ruether, Rosemary Radford, and Rosemary Skinner Keller, eds. *Women and Religion in America,* 3 vols. Harper & Row, 1981-1986.

Sarna, Jonathan D., ed. *The American Jewish Experience,* 2nd ed. Holmes and Meier, 1997.

Sernett, Milton C., ed. *Afro-American Religious History: A Documentary Witness.* Duke, 1985.

Smith, H. S., R. T. Handy, and Lefferts A. Loetscher, eds. *American Christianity: An Historical Interpretation with Representative Documents,* 2 vols. Charles Scribner's Sons, 1960.

Walch, Timothy, ed. *The Heritage of American Catholicism,* 28 vols. Garland, 1988.

(1.3) General textbooks

Ahlstrom, Sydney E. *A Religious History of the American People.* Yale, 1972.

Albanese, Catherine L. *America, Religions, and Religion,* 3rd ed. Wadsworth, 1999.

Baird, Robert. *Religion in America.* New York, 1844.

Handy, Robert T. *A History of the Churches in the United States and Canada.* Oxford, 1977.

Marty, Martin E. *Pilgrims in Their Own Land: 500 Years of Religion in America.* Penguin, 1984.

Mead, Sidney E. *The Lively Experiment: The Shaping of Christianity in America.* Harper & Row, 1963.

Noll, Mark A. *A History of Christianity in the United States and Canada.* Eerdmans, 1992.

Wells, David F., et al., eds. *Christianity in America: A Handbook.* Eerdmans, 1983.

Williams, Peter W. *America's Religions: Traditions and Cultures,* 2nd ed. Illinois, 1998.

(1.4) Readers, colloquia, collections of essays

Butler, Jon, and Harry S. Stout, eds. *Religion in American History: A Reader.* Oxford, 1998.

Fulop, Timothy E., and Albert J. Raboteau, eds. *African-American Religion: Interpretive Essays in History and Culture.* Routledge, 1997.

Hall, David D., ed. *Lived Religion in America: Toward a History of Practice.* Princeton, 1997.

Jamison, A. Leland, and John E. Smith, eds. *Religious Perspectives in American Culture.* Princeton, 1961.

Johnson, Paul E., ed. *African-American Christianity: Essays in History.* California, 1994.

Juster, Susan, and Lisa MacFarlane, eds. *A Mighty Baptism: Race, Gender, and the Creation of American Protestantism.* Cornell, 1996.

Kuklick, Bruce, and D. G. Hart, eds. *Religious Advocacy and American History.* Eerdmans, 1997.

Mulder, John M., and John F. Wilson, eds. *Religion in American History: Interpretive Essays.* Prentice-Hall, 1978.

Stout, Harry S., and D. G. Hart, eds. *New Directions in American Religious History.* Oxford, 1997.

Tweed, Thomas A., ed. *Retelling U.S. Religious History.* California, 1997.

Wells, Ronald A., ed. *History and the Christian Historian.* Eerdmans, 1998.

(1.5) Thematic narratives spanning large periods

Beaver, R. Pierce. *American Protestant Women in World Missions,* 2nd ed. Eerdmans, 1980.

Bellah, Robert N., and Frederick E. Greenspahn, eds. *Uncivil Religion: Interreligious Hostility in America.* Crossroad, 1987.

Bendroth, Margaret. *Fundamentalism and Gender, 1875 to the Present.* Yale, 1995.

Blumhofer, Edith, and Randall Balmer, eds. *Modern Christian Revivals.* Illinois, 1993.

Bowden, Henry Warner. *American Indians and Christian Missions.* Chicago, 1981.

Boyer, Paul S. *When Time Shall Be No More: Prophecy Belief in Modern American Culture.* Harvard, 1994.

Brereton, Virginia. *From Sin to Salvation: Stories of Women's Conversions, 1800 to the Present.* Indiana, 1991.

Butler, Jon. *Awash in a Sea of Faith: Christianizing the American People.* Harvard, 1992.

Butler, Jon, and Harry S. Stout, eds. *Religion in American Life,* 17 vols. (for young adults). Oxford, 1999-2002.

Carpenter, Joel A., and Wilbert R. Shenk, eds. *Earthen Vessels: American Evangelicals and Foreign Missions, 1880-1980.* Eerdmans, 1990.

Cohen, Naomi. *Jews in Christian America.* Oxford, 1992.

Demerath, N. J., et al., eds. *Sacred Companies: Organizational Aspects of Religion and Religious Aspects of Organizations.* Oxford, 1998.

Ernst, Eldon G., and Douglas Firth Anderson. *Pilgrim Progression: The Protestant Experience in California.* Fithian, 1993.

Fairbank, John King, ed. *The Missionary Enterprise in China and America.* Harvard, 1974.

Finke, Roger, and Rodney Stark. *The Churching of America, 1776-1990.* Rutgers, 1992.

Gutjahr, Paul C. *An American Bible: A History of the Good Book in the United States, 1777-1880.* Stanford, 1999.

Handy, Robert. *A Christian America: Protestant Hope and Historical Realities,* 2nd ed. Oxford, 1984.

Hart, D. G. *The University Gets Religion: Religious Studies in American Higher Education.* Johns Hopkins, 1999.

Hatch, Nathan O., and Mark A. Noll, eds. *The Bible in American Culture.* Oxford, 1982.

Hawley, Louise, and James C. Juhnke, eds. *Nonviolent America: History Through the Eyes of Peace.* Bethel College (KS), 1993.

Holifield, E. Brooks. *A History of Pastoral Care in America: From Salvation to Self-Realization.* Abingdon, 1983.

Hughes, Richard T., and C. Leonard Allen. *Illusions of Innocence: Protestant Primitivism in America, 1630-1875.* Chicago, 1985.

Hutchison, William R. *Errand to the World: American Protestant Thought and Foreign Missions.* Chicago, 1987.

Hutchison, William R., ed. *Between the Times: The Travail of the Protestant Establishment, 1900-1960.* Cambridge, 1989.

Johnson, James T., ed. *The Bible in American Law, Politics, and Political Rhetoric.* Fortress, 1985.

Lasch, Christopher. *The True and Only Heaven: Progress and Its Critics.* Norton, 1991.

Lindley, Susan. *You Have Stept Out of Your Place: A History of Women and Religion in America.* Westminster/John Knox, 1996.

Marsden, George. *Understanding Fundamentalism and Evangelicalism.* Eerdmans, 1991.

Marty, Martin E. *Protestantism in the United States: Righteous Empire,* 2nd ed. Scribner's, 1986.

McDannell, Colleen. *Material Christianity: Religion and Popular Culture in America.* Yale, 1995.

McLoughlin, William G. *Modern Revivalism: Charles Grandison Finney to Billy Graham.* Ronald, 1959.

McLoughlin, William G. *Revivals, Awakenings, and Reform, 1607-1977.* Chicago, 1978.

Miller, Randall M., and Thomas D. Marzik. eds. *Immigrants and Religion in Urban America.* Temple, 1977.

Moore, R. Laurence. *Religious Outsiders and the Making of Americans.* Oxford, 1986.

Moore, R. Laurence. *Selling God: American Religion in the Marketplace of Culture.* Oxford, 1994.

Niebuhr, H. Richard. *The Kingdom of God in America.* Willett, Clark, and Co., 1937.

Niebuhr, Reinhold. *The Irony of American History.* Charles Scribner's Sons, 1952.

Noll, Mark A., George M. Marsden, and Nathan O. Hatch. *The Search for Christian America,* 2nd ed. Helmers and Howard, 1989.

Noll, Mark A., David W. Bebbington, and George A. Rawlyk, eds. *Evangelicalism:*

Comparative Studies of Popular Protestantism in North America, the British Isles, and Beyond, 1700-1990. Oxford, 1994.

Phillips, Kevin. *The Cousins' Wars: Religion, Politics, Civil Warfare and the Triumph of Anglo-America.* Basic, 1999.

Richey, Russell E., and Donald G. Jones, eds. *American Civil Religion.* Harper & Row, 1974.

Robert, Dana Lee. *American Women in Mission.* Mercer, 1996.

Sandeen, Ernest, ed. *The Bible and Social Reform.* Fortress, 1982.

Sarna, Jonathan, ed. *Minority Faiths and the Protestant Mainstream.* Illinois, 1998.

Schmidt, Leigh Eric. *Hearing Things: Religion, Illusion, and the American Enlightenment.* Harvard, 2000.

Synan, Vinson. *The Holiness-Pentecostal Tradition: Charismatic Movements in the Twentieth Century,* 2nd ed. Eerdmans, 1997.

Taves, Ann. *Fits, Trances, and Visions: Experiencing Religion and Explaining Experience from Wesley to James.* Princeton, 1999.

Thuesen, Peter J. *In Discordance with the Scriptures: American Protestant Battles over Translating the Bible.* Oxford, 1999.

Turner, James. *Without God, Without Creed: The Origins of Unbelief in America.* Johns Hopkins, 1985.

Wells, Ronald A., ed. *The Wars of America.* Eerdmans, 1981.

Westerkamp, Marilyn J. *Women and Religion in Early America, 1600-1850.* Routledge, 1999.

Williams, Peter W. *Region, Religion, and Architecture in the United States.* Illinois, 1997.

(2) PERIODS/ERAS

(2.1) Colonial Outside of New England

Balmer, Randall H. *A Perfect Babel of Confusion: Dutch Religion and English Culture in the Middle Colonies.* Oxford, 1989.

Bonomi, Patricia U. *Under the Cope of Heaven: Religion, Society, and Politics in Colonial America.* Oxford, 1986.

Bridenbaugh, Carl. *Mitre and Sceptre: Transatlantic Faiths, Ideas, Personalities, and Politics, 1689-1775.* Oxford, 1962.

Holifield, E. B. *Era of Persuasion: American Thought and Culture, 1521-1680.* Twayne, 1989.

Lippy, C. H., R. Choquette, and S. Poole. *Christianity Comes to the Americas.* Paragon House, 1982.

Longenecker, Stephen L. *Piety and Tolerance: Pennsylvania German Religion, 1700-1850.* Scarecrow, 1994.

Marietta, Jack D. *The Reformation of American Quakerism, 1748-1783*. Pennsylvania, 1984.

Pointer, Richard W. *Protestant Pluralism and the New York Experience*. Indiana, 1988.

"Religion in Early America," special issue of *William and Mary Quarterly* 54 (Oct. 1997): 693-848.

Roeber, A. G. *Palatines, Liberty, and Property: German Lutherans in Colonial British America*. Johns Hopkins, 1993.

Rothermund, Dieter. *The Layman's Progress: Religious and Political Experience in Colonial Pennsylvania, 1740-1770*. Pennsylvania, 1961.

Schmidt, Leigh Eric. *Holy Fairs: Scottish Communions and American Revivals in the Early Modern Period*. Princeton, 1989.

Schwartz, Sally. *"A Mixed Multitude": The Struggle for Toleration in Colonial Pennsylvania*. New York University, 1987.

Stoeffler, F. Ernest, ed. *Continental Pietism and Early American Christianity*. Eerdmans, 1976.

Thwaites, R. G., ed. *Jesuit Relations and Allied Documents*. Burrows Brothers, 1896-1901.

Tolles, Frederick B. *Meetinghouse and Countinghouse: The Quaker Merchants of Philadelphia, 1682-1763*. North Carolina, 1948.

Trinterud, Leonard J. *The Forming of an American Tradition: A Re-examination of Colonial Presbyterianism*. Westminster, 1949.

(2.2) New England and the Puritans

Boyer, Paul S., and Stephen Nissenbaum. *Salem Possessed: The Social Origins of Witchcraft*. Harvard, 1974.

Cohen, Charles L. *God's Caress: The Psychology of Puritan Religious Experience*. Oxford, 1986.

Fiering, Norman. *Moral Philosophy at Seventeenth-Century Harvard*. North Carolina, 1981.

Foster, Stephen. *The Long Argument: English Puritanism and the Shaping of New England Culture, 1570-1700*. North Carolina, 1991.

Gaustad, E. S. *Liberty of Conscience: Roger Williams in America*. Eerdmans, 1991.

Hall, David D. *Worlds of Wonders, Days of Judgment: Popular Religious Belief in Early New England*. Knopf, 1989.

Hambrick-Stowe, Charles E. *The Practice of Piety: Puritan Devotional Disciplines in Seventeenth-Century New England*. North Carolina, 1982.

Heimert, Alan, and Andrew Delbanco, eds. *The Puritans in America: A Narrative Anthology*. Harvard, 1985.

Holifield, E. Brooks. *The Covenant Sealed: The Development of Puritan Sacramental Theology in Old and New England, 1570-1720*. Yale, 1974.

Karlsen, Carol F., and Laurie Crumpacker, eds. *The Journal of Esther Edwards Burr, 1754-1757.* Yale, 1984.

McLoughlin, William G. *New England Dissent: The Baptists and the Separation of Church and State,* 2 vols. Harvard, 1971.

McGiffert, Michael, ed. *God's Plot: Puritan Spirituality in Thomas Shepard's Cambridge,* 2nd ed. Massachusetts, 1994.

Middlekauf, R. *The Mathers: Three Generations of Puritan Intellectuals, 1596-1728.* Oxford, 1971.

Miller, Perry G. *Errand into the Wilderness.* Harvard, 1956.

Miller, Perry G. *The New England Mind,* 2 vols. Macmillan, 1939; Harvard, 1953.

Miller, Perry G., and Thomas H. Johnson, eds. *The Puritans,* 2nd ed., 2 vols. Harper & Row, 1963.

Morgan, Edmund S. *The Puritan Dilemma: The Story of John Winthrop.* Little, Brown, 1958.

Morgan, Edmund S. *The Puritan Family.* Boston Public Library, 1943.

Morgan, Edmund S. *Visible Saints: The History of a Puritan Idea.* New York University, 1963.

Morgan, Edmund S., ed. *Puritan Political Ideas.* Bobbs-Merrill, 1965.

Pope, Robert G. *The Half-Way Covenant: Church Membership in Puritan New England.* Princeton, 1969.

Porterfield, Amanda. *Female Piety in Puritan New England.* Oxford, 1992.

Stout, Harry S. *The New England Soul: Preaching and Religious Culture in Colonial New England.* Oxford, 1986.

Ulrich, Laurel Thatcher. *Good Wives: Image and Reality in the Lives of Women in Northern New England, 1650-1750.* Knopf, 1982.

Winslow, Ola. *Meetinghouse Hill, 1630-1783.* Macmillan, 1952.

(2.3) The era of the Great Awakening, 1735-1760

Bushman, Richard L., ed. *The Great Awakening: Documents on the Revival of Religion, 1740-1745.* Atheneum, 1969.

Crawford, Michael. *Seasons of Grace: Colonial New England's Revival Tradition in Its British Context.* Oxford, 1991.

Dallimore, Arnold A. *George Whitefield,* 2 vols. Banner of Truth, 1989-1990.

Gaustad, Edwin S. *The Great Awakening in New England.* Quadrangle, 1957.

Goen, C. C. *Revivalism and Separatism in New England, 1740-1800.* Yale, 1962.

Hall, Timothy D. *Contested Boundaries: Itinerancy and the Reshaping of the Colonial American Religious World.* Duke, 1994.

Heimert, Alan, and Perry Miller, eds. *The Great Awakening: Documents Illustrating the Crisis and Its Consequences.* Bobbs-Merrill, 1967.

Lambert, Frank. *Pedlar in Divinity: George Whitefield and the Transatlantic Revivals, 1737-1770*. Princeton, 1994.

Stout, Harry S. *The Divine Dramatist: George Whitefield and the Rise of Modern Evangelicalism*. Eerdmans, 1991.

Tracy, Joseph. *The Great Awakening: A History of Religion in the Time of Edwards and Whitefield*. Tappan and Dennet, 1842.

Westerkamp, Marilyn J. *Triumph of the Laity: Scots-Irish Piety and the Great Awakening, 1625-1760*. Oxford, 1988.

(2.4) The era of the American Revolution, 1760-1789

Bloch, Ruth H. *Visionary Republic: Millennial Themes in American Thought, 1756-1800*. Cambridge, 1988.

Davis, David Brion. *The Problem of Slavery in the Age of Revolution, 1770-1823*. Cornell, 1975.

Davis, Derek H. *Religion and the Continental Congress, 1774-1789: Contributions to Original Intent*. Oxford, 2000.

Grasso, Christopher. *A Speaking Aristocracy: Transforming Public Discourse in Eighteenth-Century Connecticut*. North Carolina, 1999.

Hanson, Charles B. *Necessary Virtue: The Pragmatic Origins of Religious Liberty in New England*. Virginia, 1998.

Hatch, Nathan O. *The Sacred Cause of Liberty: Republican Thought and the Millennium in Revolutionary New England*. Yale, 1977.

Heimert, Alan. *Religion and the American Mind, from the Great Awakening to the Revolution*. Harvard, 1966.

Hoffman, Ronald, ed. *Religion in a Revolutionary Age*. Virginia, 1994.

Hutson, James H., ed. *Religion and the New Republic: Faith in the Founding of America*. Rowman & Littlefield, 2000.

Isaac, Rhys. *The Transformation of Virginia, 1740-1790*. North Carolina, 1982.

Juster, Susan. *Disorderly Women: Sexual Politics and Evangelicalism in Revolutionary New England*. Cornell, 1994.

MacMaster, Richard K., ed. *Conscience in Crisis: Mennonites and Other Peace Churches in America, 1739-1789*. Herald, 1979.

Marini, Stephen A. *Radical Sects in Revolutionary New England*. Harvard, 1982.

McLoughlin, William G. *Isaac Backus and the American Pietistic Tradition*. Little, Brown, 1967.

Noll, Mark A. *Christians in the American Revolution*. Eerdmans, 1977.

Sandoz, Ellis, ed. *Political Sermons of the American Founding Era, 1730-1805*, 2nd ed. Liberty Fund, 1998.

Valeri, Mark. *Law and Providence in Joseph Bellamy's New England: The Origins of the New Divinity in Revolutionary America*. Oxford, 1994.

(2.5) 1789-1860

Bilhartz, Terry D. *Urban Religion and the Second Great Awakening: Church and Society in Early National Baltimore.* Fairleigh Dickinson, 1986.

Billington, Ray Allen. *The Protestant Crusade, 1800-1860* [anti–Roman Catholicism]. Rinehart, 1938.

Brekus, Catherine. *Strangers and Pilgrims: Female Preaching in America, 1740-1845.* North Carolina, 1998.

Bruce, Dickson D. *And They All Sang Hallelujah: Plain-folk Camp-meeting Religion, 1800-1845.* Tennessee, 1981.

Brumberg, Joan Jacobs. *Mission for Life: The Judson Family and American Evangelical Culture.* New York University, 1980.

Carwardine, Richard. *Evangelicals and Politics in Antebellum America.* Yale, 1993.

Carwardine, Richard. *Transatlantic Revivalism: Popular Evangelicalism in Britain and America, 1790-1865.* Greenwood, 1978.

Caskey, Marie. *Chariot of Fire: Religion and the Beecher Family.* Yale, 1978.

Cott, Nancy R. *The Bonds of Womanhood: "Women's Sphere" in New England, 1780-1835,* 2nd ed. Yale, 1997.

Dolan, Jay P. *The Immigrant Church: New York's Irish and German Catholics, 1815-1865.* Johns Hopkins, 1975.

Foster, Charles I. *An Errand of Mercy: The Evangelical United Front, 1790-1837.* North Carolina, 1960.

Gäbler, Ulrich. *Auferstehungszeit: Erweckungsprediger des 19. Jahrhunderts.* Munich: C. H. Beck, 1991.

Hambrick-Stowe, Charles E. *Charles G. Finney and the Spirit of American Evangelicalism.* Eerdmans, 1996.

Hanley, Mark Y. *Beyond a Christian Commonwealth: The Protestant Quarrel with the American Republic, 1830-1860.* North Carolina, 1994.

Hardesty, Nancy A. *Women Called to Witness: Evangelical Feminism in the Nineteenth Century,* 2nd ed. Tennessee, 1999.

Hatch, Nathan O. *The Democratization of American Christianity.* Yale, 1989.

Howe, Daniel Walker. *Making the American Self: Jonathan Edwards to Abraham Lincoln.* Harvard, 1997.

Howe, Daniel Walker. *The Political Culture of the American Whigs.* Chicago, 1979.

Johnson, Curtis. *Islands of Holiness: Rural Religion in Upstate New York, 1790-1860.* Cornell, 1989.

Johnson, Curtis. *Redeeming America: Evangelicals and the Road to the Civil War.* I. R. Dee, 1993.

Johnson, Paul. *A Shopkeeper's Millennium: Society and Revivals in Rochester, New York, 1815-1837.* Hill & Wang, 1978.

Kling, David. *A Field of Divine Wonders: The New Divinity and Village Revivals in Northwestern Connecticut, 1792-1822.* Penn State, 1993.

Kraditor, Aileen. *Means and Ends in American Abolitionism: Garrison and His Critics on Stategy and Facts, 1834-1850.* Pantheon, 1969.

Lazerow, Jama. *Religion and the Working Class in Antebellum America.* Smithsonian Institution, 1995.

Long, Kathryn Teresa. *The Revival of 1857-58.* Oxford, 1998.

Lundin, Roger. *Emily Dickinson and the Art of Belief.* Eerdmans, 1998.

McKivigan, John R., and Mitchell Snay, eds. *Religion and the Antebellum Debate Over Slavery.* Georgia, 1998.

McLoughlin, William G. *Cherokees and Missionaries, 1789-1839.* Yale, 1984.

Marsden, George M. *The Evangelical Mind and the New School Presbyterian Experience.* Yale, 1970.

Mathews, Donald G. *Slavery and Methodism . . . 1780-1845.* Princeton, 1965.

Noll, Mark A. *Princeton and the Republic, 1768-1822: The Search for a Christian Enlightenment in the Era of Samuel Stanhope Smith.* Princeton, 1989.

Oden, Thomas C., ed. *Phoebe Palmer: Selected Writings.* Paulist, 1988.

Roth, Randolph. *The Democratic Dilemma: Religion, Reform, and the Social Order in the Connecticut River Valley of Vermont, 1791-1850.* Cambridge, 1987.

Ryan, Mary. *Cradle of the Middle Class: The Family in Oneida County, New York, 1790-1865.* Cambridge, 1981.

Smith, Timothy L. *Revivalism and Social Reform: American Protestantism on the Eve of the Civil War.* Harper & Row, 1957.

Sutton, William R. *Journeymen for Jesus: Evangelical Artisans Confront Capitalism in Jacksonian Baltimore.* Penn State, 1998.

Ulrich, Laurel Thatcher. *A Midwife's Tale: The Life of Martha Ballard, 1785-1812.* Knopf, 1990.

West, John G. *The Politics of Revelation and Reason: Religion and Civic Life in the New Nation.* Kansas, 1996.

Wiebe, Robert. *The Opening of American Society: From the Adoption of the Constitution to the Era of Disunion.* Knopf, 1984.

Wood, Gordon S. *The Radicalism of the American Revolution.* Vintage, 1991.

Wyatt-Brown, Bertram. *Lewis Tappan and the Evangelical War Against Slavery.* Case Western Reserve, 1969.

(2.6) The era of the Civil War, 1860-1865

Cheseborough, David. *"God Ordained This War": Sermons on the Sectional Crisis, 1830-1865.* South Carolina, 1991.

Faust, Drew. *A Sacred Circle: The Dilemma of the Intellectual in the Old South, 1840-1860.* Johns Hopkins, 1977.

Fredrickson, George M. *The Inner Civil War: Northern Intellectuals and the Crisis of the Union.* Harper & Row, 1965.

Genovese, Eugene D. *A Consuming Fire: The Fall of the Confederacy in the Mind of the White Christian South*. Georgia, 1999.

Goen, C. C. *Broken Churches, Broken Nation: Denominational Schisms and the Coming of the American Civil War*. Mercer, 1985.

Guelzo, Allen C. *Abraham Lincoln: Redeemer President*. Eerdmans, 1999.

Miller, Randall M., Harry S. Stout, and Charles Reagan Wilson, eds. *Religion and the American Civil War*. Oxford, 1998.

Moorhead, James. *American Apocalypse: Yankee Protestants and the Civil War*. Yale, 1978.

Rose, Anne C. *Victorian America and the Civil War*. Cambridge, 1992.

Silver, James W. *Confederate Morale and Church Propaganda*. Norton, 1957.

Snay, Mitchell. *Gospel of Disunion: Religion and Separatism in the Antebellum South*. Cambridge, 1993.

(2.7) 1865-1914

Bordin, Ruth. *Frances Willard: A Biography*. North Carolina, 1986.

Brereton, Virginia Lieson. *Training God's Army: The American Bible School, 1880-1940*. Indiana, 1990.

Carter, Paul. *The Spiritual Crisis of the Gilded Age*. Northern Illinois, 1971.

Croce, Paul Jerome. *Science and Religion in the Era of William James*. North Carolina, 1995.

Dieter, Melvin E. *The Holiness Revival of the Nineteenth Century*. Scarecrow, 1980.

Dorn, Jacob H. *Washington Gladden: Prophet of the Social Gospel*. Ohio State, 1968.

Epstein, Barbara Leslie. *The Politics of Domesticity: Women, Evangelicalism and Temperance*. Wesleyan, 1981.

Findlay, James F. *Dwight L. Moody: American Evangelist, 1837-1899*. Chicago, 1969.

Fox, Richard Wightman. *Trials of Intimacy: Love and Loss in the [Henry Ward] Beecher-Tildon Scandal*. Chicago, 1999.

Frank, Douglas W. *Less Than Conquerors: How Evangelicals Entered the Twentieth Century*. Eerdmans, 1986.

Handy, Robert T. *Undermined Establishment: Church-State Relations in America, 1880-1920*. Princeton, 1991.

Hill, Patricia. *The World Their Household: The American Women's Foreign Mission Movement and Cultural Transformation, 1870-1922*. Michigan, 1985.

Hopkins, Charles Howard. *The Rise of the Social Gospel in American Protestantism, 1865-1915*. Yale, 1940.

Hutchison, William R. *The Modernist Impulse in American Protestantism*. Harvard, 1976.

Kuklick, Bruce. *Puritans in Babylon: The Ancient Near East and American Intellectual Life, 1880-1930*. Princeton, 1996.

Luker, Ralph. *The Social Gospel in Black and White: American Racial Reform, 1885-1912.* North Carolina, 1991.

McDannell, Colleen. *The Christian Home in Victorian America, 1840-1900.* Indiana, 1986.

McLeod, Hugh. *Piety and Poverty: Working-Class Religion in Berlin, London, and New York, 1870-1914.* Holmes & Meier, 1996.

Maffly-Kipp, Laurie F. *Religion and Society in Frontier California.* Yale, 1994.

Magnuson, Norris. *Salvation in the Slums: Evangelical Social Welfare Work, 1865-1920.* Scarecrow, 1977.

Marsden, George M. *Fundamentalism and American Culture..., 1870-1925.* Oxford, 1980.

Marty, Martin E. *Modern American Religion,* Vol. 1: *The Irony of It All, 1893-1919.* Chicago, 1986.

May, Henry F. *Protestant Churches and Industrial America.* Harper, 1949.

Minus, Paul M. *Walter Rauschenbusch: American Reformer.* Macmillan, 1988.

Sandeen, Ernest. *The Roots of Fundamentalism: British and American Millenarianism, 1800-1930.* Chicago, 1970.

Sizer, Sandra S. *Gospel Hymns and Social Religion: The Rhetoric of Nineteenth-Century Revivalism.* Temple, 1978.

Smith, Gary Scott. *The Seeds of Secularization: Calvinism, Culture, and Pluralism in America, 1870-1915.* Eerdmans, 1985.

Szasz, Ferenc Morton. *The Divided Mind of Protestant America, 1880-1930.* Alabama, 1982.

Turner, James. *The Liberal Education of Charles Eliot Norton.* Johns Hopkins, 1999.

(2.8) 1914-1945

Anderson, Robert Mapes. *Vision of the Disinherited: The Making of American Pentecostalism.* Oxford, 1979.

Blumhofer, Edith L. *Aimee Semple McPherson: Everybody's Sister.* Eerdmans, 1993.

Carpenter, Joel A. *Revive Us Again: The Awakening of American Fundamentalism.* Oxford, 1997.

De Berg, Betty. *Ungodly Women: Gender and the First Wave of American Fundamentalism.* Fortress, 1990.

Dorsett, Lyle W. *Billy Sunday and the Redemption of Urban America.* Eerdmans, 1991.

Fox, Richard Wightman. *Reinhold Niebuhr.* Harper & Row, 1985.

Hart, D. G. *Defending the Faith: J. Gresham Machen and the Crisis of Conservative Protestantism in Modern America.* Johns Hopkins, 1994.

Longfield, Bradley R. *The Presbyterian Controversy: Fundamentalists, Modernists, and Moderates.* Oxford, 1991.

Marty, Martin E. *Modern American Religion,* Vol. 2: *The Noise of Conflict, 1919-1941.* Chicago, 1991.

Miller, Robert Moats. *Harry Emerson Fosdick: Preacher, Pastor, Prophet.* Oxford, 1985.

Piper, John. *The American Churches in World War I.* Ohio, 1985.

Ribuffo, Leo P. *The Old Christian Right: The Protestant Far Right from the Depression to the Cold War.* Temple, 1983.

Russell, C. Allyn. *Voices of American Fundamentalism: Seven Biographical Studies.* Westminster, 1976.

Sittser, Gerald L. *A Cautious Patriotism: The American Churches and the Second World War.* North Carolina, 1997.

Trollinger, William. *God's Empire: William Bell Riley and Midwestern Fundamentalism.* Wisconsin, 1990.

Wacker, Grant. *Heaven Below: Early Pentecostals and American Culture.* Harvard, 2001.

(2.9) 1945-2000

Ammerman, Nancy. *Bible Believers: Fundamentalists in the Modern World.* Rutgers, 1987.

Balmer, Randall. *Mine Eyes Have Seen the Glory: A Journey into the Evangelical Subculture in America.* Oxford, 1989.

Balmer, Randall. *Grant Us Courage: Travels along the Mainline of American Protestantism.* Oxford, 1996.

Bellah, Robert, et al. *Habits of the Heart: Individualism and Commitment in American Life.* California, 1985.

Berger, Peter. *The Noise of Solemn Assemblies: Christian Commitment and the Religious Establishment in America.* Doubleday, 1961.

Brasher, Brenda R. *Godly Women: Fundamentalism and Female Power.* Rutgers, 1998.

Dayton, Donald W., and Robert K. Johnson, eds. *The Variety of American Evangelicalism.* Tennessee, 1991.

Emerson, Michael O., and Christian Smith. *Divided by Faith: Evangelical Religion and the Problem of Race in America.* Oxford, 2000.

Eskridge, Larry, and Mark A. Noll, eds. *More Money, More Ministry: Money and Evangelicals in Recent North American History.* Eerdmans, 2000.

George, Carol V. R. *God's Salesman: Norman Vincent Peale and the Power of Positive Thinking.* Oxford, 1993.

Green, John C., James L. Guth, Corwin E. Smidt, and Lyman A. Kellstedt. *Religion and the Culture Wars: Dispatches from the Front.* Rowman & Littlefield, 1996.

Griffith, R. Marie. *God's Daughters: Evangelical Women and the Power of Submission.* California, 1997.

Hadden, Jeffrey K., and Anson D. Shupe. *Televangelism, Power, and Politics on God's Frontiers.* Henry Holt, 1988.

Harrell, David Edwin. *All Things Are Possible: The Healing and Charismatic Revivals in Modern America.* Indiana, 1975.

Harrell, David Edwin. *Oral Roberts: An American Life.* Indiana, 1985.

Herberg, Will. *Protestant, Catholic, Jew.* Doubleday, 1955.

Hoge, Dean R., Benton Johnson, and Donald A. Luidens. *Vanishing Boundaries: The Religion of Mainline Protestant Baby Boomers.* Westminster/John Knox, 1994.

Hunter, James. *American Evangelicalism: Conservative Religion and the Quandary of Modernity.* Rutgers, 1983.

Marsden, George. *Reforming Fundamentalism: Fuller Seminary and the New Evangelicalism.* Eerdmans, 1987.

Marsden, George, ed. *Evangelicalism and Modern America.* Eerdmans, 1984.

Marsh, Charles. *God's Long Summer: Stories of Faith and Civil Rights.* Princeton, 1997.

Martin, William. *A Prophet with Honor: The Billy Graham Story.* Morrow, 1991.

Marty, Martin E. *Modern American Religion,* Vol. 3: *Under God, Indivisible, 1941-1960.* Chicago, 1996.

Miller, Donald E. *Reinventing American Protestantism: Christianity in the New Millennium.* California, 1997.

Noll, Mark A. *American Evangelical Christianity.* Blackwell, 2001.

Roof, Wade Clark, and William McKinney. *American Mainline Religion: Its Changing Shape and Future.* Rutgers, 1987.

Smith, Christian. *American Evangelicalism: Embattled and Thriving.* Chicago, 1998.

Voskuil, Dennis. *Mountains into Gold Mines: Robert Schuller and the Gospel of Success.* Eerdmans, 1983.

Wagner, Melinda Bollar. *God's Schools: Choice and Compromise in American Society.* Rutgers, 1980.

Warner, R. Stephen. *New Wine in Old Wineskins: Evangelicals and Liberals in a Small-Town Church.* California, 1988.

Warner, R. Stephen, and Judith G. Wittner, eds. *Gatherings in Diaspora: Communities and the New Immigration.* Temple, 1998.

Wind, James P., and James W. Lewis, eds. *American Congregations,* 2 vols. Chicago, 1994.

Witten, Marsha G. *All Is Forgiven: The Secular Message in American Protestantism.* Princeton, 1993.

Wuthnow, Robert. *Poor Richard's Principle: Recovering the American Dream through the Moral Dimensions of Work, Business, and Money.* Princeton, 1996.

Wuthnow, Robert. *The Restructuring of American Religion: Society and Faith Since World War II.* Princeton, 1988.

(3) SPECIAL SUBJECTS

(3.1) European perspectives

Pachter, Marc, ed. *Abroad in America: Visitors to the New Nation, 1776-1914.* Addison-Wesley, 1976.

Powell, Milton B., ed. *The Voluntary Church: American Religious Life, 1740-1860, Seen Through the Eyes of European Visitors*. Macmillan, 1967.

Siegfried, André. *America Comes of Age: A French Analysis*. Harcourt, Brace, 1927.

Tocqueville, Alexis de. *Democracy in America*. 1835-40. Many editions, including Knopf, 1999.

(3.2) African-American Christianity

Branch, Taylor. *America in the King Years*, Vol. 1, *Parting of the Waters, 1954-1963;* Vol. 2, *Pillar of Fire, 1963-1965*. Simon & Schuster, 1988, 1998.

Campbell, James T. *Songs of Zion: The African Methodist Episcopal Church in the United States and South Africa*. North Carolina, 1998.

Douglass, Frederick. *Narrative of the Life of Frederick Douglass*. Many editions, including Norton, 1997.

Essig, James. *The Bonds of Wickedness: American Evangelicals Against Slavery, 1770-1808*. Temple, 1982.

Felder, Cain Hope, ed. *Stony the Road We Trod: African American Biblical Interpretation*. Fortress, 1991.

Findlay, James F. *Church People in the Struggle: The National Council of Churches and the Black Freedom Movement, 1950-1970*. Oxford, 1993.

Frazier, E. Franklin, *The Negro Church in America* (orig. 1964), published with C. Eric Lincoln, *The Black Church Since Frazier*. Schocken, 1974.

Frey, Sylvia R., and Betty Wood. *Come Shouting to Zion: African American Protestantism in the American South and British Caribbean to 1830*. North Carolina, 1998.

Garrow, David J. *Bearing the Cross: Martin Luther King, Jr., and the Southern Christian Leadership Conference*. William Morrow, 1986.

Genovese, Eugene D. *Roll, Jordan, Roll: The World the Slaves Made*. Random House, 1974.

Gordon, Grant. *The Life of David George: Pioneer Black Baptist Minister*. Baptist Heritage in Atlantic Canada, 1992.

Higginbotham, Evelyn Brooks. *Righteous Discontent: The Women's Movement in the Black Baptist Church, 1880-1920*. Harvard, 1993.

Houchins, Sue E., ed. *Spiritual Narratives* (Maria Stewart, 1835; Jarena Lee, 1849; Julia Foote, 1886; Virginia Broughton, 1907). Oxford, 1988.

Jacobs, Sylvia M. *Black Americans and the Missionary Movement in Africa*. Greenwood, 1982.

Johnson, James Weldon. *The Book of American Negro Spirituals*. Viking, 1925.

King, Martin Luther, Jr. *The Papers of Martin Luther King, Jr.,* ed. Ralph Luker et al. California, 1992ff.

Lincoln, C. Eric, and Lawrence H. Mamiya. *The Black Church in the American Experience*. Duke, 1990.

Lischer, Richard. *Preacher King: Martin Luther King, Jr. and the Word That Moved America.* Oxford, 1997.

Raboteau, Albert J. *Slave Religion: The "Invisible Institution" in the Antebellum South.* Oxford, 1978.

Sanders, Cheryl. *Saints in Exile: The Holiness Pentecostal Experience in African American Religion and Culture.* Oxford, 1996.

Scherer, Lester B. *Slavery and the Churches in Early America, 1619-1819.* Eerdmans, 1975.

Sernett, Milton C. *Bound for the Promised Land: African American Religion and the Great Migration.* Duke, 1997.

Sobel, Mechal. *Trabelin' On: The Slave Journey to an Afro-Baptist Faith.* Greenwood, 1979.

Sobel, Mechal. *The World They Made Together: Black and White Values in Eighteenth-Century Virginia.* Princeton, 1987.

Truth, Sojourner. *Narrative of Sojourner Truth,* intro. Jeffrey C. Stewart. Oxford, 1991.

(3.3) Church and state/politics and society

Bruce, Steve. *The Rise and Fall of the New Christian Right: Conservative Protestant Politics in America, 1978-1988.* Oxford, 1990.

Curry, Thomas J. *The First Freedoms: Church and State in America to the Passage of the First Amendment.* New York, 1986.

Hanna, Mary T. *Catholics and American Politics.* Harvard, 1979.

Kurland, Philip B., and Ralph Lerner, eds. *The Founders' Constitution.* Vol. 5: *Amendments I-XII.* Chicago, 1987.

Lienesch, Michael. *Redeeming America: Piety and Politics in the New Christian Right.* North Carolina, 1993.

Murray, John Courtney. *We Hold These Truths: Catholic Reflections on the American Proposition.* Sheed and Ward, 1960.

Neuhaus, Richard John. *The Naked Public Square: Religion and Democracy in America.* Eerdmans, 1984.

Neuhaus, Richard John, and Michael Cromartie, eds. *Piety and Politics: Evangelicals and Fundamentalists Confront the World.* Ethics and Public Policy Center, 1987.

Noll, Mark A. *One Nation Under God? Christian Faith and Political Action in America.* Harper & Row, 1988.

Noll, Mark A., ed. *Religion and American Politics from the Colonial Period to the 1980s.* Oxford, 1990.

Noonan, John T., Jr. *The Lustre of Our Country: The American Experience of Religious Freedom.* California, 1998.

Pfeffer, Leo. *Church, State, and Freedom.* Beacon, 1953.

Pierard, Richard V., and Robert D. Linder. *Civil Religion and the Presidency.* Zondervan, 1988.

Sarna, Jonathan D., and David G. Dalin, eds. *Religion and State in the American Jewish Experience.* Notre Dame, 1997.

Silk, Mark. *Spiritual Politics: Religion and America Since World War II.* Simon & Schuster, 1988.

Skillen, James W. *The Scattered Voice: Christians at Odds in the Public Square.* Zondervan, 1990.

Wills, Garry. *Under God: Religion and American Politics.* Simon & Schuster, 1990.

Wilson, John F., and Donald L. Drakeman, eds. *Church and State in American History.* 2nd ed. Beacon, 1987.

Wilson, John F., ed. *Church and State in America: A Bibliographical Guide,* 2 vols. Greenwood, 1986-1987.

Witte, John, Jr. *Religion and the American Constitutional Experiment: Essential Rights and Liberties.* Westview, 2000.

(3.4) Roman Catholicism in America

Allitt, Patrick. *Catholic Converts: British and American Intellectuals Turn to Rome.* Cornell, 1997.

Appleby, R. Scott. *"Church and Age Unite": The Modernist Impulse in American Catholicism.* Notre Dame, 1992.

Carey, Patrick W. *The Roman Catholics.* Greenwood, 1993.

Carey, Patrick W., ed. *American Catholic Religious Thought.* Paulist, 1987.

Chinnici, Joseph P., O.F.M. *Living Stones: The History and Structure of Catholic Spiritual Life in the United States.* Orbis, 1996.

Dolan, Jay P. *The American Catholic Experience: A History from Colonial Times to the Present.* Doubleday, 1985.

Dolan, Jay P., ed. *The Notre Dame History of Hispanic Catholics in the United States,* 3 vols. Notre Dame, 1994.

Ellis, John Tracy, ed. *Documents of American Catholic History.* Bruce, 1956.

Ferrar, Thomas J., ed. *Catholic Lives, Contemporary America.* Duke, 1997.

Franchot, Jenny. *Roads to Rome: The Antebellum Protestant Encounter with Catholicism.* California, 1994.

Glazier, Michael, and Thomas J. Shelley, eds. *Encyclopedia of American Catholic History.* Liturgical Press, 1997.

Gleason, Philip. *Contending with Modernity: Catholic Higher Education in the Twentieth Century.* Oxford, 1995.

Gleason, Philip. *Keeping the Faith: American Catholicism Past and Present.* Notre Dame, 1987.

Greeley, Andrew M. *The Catholic Myth: The Behavior and Beliefs of American Catholics.* Scribner, 1990.

Gutierrez, Ramon A. *When Jesus Came the Corn Mother Went Away: Marriage, Sexuality, and Power in New Mexico, 1500-1846.* Stanford, 1991.

Hennesey, James, S.J. *American Catholics: A History of the Roman Catholic Community in the United States.* Oxford, 1981.

McGreevy, John T. *Parish Boundaries: The Catholic Encounter with Race in the Twentieth-Century Urban North.* Chicago, 1997.

Miller, William D. *Dorothy Day: A Biography.* Harper & Row, 1982.

O'Brien, David J. *Isaac Hecker: An American Catholic,* 2nd ed. Paulist, 1992.

O'Brien, David J. *Public Catholicism,* 2nd ed. Orbis, 1996.

Orsi, Robert A. *The Madonna of 115th Street: Faith and Community in Italian Harlem, 1880-1950.* Yale, 1985.

Taves, Ann. *The Household of Faith: Roman Catholic Devotions in Mid-Nineteenth-Century America.* Notre Dame, 1986.

Tentler, Leslie Woodcock. *Seasons of Grace: A History of the Catholic Archdiocese of Detroit.* Wayne State, 1990.

Zöller, Michael. *Washington and Rome: Catholicism in American Culture.* Notre Dame, 1999.

(3.5) Histories of other denominations

(3.5.1) American denominationalism

Niebuhr, H. Richard. *The Social Sources of Denominationalism.* Henry Holt, 1929.

Mullin, Robert Bruce, and Russell E. Richey, eds. *Reimagining Denominationalism.* Oxford, 1994.

(3.5.2) Assemblies of God

Blumhofer, Edith L. *Restoring the Faith: The Assemblies of God, Pentecostalism, and American Culture.* Illinois, 1993.

Paloma, Margaret M. *The Assemblies of God at the Crossroads: Charism and Institutional Dilemmas.* Tennessee, 1989.

(3.5.3) Baptists

Ammerman, Nancy. *Southern Baptists Observed: Multiple Perspectives on a Changing Denomination.* Tennessee, 1993.

George, Timothy, and David Dockery, eds. *Baptist Theologians.* Broadman, 1990.

Harvey, Paul. *Redeeming the South: Religious Cultures and Racial Identities Among Southern Baptists, 1865-1925.* North Carolina, 1997.

Leonard, Bill, ed. *Dictionary of Baptists in America.* InterVarsity, 1994.

Wills, Gregory A. *Democratic Religion: Freedom, Authority, and Church Discipline in the Baptist South, 1785-1900.* Oxford, 1997.

(3.5.4) Christian Reformed

Bratt, James D. *Dutch Calvinism in Modern America.* Eerdmans, 1984.

(3.5.5) Congregationalists

Walker, Williston, ed. *The Creeds and Platforms of Congregationalism.* Pilgrim, 1991 [originally 1893].
Youngs, J. William T. *The Congregationalists.* Greenwood, 1998.

(3.5.6) Episcopalians

Butler, Diana Hochstedt. *Standing Against the Whirlwind: Evangelical Episcopalians in Nineteenth-Century America.* Oxford, 1995.
Holmes, David L. *A Brief History of the Episcopal Church.* Trinity Press International, 1993.
Mullin, Robert Bruce. *Episcopal Vision/American Reality: High Church Theology and Social Thought in Evangelical America.* Yale, 1986.

(3.5.7) Lutherans

Gustafson, David A. *Lutherans in Crisis: The Question of Identity in the American Republic.* Fortress, 1993.
Nelson, E. Clifford, ed. *The Lutherans in North America.* Fortress, 1980.
Tappert, Theodore G., ed. *Lutheran Confessional Theology in America, 1840-1880.* Oxford, 1972.

(3.5.8) Mennonites and Amish

Bush, Perry. *Two Kingdoms, Two Loyalties: Mennonite Pacifism in Modern America.* Johns Hopkins, 1999.
Hostetler, John A. *Amish Society,* 4th ed. Johns Hopkins, 1993.
Schlabach, Theron, ed. *The Mennonite Experience in America,* 4 vols. Herald, 1985-1996.

(3.5.9) Methodists

Andrews, Dee E. *The Methodists and Revolutionary America, 1760-1800: The Shaping of an Evangelical Culture.* Princeton, 2000.
Hyerman, Christine Leigh. *Southern Cross: The Beginnings of the Bible Belt.* Knopf, 1997.
Richey, Russell E. *Early American Methodism.* Indiana, 1991.
Richey, Russell E., and Kenneth E. Rowe, eds. *Rethinking Methodist History.* Kingswood, 1985.
Schneider, A. Gregory. *The Way of the Cross Leads Home: The Domestication of American Methodism.* Indiana, 1993.

Wigger, John. *Taking Heaven by Storm: Methodism and the Rise of Popular Christianity in America*. Oxford, 1998.

(3.5.10) Mormons

Arrington, Leonard J. *The Mormon Experience: A History of the Latter-day Saints*. Vintage, 1979.

Bushman, Richard L. *Joseph Smith and the Beginnings of Mormonism*. Illinois, 1984.

Ostling, Richard N., and Joan K. Ostling. *Mormon America: The Power and the Promise*. HarperSanFrancisco, 1999.

Shipps, Jan. *Mormonism: The Story of a New Religious Tradition*. Illinois, 1985.

(3.5.11) Nazarenes

Smith, Timothy L. *Called Unto Holiness: The Story of the Nazarenes: The Formative Years*. Nazarene Publishing House, 1962.

(3.5.12) Presbyterians

Hart, D. G., ed. *Dictionary of the Presbyterian and Reformed Tradition in America*. InterVarsity, 1999.

Mulder, John M., Milton J Coalter, and Louis B. Weeks, eds. *The Presbyterian Presence: The Twentieth-Century Experience*, 7 vols. Westminster/John Knox, 1990-1992.

(3.5.13) Restorationists (Churches of Christ, Disciples of Christ)

Harrell, David Edwin. *A Social History of the Disciples of Christ*, 2 vols. Disciples of Christ Historical Society, 1966, 1973.

Hughes, Richard T. *Reviving the Ancient Faith: The Story of Churches of Christ in America*. Eerdmans, 1996.

(3.5.14) Salvation Army

McKinley, Edward H. *Marching to Glory: The History of the Salvation Army in the United States, 1880-1992*, 2nd ed. Eerdmans, 1995.

Winston, Diane. *Red-Hot and Righteous: The Urban Religion of the Salvation Army*. Harvard, 1999.

(3.5.15) Seventh-day Adventists

Numbers, Ronald. *Prophetess of Health: Ellen G. White and the Origins of Seventh-day Adventist Health Reform*, 2nd ed. Tennessee, 1992.

Numbers, Ronald L., and Jonathan M. Butler, eds. *The Disappointed: Millerism and Millenarianism in the Nineteenth Century*. Indiana, 1987.

(3.5.16) Shakers

Stein, Stephen J. *The Shaker Experience in America*. Yale, 1992.

(3.5.17) Unitarians

Ahlstrom, Sydney E., and Jonathan S. Carey, eds. *An American Reformation: A Documentary History of Unitarian Christianity.* Wesleyan, 1985.

Wright, Conrad. *The Beginnings of Unitarianism in America.* Beacon, 1955.

(3.6) Theology and the intellectual life

(3.6.1) Reference works

Ahlstrom, Sydney E., ed. *Theology in America: The Major Protestant Voices from Puritanism to Neo-Orthodoxy.* Bobbs-Merrill, 1967.

Elwell, Walter A., ed. *Handbook of Evangelical Theologians.* Baker, 1993.

Toulouse, Mark G., and James O. Duke, eds. *Makers of Christian Theology in America.* Abingdon, 1997.

(3.6.2) Jonathan Edwards

The Works of Jonathan Edwards, ed. Perry Miller, John E. Smith, Harry S. Stout, et al. Yale, 1957- (eventually to reach 25 volumes). From this edition two short anthologies have been extracted: John E. Smith, Harry S. Stout, and Kenneth P. Minkema, eds. *A Jonathan Edwards Reader.* Yale, 1995; and Wilson H. Kimnach, Kenneth P. Minkema, and Douglas A. Sweeney, eds. *The Sermons of Jonathan Edwards: A Reader.* Yale, 1999.

Cherry, Conrad. *The Theology of Jonathan Edwards: A Reappraisal.* Doubleday, 1966.

Conforti, Joseph. *Jonathan Edwards, Religious Tradition, and American Culture.* North Carolina, 1995.

Fiering, Norman. *Jonathan Edwards's Moral Thought and Its British Context.* North Carolina, 1981.

Guelzo, Allen C. *Edwards on the Will: A Century of American Theological Debate.* Wesleyan, 1989.

Guelzo, Allen C., and Sang Hyun Lee, eds. *Edwards in Our Time: Jonathan Edwards and the Shaping of American Religion.* Eerdmans, 1999.

Haroutunian, Joseph. *Piety Versus Moralism: The Passing of the New England Theology.* Henry Holt, 1932.

Hatch, Nathan O., and Harry S. Stout, eds. *Jonathan Edwards and the American Experience.* Oxford, 1988.

Jenson, Robert. *America's Theologian: A Recommendation of Jonathan Edwards.* Oxford, 1988.

McDermott, Gerald. *One Holy and Happy Society: The Public Theology of Jonathan Edwards.* Penn State, 1992.

Miller, Perry. *Jonathan Edwards.* William Sloane, 1949.

Murray, Iain. *Jonathan Edwards.* Banner of Truth, 1987.

(3.6.3) Individual theologians and themes

Bozeman, T. D. *Protestants and the Age of Science: The Baconian Ideal and Antebellum American Religious Thought.* North Carolina, 1977.

Brown, William McAfee, ed. *The Essential Reinhold Niebuhr: Selected Essays and Addresses.* Yale, 1986.

Cashdollar, Charles. *The Transformation of Theology, 1830-1890: Positivism and Protestant Thought in Britain and America.* Princeton, 1989.

Dayton, Donald W. *Theological Roots of Pentecostalism.* Zondervan, 1987.

Holifield, E. Brooks. *The Gentlemen Theologians: American Theology in Southern Culture, 1795-1860.* Duke, 1978.

Kraus, C. Norman. *Dispensationalism in America: Its Rise and Development.* John Knox, 1958.

Kuklick, Bruce. *Churchmen and Philosophers: From Jonathan Edwards to John Dewey.* Yale, 1985.

Lacey, Michael J. *Religion and Twentieth-Century American Intellectual Life.* Cambridge, 1989.

Lundin, Roger. *The Culture of Interpretation: Christian Faith and the Postmodern World.* Eerdmans, 1993.

Madden, Edward H., and James E. Hamilton. *Freedom and Grace: The Life of Asa Mahan.* Scarecrow, 1982.

May, Henry F. *The Enlightenment in America.* Oxford, 1976.

Meyer, Donald H. *The Instructed Conscience: The Shaping of the American National Ethic.* Pennsylvania, 1972.

Mullin, Robert Bruce. *Miracles and Modern Religious Imagination.* Yale, 1996.

Noll, Mark A. *Between Faith and Criticism: Evangelicals, Scholarship, and the Bible in America,* 2nd ed. Baker, 1991.

Shea, William M., and Peter A. Huff, eds. *Knowledge and Belief in America: Enlightenment Traditions and Modern Religious Thought.* Cambridge, 1995.

Smith, H. Shelton, ed. *Horace Bushnell.* Oxford, 1965.

Walters, Kerry S., ed. *The American Deists.* Kansas, 1992.

Warren, Heather A. *Theologians of a New World Order: Reinhold Niebuhr and the Christian Realists, 1920-1948.* Oxford, 1997.

Weber, Timothy. *Living in the Shadow of the Second Coming: American Premillennialism, 1875-1982,* 3rd ed. Chicago, 1982.

(3.6.4) Education

Cherry, Conrad. *Hurrying Toward Zion: Universities, Divinity Schools, and American Protestantism.* Indiana, 1995.

Hart, D. G., and Albert Mohler, eds. *Theological Education in the Evangelical Tradition.* Baker, 1996.

Marsden, George M. *The Soul of the American University: From Protestant Establishment to Established Nonbelief.* Oxford, 1994.

Sloan, Douglas. *The Scottish Enlightenment and the American College Ideal.* Teacher's College of Columbia University, 1971.

Stevenson, Louise L. *Scholarly Means to Evangelical Ends: The New Haven Scholars and the Transformation of Higher Learning in America, 1830-1890.* Johns Hopkins, 1986.

(3.6.5) Science

Gilkey, Langdon. *Creationism on Trial: Evolution and God at Little Rock.* Winston, 1985.

Greene, John C. *The Death of Adam: Evolution and Its Impact on Western Thought.* New American Library, 1959.

Larson, Edward J. *Summer for the Gods: The Scopes Trial and America's Continuing Debate Over Science and Religion.* Basic, 1997.

Livingstone, David N. *Darwin's Forgotten Defenders: The Encounter Between Evangelical Theology and Evolutionary Thought.* Eerdmans, 1987.

Moore, James R. *The Post-Darwinian Controversies: A Study of the Protestant Struggle to Come to Terms with Darwin in Great Britain and America, 1870-1900.* Cambridge, 1979.

Numbers, Ronald L. *The Creationists.* Knopf, 1992.

Roberts, Jon H. *Darwinism and the Divine in America: Protestant Intellectuals and Organic Evolution, 1859-1900.* Wisconsin, 1988.

(3.7) The South

Calhoon, Robert M. *Evangelicals and Conservatives in the Early South, 1740-1861.* South Carolina, 1988.

Flynt, Wayne J. *Alabama Baptists: Southern Baptists in the Heart of Dixie.* Alabama, 1998.

Genovese, Eugene D. *The Slaveholders' Dilemma: Freedom and Progress in Southern Conservative Thought, 1820-1860.* South Carolina, 1992.

Hill, Samuel S. *Southern Churches in Crisis Revisited.* Alabama, 1999.

Loveland, Anne C. *Southern Evangelicals and the Social Order, 1800-1860.* Louisiana State, 1980.

Mathews, Donald G. *Religion in the Old South.* Chicago, 1977.

Startup, Kenneth. *The Root of All Evil: The Protestant Clergy and the Economic Mind of the South.* Georgia, 1997.

Wilson, Charles Reagan. *Baptized in Blood: The Religion of the Lost Cause, 1865-1920.* Georgia, 1980.

Wyatt-Brown, Bertram. *Southern Honor: Ethics and Behavior in the Old South.* Oxford, 1982.

(3.8) Canada

Airhart, Phyllis. *Serving the Present Age: Revivalism, Progressivism, and the Methodist Tradition in Canada.* McGill-Queen's, 1992.

Bibby, Reginald. *Fragmented Gods: The Poverty and Potential of Religion in Canada.* Irwin, 1987.

Burkinshaw, Robert K. *Pilgrims in Lotusland: Conservative Protestantism in British Columbia, 1917-1981.* McGill-Queen's, 1995.

Clark, S. D. *Church and Sect in Canada.* Toronto, 1948.

Desrosiers, Yvon, ed. *Religion et Culture au Québec.* Fides, 1986.

Flanagan, Thomas. *Louis "David" Riel: Prophet of the New World,* 2nd ed. Toronto, 1996.

Gauvreau, Michael. *The Evangelical Century: College and Creed in English Canada from the Great Revival to the Great Depression.* McGill-Queen's, 1991.

Grant, George Parkin. *Lament for a Nation: The Defeat of Canadian Nationalism.* D. Van Nostrand, 1965.

Grant, John Webster. *The Church in the Canadian Era,* 2nd ed. Welch, 1988.

Grant, John Webster. *Moon of Wintertime: Missionaries and the Indians of Canada in Encounter Since 1534.* Toronto, 1984.

Grant, John Webster. *A Profusion of Spires: Religion in Nineteenth-Century Ontario.* Toronto, 1988.

Lipset, Seymour Martin. *Continental Divide: The Values and Institutions of the United States and Canada.* Routledge, 1990.

Marks, Lynne. *Revivals and Roller Rinks: Religion, Leisure, and Identity in Late-Nineteenth-Century Small-Town Canada.* Toronto, 1996.

Marshall, David B. *Secularizing the Faith: Canadian Protestant Clergy and the Crisis of Belief, 1850-1940.* Toronto, 1992.

McGowan, Mark G., and David B. Marshall, eds. *Prophets, Priests, and Prodigals: Readings in Canadian Religious History, 1608 to Present.* McGraw-Hill Ryerson, 1992.

Muir, Elizabeth Gillan, and Marilyn Färdig Whitely, eds. *Changing Roles of Women within the Christian Church in Canada.* Toronto, 1995.

Murphy, Terrence, and Roberto Perin, eds. *A Concise History of Christianity in Canada.* Oxford, 1996.

Murphy, Terrence, and Gerald Stortz, eds. *Creed and Culture: The Place of English-speaking Catholics in Canadian Society, 1750-1930.* McGill-Queen's, 1993.

Rawlyk, George A. *The Canada Fire: Radical Evangelicalism in British North America, 1775-1812.* McGill-Queen's, 1994.

Rawlyk, George A. *Is Jesus Your Personal Saviour? In Search of Canadian Evangelicalism in the 1990s.* McGill-Queen's, 1996.

Rawlyk, George A., ed. *Aspects of the Canadian Evangelical Experience.* McGill-Queen's, 1997.

Rawlyk, George A., ed. *The Canadian Protestant Experience, 1760-1990.* Welch, 1990.

Semple, Neil. *The Lord's Dominion: The History of Canadian Methodism*. McGill-Queen's, 1996.

Stackhouse, John G. *Canadian Evangelicalism in the Twentieth Century*. Toronto, 1993.

Van Die, Marguerite. *An Evangelical Mind: Nathanael Burwash and the Methodist Tradition in Canada, 1839-1918*. McGill-Queen's, 1989.

Westfall, William. *Two Worlds: The Protestant Culture of Nineteenth-Century Ontario*. McGill-Queen's, 1989.

(3.9) Mexico

Baldwin, Deborah J. *Protestants and the Mexican Revolution: Missionaries, Ministers, and Social Change*. Illinois, 1990.

Bastian, Jean-Pierre. *Historia del Protestantismo en América Latina*. Mexico City: Ediciones CUPSA, 1990.

Bastian, Jean-Pierre. *Los disidentes: sociedades protestantes y revolución en México, 1872-1911*. Mexico City: Fondo de Cultura Economica, 1989.

Dussel, Enrique. *A History of the Church in Latin America: Colonialism to Liberation*. Eerdmans, 1981.

Gaxiola, Manuel Jesus. *Mexican Protestantism: The Struggle for Identity and Relevance in a Pluralistic Society*. Diss., University of Birmingham, 1989.

Gutierrez, Gustavo. *Las Casas: In Search of the Poor of Jesus Christ*. Orbis, 1993.

Lutteroth, María Alicia Puente, ed. *Hacia una Historia Mínima de la Iglesia en México*. Mexico City: JUS/CEHILA, 1993.

Martin, David. *Tongues of Fire: The Explosion of Protestantism in Latin America*. Blackwell, 1990.

Mecham, J. Lloyd. *Church and State in Latin America: A History of Politico-Ecclesiastical Relations*, 2nd ed. North Carolina, 1966.

Norman, Edward. *Christianity in the Southern Hemisphere: The Churches in Latin America and South Africa*. Clarendon, 1981.

Reich, Peter Lester. *Mexico's Hidden Revolution: The Catholic Church in Law and Politics Since 1927*. Notre Dame, 1996.

Scott, Lindy. *Salt of the Earth: A Socio-Political History of Mexico City Evangelical Protestants (1964-1991)*. Mexico City: Editorial Kyrios, 1991.

Tangeman, Michael. *Mexico at the Crossroads: Politics, the Church, and the Poor*. Orbis, 1995.

INDEX

327